Family Circle

· 1989 ·

CHRISTMAS TREASURY

EDITORIAL

Editor, Family Circle Books — Carol A. Guasti
Assistant Editor — Kim E. Gayton
Project Editor — Ceri Hadda
Book Design — Bessen, Tully & Lee
Watercolor Art — Yvonne Buchanan
Silhouette Art — Maggie Zander; plus excerpts from the books, Silhouettes: A Pictorial Archive of Varied Illustrations, copyright ©1979 by Dover Publications, Inc., and More Silhouettes: 868 Copyright-Free Illustrations for Artists and Craftsmen, copyright ©1982 by Dover Publications, Inc.;
both books edited by Carol Belanger Grafton.
Typesetting — Gary Borden, Alison Chandler, Maureen Harrington
Editorial Assistants — Kristen J. Keller, Celeste Bantz

Cover Photo — William Stites
Photographers — David Bishop; Ralph Bogertman; Fran Brennan; Ronald G. Harris; Irwin Horowitz; Lynn Karlin; Taylor Lewis; Bill McGinn; Chris Mead; Rudy Muller; Jeff Niki; Leonard Nones; Robert Perron; Dean Powell; Carin Riley; Michael Skott; Gordon E. Smith; William P. Steele; William Stites; Bob Stoller; Theo; René Velez

Contributing Food Editors: JoAnn Brett-Billowitz; Mary Caldwell; Jim Fobel; Sandra Gluck; Ceri Hadda; Joanne L. Hayes; Dora Jonassen; Michael Krondl; Diane Mogelever; Jane O'Keefe; David Ricketts; Janice Schindeler; Catherine Vosecky; Jane Weston Wilson; Lucy Wing

Contributing Crafts Editors: Vicky Babcock; Jeanne Beretta; Cari Clement; Camilla Crist; Donald Grover; Blake Hampton; Irene Miller; Patricia Mlenak; Barbara O'Connor; Lillian Pacelli; Enola Padgett; Susan Pippin; Judy Pugh; Joe Ruggiero; Frances Ryan for Bordens; Mimi Shimmin; Lynne Shipp for Coats & Clark; Susan Singer; Jane Slovachek; Constance Spates; René Velez; Val Love; Les Walker

Special Thanks to Contributing Crafts Editors: Leslie Allen At Home (pages 158-159); Susan Dalton (pages 46-48); J. Marconi-Martin (pages 49-50, 54-55, 56-57, 58-59, 60-61, 169)

MARKETING

Director, Family Circle Books & Licensing — Margaret Chan-Yip
Promotion/Fulfillment Manager — Pauline MacLean Treitler
Fulfillment/Planning Coordinator — Carrie Meyerhoff
Administrative Assistant — Lynne Bertram

Published by The Family Circle, Inc.
110 Fifth Avenue, New York, NY 10011

Copyright® 1989 by The Family Circle, Inc.

Manufactured in the United States of America

10 9 8 7 6 5 4 3 2 1

Library of Congress Cataloging in Publication Data
Main entry under title:

The Family circle christmas treasury.
Includes index.
1.Christmas decorations.   2.Christmas cookery.
I.Family circle, Inc.   II.Title: Christmas treasury.
TT900. C4F36   1989   745.594'1   86-11598
ISBN 0-933585-12-8
ISSN 0892-3604

Other Books by Family Circle

TABLE OF CONTENTS

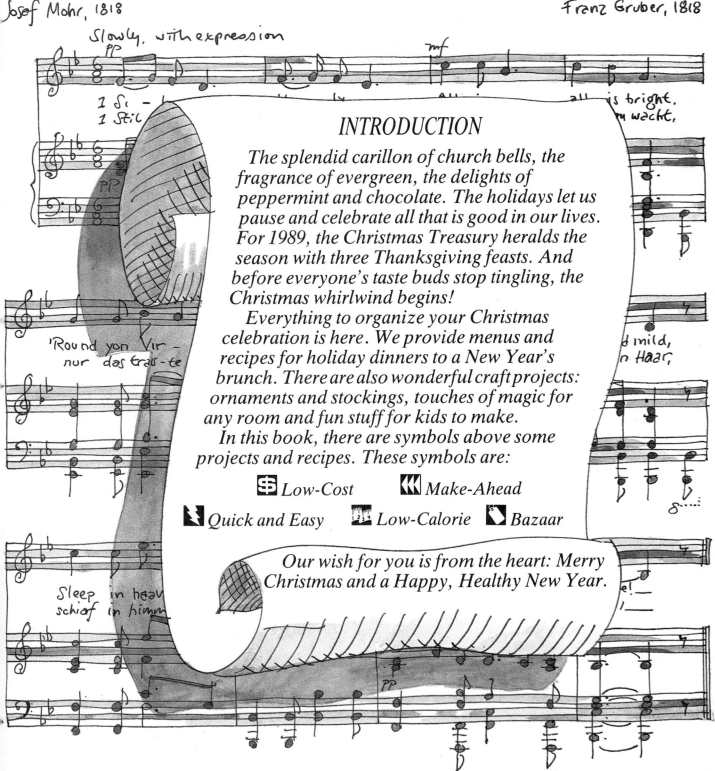

Silent Night, Holy Night

Josef Mohr, 1818

Franz Gruber, 1818

Slowly, with expression

INTRODUCTION

The splendid carillon of church bells, the fragrance of evergreen, the delights of peppermint and chocolate. The holidays let us pause and celebrate all that is good in our lives. For 1989, the Christmas Treasury heralds the season with three Thanksgiving feasts. And before everyone's taste buds stop tingling, the Christmas whirlwind begins!

Everything to organize your Christmas celebration is here. We provide menus and recipes for holiday dinners to a New Year's brunch. There are also wonderful craft projects: ornaments and stockings, touches of magic for any room and fun stuff for kids to make.

In this book, there are symbols above some projects and recipes. These symbols are:

$ Low-Cost   Make-Ahead

Quick and Easy   Low-Calorie   Bazaar

Our wish for you is from the heart: Merry Christmas and a Happy, Healthy New Year.

Over The River and Through the Wood

Lydia Maria Child

Traditional (v.s.)

1. O·ver the riv··er and through the wood to Grand·fa·ther's house we

The horse knows the way to car·ry the sleigh through the

white and drift·ed snow. _____ O·ver the riv·er and

through the wood, oh how the w

stings the toes and bites the nose as o·ver the ground we go.

WELCOME THE SEASON WITH THANKSGIVING

Thanksgiving is a sumptuous prelude to the season of family gatherings and good times. This year, why not add a little spice to the celebration? Our three harvest menus offer exciting new dishes that will send everyone back for seconds. Try our traditional "heartland" turkey dinner complete with brandied fruit stuffing, creamy green bean soup and apricot nut pie. Want something more dramatic? "A Star From the East" was inspired by the exotic flavors of the Orient. Our third Thanksgiving menu derives from the Old South where hospitality is a practiced art. This time the turkey gets a little kick from bourbon in the glaze and cranberry relish. You'll also find a step-by-step guide for carving your turkey, wonderful gifts and goodies to make and give, and beautiful decorations that say "welcome" to the most wonderful season of the year!

Shrimp & Snow Peas with Tangy Cream Sauce (recipe, page 7); Herb & Spice Cheese Balls (recipe, page 8); Red Pepper Pesto in Endive (recipe, page 7); Radishes à la Vinaigrette (recipe, page 13); Creamy Green Bean Soup (recipe, page 9); Roast Turkey with Brandied Fruit Stuffing (recipe, page 9); Red Pepper Cups with Pea Purée (recipe, page 11); Braided Wreath Bread (recipe, page 14); Bourbon Gingered Sweet Potatoes (recipe, page 12); Lemon Dilled Brussels Sprouts (recipe, page 12); Tangy Cranberry Relish (recipe, page 13); Apricot Nut Pie (recipe, page 15)

HEARTLAND THANKSGIVING DINNER

(for 8)

Shrimp & Snow Peas with Tangy Cream Sauce
Red Pepper Pesto in Endive
Herb & Spice Cheese Balls
Creamy Green Bean Soup
Roast Turkey with Brandied Fruit Stuffing
Red Pepper Cups with Pea Purée
Lemon Dilled Brussels Sprouts
Bourbon Gingered Sweet Potatoes
Radishes à la Vinaigrette
Tangy Cranberry Relish
Braided Wreath Bread
Apricot Nut Pie

WORK PLAN FOR HEARTLAND
THANKSGIVING DINNER

Up to One Month Ahead:
- Prepare and freeze the Red Pepper Pesto (without the Parmesan cheese), Creamy Green Bean Soup (without the cream), Braided Wreath Bread and Apricot Nut Pie.

Up to Several Days Ahead:
- Prepare and refrigerate the Tangy Cranberry Relish.
- Prepare the Creamy Green Bean Soup, if it was not prepared ahead and frozen.

Up to Two Days Ahead:
- Prepare and refrigerate the Brandied Fruit Stuffing.
- Prepare the Apricot Nut Pie, if it was not prepared ahead and frozen.

The Day Before:
- Prepare and refrigerate the Bourbon Gingered Sweet Potatoes.
- Cook shrimp for Shrimp & Snow Peas.
- Thaw the Red Pepper Pesto, stirring in the Parmesan cheese; refrigerate.
- Thaw the Creamy Green Bean Soup, Braided Wreath Bread and Apricot Nut Pie, if frozen. Refrigerate the soup.
- Prepare the Braided Wreath Bread, if it was not prepared ahead and frozen.
- Prepare and refrigerate the Herb & Spice Cheese Balls.
- Prepare the Radishes à la Vinaigrette.

Early in the Day:
- Rinse, dry and refrigerate the greens for the Radishes à la Vinaigrette.
- Blanch the snow peas, wrap them around the shrimp and refrigerate them.

Five Hours Before:
- Stuff the turkey and *immediately* start roasting it.

Several Hours Before:
- Unmold the Tangy Cranberry Relish and refrigerate it.
- Prepare the pea purée and the peppers for the Red Pepper Cups with Pea Purée. Cover lightly with plastic wrap.
- Clean the Brussels sprouts for the Lemon Dilled Brussels Sprouts and keep them refrigerated. Squeeze the lemon juice and slice the water chestnuts.
- Line a serving platter with lettuce, cover lightly with plastic wrap and refrigerate.

One Hour Before:
- Remove the Herb & Spice Cheese Balls from the refrigerator.
- Fill the endive leaves with the Red Pepper Pesto.

30 Minutes Before:
- Start reheating the Bourbon Gingered Sweet Potatoes.
- Prepare sauce for Shrimp & Snow Peas.
- Start reheating the Creamy Green Bean Soup, adding the cream.
- After the turkey is removed from the oven, reheat the Braided Wreath Bread.
- Prepare the Giblet Gravy; keep warm.
- Finish preparing the Lemon Dilled Brussels Sprouts.

Just Before Dinner:
- Garnish the turkey platter with the Red Pepper Cups with Pea Purée, Bourbon Gingered Sweet Potatoes and watercress.
- Top the lettuce-lined platter with the Radishes à la Vinaigrette.

During Dinner:
- Reheat the Apricot Nut Pie.

SHRIMP & SNOW PEAS WITH TANGY CREAM SAUCE

Makes 8 servings.

1¼ pounds medium-size shrimp, shelled and
        deveined (about 24 shrimp)
1   cup water
½   teaspoon salt
3   ounces snow peas, trimmed (about 24
        snow peas)
     Mustard Cream Sauce (recipe follows)

1. Cook the shrimp in boiling water to cover
   in a medium-size saucepan until they are
   pink and curled, for about 3 minutes.
   Drain the shrimp.
2. Rinse out the pot. Add the 1 cup of water
   and the salt. Bring to boiling over high
   heat. Add the snow peas and return to
   boiling. Reduce the heat to medium and
   cook for 3 minutes, or until the peas are
   tender and pliable. Drain and immerse the
   peas in very cold water to set the bright
   green color. Drain the peas well.
3. Wrap a snow pea around the center of
   each shrimp and secure it with a wooden
   pick. Cover and refrigerate the shrimp.
4. Serve with the Mustard Cream Sauce.

Mustard Cream Sauce: Melt 1½ tablespoons
of butter in a small saucepan over medium
heat. Stir in 1½ tablespoons of all-purpose
flour until blended and cook until the
mixture has thickened, for about 3 minutes.
Gradually add ½ cup of heavy or whipping
cream. Cook over medium heat, stirring
constantly, until the mixture is smooth and
thickened. Remove the saucepan from the
heat. Stir in ½ cup of dairy sour cream, 3
tablespoons of Dijon-style mustard, 4
teaspoons of balsamic vinegar, 1 tablespoon
of drained capers, ¼ teaspoon of dry
mustard powder and ¼ teaspoon of pepper.
Sprinkle with chopped parsley, if you wish.

RED PEPPER PESTO IN ENDIVE

Makes 24 servings.

Red Pepper Pesto:
1   cup water
3   large sweet red peppers (about 1⅓
        pounds), coarsely chopped
2   cloves garlic, chopped
1   teaspoon leaf basil, crumbled
½   teaspoon salt
¼   teaspoon pepper
½   cup fresh bread crumbs (1½ slices)
⅓   cup grated Parmesan cheese
2   tablespoons finely ground pine nuts
        (pignoli)

2   large heads Belgian endive (about 4½
        ounces each), separated into 24
        individual leaves

1. Prepare the Red Pepper Pesto: Bring the
   water to boiling in a 10-inch skillet. Add
   the red peppers and the garlic, and return
   to boiling. Lower the heat and cover the
   skillet. Simmer for 10 minutes, or until the
   red peppers are tender. Drain.
2. Place the cooked red peppers and garlic in
   the container of an electric blender or a
   food processor. Cover and process until
   the mixture is puréed. Return the mixture
   to the same skillet, along with the basil,
   salt and pepper. Bring to boiling. Reduce
   the heat to low and simmer for 10 minutes,
   or until the mixture thickens and most of
   the moisture is absorbed. Stir in the bread
   crumbs, Parmesan cheese and pine nuts.
   Cool slightly. Cover and refrigerate the
   pesto for several hours, or until it is
   completely cooled.
3. When ready to serve, spoon the pesto into
   a pastry bag fitted with a decorative tip.
   Pipe out about 1 scant tablespoon of pesto
   into the center of each endive leaf.

Did You Know . . .

In Canada, Thanksgiving is celebrated in October. Unlike Thanksgiving in the U.S., there are no parades, no football games, no elaborate decorative displays. Thanksgiving simply is a time for families and friends to gather together and share a special dinner thanking "Almighty God for the blessings with which the people of Canada have been favored." The date of this harvest celebration used to vary from province to province, occurring sometime between the first week of October and the second week of November. In 1957, the Canadian government set the official date as the second Monday in October.

HERB & SPICE CHEESE BALLS

Makes 6 dozen cheese balls.

Cilantro Cumin Cheese Balls:
- ⅓ cup finely chopped fresh cilantro
   OR: parsley OR: watercress
- 1 teaspoon ground cumin
- 1 pound Jarlsberg cheese
- 1 tablespoon melted butter

Ginger Sesame Cheese Balls:
- ⅓ cup sesame seeds, toasted*
- 1¼ teaspoons ground ginger
- 1¼ teaspoons soy sauce
- 1 pound mozzarella cheese
- 1 tablespoon melted butter

Paprika Pistachio Cheese Balls:
- 2 tablespoons finely ground pistachio nuts
- 2½ teaspoons paprika
- 1 pound Cheddar cheese

1. Prepare the Cilantro Cumin Cheese Balls: Mix the cilantro, parsley or watercress with the cumin in a small bowl until they are well blended. Set aside the mixture.
2. Using a ¾- or ⅞-inch melon baller, scoop out balls from the wedge of Jarlsberg cheese. (Save the scraps for shredding or snacks.)
3. With a wooden pick or skewer, dip each cheese ball into the melted butter, letting the excess drip off. Sprinkle the cilantro-cumin mixture over the entire ball, patting to help the coating adhere. Place the cheese balls on a serving platter. Cover the platter and refrigerate the cheese balls until ready to serve.
4. Prepare the Ginger Sesame Cheese Balls: Mix together the sesame seeds, ginger and soy sauce in a small bowl until they are well blended. Set aside the mixture. Proceed as in Steps 2 and 3, using the mozzarella cheese and the butter.
5. Prepare the Paprika Pistachio Cheese Balls: Mix the pistachio nuts with the paprika in a small bowl until they are well blended. Set aside the mixture. Proceed as in Steps 2 and 3, using the Cheddar cheese and omitting the butter.

Note: Toast the sesame seeds in a small, heavy skillet over medium heat until they are lightly golden, for about 2 to 3 minutes.

🍴 ◀◀◀
CREAMY GREEN BEAN SOUP

Makes 8 to 10 servings.

2 medium-size all-purpose potatoes
   (½ pound), peeled and cubed
4 cups chicken broth
2 pounds green beans, trimmed and cut into
   small pieces
1 bunch green onions, both green and white
   parts, sliced (about 8 green onions)
6 large shallots, peeled and chopped
   (about 1 cup)
1 large clove garlic, chopped
½ teaspoon leaf tarragon, crumbled
3 tablespoons butter
½ cup heavy cream OR: whipping cream
1 tablespoon lemon juice
¼ teaspoon freshly ground black pepper
   Fresh mint leaves, for garnish (optional)

1. Cook the potatoes in boiling salted water
   to cover in a medium-size saucepan until
   they are just tender, for about 15 minutes.
   Drain and set aside the potatoes.
2. Bring the broth to boiling in a large
   saucepan or Dutch oven. Add the green
   beans and return to boiling. Reduce the
   heat to low. Cover and simmer for 5
   minutes, or until just tender. Add the
   potatoes to the saucepan and reserve.
3. Meanwhile, sauté the green onion,
   shallots, garlic and tarragon in 2
   tablespoons of the butter in a medium-size
   saucepan for 8 to 10 minutes, or until the
   vegetables are tender and transparent. Stir
   in the reserved green bean mixture.
4. Pour about one third of the bean mixture
   into the container of an electric blender or
   a food processor. Cover and process until
   the mixture is puréed. Repeat with the
   remaining bean mixture. Return the purée
   to the saucepan.
5. Heat the soup to boiling. Stir in the heavy
   or whipping cream and the remaining 1
   tablespoon of butter. Lower the heat.
   Gently heat the soup; do not boil it. Stir in
   the lemon juice and the black pepper.
   Garnish with fresh mint leaves, if you wish.

🍴
ROAST TURKEY WITH BRANDIED FRUIT STUFFING

Roast at 400° for 15 minutes, then at 325° for
3¼ hours.
Makes 8 servings, with leftovers.

Brandied Fruit Stuffing:
1 box (11 ounces) dried mixed fruit, coarsely
   chopped
1 cup water
¼ cup brandy OR: orange juice
   Chicken broth OR: orange juice
1 large onion, coarsely chopped (1 cup)
¼ cup (½ stick) butter
¼ cup unsalted sunflower seeds
2 tablespoons grated orange zest
   (orange part of rind only)
½ teaspoon salt
¼ teaspoon pepper
9 slices day-old whole wheat bread, cut into
   ½-inch cubes (6 cups)

Roast Turkey:
1 turkey (about 12 pounds), thawed if frozen
   (see page 17 for how to thaw a turkey)
¾ teaspoon salt
½ teaspoon pepper
2 cups water
2 carrots, peeled and cut into 1-inch
   pieces
2 stalks celery, cut into 1-inch pieces
2 medium-size onions, peeled and quartered
4 parsley sprigs

Giblet Gravy:
   Turkey giblets
1 can (13¾ ounces) chicken broth
1 bay leaf
2 cups defatted pan drippings
2 tablespoons butter
¼ cup all-purpose flour
   Salt and pepper, to taste

   Watercress sprigs, for garnish
   Red Pepper Cups with Pea Purée,
   for garnish (recipe, page 11)

1. Prepare the Brandied Fruit Stuffing:
   Combine the mixed fruit, water and 2

tablespoons of the brandy or orange juice in a large saucepan. Bring to boiling over medium heat. Reduce the heat to low and simmer for 5 to 10 minutes, or until the fruit is just tender. Drain and reserve any remaining liquid, adding, if necessary, enough broth or orange juice to the liquid to make ½ cup. Set aside the fruit.

2. Meanwhile, sauté the onion in the butter in a large skillet for 5 minutes, or until the onion is just tender. Add the sunflower seeds and sauté for about 3 minutes, or until the seeds are lightly golden. Stir in the drained fruit, the reserved cooking liquid-broth mixture from the fruit, the remaining 2 tablespoons of brandy, the orange zest, salt and pepper.

3. Place the bread cubes in a large bowl. Pour the fruit mixture over. Toss gently with a fork to moisten all the ingredients. Set aside until you are ready to stuff the turkey. (The stuffing can be made ahead of time. Cover the bowl and refrigerate the stuffing for up to 2 days.)

4. Prepare the Roast Turkey: Preheat the oven to hot (400°). Remove the neck and giblets from the turkey and reserve them for making the gravy. Rinse the turkey well with cold water, inside and out. Pat dry with paper toweling. Sprinkle the inside of the body and neck cavities with ½ teaspoon of the salt and ¼ teaspoon of the pepper. Spoon the stuffing loosely into both cavities. Tie the legs to the tail with string and skewer the neck skin to the back. Place the turkey on a rack in a roasting pan with a tight-fitting lid. (If no lid is available, prepare a loose tent of aluminum foil sealed tightly around the rim of the pan.) Add the water, carrots, celery, onion and parsley. Sprinkle turkey with the remaining salt and pepper.

5. Roast the turkey, uncovered, in the preheated hot oven (400°) for 15 minutes. Reduce the oven temperature to slow (325°). Cover the pan with the lid or aluminum foil. Roast for 2½ hours. Uncover and roast for 45 minutes more, or until a meat thermometer inserted in the thickest part of the thigh, without touching the bone, reaches 180°. Remove the turkey from the oven. Let it stand for another 20 minutes before carving. Reserve the drippings in the roasting pan.

6. Meanwhile, prepare the Giblet Gravy: Combine the giblets (except the liver), broth and bay leaf in a medium-size saucepan. Bring to boiling over medium heat. Lower the heat, cover and simmer for 1 hour, or until tender. Add the liver and simmer for 15 minutes more. Drain the mixture, reserving the broth. Discard the bay leaf. Finely chop the giblets and set aside. Strain the drippings from the roasting pan into a 4-cup glass measure. Skim off the fat and discard. You should have at least 2 cups of drippings without fat. Add enough reserved giblet broth to make 3¾ cups.

7. Melt the butter in a small saucepan. Stir in the flour and cook for 2 minutes. Gradually stir in the broth mixture. Cook over medium heat, stirring constantly, until the mixture thickens and boils. Lower the heat, add the giblets and simmer for 5 minutes. Season with the salt and pepper. Pour gravy into a gravy boat.

8. Garnish the turkey with the watercress and Red Pepper Cups with Pea Purée. To store leftovers, remove the stuffing from the turkey and refrigerate it separately.

DON'T STUFF THE STUFFING!

Stuffing expands while the turkey roasts, so it's important not to pack it into the turkey too firmly or you'll have a minor explosion on your hands. Extra stuffing can be baked easily in a casserole dish during the last 30 to 45 minutes of roasting time. Baste the stuffing with the pan drippings or with broth to insure getting the moist, flavorful stuffing everyone loves.

THE HOT LINE

When you're feeding a crowd, it can be difficult to serve everybody while the food still is hot. Here are some pointers to keep the main course and side dishes warm.

● Cover serving platters of sliced turkey between servings.

● Transfer the stuffing, potatoes and other hot side dishes to warmed serving bowls or casserole dishes. Ovenproof casserole dishes can be warmed in a 200° oven. More delicate casserole dishes just should be rinsed with hot water and dried. Dinner plates can be heated on top of a warm stove before serving or, if they are ovenproof, in the oven on low heat.

● Heat a special "bun warmer" stone or tile in the oven and set it into a bread basket before lining the basket with a tea towel.

● Above all, don't stand on ceremony. Insist that your family and friends start eating as soon as they're served, even if you're still running in and out of the kitchen seeing to all the details.

RED PEPPER CUPS WITH PEA PURÉE

Makes 8 servings.

4	large sweet red peppers (about 2 pounds)
1	cup water
¾	teaspoon salt
3	packages (10 ounces each) frozen green peas
1	tablespoon butter
1	tablespoon grated orange zest (orange part of rind only)
1	teaspoon leaf rosemary, crumbled
¼	teaspoon freshly ground black pepper Red pepper twists, for garnish (optional)

1. Halve the red peppers crosswise. Remove the stems, seeds and white membrane. If necessary, place a small piece of red pepper in each space created by removing the stem. Set aside the red peppers.

2. Bring the water and the salt to boiling in a large saucepan over medium heat. Add the peas and return to boiling. Lower the heat to medium. Cook, covered, for 5 minutes, or until the peas are tender. Drain, reserving the cooking liquid.

3. Place the peas, 6 tablespoons of the reserved cooking liquid and the butter in the container of an electric blender or a food processor. Cover and process until the mixture is puréed. Return the pea purée to the saucepan. Stir in the orange zest, rosemary and black pepper. Heat the mixture through.

4. Meanwhile, cook the red peppers in boiling salted water to cover in a large saucepan or Dutch oven until the peppers are just tender, for about 5 minutes. Drain. Fill each red pepper with an equal amount of the pea purée. Garnish with red pepper twists, if you wish.

Microwave Instructions
(for a 650-watt variable power microwave oven)

Ingredient Changes: Reduce the water to ½ cup; reduce the rosemary to ¼ teaspoon.

Directions: Combine the peas with the water in a microwave-safe 2-quart casserole dish. Cover and microwave at full power for 10 to 12 minutes, stirring once. Drain the peas, reserving the cooking liquid. Purée the peas in an electric blender or a food processor with the butter and the reserved cooking liquid as in Step 3 above. Stir in the salt, orange zest, rosemary and black pepper. Spoon the pea purée into the red pepper cups. Arrange the filled cups around the edge of a microwave-safe 12-inch quiche pan. Cover with wax paper. Microwave at full power for 8 minutes, rotating the pan one quarter turn after 4 minutes. Let stand for 2 minutes.

LEMON DILLED BRUSSELS SPROUTS

Makes 10 to 12 servings.

1½ cups water
¾ teaspoon salt
3 containers (10 ounces each) Brussels
    sprouts, trimmed OR: 3 packages (10
    ounces each) frozen Brussels sprouts
¼ cup butter
2 tablespoons snipped fresh dill OR:
    1½ teaspoons dried dillweed, crumbled
1 tablespoon fresh lemon juice
1 can (8 ounces) sliced water chestnuts,
    drained

1. Bring the water and the salt to boiling in a
large saucepan. If using fresh Brussels
sprouts, cut an X in the stem ends. Add
the sprouts to the saucepan. Cover and
return to boiling.
2. Lower the heat and simmer, covered, until
the sprouts are tender, for about 12 to 15
minutes. Drain. Return the sprouts to the
saucepan.
3. Meanwhile, melt the butter in a small
saucepan. Add the dill, lemon juice and
water chestnuts. Set aside the mixture.
4. To serve, pour the butter-dill mixture over
the Brussels sprouts and toss together
until the sprouts are well coated.

Did You Know . . .

*The earliest American Thanksgivings were
centered around two lengthy church services,
with dinner served in between.*

BOURBON GINGERED SWEET POTATOES

Bake at 350° for 30 minutes.
Makes 8 servings.

3 pounds sweet potatoes, scrubbed
    (6 to 8 medium-size potatoes)
¼ cup bourbon whiskey
1 tablespoon butter, melted
1 tablespoon light brown sugar
1 tablespoon finely chopped, peeled fresh
    gingerroot
½ to 1 teaspoon salt
8 walnut halves OR: pecan halves,
    for garnish (optional)

1. Cook the sweet potatoes in boiling salted
water to cover in a large saucepan or
Dutch oven for 30 minutes, or until the
potatoes are tender. Drain. When the
potatoes are cool enough to handle, peel
them.
2. Place half the peeled potatoes in the
container of an electric blender or a food
processor. Cover and process until the
potatoes are puréed. Transfer the potato
purée to a large bowl. Repeat with the
remaining potatoes.
3. Preheat the oven to moderate (350°).
4. Stir the bourbon, butter, brown sugar,
ginger and salt into the puréed potatoes.
5. Using a pastry bag fitted with a large star
tip, pipe the potato mixture into 8 large
swirls in a shallow, round, 1½-quart
baking dish.
6. Bake in the preheated moderate oven
(350°) for 30 minutes, or until the potatoes
are hot. Garnish each swirl with a walnut
or pecan half, if you wish.

*Note: The Bourbon Gingered Sweet Potatoes
shown in the photo on page 4 are in a
different type of baking dish than called for in
the recipe. The potato swirls can be prepared
up to 1 day ahead of time. Cover and
refrigerate them.*

OPEN SESAME

Oriental sesame oil is wonderfully pungent and full of flavor—just a few drops impart a rich sesame taste to any dish. It also is darker in color than regular sesame oil. Oriental sesame oil can be found in the Oriental food section of many supermarkets or in Oriental specialty food stores.

RADISHES À LA VINAIGRETTE

Makes 8 servings.

 3 **tablespoons walnut oil**
 8 **teaspoons raspberry vinegar**
 4½ **teaspoons sesame seeds, toasted***
 4½ **teaspoons chopped fresh or freeze-dried chives**
 ½ **teaspoon salt**
 ¾ **teaspoon grated lemon zest (yellow part of rind only)**
 ¼ **teaspoon freshly ground black pepper**
 ¼ **teaspoon sugar**
 ¼ **teaspoon Oriental sesame oil**
 4 **cups thinly sliced radishes (3 to 4 bunches)**
   Lettuce leaves (optional)

1. Whisk together the walnut oil, vinegar, sesame seeds, chives, salt, lemon zest, black pepper, sugar and Oriental sesame oil in a large bowl until all the ingredients are well blended.
2. Add the radishes and toss until they are well coated with the salad dressing. Cover and refrigerate the salad for at least 3 hours before serving, tossing occasionally.
3. Serve the salad on a bed of lettuce leaves arranged on a serving platter, if you wish.

Note: Toast the sesame seeds in a small, heavy skillet over medium heat until they are lightly golden, for about 2 minutes.

TANGY CRANBERRY RELISH

Makes 12 servings.

 1 **package (12 ounces) whole cranberries, picked over and rinsed**
 ⅔ **cup granulated sugar***
 1 **cup water**
 1½ **envelopes unflavored gelatin (about 4½ teaspoons)**
 ⅓ **cup firmly packed light brown sugar**
 1 **can (6 ounces) unsweetened pineapple juice**
 2 **tablespoons red wine vinegar**
 2 **cups coarsely chopped peeled and cored cooking apples, such as McIntosh (2 medium-size apples)**
 1 **tablespoon prepared horseradish**
   Green apple skin roses, for garnish (optional)
   Additional whole cranberries, for garnish (optional)

1. Cook the cranberries, granulated sugar and ¼ cup of the water in a medium-size saucepan over medium-high heat, stirring occasionally, for about 10 minutes, or until the cranberries begin to pop and the mixture starts to thicken. Set aside the cranberry mixture to cool completely.
2. Meanwhile, sprinkle the gelatin over ¼ cup of the water in a small saucepan. Let stand until the gelatin softens, for about 5 minutes.
3. Add the remaining ½ cup of water and the brown sugar to the gelatin. Place the saucepan over low heat and cook, stirring occasionally, until the gelatin and the brown sugar are dissolved completely. Stir in the pineapple juice and the vinegar.
4. Pour the gelatin mixture into a large bowl and refrigerate until it is partially set, for about 45 to 60 minutes (the mixture will mound slightly when dropped from a spoon).
5. When the gelatin mixture has thickened, fold in the cranberry mixture, apples and horseradish. Pour the cranberry-gelatin

SLIP-SLIDING: A WAY

When you're ready to serve a gelatin-based salad or relish, moisten the plate onto which you'll be unmolding the salad. This will enable you to move the mold on the plate, if necessary, to center it.

mixture into a 5- or 6-cup non-aluminum decorative mold. Chill overnight, or until the gelatin is firm.

6. To unmold, gently and carefully loosen the edges of the gelatin from the sides of the mold with your fingertips. Dip a cloth towel in hot water, squeeze out the excess water and wrap the towel around the outside of the mold to loosen the gelatin. Invert the mold onto a serving platter. Repeat the procedure, if necessary, to loosen the gelatin completely. Garnish the relish with green apple skin roses and whole cranberries, if you wish.

Note: For a more tart flavor, use only ½ cup of sugar.

Microwave Instructions
(for a 650-watt variable power microwave oven)

Directions: Combine the cranberries, granulated sugar and ¼ cup of the water in a microwave-safe 2-quart casserole dish. Cover and microwave at full power for 6 minutes, stirring once. Soften the gelatin in ¼ cup of the water in a small bowl. Stir the softened gelatin into the hot cranberry mixture until the gelatin is dissolved. Stir in the brown sugar until it is dissolved. Stir in the remaining ½ cup of water, the pineapple juice and vinegar. Refrigerate the mixture until it thickens slightly. Fold in the apples and the horseradish. Pour the mixture into a 6-cup mold. Chill overnight or until firm, and unmold as in Step 6 above.

BRAIDED WREATH BREAD

Bake at 350° for 35 minutes.
Makes 2 wreaths (16 servings each).

7½ cups sifted all-purpose flour
3 tablespoons sugar
4½ teaspoons salt
3 packages active dry yeast
3½ cups very warm to hot water (120° to 130°)
6 tablespoons butter, softened
5 tablespoons dark molasses
1½ cups whole wheat flour, stirred
3 tablespoons unsweetened cocoa powder
1½ cups rye flour, stirred
1 egg
1 tablespoon water

1. Combine 3½ cups of the all-purpose flour, the sugar, salt and yeast in a large bowl. Stir in the 3½ cups of water and the butter. Beat with an electric mixer at medium speed for about 2 minutes, scraping the sides of the bowl occasionally. Add 1½ cups of the remaining all-purpose flour. Beat at high speed for 2 minutes, scraping the sides of the bowl occasionally.

2. Divide the dough into thirds, placing 2 of the thirds in two medium-size bowls, about 2 cups per bowl. Set aside the medium-size bowls. Stir 1 tablespoon of the molasses and the whole wheat flour into the remaining third of dough. Add enough of the remaining all-purpose flour to make a very soft dough.

3. Turn out the dough onto a floured surface and knead until the dough is smooth and satiny, for about 5 minutes. Wash, dry and grease the bowl. Return the dough to the greased bowl and turn the dough greased side up. Cover the bowl with a towel and set aside.

4. Stir the cocoa, the remaining 4 tablespoons of molasses and the rye flour into one of the remaining thirds of dough. Add enough of the remaining all-purpose flour to make a very soft and slightly sticky dough. Proceed as in Step 3.

5. Add enough of the remaining all-purpose flour to the remaining third of dough to make a very soft dough. Proceed as in Step 3.

6. Let all 3 bowls of dough rise in a warm place, away from drafts, until the doughs are doubled in bulk, for about 1 hour.

7. Punch down the doughs. Divide each in half and let rest for 10 minutes. Roll each half into a 24-inch-long rope.

8. Place 1 whole wheat, 1 white and 1 rye rope side by side on a lightly greased baking sheet. Beginning in the middle, braid the ropes together to one end. Then braid from the middle to the other end; try not to stretch the dough. Form the braid into a round ring, pinching the ends together to seal them. Repeat with the remaining ropes. Cover the wreaths and let them rise in a warm place, away from drafts, until they are doubled in bulk, for about 35 to 40 minutes.

9. Preheat the oven to moderate (350°).

10. Beat together the egg and the 1 tablespoon of water in a small bowl. Brush each ring with the egg mixture.

11. Bake in the preheated moderate oven (350°) for 35 minutes, or until the wreaths are golden brown and sound hollow when tapped with your fingertips. Remove the wreaths to a wire rack to cool. Serve the bread warm or at room temperature.

Did You Know . . .

Benjamin Franklin was a stalwart champion of our native bird, the turkey " . . . a true, original native of America who would not hesitate to attack a grenadier of the British guard who should presume to invade the farmyard with a red coat on."

APRICOT NUT PIE

Bake at 350° for 1½ hours.
Makes one 9-inch pie (10 servings).

Lemon-Flecked Pastry Crust:
2   cups unsifted all-purpose flour
2   tablespoons grated lemon zest (yellow part of rind only)
½   teaspoon salt
⅔   cup margarine, softened
3   tablespoons ice water
1   to 2 tablespoons lemon juice

Apricot Raisin Nut Filling:
1   package (16 ounces) dried apricots
    Water
¾   cup sugar
3   tablespoons quick-cooking tapioca
2   tablespoons butter or margarine, softened
1   teaspoon grated lemon zest (yellow part of rind only)
¼   teaspoon ground cinnamon
¼   teaspoon ground nutmeg
¼   teaspoon salt
1   cup golden raisins
½   cup coarsely chopped walnuts

1   egg
1   tablespoon water

1. Prepare the Lemon-Flecked Pastry Crust: Combine the flour, lemon zest and salt in a medium-size bowl. Cut in the margarine with a pastry blender or 2 knives until the mixture is crumbly. Gradually add the ice water and the lemon juice, 1 tablespoon at a time, stirring with a fork until the dough leaves the sides of the bowl clean and can be gathered into a ball.

2. Divide the pastry into 2 pieces, one slightly larger than the other. Wrap the smaller portion in plastic wrap and refrigerate it. Roll out the larger portion to a 13-inch circle. Fold the circle in quarters and place it in a 9-inch pie plate. Gently unfold and press the pastry into the pie plate, being careful not to stretch

the dough. Using a knife or scissors, trim the pastry even with the pie plate. Cover with plastic wrap and refrigerate the pastry until ready to fill it. Reserve the scraps, covered, in the refrigerator.

3. Prepare the Apricot Raisin Nut Filling: Place the apricots in a large saucepan with enough water to cover. Bring to boiling over high heat. Reduce the heat to medium and cook until the apricots are just tender, for 5 to 10 minutes. Drain the apricots, reserving 1¼ cups of the cooking liquid.

4. Combine the sugar, tapioca, butter or margarine, lemon zest, cinnamon, nutmeg and salt in a large bowl. Add the apricots and the reserved cooking liquid, stirring until all the ingredients are well mixed. Set aside the mixture for 20 minutes.

5. Meanwhile, prepare the decorative top crust: Roll out the remaining pastry to a ⅛- to ¼-inch thickness. Using a fluted pastry wheel, cut fifteen ½-inch strips, 4¾ to 5 inches long. Cut the remaining dough into 46 stars, using a ¾-inch star-shaped cookie or candy cutter, and 18 circles, using a fluted 1-inch cookie or candy cutter. Reroll the reserved scraps, if necessary, to cut enough stars and circles. Set aside the strips and shapes, and cover them with lightly dampened paper toweling.

6. Add the golden raisins and the walnuts to the apricot filling and stir until the ingredients are well mixed. Spoon the filling into the pie shell.

7. Preheat the oven to moderate (350°).

8. Place the fluted strips on the pie in a wheel-spoke design, twisting each strip, and have them meet in the center but overlap in as few places as possible. If the strips extend beyond the edge of the pie plate, trim them flush with the pie plate. Seal the edge of the bottom pastry, using a dab of water, if necessary. Place the stars, overlapping slightly, around the outer edge of the pastry, using a dab of water to seal them. Using a rolling pin,

DOUGHS AND DON'TS

To help make pastry flaky, light and picture-perfect, use ice water to prepare the dough, and handle the dough as little as possible. Unlike bread dough, pastry dough that is overhandled becomes tough. Chilling the dough before rolling it out allows the dough to relax, producing a more tender, flaky crust.

lightly roll over each fluted circle to slightly flatten and enlarge it. Slightly overlap 6 circles, one at a time, holding them between your thumb and forefinger, to form a solid circle of discs. With the index finger of your opposite hand, gently push in the center of the circle to form a slight stem on the underside. With your fingers, shape the top of the circle to form a flower, pinching the discs together to seal them. Place the dough flower in the center of the pie, using a dab of water, if necessary, to seal the strips. Repeat 2 times more with the remaining circles of dough.

9. Beat together the egg and the 1 tablespoon of water in a small glass measuring cup. With a pastry brush, carefully brush the pastry with the egg mixture.

10. Bake the pie on the bottom rack of the preheated moderate oven (350°) for 1½ hours, or until the crust is golden and the filling is bubbly. (If the crust begins to brown too much, cover the darker spots with aluminum foil.)

11. Cool the pie slightly on a wire rack. Serve the pie warm, or cool it completely and serve it at room temperature.

TALKING TURKEY

Here are some holiday-tested hints to make your Thanksgiving meal a gobbling success!

BUYING AND PREPARING THE BIRD

• When choosing a turkey, allow one pound per serving if the bird weighs 12 pounds or less, ½ pound per serving if the bird weighs more than 12 pounds.

• Remember, a bigger turkey is a better buy and will provide you with leftovers.

• For just two people, consider buying a frozen boneless turkey or turkey roll. A small family with a preference for white meat would enjoy a roasted turkey breast.

STORING

Fresh Turkey: Refrigerate it at all times. Cook it within 1 to 2 days of purchase.

Frozen Whole Turkey: Store it in its original wrapper for up to 12 months at 0° or lower.

THAWING

The National Turkey Federation recommends these two methods.

Conventional (long) Method:
Thawing time—3 to 4 days, about 24 hours for each 5 pounds of whole frozen turkey.

• Leave the turkey in its original wrapper.

• Place the frozen turkey on a tray in the refrigerator.

Cold Water (short) Method:
Thawing time—about 30 minutes per pound of whole frozen turkey.

• Leave the turkey in its original wrapper.

• Place the turkey in a sink or large pan.

• Completely cover with cold water.

• Change the water every 30 minutes.

• Keep the turkey immersed in the cold water at all times.

Note: Never thaw a turkey at room temperature. Once thawed, cook or refrigerate the turkey immediately.

STUFFING

When? Just before roasting the turkey is the time to stuff it. You run the risk of getting food poisoning if this is done earlier.

How much? Allow ¾ cup of stuffing per pound of bird for turkeys weighing more than 10 pounds, ½ cup of stuffing per pound for smaller turkeys.

Note: Never freeze stuffing that is in a cooked or raw bird. Remove all the stuffing from a cooked bird, wrap it separately and refrigerate it.

TIMETABLE FOR ROASTING TURKEY (325°)

BIRD WEIGHT (pounds)	STUFFED (hours)	UNSTUFFED (hours)
6 to 8	3 to 3½	2½ to 3½
8 to 12	3½ to 4½	3 to 4
12 to 16	4 to 5	3½ to 4½
16 to 20	4½ to 5½	4 to 5
20 to 24	5 to 6½	4½ to 5½

• Do not roast turkey overnight at very low oven temperatures.

GOOD GRAVY!

To many people, the Thanksgiving bird is naked without delicious creamy gravy on top. Here are some quick tips to make holiday-perfect gravy every time.

Lumpy Gravy: Force the gravy through a sieve with a rubber spatula, or whirl it in an electric blender or a food processor until smooth. Return the gravy to the saucepan and gently simmer until it is heated through.

Too-thick Gravy: Transfer the gravy to a saucepan. Whisk in the liquid used to make the gravy, 1 tablespoon at a time, until the gravy reaches the desired consistency.

Too-thin Gravy: Transfer the gravy to a saucepan. Gently boil until the gravy is reduced to the desired consistency. Or add small pieces of Instant Thickener *(recipe follows)* into the gravy, whisking after each addition, until the gravy thickens to the desired consistency.

Instant Thickener: This is a quickly made thickening agent (known as *beurre manié*) that can be added to any liquid to turn it into a gravy. Freeze small amounts to have on hand.

Makes enough to thicken 4 to 6 cups of very thin liquid.

¼ cup (½ stick) unsalted butter, softened
¼ cup all-purpose flour

1. Mix together the butter and the flour in a small bowl to form a smooth paste.
2. To freeze Instant Thickener, scoop it with a measuring tablespoon and spatula onto a wax paper-lined baking sheet. Place the baking sheet in the freezer until the thickener is hard. Remove the frozen mounds to a freezer bag. Store Instant Thickener in the freezer for up to 3 months. One tablespoon is enough to thicken 1 to 2 cups of liquid.

TESTING FOR DONENESS

• A meat thermometer inserted in the meatiest part of the thigh, without touching the bone, reads 180° to 185°.
• The turkey juices run clear.
• The drumsticks move up and down easily.

RESTING PERIOD

Let the turkey stand at room temperature for 20 minutes. This allows the juices to settle and the meat to firm up for easier carving.

GOT A QUESTION?

• The toll-free U.S.D.A. Meat and Poultry Hotline at 1-800-535-4555 will answer questions about your holiday bird from 10 A.M. to 4 P.M. (EST), Monday-Friday, no weekends or holidays.
• The toll-free Butterball Turkey Talk-line at 1-800-323-4848 will answer any questions about preparing a holiday turkey and trimmings. The Talk-line will operate from November 2 through December 24, Monday-Friday, 8 A.M. to 8 P.M. (CST), Thanksgiving Day, 6 A.M. to 7 P.M. (CST) and Christmas Eve, 8 A.M. TO 6 P.M. (CST).

MICROWAVE COOKING DIRECTIONS FOR TURKEY

(625- to 700-watt microwave ovens)

If frozen, thaw the turkey as directed in the general directions on page 17. Thawing a turkey in the microwave is not recommended.

Preparation:
1. Free the legs from the tucked position. Do not cut the band of skin.
2. Remove the neck meat and giblets from the neck and body cavities. To microwave these, place 3 cups of water, ½ teaspoon of salt, the neck, gizzard and heart in a microwave-safe 2-quart casserole dish. Cover and microwave at half power for 35 minutes. Add the liver, cover and microwave for 10 minutes more. The cooked neck, giblets and stock may be used to make the turkey gravy or be mixed together with the stuffing.
3. Rinse the turkey and drain it well.

4. If you wish, loosely stuff the neck and body cavities. Cover any exposed stuffing with plastic wrap.

5. Turn back the wings to hold the neck skin in place. Return the legs to the tucked position. No trussing is necessary.

6. Make the Browning Sauce: Microwave ½ stick of butter in a microwave-safe bowl at full power for 30 to 40 seconds, or until the butter has melted. Blend in ¼ teaspoon of paprika and ⅛ teaspoon of browning and seasoning sauce. Stir well before using.

Cooking:

1. Place the turkey, breast side down, in a microwave-safe dish. If the turkey tips, level it with a microwave-safe item so it will cook evenly.

2. Brush the back of the turkey with 1 tablespoon of the Browning Sauce.

3. See the Microwave Oven Cooking Schedule, below, for the cooking time. Use the schedule closest to the weight of the turkey. Follow Part I and Part II Cooking Times without any delaying interruptions.

4. Microwave at full power for Time 1. Rotate the turkey one half turn. Microwave for Time 2. Remove and discard the pan drippings.

5. Turn the turkey breast side up. If the turkey is stuffed, remove the plastic wrap. Brush with the Browning Sauce. Level if the turkey tips.

6. Microwave at half power for Times 3, 4 and 5. At the end of each Time, rotate the turkey one quarter turn, discard the pan drippings and brush the turkey with the Browning Sauce. If overbrowning occurs, shield the turkey with small pieces of aluminum foil. After Time 5, check for doneness. A meat thermometer inserted in the thickest part of the thigh, without touching the bone, should register 180° to 185°; in the thickest part of the breast, 170°; in the center of the stuffing, 160° to 165°. If any of these temperatures have not been reached, cook for Time 6. Recheck the temperature and cook longer, if necessary.

7. Cover the turkey with aluminum foil. Let it stand for 20 minutes before carving.

MICROWAVE OVEN COOKING SCHEDULE
for Stuffed or Unstuffed Turkey
Approximate cooking time in 625- to 700-watt microwave ovens

Weight		4 lb.	5 lb.	6 lb.	7 lb.	8 lb.	9 lb.	10 lb.	11 lb.	12 lb.
Times		**Part I—Breast down at full power**								
	1	8 min	10 min	12 min	14 min	16 min	18 min	20 min	22 min	24 min
	2	8 min	10 min	12 min	14 min	16 min	18 min	20 min	22 min	24 min
		Part II — Breast up at half power								
	3	8 min	10 min	12 min	14 min	16 min	18 min	20 min	22 min	24 min
	4	8 min	10 min	12 min	14 min	16 min	18 min	20 min	22 min	24 min
	5*	8 min	10 min	12 min	14 min	16 min	18 min	20 min	22 min	24 min
	6	8 min	10 min	12 min	14 min	16 min	18 min	20 min	22 min	24 min
Total Cooking Time		48 min	60 min	72 min	84 min	96 min	108 min	120 min	132 min	144 min

*Check for doneness after Time 5

CARVING A TURKEY

There's no mystery to being a master carver—just follow our simple step-by-step directions.*

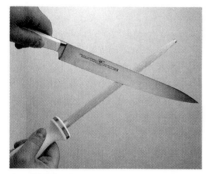

1. SHARPEN THE KNIFE:
Place the base of the blade at a 20° angle to the tip of a sharpener. Pull the blade's cutting edge across and down the sharpener toward the base. Now place the opposite side of the blade on the underside of the sharpener and repeat the motion. Do each edge several times.

2. REMOVE THE TURKEY FROM THE PAN: To make it easy to remove the cooked turkey, line the roasting pan across its width with a strip of folded heavy-duty aluminum foil before placing the turkey in the pan. When the turkey is cooked, lift it out by the foil ends and let it rest for 15 to 30 minutes before carving it. Remove the stuffing. Carve one side of the bird at a time.

3. REMOVE THE LEG:
Place the turkey, breast side up, on a cutting board. Steady the bird with the back of the carving fork to avoid sticking the tines into the meat and releasing the juices. Slice through the skin between the breast and the thigh. Pull the leg back to locate the joint. Cut through the joint to remove the leg.

*Note: Our carver is left-handed.

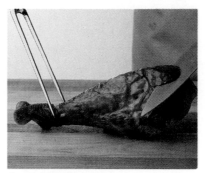

4. DIVIDE THE LEG: To separate the drumstick and the thigh for carving, slightly stretch apart the drumstick and thigh, and find the joint. With a firm downward movement of the knife, cut through the joint.

5. CARVE THE DRUMSTICK: Position the narrow end of the leg between the tines of the carving fork to avoid piercing the meat. Holding the carving knife parallel to the bone, cut slices from the drumstick.

6. CARVE THE THIGH AND WING: Moving parallel to the bone, cut slices from the thigh. To remove the wing (not pictured), cut through the skin at the corner of the breast around the wing. Move the wing to locate the joint. Cut through the joint to remove the wing with a small part of the breast.

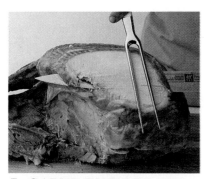

7. CARVE THE BREAST: Starting at the outside of the breast, cut diagonally downward to produce thin slices. Steady the turkey with the back of the carving fork to avoid sticking the tines into the meat. Repeat all the carving steps with the other side of the turkey when you refill the serving platter.

Marinated Vegetable Salad (recipe, page 30)

"A STAR FROM THE EAST" THANKSGIVING DINNER

(for 8)

Seafood Pâté Loaf with Beurre Blanc Sauce
Roast Turkey with Honey Soy Glaze
Sausage, Rice and Shiitake Mushroom Stuffing
Broccoli with Black Beans and Water Chestnuts
Ginger-Glazed Carrots and Onions
Marinated Vegetable Salad
Kumquat Pecan Pie
Gingered Pumpkin Cheesecake
Praline Lace Cookies

WORK PLAN FOR "A STAR FROM THE EAST" THANKSGIVING DINNER

Up to One Month Ahead:
- Prepare and freeze the Kumquat Pecan Pie.

Up to Several Days Ahead:
- Prepare the Kumquat Pecan Pie, if it was not prepared ahead and frozen.
- Prepare and refrigerate the Gingered Pumpkin Cheesecake. Prepare the Praline Lace Cookies; store in an airtight container.

The Day Before:
- Chop the green onions for the Beurre Blanc Sauce.
- Prepare and refrigerate the Seafood Pâté Loaf.
- Thaw the Kumquat Pecan Pie, if frozen.

Early in the Day:
- Prepare the Sausage, Rice and Shiitake Mushroom Stuffing.
- Prepare the Marinated Vegetable Salad.
- Remove the side of the springform pan from the Gingered Pumpkin Cheesecake, place the cheesecake on a serving platter, cover the cheesecake loosely with plastic wrap and return it to the refrigerator.

Five Hours Before:
- Stuff the turkey and *immediately* start roasting it, basting with the Honey Soy Glaze during the last half hour of roasting time. (Allow the roast turkey to rest for 20 minutes before carving it.)

Several Hours Before:
- Prepare the ingredients for the Ginger-Glazed Carrots and Onions, and for the Broccoli with Black Beans and Water Chestnuts.

One Hour Before:
- Remove the Seafood Pâté Loaf from the refrigerator.

30 Minutes Before:
- Reheat the Seafood Pâté Loaf in a slow oven.
- Prepare the Beurre Blanc Sauce.
- Prepare the Ginger-Glazed Carrots and Onions, and the Broccoli with Black Beans and Water Chestnuts.
- Remove the Marinated Vegetable Salad from the refrigerator.

Just Before Dinner:
- Finish preparing the Marinated Vegetable Salad.
- Remove the Gingered Pumpkin Cheesecake from the refrigerator; garnish with the Praline Lace Cookies.

During Dinner:
- Reheat the Kumquat Pecan Pie.

SEAFOOD PÂTÉ LOAF

Have the eggs, fish and cream well chilled before blending them.

Bake at 350° for 45 minutes.
Makes 8 servings.

1	**tablespoon butter**
½	**cup finely chopped shallots**
2	**tablespoons chopped celery**
2	**teaspoons finely chopped fresh gingerroot**
1	**teaspoon finely chopped garlic**
¾	**pound firm white fish fillets, such as sole, halibut or scrod**
½	**pound shrimp, shelled and deveined**
1	**egg yolk**
2	**egg whites**
1	**cup heavy cream OR: whipping cream**
2	**tablespoons dry sherry**
¼	**pound bay scallops OR: quartered sea scallops**
⅓	**cup finely chopped fresh parsley**
	Salt and freshly ground white pepper, to taste
	Beurre Blanc Sauce (recipe, page 26)
	Parsley sprigs and additional cooked shrimp, for garnish (optional)

1. Melt the butter in a small sauté pan. Add the shallots, celery, ginger and garlic. Cover and cook over low heat for 2 minutes. Uncover and sauté for 2 minutes more. Remove the vegetables from the heat and cool them.
2. Preheat the oven to moderate (350°). Lightly butter the sides and bottom of an 8 x 4-inch loaf pan.
3. Place the fish fillets, half the shrimp, the sautéed vegetables and the egg yolk in the container of a food processor. Process the mixture until it is puréed. With the motor running, add the egg whites, one at a time, then the heavy or whipping cream mixed with the sherry, scraping down the sides of the bowl once or twice with a rubber spatula. Transfer the puréed mixture to a large bowl.
4. Coarsely chop the remaining shrimp and add them, along with the scallops, parsley and salt and white pepper, to the puréed mixture. Gently mix together all the ingredients with the spatula.
5. Spoon the mixture into the prepared pan, smoothing the top. Bang the bottom of the pan against the counter once or twice to eliminate air bubbles. Cover the top of the pan with a piece of buttered aluminum foil and place the pan inside a baking pan. Place the baking pan on an oven rack. Pour hot water into the baking pan until the water is halfway up the sides of the loaf pan.
6. Bake in the preheated moderate oven (350°) for 45 minutes, or until a skewer inserted in the center of the loaf comes out clean. Cool the loaf in the pan on a wire rack for 15 minutes, then unmold it.
7. Serve slices of the loaf hot or tepid with the Beurre Blanc Sauce. Garnish with parsley and additional cooked shrimp, if you wish.

Did You Know . . .

The idea of a festival in thanks for the harvest is found in almost every culture. The ancient Hebrews celebrated a Feast of Tabernacles, the Greeks had a festival honoring Demeter, the goddess of the harvest, and the Romans had the Cerealia in honor of Ceres, the goddess of grain. But, in this country, the best known celebration by far is the three-day feast celebrated in the fall of 1621 by the settlers of Plymouth, Massachusetts.

BEURRE BLANC SAUCE

Gingerroot adds a zippy undernote.

Makes 8 servings.

- ½ cup dry white wine
- ½ cup rice wine vinegar
- ½ cup finely chopped shallots
- ¾ cup finely chopped green onion
- 2 tablespoons finely chopped fresh gingerroot
- 1 cup (2 sticks) unsalted butter, well chilled
   Salt and pepper, to taste

1. Place the wine, vinegar, shallots, ¼ cup of the green onion and the ginger in a small, heavy saucepan. Bring to boiling over high heat. Boil for 2 to 4 minutes, or until the mixture reduces to about ¼ cup with a thick, glaze-like consistency. (The sauce can be made in advance up to this point, but reduce the mixture only to ⅓ cup, since it will need to be heated again.)
2. Meanwhile, cut each stick of butter into 8 slices, but do not let the slices get soft.
3. When the wine mixture is reduced, quickly beat in 2 squares of the butter with a wire whisk, beating until the butter is creamy. Continue adding the butter, bit by bit, over the lowest possible heat, until the butter does not melt completely but softens enough to reach the consistency of a heavy cream sauce. Taste and season with the salt and pepper. Stir in the remaining ½ cup of green onion. Serve the sauce at once.

GLAZING GLITCHES

Glazes that contain sugar, honey or preserves should be brushed onto roasting meats only during the last half hour of roasting time, or the glazes will burn.

ROAST TURKEY WITH HONEY SOY GLAZE

Roast at 400° for 15 minutes, then at 325° for 3¼ hours.
Makes 8 servings, with leftovers.

- 1 12-pound turkey
   Sausage, Rice and Shiitake
      Mushroom Stuffing (recipe, page 27)
   Honey Soy Glaze (recipe follows)

1. Follow the directions for Roast Turkey with Brandied Fruit Stuffing *(recipe, page 9)*, substituting Sausage, Rice and Shiitake Mushroom Stuffing for the fruit stuffing. During the last half hour of roasting, brush the turkey every 10 minutes with the Honey Soy Glaze.
2. Top each serving of turkey with any remaining Honey Soy Glaze.

HONEY SOY GLAZE

This glaze can be made ahead and refrigerated for 2 to 3 days before using it.

Makes 3 cups.

- 1 cup honey
- 1 cup soy sauce
- 1 cup dry sherry
- 2 green onions, chopped
- 2 cloves garlic, finely chopped

Combine the honey, soy sauce, sherry, green onion and garlic in a small saucepan. Bring the mixture to boiling over medium heat, stirring. Remove the saucepan from the heat. Brush the glaze on the turkey every 10 minutes during the last half hour of roasting.

TROT OUT THE TURKEY

Stuffing Sense: No matter what recipe you choose, stuffing always should be kept very hot or very cold. If left for extended periods at in-between temperatures, stuffing can develop bacteria that causes food poisoning. For the same reason, always store stuffing separately from the bird both before and after roasting.

There's no rule that says you have to cook the stuffing *in* the turkey. As an alternative, pack the stuffing into the pan around the bird 2 hours before the end of the roasting time, and baste it with the pan juices.

Trusty Trussing: A trussed turkey keeps its shape better during roasting. Set the turkey, seasoned and stuffed as you like, in a large roasting pan. Tie the ends of the legs together with kitchen twine or unwaxed dental floss. Tuck the wings underneath the bird, or fold them across the breast and secure them with a long piece of twine wrapped around the bird.

Basting Basics: To keep the bird moist, baste it with the pan juices every half hour during roasting. Begin by brushing with melted butter until sufficient juices accumulate in the pan. Set an aluminum foil "tent" on top of the bird to prevent it from browning too quickly.

Is It Turkey Yet? Plan on a roasting time of 15 to 20 minutes per pound for a stuffed bird, or about 12 minutes per pound if the bird is not stuffed. To test for doneness, pierce the bird with a thin skewer at the point where the thigh meets the body. When the juices run clear (not pink), the bird is done. Meat on the inner part of the thigh should register 180° to 185°. Set aside the roasted bird on a board or warm platter for 15 to 20 minutes before carving it.

SAUSAGE, RICE AND SHIITAKE MUSHROOM STUFFING

Use long-grain rice instead of the sticky kind, if you prefer.

Makes enough stuffing for a 10- to 12-pound turkey (8 servings).

- 3 **cups glutinous or sticky rice***
- 3 **ounces dried shiitake mushrooms***
- 2 **cups chicken broth**
- ¼ **cup (½ stick) butter**
- 2 **cups chopped onion**
- 1 **cup chopped celery**
- ¾ **pound Chinese pork sausage, thinly sliced***
- 1 **tablespoon finely chopped garlic**
- 1 **tablespoon finely chopped fresh gingerroot**
- 1 **cup chopped green onions**
- 1 **cup chopped water chestnuts**
- 2 **tablespoons Oriental sesame oil***
- 2 **tablespoons soy sauce**
- 1 **teaspoon cracked black pepper**
- 2 **eggs, slightly beaten**

1. Rinse the rice in a colander under cold running water, running your fingers through the rice, until the water runs clear. Drain the rice.
2. Meanwhile, soak the mushrooms in hot water to cover in a medium-size bowl for 30 minutes, or until they are softened. Cut off the tough stems, then slice the caps into julienne sticks.
3. Combine the rice with 1½ cups of the broth in a medium-size saucepan over medium heat. Bring to boiling, lower the heat and cover. Simmer for 10 to 12 minutes, or until the liquid is absorbed and the rice is slightly tender. (It will continue cooking in the turkey.) Remove the rice from the heat and let stand, covered, for 10 minutes. Fluff the rice with a fork.
4. Melt the butter in a large saucepan over medium heat. Sauté the onion and the celery for 5 minutes, or until they are translucent. Add the sausage and sauté for 3 minutes. Add the mushroom sticks, garlic and ginger, and sauté for 2 minutes

more. Remove the sausage-mushroom mixture from the heat.

5. Add the rice, green onion, water chestnuts, Oriental sesame oil, soy sauce and black pepper. Mix with your fingers until the ingredients are well blended. (The recipe can be made ahead up to this point. Cover the stuffing with plastic wrap and refrigerate it.)

6. When ready to stuff the turkey, add the eggs to the rice mixture and mix until the ingredients are well blended.

7. Very loosely stuff the turkey with the rice mixture (because it is only partially cooked, the rice will expand in the turkey as it cooks). Roast the turkey following the directions on page 17.

8. Place any leftover stuffing in a casserole dish and pour over the remaining ½ cup of broth. Place the casserole dish in the oven during the last 45 minutes of roasting time, basting with ½ cup of pan drippings.

Note: These ingredients are available in Oriental food stores.

DEEP FREEZE

Let your freezer help you make the most of holiday leftovers. When you bone a turkey or cut up a leftover ham, divide the small chunks into the right size portions for your favorite recipes. Then freeze the packets until needed.

BROCCOLI WITH BLACK BEANS AND WATER CHESTNUTS

Preserved in salt, fermented black beans must be rinsed before using.

Makes 8 servings.

- ⅓ **cup finely chopped green onion**
- 3 **tablespoons fermented black beans* (salted black beans), rinsed, drained and finely chopped**
- 1 **tablespoon finely chopped fresh gingerroot**
- 1 **tablespoon finely chopped garlic**
- 2 **tablespoons peanut OR: corn oil**
- 1 **cup chicken broth**
- 2 **tablespoons soy sauce**
- 1 **tablespoon cornstarch**
- 2 **heads broccoli, broken into flowerets and stem pieces**
- 1 **cup sliced water chestnuts**
  Sweet red pepper strips, for garnish

1. Sauté the green onion, black beans, ginger and garlic in the peanut or corn oil in a small saucepan over medium heat for 30 seconds.

2. Add the broth, soy sauce and cornstarch. Continue cooking, stirring, until the sauce thickens. Remove sauce from the heat.

3. Steam or simmer the broccoli stem pieces in a wok or very large saucepan for 4 minutes. Add the floweret pieces and continue cooking until the broccoli is crisply tender.

4. Add the black bean sauce and the water chestnuts. Cook over low heat, tossing gently, until the broccoli is evenly coated. Garnish with the red pepper strips.

Note: Black beans are available in Oriental food stores.

Ginger-Glazed Carrots and Onions

GINGER-GLAZED CARROTS AND ONIONS

Makes 8 servings.

2	*pounds baby carrots, trimmed and peeled*
1/2	*pound baby onions, parboiled and peeled*
2	*tablespoons sugar*
1	*tablespoon finely chopped fresh gingerroot*
3	*tablespoons butter*
1	*piece lemon zest (yellow part of rind only)*
	Salt, to taste
1	*bunch green onions*
1/4	*cup plum wine OR: sweet sherry*
1	*tablespoon lemon juice*
2	*tablespoons finely chopped crystallized ginger*

1. Place the carrots and the baby onions in a large, heavy saucepan. Add 1 tablespoon of the sugar, the fresh ginger, 1 tablespoon of the butter, the lemon zest, 2 cups of water and the salt. Bring the mixture to boiling over medium heat. Cover and lower the heat.
2. Simmer for 10 minutes, or until the carrots and baby onions are tender but still a bit crunchy. Drain and set aside.
3. Place the remaining butter and sugar in the saucepan and place the saucepan over medium heat. Cook, stirring, until the butter melts and dissolves the sugar. Add the carrots, baby onions and green onion. Cook, tossing, until the vegetables are coated with the butter and sugar. Add the wine or sherry, the lemon juice and the crystallized ginger. Cook and toss until the vegetables are heated through.

MARINATED VEGETABLE SALAD

Remove the salad from the refrigerator half an hour before serving time.

Makes 8 servings.

- ½ **pound snow peas, trimmed, strings removed**
- 4 **large sweet red, green and/or yellow peppers, halved, seeded and cut into julienne sticks**
- ¼ **cup red wine vinegar**
- ¼ **cup peanut oil**
- 3 **tablespoons soy sauce**
- 1 **clove garlic, crushed but left whole**
- 1 **quarter-size slice fresh gingerroot, peeled and crushed but left whole**
- ½ **teaspoon crushed red pepper flakes**
- ¼ **pound mung bean sprouts (optional)**
- 1 **cup chopped green onion**
- 2 **tablespoons chopped fresh Chinese parsley (cilantro) OR: regular parsley**

1. Combine the snow peas with the red, green or yellow pepper sticks in a large bowl.
2. Beat together the vinegar, oil, soy sauce, garlic, ginger and red pepper flakes in a small bowl. Pour the marinade over the vegetables and toss to combine. Cover the salad and refrigerate, tossing occasionally, until 30 minutes before serving time.
3. At serving time, remove the garlic and the ginger. Sprinkle the salad with bean sprouts, if you wish, and with the green onion and the parsley.

KUMQUAT PECAN PIE

Look for fresh kumquats, because they really make a difference in this recipe. If they're not available, use prepared kumquats and omit the sugar in the recipe.

Bake at 375° for 45 minutes.
Makes 8 servings.

- **Butter Crust (recipe, page 31)**
- ½ **pound fresh kumquats, halved, pitted and chopped OR: 1 jar (8 ounces) kumquats, drained, halved, pitted and chopped**
- 2 **cups golden raisins**
- ½ **cup Grand Marnier OR: other orange-flavored liqueur**
- ½ **cup dark rum Grated zest of 1 orange (orange part of rind only)**
- 2 **Granny Smith apples (about ½ pound)**
- ¼ **cup sugar (omit if using prepared kumquats)**
- ½ **cup orange juice**
- 2 **tablespoons cornstarch**
- 2 **cups chopped toasted pecans***
- 1 **egg**
- 1 **tablespoon water**

1. Prepare the Butter Crust. Wrap the crust in plastic wrap and refrigerate it for 4 hours.
2. Combine the kumquats, raisins, Grand Marnier or other orange-flavored liqueur, rum and orange zest in a medium-size saucepan. Toss to blend the ingredients. Cover with plastic wrap and let stand for 4 hours, stirring occasionally.
3. Remove the plastic wrap from the saucepan. Halve, core, peel and chop the apples. Stir them into the kumquat mixture along with the sugar, orange juice and cornstarch. Cook over medium heat, stirring constantly, until the mixture thickens and bubbles. Remove the saucepan from the heat and cool the mixture completely.
4. Preheat the oven to moderate (375°). Roll out half the dough on a lightly floured surface to an 11-inch circle. Press the circle into a 9-inch pie pan and trim the overhang to 1 inch.

5. Stir the pecans into the cooled filling and spread the filling over the bottom crust.

6. Roll out the remaining dough to a ⅛-inch thickness and cut into ½-inch-wide strips. Arrange the strips in a lattice pattern over the filling and trim the strips flush with the edge of the bottom crust. Fold the bottom edge over the strips and crimp all around.

7. Beat together the egg and water. Brush the egg mixture over the top of the pie.

8. Bake in the preheated oven (375°) for 45 minutes, or until the filling bubbles up and the pastry is golden brown.

Note: Toast the pecans in a baking pan in a preheated, slow oven (300°), stirring occasionally, for 10 to 15 minutes, or until the edges are golden and the pecans smell toasted. Cool the pecans completely before adding them to the pie filling.

BUTTER CRUST

Makes 1 crust for a 9-inch pie.

2½ cups unbleached all-purpose flour
⅓ cup sugar
  Pinch salt
¾ cup (1½ sticks) frozen unsalted butter, cut into ½-inch pieces
5 to 6 tablespoons ice water

1. Place the flour, sugar and salt in the workbowl of a food processor. Add the butter. Process until the mixture resembles coarse crumbs.

2. With the motor running, pour the ice water through the feed tube. Continue pulse-processing for 30 seconds, or just until the dough forms a ball. Do not overprocess the dough.

3. Remove the dough from the processor. Flatten it into a disk and wrap it in plastic wrap. Refrigerate the dough for 3 hours.

Note: To make Cinnamon Butter Crust, add 2 teaspoons of ground cinnamon to the flour and sugar.

Did You Know . . .

Sarah Josepha Hale, the editor of Godey's Lady's Book, an important magazine of the 19th century, was the driving force behind our modern Thanksgiving celebration. In 1846, Mrs. Hale began devoting every November issue of the magazine to the idea of establishing the last Thursday in November as our official day of thanks. She felt that such a celebration might help promote a spirit of national unity in a country suffering from civil strife. And in 1863, President Abraham Lincoln proclaimed our first official Thanksgiving.

FROZEN ASSETS

When preparing pastry doughs in a food processor, freeze the butter or shortening ahead of time. This will produce a very short, crisp crust.

Gingered Pumpkin Cheesecake

GINGERED PUMPKIN CHEESECAKE

A creamy, rich dessert that will disappear quickly.

Bake at 325° for 1¾ hours.
Makes 12 servings.

1½   **cups crushed gingersnaps OR: graham cracker crumbs**
1   **cup granulated sugar**
6   **tablespoons butter, melted**
3   **packages (8 ounces each) cream cheese, softened**
¾   **cup firmly packed light brown sugar**
5   **eggs**
1   **can (16 ounces) pumpkin purée (not pumpkin pie filling)**
¼   **cup finely chopped crystallized ginger**
1½   **teaspoons pumpkin pie spice**
¼   **cup heavy cream OR: whipping cream Praline Lace Cookies, for garnish (recipe follows)**

1. Blend the crumbs, ¼ cup of the granulated sugar and the butter in a bowl. Firmly press the mixture over the bottom and up the sides of a lightly buttered 9-inch springform pan. Chill the crust.
2. Preheat the oven to slow (325°).
3. Beat the cream cheese with an electric mixer at medium speed until the cheese is smooth. Gradually add the remaining granulated sugar and the brown sugar, beating until the ingredients are well mixed. Beat in the eggs, one at a time, until the mixture is light and fluffy. At low speed, beat in the pumpkin, crystallized ginger, pumpkin pie spice and the heavy or whipping cream. Pour the filling into the prepared pan.
4. Bake in the preheated slow oven (325°) for 1¾ hours. Cool the cheesecake on a wire rack and refrigerate it for 6 hours, or overnight.
5. Garnish the cheesecake with the Praline Lace Cookies.

SOFT STEP

If you have a microwave oven, use it to soften butter and cream cheese for ease in baking. Remember that all aluminum foil wrappers must be removed before the cream cheese or butter is placed in the microwave oven.

PRALINE LACE COOKIES

Delicate and delicious cookies.

Bake at 300° for 10 minutes.
Makes 36 cookies.

¼   **cup (½ stick) butter, softened**
½   **cup firmly packed light brown sugar**
1   **egg**
¼   **cup finely chopped pecans**
2   **tablespoons all-purpose flour**
¼   **teaspoon salt**

1. Preheat the oven to slow (300°). Lightly grease 2 baking sheets.
2. Beat the butter with the brown sugar in a small bowl with an electric mixer at high speed until the mixture is fluffy. Beat in the egg. Stir in the pecans, flour and salt.
3. Drop the dough by half-teaspoonfuls, 5 inches apart, on one of the baking sheets. Spread each into a very thin 2½-inch round. (Make only two at a time for easy handling.) While the cookies bake, shape another batch on the second baking sheet.
4. Bake in the oven (300°) for 10 minutes, or until golden brown. Cool the cookies on the baking sheet for 1 minute, or just until they are firm enough to hold their shape.
5. Cut the cookies in half with a sharp knife, then loosen them from the baking sheet with a metal spatula. Cool on wire racks. Store cookies in an airtight container.

Sweet Potato Rolls (recipe, page 39) with Nutmeg Butter (recipe, page 40)

SOUTHERN HOSPITALITY THANKSGIVING DINNER

(for 8)

Shrimp and Saffron Bisque
Roast Turkey with Bourbon Glaze
Chili Corn Bread Stuffing
Spicy Southern Green Beans
Sweet Potato Rolls with Nutmeg Butter
Cranberry Bourbon Relish
Cranberry Apple Turnovers
Cinnamon Ice Cream
Harlequin Pumpkin Mousse

WORK PLAN FOR SOUTHERN HOSPITALITY THANKSGIVING DINNER

Up to Several Weeks Ahead:
- Prepare and freeze the corn bread for the Chili Corn Bread Stuffing.
- Prepare and freeze the Sweet Potato Rolls, Nutmeg Butter, Cranberry Apple Turnovers and Cinnamon Ice Cream.

Up to a Week Ahead:
- Prepare and refrigerate the Cranberry Bourbon Relish.
- Prepare and freeze the chocolate wedges to garnish the Harlequin Pumpkin Mousse.

Up to Several Days Ahead:
- Prepare the Cinnamon Ice Cream, if it was not prepared ahead.

Up to Two Days Ahead:
- Prepare the corn bread for the Chili Corn Bread Stuffing, if it was not prepared ahead and frozen, or thaw the corn bread, if frozen; let it dry.

The Day Before:
- Prepare the Butter Dough and filling for the Cranberry Apple Turnovers, if they were not prepared ahead and frozen; bake the turnovers the night before.
- Prepare and refrigerate the Chili Corn Bread Stuffing.
- Prepare and refrigerate the Bourbon Glaze.
- Thaw the Cranberry Apple Turnovers, Nutmeg Butter and Sweet Potato Rolls, if frozen.
- Prepare and refrigerate the Harlequin Pumpkin Mousse.
- Cook and mash the sweet potatoes for the Sweet Potato Rolls, if they were not prepared ahead and frozen.

Early in the Day:
- Prepare the Sweet Potato Rolls and Nutmeg Butter, if they were not prepared ahead and frozen.

Five Hours Before:
- Stuff the turkey and *immediately* start roasting it, basting with the Bourbon Glaze during the last half hour of roasting time. (Allow the roast turkey to rest for 20 minutes before carving it.)

Several Hours Before:
- Prepare the ingredients for the Spicy Southern Green Beans.
- Prepare the shrimp and shells for the Shrimp and Saffron Bisque.
- Prepare the chocolate wedges to garnish the Harlequin Pumpkin Mousse, if they were not prepared ahead and frozen.

One Hour Before:
- Unmold the Harlequin Pumpkin Mousse, loosely cover it with plastic wrap and return it to the refrigerator.
- Whip and refrigerate the cream to garnish the Harlequin Pumpkin Mousse.

Just Before Dinner:
- Finish preparing the Shrimp and Saffron Bisque.
- Prepare the Spicy Southern Green Beans.

During Dinner:
- Reheat the Cranberry Apple Turnovers.

Just Before Dessert:
- Decorate the Harlequin Pumpkin Mousse.

SHRIMP AND SAFFRON BISQUE

Makes 8 servings.

- 2   quarts water
- 1   small onion, sliced
- 1   bay leaf
- 1   stalk celery with leaves, cut up
- 1   tablespoon salt
- 6   whole peppercorns
- 2   pounds shrimp
- ½   lemon
- 6   cups milk
- ½   teaspoon saffron strands
- ½   cup (1 stick) butter
- ½   cup chopped shallots
- 1   pint heavy cream
- ⅓   cup dry sherry
     Juice of ½ lemon
     Ground hot red pepper
     Pinch nutmeg
     Salt and freshly ground white pepper, to taste
     Fresh chives, for garnish

1. Combine the water, onion, bay leaf, celery, the 1 tablespoon of salt and the peppercorns in a large saucepan. Bring the mixture to boiling. Lower the heat and simmer for 10 minutes. Add the shrimp and the lemon. Simmer for 5 minutes, or until the shrimp are pink and opaque. Drain. Shell and devein the shrimp, reserving half the shells. Reserve 4 shrimp for garnish. Finely pulse-chop remaining shrimp in a food processor and set aside.
2. Process reserved shells in the workbowl of a food processor until finely chopped.
3. Place the shells, milk and saffron in a medium-size saucepan. Heat gently just enough to warm the milk, for about 5 minutes. Remove the mixture from the heat and let stand for 30 minutes.
4. Meanwhile, melt the butter in the top of a double boiler over medium heat. Sauté the shallots for 2 minutes. Cover the double boiler top, lower the heat and simmer for 10 minutes. Uncover and place the double boiler top over boiling water.
5. Strain the warm milk through a cheesecloth-lined sieve into the double boiler top. Add the chopped shrimp. Cook, stirring occasionally, for 3 minutes.
6. Add the cream and heat the mixture, but do not allow it to boil. Stir in the sherry, lemon juice, ground hot pepper, nutmeg, salt and white pepper. Halve the reserved shrimp lengthwise. Garnish each portion of soup with chives and a shrimp half.

💲 ROAST TURKEY WITH BOURBON GLAZE

Roast at 400° for 15 minutes, then at 325° for 3¼ hours.
Makes 8 servings, with leftovers.

- 1   10- to 12-pound turkey
     Chili Corn Bread Stuffing (recipe, page 38)
     Bourbon Glaze (recipe follows)

1. Follow the directions for Roast Turkey with Brandied Fruit Stuffing (page 9), substituting Chili Corn Bread Stuffing for the fruit stuffing. During the last half hour of roasting, brush the turkey every 10 minutes with the Bourbon Glaze.
2. Top each serving of turkey with any remaining Bourbon Glaze.

BOURBON GLAZE

Makes 3 cups.

- 1   cup dry red wine
- 1   cup bourbon whiskey
- 1   cup apricot preserves
- 2   tablespoons Dijon-style mustard

Combine the wine, bourbon, preserves and mustard in a small saucepan over low heat. Bring the mixture to boiling, stirring, and remove the saucepan from the heat. Brush the glaze on the turkey every 10 minutes during the last half hour of roasting.

CHILI CORN BREAD STUFFING

Extra stuffing can be baked in a greased baking dish during the last 45 minutes to 1 hour of roasting. For best results, bake the Double Corn Bread a day or two in advance to give it time to dry out enough for the stuffing.

Makes enough stuffing for a 10- to 12-pound turkey (8 servings).

    Double Corn Bread (recipe at right)
½   cup (1 stick) unsalted butter
1½ cups chopped onion
1   cup chopped celery
1   small red pepper, halved, seeded and
        chopped
1   clove garlic, finely chopped.
1   can (4 ounces) mild chili peppers, rinsed,
        seeded and chopped
1   to 1½ cups chicken broth
1   tablespoon leaf thyme, crumbled
3   eggs, slightly beaten
    Salt and freshly ground pepper, to taste

1. Prepare the Double Corn Bread a day or two in advance. Cover it and let stand. When you are ready to prepare the stuffing, break up the bread into the work-bowl of a food processor; if the workbowl is small, you may have to work in two batches. Pulse-chop the bread to form crumbs and transfer them to a large bowl.
2. Melt the butter in a large skillet. Sauté the onion and the celery until they are almost soft and translucent, for about 5 minutes. Add the red pepper and sauté for 10 minutes, or until the vegetables are very soft. Add the garlic and sauté for 1 minute more.
3. Add the sautéed vegetables, chili peppers, broth, thyme and eggs to the crumbs in the bowl. Mix until the ingredients are well blended. Add the salt and pepper. Cool completely before stuffing the turkey.

DOUBLE CORN BREAD

This recipe also can be used to make corn muffins.

Bake at 375° for 25 minutes.
Makes 10 servings.

2   cups yellow cornmeal
½   cup all-purpose flour
1   tablespoon baking powder
1   tablespoon sugar
1   teaspoon baking soda
1   teaspoon ground cumin
1   teaspoon salt
3   eggs
1½   cups milk
¼   cup (½ stick) butter, melted
1½   cups fresh or frozen whole kernel corn
1   small red onion, finely chopped

1. Preheat the oven to moderate (375°). Grease a 9 x 13-inch baking pan.
2. Combine the cornmeal, flour, baking powder, sugar, baking soda, cumin and salt in a medium-size bowl.
3. Beat together the eggs, milk and butter in a small bowl and pour them over the dry ingredients. Mix all the ingredients gently but thoroughly. Fold in the corn and the onion. Pour the batter into the prepared pan.
4. Bake in the preheated moderate oven (375°) for 25 minutes, or until a wooden pick inserted in the center of the cornbread comes out clean. Serve the cornbread warm, or cool it to make stuffing crumbs.

DRY IT, YOU'LL LIKE IT!

Stuffings are best if they're made with 1- or 2-day-old bread. If you have only fresh bread, use your microwave or oven to dry it out a bit.

ONE POTATO, TWO POTATO . . .

Potatoes, both sweet and regular, add great texture and moistness to yeast breads and rolls. For extra flavor and nutrients, use the water in which the potatoes have cooked as part of the liquid in the dough.

SPICY SOUTHERN GREEN BEANS

Asparagus also is delicious when prepared in this fashion.

Makes 8 servings.

8   slices bacon, chopped
2   bunches green onions, trimmed and
        chopped
2   cloves garlic, finely chopped
2   tablespoons Dijon-style mustard
2   teaspoons Worcestershire sauce
        Large pinch ground hot red pepper
3   pounds green beans, trimmed
½   cup roasted peanuts, finely
        chopped

1. Sauté the bacon until crisp in a medium-size skillet. Remove the bacon with a slotted spoon to paper toweling and reserve the fat.
2. Sauté the green onion in the reserved bacon fat until it is soft, for 5 minutes. Add the garlic and sauté for 1 minute more. Stir in the mustard, Worcestershire sauce and ground hot red pepper.
3. Meanwhile, steam the green beans until they are crisply tender. Transfer them to a heated large serving bowl and toss them with the green onion mixture. Crumble the bacon. Sprinkle the bacon and the peanuts over the beans.

SWEET POTATO ROLLS

The dough for these tasty rolls tends to be rather sticky.

Bake at 375° for 30 to 40 minutes.
Makes 32 rolls.

¾   cup milk
¼   cup (½ stick) plus 2 tablespoons butter
3   tablespoons sugar
        Grated zest of ½ orange (orange part of
        rind only)
¾   teaspoon salt, preferably coarse kosher
1   package active dry yeast
¼   cup warm water
1   cup mashed cooked sweet potato
½   cup fresh orange juice
½   cup cornmeal, plus more for shaping rolls
4½   to 5½ cups unbleached all-purpose flour
        Nutmeg Butter (recipe, page 40)

1. Scald the milk in a small saucepan over medium heat. Stir in ¼ cup of the butter, the sugar, orange zest and salt. Cool the mixture to lukewarm.
2. Sprinkle the yeast over the warm water in a medium-size bowl and let it stand for 5 minutes. Add the milk mixture, sweet potato and orange juice. Beat the mixture with a large wooden spoon until all the ingredients are blended.
3. Add ½ cup of the cornmeal and half the flour. Beat the mixture with a spoon until it is well blended. Add enough of the remaining flour to make a soft dough.
4. Turn out the dough onto a floured surface. Knead until the dough is smooth and pliable, for about 8 minutes, adding more flour as needed to prevent the dough from sticking.
5. Place the dough in a greased bowl and turn the greased side up. Cover the bowl and let the dough rise in a warm place, away from drafts, for 1 hour, or until it is doubled in bulk.
6. Melt the remaining 2 tablespoons of butter in a small saucepan over low heat.
7. Punch down the dough. Knead the dough on a lightly floured surface. Roll out the

dough, half at a time, into a 2 inch-thick cylinder. Cut each cylinder into 16 equal pieces. Shape each piece into a ball. For soft rolls, place half the balls into each of two 9-inch round baking pans that have been brushed with some of the melted butter and sprinkled with some of the remaining cornmeal. Brush the tops with more butter. For crustier rolls, place the balls, 2 inches apart, on baking sheets that have been brushed with the melted butter and sprinkled with the cornmeal. Brush the tops with more butter and sprinkle with more cornmeal. Cover the pans or sheets and let the dough rise in a warm place, away from drafts, until it is nearly doubled in bulk, for about half an hour.

8. Preheat oven to moderate (375°).
9. Bake in the preheated moderate oven (375°) until the rolls are golden, for about 30 minutes for the rolls on baking sheets, 40 minutes for the rolls in pans. Cool the baking sheet rolls on the baking sheets on wire racks. Let the pan rolls cool in the pans for 5 minutes. Gently invert the rolls onto wire racks, turn them right side up and let cool. Serve with Nutmeg Butter.

Note: For pull-apart rolls, melt ¼ cup (½ stick) of butter instead of the 2 tablespoons. Divide the dough in half. Roll out each half to a ½-inch-thick rectangle and brush it with the butter. Cut each rectangle into 7 lengthwise strips, stack the strips and cut them into 16 pieces. Place the pieces, layered side up, into muffin pan cups that have been buttered and sprinkled with cornmeal. Brush the pieces with more butter. Let them rise, and bake as for the crustier rolls.

NUTMEG BUTTER

Freshly grated nutmeg really makes a difference in this delightfully simple accompaniment.

Makes 1¼ cups.

- 1 **cup (2 sticks) unsalted butter, softened**
- ¼ **cup honey**
- ½ **teaspoon freshly grated nutmeg**

Blend the butter, honey and nutmeg in a small bowl and chill the mixture.

CRANBERRY BOURBON RELISH

A pleasantly tart relish that also is good as a topping for vanilla ice cream or plain cake. For a sweeter condiment, increase the sugar by ⅓ cup.

Makes about 3 cups.

- 1⅓ **cups sugar**
- 1 **orange**
- 1 **lemon**
- 5 **cups raw cranberries (1⅓ pounds)**
- 1 **cup raisins**
- ½ **cup bourbon whiskey**

1. Place ⅓ cup of the sugar in the container of a food processor. Strip the zests from the orange and the lemon (orange and yellow parts of the rinds only), using a swivel-bladed vegetable peeler, and add the zests to the sugar. Process until the zests are finely chopped. Squeeze the juice from the orange and the lemon.
2. Mix together the citrus-flavored sugar, the orange and lemon juices, the remaining sugar, the cranberries, raisins and bourbon in a medium-size saucepan. Let mixture stand for 1 hour, stirring occasionally.
3. Bring the mixture to boiling over medium heat. Lower the heat and simmer for 5 to 10 minutes, or until some of the berries have popped but others remain whole.
4. Place the relish in clean glass jars, cover the jars and refrigerate the relish.

CRANBERRY APPLE TURNOVERS

These tasty turnovers also can be made with dried cranberries.

Bake at 450° for 20 minutes.
Makes 20 turnovers.

1 **pound Golden Delicious apples**
1 **pound tart green apples**
½ **cup sugar**
¼ **cup (½ stick) butter**
  Juice of 1 lemon
1 **teaspoon grated lemon zest (yellow part of rind only)**
1 **cup cranberries**
2 **tablespoons dark rum**
  Cinnamon Butter Crust (recipe, page 31)
1 **egg, slightly beaten with 1 teaspoon water**
  Cinnamon Ice Cream (recipe follows)

1. Peel, core and chop the apples. Place them in a large saucepan along with the sugar, butter, lemon juice and zest. Cover the saucepan and cook the mixture over medium heat until juices form, for about 5 minutes. Uncover the saucepan and continue cooking until the apples are almost soft but still hold their shape. Add the cranberries when the juices still are a bit thin, so the berries will cook. Continue cooking until the cranberries pop, for about 5 minutes. Remove the saucepan from the heat and cool the mixture completely. Stir in the rum.

2. Prepare the Cinnamon Butter Crust. Roll out the dough on a lightly floured surface to a ⅛-inch-thick rectangle. Cut out 20 circles with a 4-inch round cookie cutter, or use a ravioli wheel to make squares.

3. Preheat the oven to very hot (450°). Butter 2 or 3 baking sheets.

4. Place 1 tablespoon of the filling on each pastry circle or square. Brush the border of the dough with the egg and water mixture. Fold the pastry over to form semicircles or triangles and press the edges together with your fingertips. Repeat the pressing with the tines of a fork. Brush the tops of the turnovers with the egg mixture. Poke a ⅛-inch hole through the top of each turnover and place the turnovers on the prepared baking sheets.

5. Bake the turnovers in the preheated oven (450°), turning the baking sheets once halfway through the baking, for 20 minutes, or until the pastry is golden brown. Serve turnovers warm or at room temperature with Cinnamon Ice Cream.

CINNAMON ICE CREAM

For a special treat, try serving this ice cream topped with hot sautéed apples and toasted pecans.

Makes 1 quart.

2 **cups milk**
2 **pieces (2 to 3 inches each) stick cinnamon**
3 **egg yolks**
½ **cup sugar**
¼ **teaspoon salt**
1 **cup heavy cream OR: whipping cream**
1 **tablespoon dark rum**
1 **teaspoon vanilla**
1 **teaspoon ground cinnamon**

1. Combine the milk with the cinnamon sticks in a small, heavy saucepan over medium heat and bring the mixture just to a simmer. Remove the saucepan from the heat.

2. Beat together the egg yolks, sugar and salt with a wire whisk in a second small saucepan. Gradually stir in 1 cup of the milk, reserving the cinnamon sticks. Place the mixture over low heat, stirring constantly, just until the sugar dissolves. Pour the mixture into a medium-size bowl, add the reserved cinnamon sticks and refrigerate the mixture until it is very cold.

3. Remove and discard cinnamon sticks. Stir in the remaining milk, the heavy or whipping cream, rum, vanilla and ground cinnamon. Pour into a hand-cranked or electric ice cream freezer and freeze, following manufacturer's directions.

Harlequin Pumpkin Mousse

HARLEQUIN PUMPKIN MOUSSE

Makes 10 servings.

2 tablespoons unflavored gelatin
½ cup very cold water
1 teaspoon grated orange zest (orange part of rind only)
¾ cup orange juice
1 tablespoon lemon juice
1 teaspoon ground cinnamon
1 teaspoon ground ginger
¼ teaspoon ground nutmeg
1 tablespoon brandy
½ cup granulated sugar
1 cup heavy cream OR: whipping cream
2 tablespoons 10X (confectioners' powdered) sugar
2 cups canned pumpkin purée (not pumpkin pie filling)
1 cup dairy sour cream
¾ cup glacé cherries and pineapple, cut into small pieces
2 squares (1 ounce each) semisweet chocolate
1 cup heavy cream OR: whipping cream, whipped, for garnish
Candied orange rind, for garnish (optional)

1. Lightly oil a 6-cup soufflé dish or other straight-sided round mold. Set aside.

2. Sprinkle the gelatin over the cold water in a small saucepan and let stand to soften the gelatin, for about 5 minutes. Place the saucepan over low heat and stir to dissolve the gelatin. Add the orange zest and juice, the lemon juice, cinnamon, ginger and nutmeg. Stir until the ingredients are blended. Remove the saucepan from the heat. Stir in the brandy and the granulated sugar. Chill for 8 to 10 minutes, stirring occasionally, or until the mixture is slightly syrupy.

3. Meanwhile, beat the heavy or whipping cream with the 10X (confectioners' powdered) sugar in a small bowl until stiff peaks form (do not overbeat).

4. Combine the pumpkin with the sour cream in a small bowl. Fold in the sweetened whipped cream and the glacé fruits. Fold in the gelatin mixture until it is well blended. Pour the pumpkin mixture into the prepared mold and chill the mixture until it is set, for several hours or overnight.

5. Line the bottom of a 7-inch tart pan with a removable bottom, or other 7-inch circular pan, with wax paper.

6. Melt the chocolate in the top of a double boiler or in a small bowl over simmering water. Beat the chocolate until it is shiny, then spread it evenly over the lined circle. Refrigerate the chocolate until it just begins to set, for about 10 minutes. Cut the chocolate into 8 equal wedge-shaped triangles, and return it to the refrigerator to finish setting, for about 1 hour.

7. Run a thin-bladed knife around the sides of the mold. Dip the mold briefly in hot water and invert it onto a serving plate.

8. To garnish, peel the wax paper from the chocolate triangles. Place a small dot of whipped cream in the center of each triangle. Gently press the triangles against the mousse along the outside, pointed ends up and wide bases almost touching each other. Garnish the top of the mousse with candied orange rind, if you wish. Pipe whipped cream rosettes around the base and top edge of the mousse.

ℒET THE CRAFTING BEGIN!

Celebrate the season with the joy of giving: Presents to make ahead.

CRANBERRY HEART

Easy: Achievable by anyone.

Materials: One package of fresh cranberries; heavy-gauge floral wire (a little lighter than coat hanger wire); wire cutters; paper and pencil.

Directions:

1. On paper, sketch a heart in the size you want.

2. Using the wire cutters, cut a length of wire long enough to go around the heart shape, plus 3 inches.

3. Bend the wire to the shape, leaving one end 2 inches too long and the other 1 inch. Bend the 1-inch end into a hook.

4. Push the cranberries onto the wire as if threading beads. Hook the 1-inch end around the 2-inch end and press closed. Bend the 2-inch end into a hook to hang the heart.

Note: *To make a holiday garland, string whole cranberries and clementines on floral wire, intersperse with cranberry hearts, and add a leaf or two as desired.*

💲 📦
PINE CONE WREATH

Easy: Achievable by anyone.

Materials (Gather the materials available from a walk in the woods or your backyard before buying anything): Pine cones (include enough large cones to fill the body of the wreath); any of the following: Brazil nuts, walnuts, almonds, pecans, grasses, horse chestnuts, milkweed pods; ribbon for bow *(optional)*; craft glue; floral wire or picks; Styrofoam® wreath form of desired size; heavy-gauge wire (coat-hanger weight).

Directions:

Follow the Method for Styrofoam® wreath forms on page 45. Begin to form the wreath body with the largest size pine cones and any other large dried pieces. Fill in all the gaps, being careful to keep the look of the wreath balanced. Use the floral wire or picks to add the remaining details. If you wish, tie the ribbon into a large bow, insert a piece of floral wire through the bow back and twist the wire ends around the wreath to secure the bow to the wreath. With the heavy-gauge wire, form a loop for hanging. Poke holes in the back of the wreath form where you want to place the loop, dip the ends of the loop in glue and insert the loop into the holes. Let the glue dry.

Pine Cone Wreath (directions, page 44)

WREATH-MAKING MATERIALS AND FORMS

These materials are available at florists and garden centers, or through mail order (see Materials Shopping Guide, page 274).

Floral picks: Three to four inches long, painted green, wire already is attached to secure ornaments or bows.

Floral wire: Spools or 18-inch lengths.

Wire cutters: Available at hardware stores.

Pruning shears: To trim greenery.

Styrofoam® wreath forms: Size and thickness vary depending on supplier.

Method for Styrofoam® wreath forms: Poke holes in the forms with an ice pick or skewer where the greenery is to go. Dip the stems of the greenery in glue before inserting them into the holes. Let the glue dry. Attach ornaments or bows with floral picks.

EVER GREEN

• Cut fresh greenery early in the morning or in the evening, while it is moist. If you are buying greenery, make sure it still is supple and has a rich green color.

• Carry, or have nearby, a deep container full of water. Immediately after cutting, submerge the greenery in the water.

• If you are not using the greenery (fresh picked or bought) immediately, smash the end of each branch with a hammer and keep the branches in the container of water until they are needed. This keeps the veins open to absorb the water.

• Once the greenery is arranged, spray it with an evaporation-prevention spray available at garden centers and florists. You also can use the spray on Christmas trees to slow the drying process.

Rudolph the Red-Nosed Reindeer Sweater

RUDOLPH THE RED-NOSED REINDEER SWEATER

Challenging: Requires more experience in knitting.

Directions are given for Size 2. Changes for Sizes 4 and 6 are in parentheses.

Materials: Brunswick Rugger Bulky Yarn (1¾-oz ball): 3 (3,4) balls each of Teal (A) and Tan (B), 1 ball each of White (C), Bright Red (D) and Beige (E), scrap of black yarn for eyes (F); 1 pair size 10½ knitting needles, OR ANY SIZE NEEDLES TO OBTAIN GAUGE BELOW; one ⅜-inch-diameter button for back opening; tapestry needle; size G crochet hook.

Gauge: In Stockinette Stitch (st st), 7 sts = 2 inches; 10 rows = 2 inches.

SIZES:	(2)	(4)	(6)
BODY CHEST:	21″	23″	25″
FINISHED MEASUREMENTS:			
CHEST:	22″	24″	26″
WIDTH ACROSS BACK OR FRONT AT UNDERARMS:	11″	12″	13″
WIDTH ACROSS SLEEVE AT UPPER ARMS:			
	11½″	11½″	11½″

Note 1: The body and sleeves are worked in one piece, starting at the lower edge of the Front and ending at the lower edge of the Back. The sweater has side seams and a back opening.

Note 2: The Reindeer design is worked in stockinette stitch (st st; k 1 row, p 1 row), following FIGS. I, 1 and 1a. When changing colors, pick up the color to be used under the color previously used, twisting the yarns on the wrong side to prevent holes in the work. Carry the unused colors loosely on the wrong side of the work, being careful to maintain the gauge specified and making sure to keep the work flat. Attach 1 ball of A at each side of the reindeer and 1 ball between the antlers.

Note 3: The eyes, nose, berries and outline of the jawline are added when the sweater is completed.

Directions:

1. *Body, Front:* Starting at lower edge of the Front with A, cast on 40 (44, 48) sts. Work in k 1, p 1 ribbing for 6 rows, decreasing 1 st at the end of the last row worked—39 (43, 47) sts. Cut A. Work in garter stitch (k every row) in the following striped pattern: Work 2 rows C, 2 rows D, 2 rows C, ending with 0 (2, 2) rows D and 0 (0, 2) rows C. Now beg Reindeer design, following FIG. I, 1, starting with Row 1 at size indicated. Continue to follow FIG. I, 1 until Row 32 is completed. *Do not* fasten off.

2. *Sleeves, Rows 33 and 34:* Continuing to follow FIG. I, 1, cast on 26 (29, 32) sts at beg of next 2 rows for each sleeve—91 (101, 111) sts. Follow FIG. I, 1 until Row 54 is completed.

3. *Neck Shaping, Row 55:* Following FIG. I, 1, k across first 38 (42, 46) sts, bind off 15 (17, 19) sts for front neck, join new ball and k rem 38 (42, 46) sts. Working both sides at the same time with separate balls, follow FIG. I, 1 until Row 61 is completed. *Do not* fasten off.

4. *Back:* Beg Reindeer design, following FIG. I, 1a, starting with Row 1 at size indicated and working both sides at the same time with separate balls until Row 7 is completed. *Row 8:* Continuing to follow FIG. I, 1a, cast on 8 (9, 10) sts at each neck edge for center back. Keeping back opening as established, work until Row 19 is completed. Continue to follow FIG. I, 1a, working across all sts until Row 27 is completed. *Rows 28 and 29:* Bind off 26 (29, 32) sts at beg of next 2 rows to complete sleeves—39 (43, 47) sts. Follow FIG. I, 1a until Row 61 is completed. Work in garter st following the same striped pattern as for lower Front, increasing 1 st at end of last row worked—40 (44, 48) sts. With A, work in k 1, p 1 ribbing for 6 rows. Bind off loosely in ribbing.

5. *Sleeve Cuffs:* With A, pick up 28 sts along the end of each sleeve. Work in k 1, p 1 ribbing for 6 rows. Bind off loosely in ribbing.

6. *Finishing:* Sew the side and underarm seams. Block the sweater lightly without placing the iron directly on the yarn. Sew the button onto the top right edge of the back opening and loosen the stitch at the opposite edge for a button loop.

7. *Facial Features, Jaw:* With C yarn, work a crocheted chain stitch to outline the Reindeer jaw (*see* FIG. I, 1). *Nose:* Make a pompon with D yarn and tack it to the front of the sweater (*see photo*). *Eyes:* With F yarn, make 9 straight stitches for the pupil of each eye. *Antlers:* With E yarn, work large horizontal whip stitches, around each antler (*see photo*). *Holly:* Embroider French knots with D for holly berries.

FIG. I, 1 & 1a RUDOLPH THE RED-NOSED REINDEER SWEATER

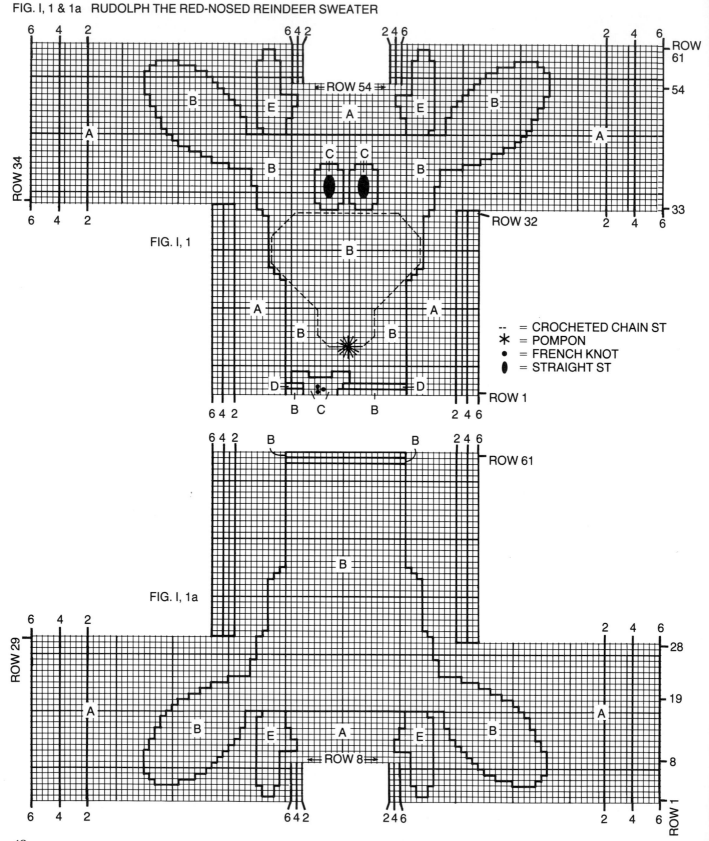

= CROCHETED CHAIN ST
= POMPON
= FRENCH KNOT
= STRAIGHT ST

FIG. I, 1

FIG. I, 1a

Candy Striped Baskets

CANDY STRIPED BASKETS

Average: For those with some experience in sewing.

Materials: Baskets; red mattress ticking fabric; thread. *(See Methods for shapes and amounts of all Materials).*

General Directions:
Three methods for three basic basket shapes are given, plus variations for one or two handles. When possible, take all measurements from the bottom or outside surface of the basket to determine fabric amounts.

Method 1:
Circular basket with spherical bottom, one handle.
1. Measure the distance across the bottom of the basket from one side to the other and add 2 inches. Using this measurement as the lengths, cut 2 squares from the fabric. Fold the squares together into quarters and trim them to create quarter circles. Open up the two circles.
2. For the length of the ruffle, measure the circumference of (or distance around) of the basket top edge and add half as much. Cut a rectangular piece of fabric the length of the ruffle by 3 inches. Seam short ends together, right sides facing. Press

the seam open. Fold the ruffle in half lengthwise and press again. Baste ½ inch from the raw edges of the ruffle and gather the ruffle to fit the circumference of the fabric circles. Pin the ruffle to the right side of one circle, raw edges matching, folded edge facing inward.
3. For each bow tie, cut two 12 x 3-inch pieces of fabric. Fold each piece in half lengthwise, right sides facing, and pin. Stitch a ¼-inch seam across one end and down the length. Turn right side out and press.
4. Pin the ties as pairs, on top of the ruffle, on opposite sides of the circle to match the position of the basket handle. The ties'

raw edges should align with the raw edges of the ruffle and circle. Using a basting stitch, sew all around ½ inch from the edges.

5. Place the second circle over the first, right sides facing, and pin in position. Sew a ⅝-inch seam around, leaving 4 inches open. Trim the seam to ⅜ inch. Turn and slipstitch the opening closed. Place the liner in the basket and tie a bow around the sides of the handle.

Method 2:
Circular tapered basket with one handle; variation for 2 handles.
1. Trace the bottom of the basket on the wrong side of the fabric and cut out.
2. Measure the circumference of the basket top edge and add half again as much for the total length. Measure the height of the basket and add 5 inches for the total depth. From the fabric, cut out a rectangle using the length and depth. Fold in half lengthwise, right sides facing, and pin. Stitch a ½-inch seam. Press the seam open. Fold under to one side and press ¼ inch, then 2 inches. Pin and topstitch down along the hemline fold. Using a basting stitch, gather just above the topstitching to fit the top basket edge. Gather ½ inch from the opposite edge with the basting stitch to fit the fabric circle and pin into place. Stitch a ½-inch seam all around.
3. Repeat Step 3, Method 1. Sew the ties, in pairs on opposite sides, to the top side of the ruffle along the gathering stitches.
Variation for two handles: Repeat Steps 1 and 2 above. Follow Step 3 above, sewing the

ties to the underside of the ruffle gathering. Thread one tie through the basket, centered under the handle, and tie a bow.

Method 3:
Rectangular or square basket with straight sides, one handle.
1. Measure the circumference of the basket top edge and add 1 inch. Measure the basket height and add 1½ inches. Cut 2 rectangles from the fabric, using the measurements as the length and width. Fold each rectangle in half lengthwise, right sides facing, and pin. Sew a ½-inch seam. Press the seam open.
2. Follow Step 2, Method 1, fitting the ruffle to the long edge of one rectangle.
3. Follow Step 3, Method 1.
4. Follow Step 4, Method 1.
5. Place the second rectangle over the first, right sides facing, and pin in position. Sew a ⅝-inch seam all around, leaving 4 inches open. Trim the seam to ⅜ inch. Turn and slipstitch the opening closed.
6. Trace the basket bottom on the wrong side of the fabric and cut out. Pin the raw edges of the rectangles to the raw edges of the basket bottom, with right sides facing.
7. Place the liner in the basket and tie a bow around the sides of the handle. Sew a ½-inch seam to finish.

"BABY LOVE" BISCUIT COMFORTER
(39 x 46 inches)

Average: For those with some experience in patchwork.

Materials: (44/45-inch-wide fabric) ⅝ yard each of rose and white for patches, ¾ yard of unbleached muslin, ⅝ yard of blue, and 1⅝ yards of rose for the quilt back; batting; stuffing material; threads to match; iron-on patching material *(optional).*

Directions (½-inch seams allowed):
1. Cut 18 rose and 17 white patches, each 6-inches square. Cut 35 muslin patches, 5-inches square. Cut four 5½-inch-wide blue borders, two 26-inches and two 45-inches long. Cut a rose quilt back 43 x 53 inches. Cut four 7-inch wide strips of batting, two 45-inch and two 35-inches long.
2. ***"Biscuits":*** Pin each 6-inch patch to a muslin 5-inch patch, wrong sides together, with the corners matching. Fold the extra colored fabric into a tuck at the center of each edge. Topstitch around all four sides, ½ inch from the cut edge, through all the layers.
3. Seam seven horizontal rows of five patches each, starting four of the rows with the rose fabric, and alternating the colors. Seam one row beneath the other, alternating the colors. To each short end of the patchwork, seam a shorter blue border; to the longer sides, seam the longer borders.
4. Into the muslin back only of each biscuit patch pocket, cut a

"Baby Love" Biscuit Comforter (directions, page 50); Patchwork Pals Pillows (directions, page 52) and Nine-Patch Pillow (directions, page 53)

short (less than an inch) slash. Stuff each patch pocket through the slash to "raise the biscuit." Close the slash with a few stitches or a scrap of iron-on fabric.

5. Place the quilt top in the center of the quilt back, wrong sides together. The rose fabric will extend 4 inches on each side for use in binding. First pin, then topstitch along the inside border seams through both layers.

6. Place the batting strips under the borders (the batting will extend 2 inches beyond the border). Pin the outside border edges to the quilt back (through the batting) and topstitch ½ inch from the cut edge of the blue fabric.

7. Turn under the rose fabric ½ inch at the short edges of the quilt back. Fold the edge over to the right side and pin the turned-under edge to the previous topstitching; edgestitch. Repeat the process on the remaining two edges.

FIG. I, 2 PATCHWORK PALS PILLOWS   1 SQ. = 2"

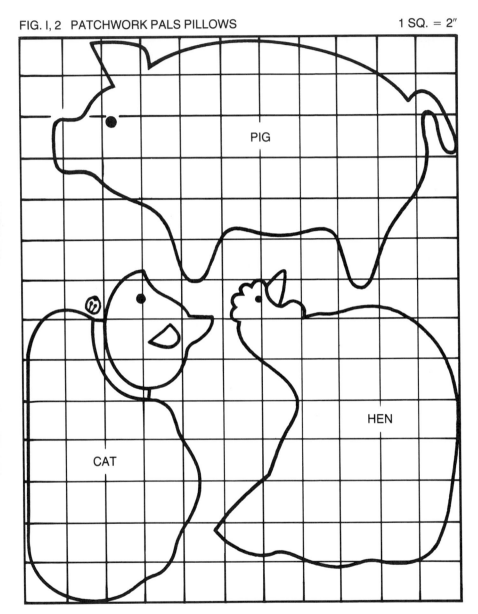

PIG

CAT

HEN

PATCHWORK PALS PILLOWS
(39 x 46 inches)

Easy: Achievable by anyone.

Materials: ⅜ yard of 45-inch-wide muslin for each pillow; scraps of printed pastel fabric; stuffing; fusible webbing; scrap of black, iron-on fabric; iron; batting *(optional);* paper hole punch; threads to match.

Directions:
1. Enlarge the patterns in Fɪɢ. I, 2, following the directions on page 271. Fold the muslin in half, bringing the selvage edges together. Trace the pattern pieces onto the muslin. Cut out the pattern pieces through both layers of muslin, cutting ¼-inch beyond the traced lines. Cut 2-inch square patches from the assorted print fabrics and the fusible webbing.
2. Lightly mark the grainline (a gridline up and down the body) on one animal pillow front. Pin the colored patches along the grainline of the muslin, with a patch of the fusible webbing between each patch and the muslin. Alternate the patches to the right and left of the grainline. Following the same line-up, pin the rest of the patches in place and press with an iron to fuse them in place. Edgestitch or zig-zag stitch the raw edges of the patches to secure them to the muslin. For the hen pillow, fuse the yellow beak to the muslin in the same fashion as the patches.
3. Lightly draw lines that connect the opposite corners of the patches. Repeat the lines in the opposite direction, making lines

that are at right angles to each other to form squares. Baste the batting to the wrong side of the patched fabric. Topstitch along the drawn lines to quilt.

4. With the right sides together, seam (¼-inch allowance) the pillow front to the pillow back, leaving about 3 inches open at the bottom edge. Turn the pillow right side out; stuff the pillow firmly and slipstitch the opening closed.

5. With the paper hole punch, cut an "eye" from the iron-on fabric. Fuse the eye to the pillow as indicated on the pattern. For the cat, cut an ear from a piece of colored fabric and a corresponding piece of fusible webbing. Fuse the cat's ear to the pillow front as indicated on the pattern. Slipstitch the edges of the eye and the ear to secure them to the pillow.

NINE-PATCH PILLOW
(39 x 46 inches)

Easy: Achievable by anyone.

Materials: ½ yard blue and ¾ yard muslin (44/45-inch fabric); stuffing; batting *(optional)*; compass; ruler; hard pencil; threads to match.

Directions (¼-inch seams allowed):

1. From the blue fabric, cut one 12½-inch square, twenty 2½-inch squares and four 2½ x 12½-inch strips. From the muslin, cut eight 2½-inch squares and a 24½-inch square pillow back.

2. **Nine-Patch block:** Seam one small muslin square between two small blue fabric squares; repeat. Seam one small blue square between two small muslin squares. Seam the three rows, one below the other with a small blue square in the center. Make three more patch blocks in the same fashion, one for each corner.

3. Seam a blue fabric strip between two muslin strips. Repeat the strip blocks three times for four strip blocks.

4. Seam a strip block to two opposite sides of the large blue fabric square.

5. Seam a nine-patch block at each end of the two remaining strip blocks and seam them to the large blue fabric square and previously attached strip blocks to complete the pillow top.

6. Baste the batting to the back of the pillow top. Using the compass and hard pencil, lightly draw overlapping 5-inch circles in the center of the large blue square. Lightly rule diagonal lines across the border strip blocks. Sew running stitches along the drawn lines to quilt.

7. Pin the pillow top to the pillow back, with right sides together. Seam (¼-inch) around three sides and four corners of the pillow. Turn the pillow right side out, stuff firmly, turn under the open edge and slipstitch the opening closed.

Reindeer and Snowflake Pillows

REINDEER AND SNOWFLAKE PILLOWS

Challenging: Requires more experience in knitting.

Materials for Two Pillows: Reynolds Icelandic Lopi: 1 skein each of Red (MC) and Black (CC); 1 pair size 9 knitting needles, OR ANY SIZE NEEDLES TO OBTAIN GAUGE BELOW; 1 yard of 54-inch-wide red gabardine; 4 yards of 1/4-inch-wide covered cording in any color; two 16-inch square pillow forms or loose stuffing.
Gauge: In Stockinette Stitch (st st), 3½ stitches = 1 inch; 4 rows = 1 inch.

Directions:

1. With MC, cast on 53 sts for Reindeer Pillow and 55 sts for Snowflake Pillow. Working in st st, follow reindeer or snowflake chart in Figs. I, 3 and 3a. Always pick up new color from under previous color, twisting yarns on wrong side to avoid holes. Bind off loosely. Block the piece to measure 15 x 15 inches.

2. Cut two pieces of red fabric 17 x 17 inches for each pillow. Pin the blocked pillow front right side up on a fabric square. With a sewing machine, zigzag-stitch the knitted piece to the fabric around all the edges to back the knitted piece.

3. Pin the cording over edges of knitting, seam allowance facing out. Stitch close to cording all around. Place second square of fabric over knitted piece, right sides together. Stitch around cording edge on *three* sides. Trim excess; turn pillow right side out. Insert pillow form or stuffing. Slipstitch fourth side closed. Repeat for second pillow.

FIG. I, 3 & 3a REINDEER AND SNOWFLAKE PILLOWS

COLOR KEY: ⊠ = BLACK, ☐ = RED

HATBOX HEAVEN

Easy: Achievable by anyone.

Materials: Old or new hatbox *(see Materials Shopping Guide, page 274)*; wallpaper; sponge; utility knife; wallpaper paste or manufacturer's recommended adhesive; paint brush; scissors; pencil; contact cement for repairs; paint primer, applied to hatboxes with a glossy surface so paste will adhere.

Directions:
1. Remove any dust or mildew from the hatbox with a damp sponge. Repair any damaged cardboard with the cement.
2. To cover the side surfaces of the box, cut a strip of wallpaper the circumference of the bottom plus 2 inches for the length and the height of the box plus 4 inches for the width. Draw a light pencil line 2 inches in from each long edge as a guide for the box.
3. Apply an even coat of paste to the strip and let it rest for 2 to 3 minutes.
4. Using the pencil lines, center the box on its side on the paper. Wrap the paper around the box, allowing 2 inches to be turned in on the inside top, and overlap the side seam. At the overlap, cut through both thicknesses with the utility knife, being careful not to cut through the box. Lift the paper, remove the excess pieces and smooth the edges back in place to make a butted seam.
5. Smooth out any air bubbles on the sides. Fold over the paper inside the box, making small cuts on the inside flap where needed to flatten the paper.
6. With the scissors, make cuts every inch on the lower extension, up to the lower edge of the box. Fold the strips onto the bottom, overlapping the cuts. Add more paste, if necessary.
7. Trace the bottom of the box on the wrong side of the wallpaper and cut it out with the utility knife. Apply the paste, let it rest and apply the paper to the box bottom. Wipe off extra paste before it dries with a clean, damp sponge.
8. To cover the side surface of the lid, carefully match the pattern and cut a strip of wallpaper the circumference of the lid plus 2 inches for the length, the height of the top plus 4 inches for the width. Apply paste to the strip and let it rest. Center the lid on the paper, allowing 2 inches for turning under on the inside of the lid. Overlap the side seam and finish as described for the box bottom in Step 7.
9. Turn the paper under onto the inside of the lid, making small cuts as needed in the paper where it overlaps inside the lid. On the outside of the lid, make cuts with the scissors every inch up to the top edge of the lid. Fold the paper strips onto the top, overlapping the cuts. Smooth the paper and add paste where needed.
10. Place the lid, top side down, on the wrong side of the wallpaper. Trace the exact size of the lid and cut it out with the utility knife. Apply paste to the paper, let it rest and paste the paper to the top of the lid, smoothing out the wrinkles. Wipe the top with a clean, damp sponge to remove any excess paste.

Hatbox Heaven

HEARTS 'N FLOWERS ROCKING CHAIR

Easy: Achievable by anyone.

The stencils also work well for creating a decorative border on walls or around windows.

Materials: Child's chair, painted or unfinished; clean cotton rags or paper toweling; rubbing alcohol; acetate sheets; utility knife; masking tape; red, green, white and blue acrylic stencil paints; 4 stencil brushes; polyurethane spray *(optional)*.

Directions:

1. Make sure the finish on the chair is clean and smooth. Have the rubbing alcohol and rags or paper toweling ready to clean the stencils as they are used.

2. Make one acetate stencil for each color in each design. Trace the actual size designs in Fig. I, 4 onto acetate sheets and lightly sketch the grid onto each sheet. Layer the sheets so each design lines up properly; use the grid to help you line up the layers. Cut out the details (not the grid) on each sheet using the utility knife and working on a hard surface; the knife will scratch the surface below the acetate.

3. Starting with the darkest paint color, tape the stencil for that color in place. Dip a stencil brush in the paint and rub the brush on the rags or paper toweling in a circular motion until the brush is almost dry. Apply a thin coat of the paint to the stencil, starting at the edges of the cutout and working toward the center. Allow the paint to dry and apply more coats until the desired color depth is achieved. Repeat the process until all the colors are used, using a different stencil brush for each color, and allowing adequate drying time between coats.

4. If you wish, apply polyurethane spray to act as a protective coating for the design.

5. Clean the stencils with the rags or paper toweling soaked in rubbing alcohol. Clean the brushes with soap and water until the rinse water runs clear.

6. Store the cleaned stencils between layers of cardboard for future use.

FIG. I, 4 HEARTS 'N FLOWERS ROCKING CHAIR STENCIL PATTERN

COLOR ORDER:

VINE IN GREEN
HEART AND FLOWERS IN RED
SWIRLS IN WHITE
BERRIES IN BLUE

BOTTOM BACK AND SEAT

BACK RUNGS

TOP BACK

Hearts 'N Flowers Rocking Chair

Christmas Goose Stocking

CHRISTMAS GOOSE STOCKING

Challenging: Requires more experience in knitting and some experience in crocheting.

Materials: Worsted weight wool: 1 skein each of Natural, Red and Gray, partial skeins each of Turquoise, Orange and Dark Green; 1 pair size 7 knitting needles, OR ANY SIZE NEEDLES TO OBTAIN GAUGE BELOW; 1 tapestry needle; 1 double-pointed needle in any size; 1 stitch holder; size 5 or F crochet hook.

Gauge: In Stockinette Stitch (st st), 5 sts = 1 inch.

Notes: When changing color, pick up new color from under color previously used, twisting yarns on wrong side to prevent holes in work. Carry colors loosely on back of work. When possible, use bobbins to eliminate bulk in knit work (for geese beaks and feet, hearts, trees).

The chart in FIG. I, 5 *is shown upside down because the stocking is worked from the top (the cuff) down to the toe. Each square on the graph represents one stitch.*

Directions:

1. Cuff and Stocking: With Red yarn, cast on 52 sts. Work in k 1, p 1 ribbing for 1½ inches. Change to Natural. Starting with row 1 and working in st st, follow FIG. I, 5 to row 82. Follow the color key for color changes.

2. Heel: Take first 13 sts from single-pointed needle and put on double-pointed needle; the next 26 sts (for instep) are put on stitch holder. Join Natural and k rem 13 sts. Turn the double-pointed needle around and with single-pointed needle k the 13 sts off the other side of the double-pointed needle. This will close the heel. Continue on these 26 sts in st st (k 1 row, p 1 row) for 3 inches, ending with a k row.

To shape heel, p 23, p 2 tog, p 1, turn. *Slip the first st as if to p, k until 3 rem, k 2 tog, k 1, turn. Slip the first st as if to p, p until 3 sts rem, p 2 tog, p 1, turn. Repeat from * until 16 sts rem. K last row.

Do not turn work. Pick up and k 10 sts on right side of heel. Turn and p back across heel (26 sts). Pick up and p 10 sts from left side of heel (36 sts). K 1 row. On next row and each k row, k 2 tog at each end 5 times (26 sts). Work the 11 rows from the Instep Hearts chart shown within the stocking chart in FIG. I, 5, beginning and ending with 3 or 4 sts in Natural. P 1 row. Break off Natural, attach Red. Work in st st on 26 sts for 2½ inches.
3. Toe, Row 1: *K 1, k 2 tog, work to last 3 sts, k 2 tog, k 1.
Row 2: P. Repeat from * until 8 sts remain. Bind off.
4. Top of Foot: Using Natural, pick up 26 sts from holder and work in st st. When work is same length to beg of Instep Hearts on foot bottom, repeat Instep. Change to Red and shape toe as stated in Step 3.
5. Finishing: Block the stocking lightly. Sew the back seam using matching yarn. Draw Red yarn through the bound off stitches on the toe to close opening; secure. Use matching yarns to sew foot seams. Use Red yarn also to sew top 1½ inches of ribbing; leave the end loose. With crochet hook, chain 4 inches with Red. Attach to the seam to form a hanging loop. Fasten off.

FIG. I, 5 CHRISTMAS GOOSE STOCKING ▲ROW 82

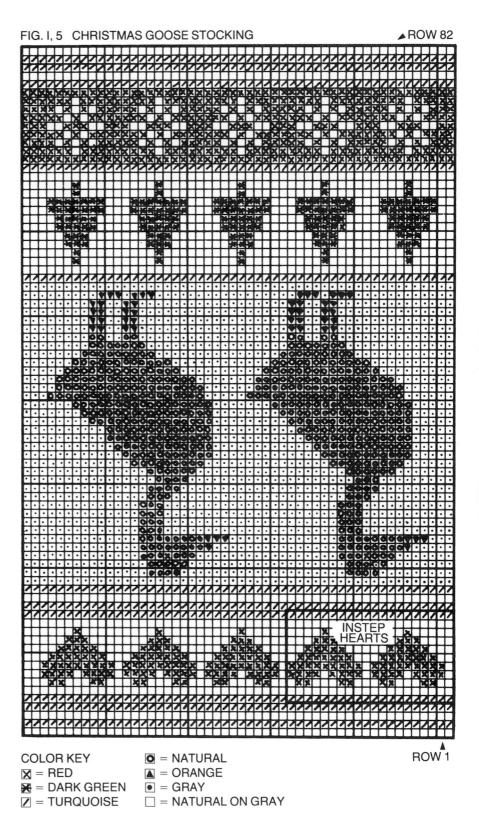

INSTEP HEARTS

▲
ROW 1

COLOR KEY
⊠ = RED
⊠ = DARK GREEN
⊡ = TURQUOISE
◉ = NATURAL
▲ = ORANGE
● = GRAY
☐ = NATURAL ON GRAY

FOOD GIFTS OF THE SEASON

Wonderful goodies from your hearth to delight friends and family alike.

Chocolate-Dipped Orange Cookies (recipe, page 63);
Coconut Almond Macaroons (recipe, page 64)

CHOCOLATE-DIPPED ORANGE COOKIES

You can prepare these cookies in three stages, baking, sandwiching and dipping them as time permits.

Bake at 350° for 12 to 14 minutes.
Makes 24 sandwich cookies.

1 **cup (2 sticks) unsalted butter, at room temperature**
⅔ **cup sugar**
4 **egg yolks**
  Grated zest of 1 orange (orange part of rind only)
1 **teaspoon vanilla**
⅔ **cup all-purpose flour**
1 **cup apricot preserves OR: sweet orange marmalade**
1 **package (12 ounces) semisweet chocolate pieces**
2 **tablespoons vegetable shortening**

1. Preheat the oven to moderate (350°). Lightly grease 2 aluminum foil-lined baking sheets. Also grease 3 to 4 other pieces of aluminum foil cut to fit the baking sheets.
2. Beat the butter until it is creamy in a medium-size bowl with an electric mixer at high speed. Beat in the sugar and continue beating until mixture is very light. Beat in the egg yolks, orange zest and vanilla. Lower mixer speed and beat in the flour.
3. Drop the batter by rounded teaspoonfuls, 3 inches apart, on the baking sheets.
4. Bake in the oven (350°) for 12 to 14 minutes, or until cookie edges are golden brown. Transfer cookies with a metal spatula to wire racks and let cool completely.
5. Simmer the preserves or marmalade in a small saucepan over medium heat. Strain the preserves through a fine sieve into a bowl and return them to the saucepan. Simmer for 1 minute, or until the preserves are slightly thickened.
6. Sandwich the cookies, bottoms together, with the preserves. Let the sandwiches stand for at least 1 hour.

CHOCOLATE BY ANY NAME . . .

Baking chocolate is unsweetened and consists mostly of chocolate liquor, with very little cocoa butter.

Bittersweet or *semisweet chocolate* contains chocolate liquor, cocoa butter, sugar and vanilla or vanilla flavoring.

Sweet dark chocolate contains more sugar and less chocolate liquor.

Milk chocolate contains cocoa butter, sugar, milk, vanilla, and less chocolate liquor than sweet dark chocolate has.

White chocolate contains no chocolate liquor, only cocoa butter, milk, sugar and vanilla.

Cocoa powder is unsweetened chocolate liquor with most of the cocoa butter removed. To substitute cocoa powder for unsweetened baking chocolate, use 3 tablespoons of cocoa powder plus 1 tablespoon of butter, margarine or shortening, for every 1 ounce (1 square) of baking chocolate.

Dutch-processed cocoa has a slightly different taste. It's processed with alkali to neutralize some of the acid and has a slightly higher fat content than regular cocoa.

7. Melt the chocolate pieces and shortening in a small, heavy saucepan over low heat. Remove saucepan from heat and transfer the melted chocolate to a small bowl.
8. Dip the cookies, one at a time, halfway into the melted chocolate, letting excess chocolate drip back into the bowl. Place cookies on wax paper-lined baking sheets.
9. Refrigerate the dipped cookies until the chocolate sets. Gently lift the cookies from the paper and transfer them to a wax paper-lined container, separating the layers with additional wax paper or plastic wrap. Refrigerate or freeze the cookies until serving time.

STORING COOKIES

- To keep cookies crisp, store them between layers of wax paper in a metal or glass container with a tight-fitting lid. Keep the container in a cool, dry place.
- To keep cookies soft, store them in a tin with an apple wedge or a piece of soft white bread to add moisture; be sure to replace the apple or bread often.
- To freshen soft cookies, place them in a casserole dish, cover the dish and heat the cookies at 300° for 8 to 10 minutes.
- To freshen crisp cookies before serving them, place them on a baking sheet and heat them at 300° for 3 to 5 minutes.

COCONUT ALMOND MACAROONS

Toasting the almonds brings out their special flavor.

Toast the almonds at 300° for 10 to 15 minutes; bake the macaroons at 300° for 30 to 40 minutes. Makes 12 macaroons.

- 1   *can (8 ounces) sliced almonds*
- 1   *bag (7 ounces) sweetened flaked coconut*
- 1½   *cups sugar*
- 6   *egg whites*
- ½   *teaspoon almond extract*
- 1   *bag (6 ounces) semisweet chocolate pieces*
- 1   *tablespoon butter*

1. Preheat the oven to slow (300°). Toast the almonds in the oven as it preheats: Place almonds in a single layer on a baking sheet and bake, stirring often, for 10 to 15 minutes, or until they are golden. Remove almonds from the oven and cool them while preparing remaining ingredients. Butter and lightly flour 2 baking sheets.

2. Combine the coconut, sugar and egg whites in a saucepan. Cook over low heat, stirring constantly, for about 12 minutes, or until mixture retains the mark of a spoon when the spoon is drawn through it. Remove mixture from heat and stir in the almond extract and the almonds.

3. Divide the mixture into 12 mounds, 2 inches apart, on the baking sheets. Cool the mixture slightly and shape it into smoother mounds with your fingers. Let the mounds stand for 20 minutes.

4. Bake in the slow oven (300°) for 30 to 40 minutes or until macaroons are golden and firm. Let stand on baking sheets on wire racks for 1 minute, then gently loosen and remove to wire racks with a metal spatula. Cool completely, for at least 1 hour.

5. Melt the chocolate with the butter in a small, heavy saucepan over low heat. Dip the macaroons into melted chocolate and place them on a wax paper-lined baking sheet. Let the macaroons stand for at least 1 hour, or until the chocolate sets. Store the macaroons between sheets of wax paper in an airtight container.

BERRIED TREASURE LIQUEUR

Easy, but definitely a make-ahead treat.

Makes 5 cups.

- ½ pound fresh cranberries
- ½ pint fresh raspberries
  Stripped zest of 1 navel orange (orange part of rind only)
- 1 bottle (750 ml) vodka
- ½ cup kirsch (cherry eau-de-vie; optional)
- 1½ cups sugar
- ¾ cup water

1. Coarsely chop the cranberries. Crush the raspberries slightly. Place the cranberries, raspberries, orange zest, vodka and kirsch in a glass or ceramic 1-gallon container.
2. Cover the container and let it stand at room temperature for 3 to 4 weeks.
3. Strain the cranberry-raspberry mixture into a clean container and filter off the liquid if it is cloudy.
4. Combine the sugar with the water in a saucepan. Bring mixture to boiling over high heat and boil for 1 minute. Remove from heat and cool the sugar syrup.
5. Stir sugar syrup into cranberry-raspberry liquid. Taste. To add more syrup, use 2-parts-sugar to 1-part-water ratio.
6. Pour the liqueur into five sterilized 1-cup bottles. Cover the bottles. Let stand for at least 3 weeks, and up to 6 months.

Variations: For *Cranberry Orange Liqueur,* omit the raspberries and use 1 pound of cranberries. Use the stripped zests of 2 oranges and omit the kirsch.
For *Raspberry Liqueur,* omit the cranberries and use 1 pint of raspberries.
For *Double Berry Liqueur,* omit the cranberries and use ½ pint each of raspberries and blackberries.
For *Spiced Berry Liqueur,* tie 4 whole cloves and one 3-inch piece of stick cinnamon in a square of cheesecloth. Add the cheesecloth square to the boiling sugar syrup. Let syrup cool and remove cheesecloth square before combining syrup with the fruit liquid.

BRANDIED FRUIT SAUCE

The sauce is delicious over ice cream or crêpes.

Makes 3½ cups.

- ½ pound dried apricots
- 1 cup golden raisins
- 1 cup water
- 1 can (1 pound) pear halves in syrup
- ⅓ cup sugar
- 1 3-inch piece stick cinnamon
- ½ cup brandy

1. Combine the apricots, raisins and water in a medium-size saucepan. Let the mixture stand for 10 minutes to soften the fruits.
2. Drain the syrup from the pears into the saucepan. Add the sugar and the cinnamon stick. Bring the mixture to boiling over medium heat. Lower the heat and simmer for 5 minutes, or until the apricots are soft but not mushy.
3. Chop the pears and add them to the saucepan along with the brandy. Pour the sauce into a container and cover the container. Refrigerate the sauce for at least a week.
4. Spoon the sauce into decorative jars.

Variations: Substitute canned peaches for the pears in the above recipe.
For *Dark Brandied Fruit Sauce,* substitute pitted prunes for the dried apricots, raisins for the golden raisins and 1 can of purple plums for the pears in the above recipe.

HERE COMES SANTA CLAUS!

Tuck antique or new Santa chocolate molds into stockings, gift baskets or bows on gift boxes. Try them as tree ornaments, too!

Gingered Nut Mix

DOUBLE YOUR PLEASURE

What could be nicer than giving wonderful food gifts or surprising your guests with some "incredible edibles." Once you make these delectable holiday goodies, you'll always have something very special on hand to give or serve — or make a double batch and do both!

GINGERED NUT MIX

Candied ginger gives new sparkle to a party mix.

Makes 2½ pounds.

- ½ **pound shelled peanuts, salted or unsalted**
- ½ **pound unsalted almonds**
- ½ **pound unsalted pecans**
- ½ **pound golden raisins**
- ¼ **pound hulled, unsalted pumpkin seeds (pepitas; optional)**
- ¼ **pound candied ginger, chopped**

Thoroughly combine all the ingredients in a large bowl. Place the mix in tightly covered containers and refrigerate or freeze it. The nut mix defrosts in about 4 hours in the refrigerator.

HOLIDAY SPICED FRUIT

Serve this spicy fruit mixture with ham or turkey.

Bake at 350° for 40 to 55 minutes.
Makes 16 servings.

1½ tablespoons finely chopped candied ginger
½   pound dried pears, halved or cut into
      thirds
½   pound dried apricots, halved or whole
¼   pound golden raisins
1   can (16 ounces) fruit cocktail OR: fruit
      for salad, with juice (remove
      maraschino cherries)
1   cup apple cider OR: apple juice
½   cup brandy (optional)
2   teaspoons ground allspice
2   teaspoons ground cardamom
1   tablespoon curry powder
2   unpeeled green apples, cored and sliced
⅓   cup fresh cranberries, rinsed and picked
      over

1. Preheat the oven to moderate (350°).
2. Combine all the ingredients except the
   apples and the cranberries in a large
   casserole dish, and cover the dish.
3. Bake in the preheated moderate oven
   (350°), stirring frequently, for 30 to 45
   minutes, or until the fruit softens but still
   retains its shape. (Or cook the fruit in a
   saucepan over very low heat, stirring
   constantly.)
4. Add the apples and the cranberries.
   Continue baking until the apples are
   slightly tender and the cranberries pop,
   for about 10 minutes more.
5. Remove the casserole dish from the oven
   and transfer the fruit mixture to a
   container with a lid. Cool the fruit and
   cover the container. Refrigerate the fruit
   for up to several weeks, or freeze it.

BRANDIED CRANBERRIES

A delicacy over ice cream, pound cake or cheesecake.

Makes 1½ quarts.

2   bags (12 ounces each) fresh or thawed
      frozen cranberries
2   jars (12 ounces each) red currant jelly
½   cup sugar
1   cup light rum
1   cup brandy
    Grated or finely chopped zest of 2 oranges
      (orange part of rind only)

1. Combine the cranberries, jelly, sugar,
   rum, brandy and orange zest in a large
   saucepan over medium heat. Bring the
   mixture to boiling.
2. Cook, stirring constantly, for about 5
   minutes, or until the sauce thickens and
   some, but not all, of the berries pop. Cool
   the sauce slightly, transfer it to sterilized
   jars and refrigerate it.

Brandied Cranberries

APRICOT PECAN LOAF

This dense, moist loaf is best cut into very thin slices.

Bake at 350° for 50 to 60 minutes.
Makes 1 large loaf (20 slices) or 2 small loaves.

1½   **cups water OR: 1 cup apricot nectar plus**
　　　　½ cup water
2   **tablespoons unsalted butter**
⅓   **cup firmly packed light brown sugar**
2   **cups finely chopped dried apricots**
1¼   **cups unbleached all-purpose flour**
1   **cup whole wheat pastry flour**
2   **teaspoons baking powder**
½   **teaspoon salt**
2   **large eggs, well beaten**
1   **teaspoon lemon extract**
½   **cup chopped pecans**
　　Nonstick vegetable cooking spray

1. Combine the water or nectar, the butter and brown sugar in a medium-size saucepan and bring the mixture to boiling. Continue boiling, stirring occasionally, for 1 minute. Remove the pan from the heat and add the apricots. Let the mixture cool for 30 to 45 minutes.
2. Sift together the all-purpose and whole wheat flours, the baking powder and salt into a medium-size bowl. Add the cooled apricots and their liquid.
3. In another medium-size bowl, beat the eggs with an electric mixer at high speed until they quadruple in volume, for about 5 minutes. Add the beaten eggs to the apricot mixture along with the lemon extract. Mix all the ingredients well. Stir in the pecans.
4. Spray a 9 x 5 x 3-inch loaf pan with nonstick vegetable cooking spray and line the pan with parchment paper. Pour in the batter and let it stand for 30 minutes.
5. Preheat the oven to moderate (350°).
6. Bake in the preheated moderate oven (350°) for 50 to 60 minutes, or until a skewer inserted in the center of the loaf comes out clean. Immediately turn out the loaf onto a wire rack; cool for 15 minutes.

Apricot Pecan Loaves

7. Remove the paper, wrap the loaf in plastic wrap and let it stand overnight before slicing. At this point, the bread may be tightly wrapped in plastic freezer wrap and frozen. Thaw the loaf overnight in the refrigerator.

Variations: For *Pineapple Date Bread*, substitute 1 cup each of coarsely chopped dried pineapple and dates for the apricots and 1 cup of pineapple juice for the apricot nectar.
For *Peach and Pear Bread*, substitute 1 cup each of coarsely chopped dried peaches and pears for the apricots and 1 cup of pear nectar for the apricot nectar.

FOOD TO GO—SENDING FOOD BY MAIL

Be sure to choose the right cakes, breads and cookies to mail. Foods to be mailed must be sturdy and should keep well. Soft drop, bar and fruit cookies are good travelers, as as are fruit-cakes and pound cakes, and all kinds of breads. Give your crisper cookies and tender pies to neighbors and nearby family members.

Cylindrical containers in quart and half-gallon sizes are good choices for packing nuts, candies and cookies. Many come printed with holiday designs.

For Cookies: Use empty metal coffee or shortening cans as containers. Wrap two drop cookies back to back, and bar cookies individually, with aluminum foil, and seal them with cellophane tape.

For Breads and Cakes: Send these in strong cardboard boxes after first wrapping the foods in plastic wrap or strong plastic bags, and then again in aluminum foil.

To Pack:

• Line the containers with waterproof plastic wrap, wax paper or aluminum foil. As filler, use crumpled aluminum foil, tissue paper or wax paper. Do *not* pack unsalted popcorn this way; it can become moldy, especially if the package is sent overseas.

• Pack cookies close together in order to leave as little empty space as possible; shifting will cause cookies to break. If you're sending a variety of cookies, place the heaviest ones on the bottom. Place wrapped cakes and breads in a filler-lined box.

• Add more filler to the container, packing it down to minimize shifting and breakage. The box should be so full that you have to use pressure to tape it shut.

• If you can, wrap your package in corrugated cardboard, then in a double layer of brown paper.

• Label only the top of the package with the address of your friend or family member. Write "Fragile—Handle with Care" and "Perishable—Keep from Heat" on the top and sides of the package.

• Send overseas packages by air whenever possible, to avoid spoilage.

Here we Come a-wassailing

THERE'S CHRISTMAS IN THE AIR!

The scent of pine trees and the sound of joyful carols— they're a sure sign it's December, and there's Christmas in the air! To start off this chapter, we bring you warm, woolly sweaters, scarves, mittens and leg warmers, so you can bundle up to go caroling through the neighborhood. Of course, these warm woollies make ideal gifts for Christmas too! As December 25th draws closer, invite friends and family over for a "Come Trim The Tree" party, to get everyone in the holiday spirit. You'll find ornaments to make ahead, or you can ask your guests to help you make them. And since you can't have a great party without great food, we have six different soul-warming chilis and a medley of Christmas cookie hits. Finally, to get you through this month in stride, we show you how to wrap gifts of any shape or size, and give you a complete mailing schedule to help you send out those special gifts on time.

HERE WE COME A' WASSAILING

*Fill the air with the sounds of Christmas—
the most joyous season of the year!*

MAKE A JOYFUL NOISE!

Be sure to have on hand the words and music to some of these favorites.

Silent Night
The First Noël
Joy to the World
O Little Town of Bethlehem
The Holly and the Ivy
Coventry Carol
Angels We Have Heard on High
Hark! The Herald Angels Sing
Good King Wenceslas
We Three Kings of Orient Are
O Tannenbaum
O Come All Ye Faithful
God Rest Ye Merry Gentlemen

We Wish You a Merry Christmas
Deck the Hall
I Saw Three Ships
White Christmas
Silver Bells
Jingle Bells
Winter Wonderland
Jingle Bell Rock
The Christmas Song
   ("Chestnuts roasting on an
   open fire")
Rudolph the Red-Nosed Reindeer
Santa Claus is Coming to Town
The Twelve Days of Christmas

Frosty & Friends Pullover (directions, page 74); Jingle Bell Cardigan (directions, page 75);
Let It Snow! Cap and Mittens (directions, page 77)

FIG. II, 1 FROSTY & FRIENDS PULLOVER

▲
CENTER

⊡ = WHITE
Ⅴ = ORANGE
☒ = BLACK
▲ = GREEN
■ = BLUE

FROSTY & FRIENDS PULLOVER

Challenging: Requires more experience in knitting.

Directions are given for Child's Size 4. Changes for Sizes 6, 8, 10, 12 are in parentheses.

Materials: Coats & Clark 2-ply Red Heart Sport yarn (2-oz skein): 2 (3, 3, 4, 4) skeins of Red, 1 skein of White, 1 ounce each of Periwinkle, Orange, Bright Green and Black; 1 pair each size 4 and size 5 knitting needles, OR ANY SIZE NEEDLES TO OBTAIN GAUGE BELOW; tapestry needle.

Gauge: On size 5 needles in Stockinette Stitch (st st), 6 sts = 1 inch; 8 rows = 1 inch.

SIZES:	4	6	8	10	12
BODY CHEST:	23″	25″	27″	28½″	30″
FINISHED MEASUREMENTS:					
CHEST:	26½″	27″	28½″	30″	31″
WIDTH ACROSS BACK OR FRONT AT UNDERARMS:					
	13¼″	13½″	14¼″	15″	15½″
WIDTH ACROSS SLEEVE AT UPPER ARMS:					
	10½″	11½″	12″	13″	13½″

Note: The snowmen and snowflakes are worked in duplicate stitch.

Directions:
1. Back: With size 4 needles and Red, cast on 76 (78, 82, 86, 90) sts. Work in k 1, p 1 ribbing for 2 (2, 2, 2½, 2½) inches, inc 4 sts evenly spaced across last row—80 (82, 86, 90, 94) sts. Change to size 5 needles and st st (k 1 row, p 1 row). Work until 13½ (14, 15, 16, 16½) inches from beg. Work in k 1, p 1 ribbing for 1½ inches. Bind off loosely in ribbing.

2. Front: Work same as Back.

3. Sleeves: With size 4 needles and Red, cast on 46 (48, 50, 52, 54) sts. Work in k 1, p 1 ribbing for 2 (2, 2½, 2½, 2½) inches, inc 4 (6, 6, 8, 8) sts evenly spaced across last row—50 (54, 56, 60, 62) sts. Change to size 5 needles and work in st st for 8 rows. Inc one st each edge every 4 rows until there are 64 (68, 72, 78, 80) sts. Work until 10 (11, 12, 13, 14) inches from beg. Work in k 1, p 1 ribbing for 1¼ inches. Bind off loosely in ribbing.

4. Finishing: Wet all the pieces, pin them to the finished measurements and let them dry completely. *Duplicate St:* With contrasting color thread, baste a line up center st from bottom to top on Front of sweater. Matching marked center st in Fig. II, 1 to basting line, work duplicate st snowmen on Front of sweater. The snowflakes are scattered; there is no set pattern. The chart in Fig. II, 1 shows an arrangement of snowflakes for the smallest size; for larger sizes, move the motifs further to the sides and top to fill the space. Work 12 to 15 duplicate st snowflakes scattered on each Sleeve. When duplicate st is completed, block again, if necessary.

Sew Front and Back tog for 1 (1, 1¼, 1½, 1½) inch(es) at each shoulder. Sew Sleeves in place for 5¼ (5¾, 6, 6¼, 6¾) inches below shoulder seams. Sew underarm and side seams.

JINGLE BELL CARDIGAN

Challenging: Requires more experience in knitting.

Directions are given for Child's Size 4. Changes for Sizes 6, 8, 10, 12 are in parentheses.

Materials: Coats & Clark Red Heart Premier yarn (3½-oz skein): 5 (5, 6, 6, 7) skeins of Jockey Red, 1 skein each of White and Jade; 1 pair each size 6 and size 8 knitting needles, OR ANY SIZE NEEDLES TO OBTAIN GAUGE BELOW; stitch holders; 6 silver jingle bells; 6 small plastic shanks, or matching yarn to attach bells.

Gauge: On size 8 needles in Stockinette Stitch (st st), 9 sts = 2 inches; 6 rows = 1 inch.

SIZES:	4	6	8	10	12
BODY CHEST:					
	23"	25"	27"	28½"	30"
FINISHED MEASUREMENTS:					
GARMENT SIZE, BUTTONED:					
	27½"	28½"	29½"	31"	32½"
WIDTH ACROSS BACK AT UNDERARMS:					
	13¾"	14¼"	14¾"	15½"	16¼"
WIDTH ACROSS SLEEVE AT UPPER ARMS:					
	10½"	11½"	12"	13½"	14"

Note: The reindeer and snowflakes are worked in duplicate stitch.

Directions:

1. Back: With size 6 needles and Red, cast on 60 (62, 64, 68, 72) sts. Work in k 1, p 1 ribbing for 2 (2, 2½, 2½, 2½) inches, inc 1 st each edge on last row—62 (64, 66, 70, 74) sts. Change to size 8 needles and st st (k 1 row, p 1 row). Continue until 12 (13, 14, 15, 16) inches from beg, end with a k row. Work 4 rows garter stitch (k each row). Continue in st st until 15 (16, 17, 18, 19) inches from beg, end with a k row.

2. Neck Shaping: P 22 (22, 23, 23, 24) sts, join another ball of yarn, p 18 (20, 20, 24, 26) and sl these sts to a holder for back of neck, p 22 (22, 23, 23, 24). Working both sides at the same time, dec 1 st each neck edge on next 2 rows—20 (20, 21, 21, 22) sts each side. Work 2 rows even. Bind off.

3. Left Front: With size 6 needles and Red, cast on 37 (39, 41, 43, 45) sts. Work in k 1, p 1 ribbing for 2 (2, 2½, 2½, 2½) inches, inc one st on last row—38 (40, 42, 44, 46) sts. Change to size 8 needles and k to last 7 sts; sl these sts to a holder for Front border to be worked later—31 (33, 35, 37, 39) sts remain. Continue in st st until same length as Back to garter stitch rows. Work 4 rows garter stitch. Work until 13½ (14, 15, 16, 17) inches from beg, end at neck edge.

4. Neck Shaping: Work across 6 (6, 6, 7, 8) sts and sl these sts to a holder for front of neck, work rem 25 (27, 29, 30, 31) sts. Dec 1 st each neck edge row until 20 (20, 21, 21, 21) sts remain. Work until same length as Back to shoulder. Bind off.

5. Right Front: Work ribbing same as Left Front until ¾ inches from beg, end at Front edge.

FIG. II, 2 JINGLE BELL CARDIGAN, POCKET

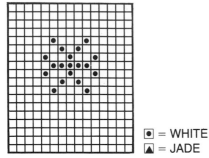

◉ = WHITE
▲ = JADE

FIG. II, 3 JINGLE BELL CARDIGAN, BACK YOKE

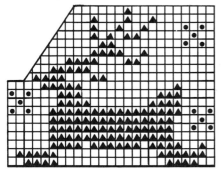

FIG. II, 4 JINGLE BELL CARDIGAN, LEFT FRONT YOKE

6. Buttonhole Row: Work 2 sts in ribbing, bind off 3 sts, work in ribbing across. *Next Row:* Work in ribbing as established, cast on 3 sts over bound-off sts. Continue in ribbing until same depth as Left Front. Slipping 7 front sts to a holder as before, complete same as Left Front, reversing the shaping.

7. Sleeves: With size 6 needles and Red, cast on 36 (36, 38, 40, 42) sts. Work in k 1, p 1 ribbing for 2 (2½, 3, 3, 3) inches, inc 2 (2, 2, 4, 4) sts evenly spaced across last row—38 (38, 40, 44, 46) sts. Change to size 8 needles and beg st st. Inc 1 st each edge every 6th row until there are 48 (52, 54, 60, 62) sts. After last inc, continue until 11 (12, 13, 14, 15) inches from beg. Bind off.

8. Finishing Left Front Border, Buttonband: Sl 7 sts for Left Front border to size 6 needles. Continue working k 1, p 1 ribbing as established until band, very slightly stretched, reaches neck. Sl sts to a holder. Sew band to Front edge. Mark for 5 buttons (jingle bells) evenly spaced, the first ½ inch above ribbing, the last at garter stitch rows, the rem evenly spaced between (the sixth button goes in the neck ribbing).

9. Right Front Border, Buttonhole Band: Work same as buttonband. Opposite markers, work buttonholes as follows: rib 2 sts, bind off 3 sts, rib 2 sts. *Next 2 Rows:* Work in ribbing as established, cast on 3 sts over bound-off sts. When band reaches neck, sl sts to a holder. Sew band to Front of cardigan. Sew Front and Back tog at shoulders. Sew Sleeves in place 5¼ (5¾, 6, 6¾, 7) inches below shoulder seams. Sew underarm and side seams.

10. Neckband: With size 6 needles and Red, pick up 83 (87, 93, 99, 105) sts from around neck edge, including all sts on holders. Work in k 1, p 1 ribbing for 3 rows. Work another buttonhole in Right Front band.

Continue in ribbing until 1 (1, 1¼, 1½, 1½) inch(es) from beg. Bind off loosely in ribbing.

11. Sleeve Pocket: With size 8 needles and Jade, cast on 15 sts. Work in garter stitch for 4 rows. Keeping 2 sts each edge in garter st and center 11 sts in st st, work until 3 inches from beg. Work in k 1, p 1 ribbing for ½ inch. Bind off loosely in ribbing. **Duplicate St:** Following FIG. II, 2 with White, work duplicate st on pocket. Sew pocket to Left Sleeve at elbow.

12. Duplicate St, Back Yoke: On yoke of Back (above garter stitch border), using FIG. II, 3 as a guide, work 18 to 20 White snowflakes in duplicate st. The snowflakes are scattered; there is no set pattern.

13. Front Yoke (the reindeer and snowflakes are worked on both Front yokes. FIG. II, 4 shows reindeer for Left Front; reverse to work Right Front): With contrasting color thread, baste a line up center st of yoke (area above garter stitch); make count on st st section only and do not count border sts. Beginning 1 (1, 2, 2, 3) row(s) up from garter stitch border, working duplicate st in Jade and matching marked center st on chart to basting line, embroider the reindeer. The snowflakes are worked in White and scattered; for larger sizes, move the snowflakes closer to the edges.

14. Bottom Front Snowflakes: FIG. II, 5 shows arrangement of snowflakes below the yoke. With contrasting color thread, baste a line up center st of Front to yoke (do not count Front border sts).

15. Left Front: Using Fig. II, 5 as a general guide, match basting line to marked center st. With White in duplicate st, embroider large, medium, and small snowflakes. The chart shown is for the smallest size; for larger sizes, scatter the motifs closer to the edges.

16. Right Front: Work the exact arrangement of snowflakes on the Left Front in reverse (note that the Left and Right Fronts are mirror images).

With the shanks, or matching yarn, join the jingle bells opposite the buttonholes.

FIG. II, 5   JINGLE BELL CARDIGAN, LEFT BOTTOM YOKE

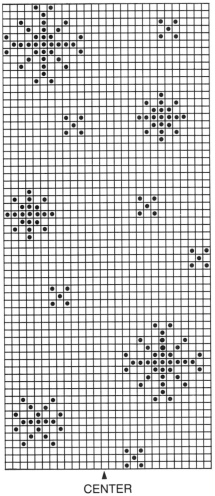

▲
CENTER

LET IT SNOW! CAP AND MITTENS

Average: For those with some experience in knitting.

Fits Child's Sizes 4 to 12.

Materials: Same yarn as Frosty & Friends Pullover (2-oz skein): 2 skeins of Red, 1 skein of White; 1 pair each size 3 and size 5 knitting needles, OR ANY SIZE NEEDLES TO OBTAIN GAUGE BELOW; stitch markers; stitch holders; small amount of sewing elastic.

Gauge: On size 5 needles in Stockinette Stitch (st st), 6 sts = 1 inch; 8 rows = 1 inch.

Directions:

1. Cap: With size 3 needles and Red, cast on 122 sts. Work in k 1, p 1 ribbing for 2 inches. Change to size 5 needles and work in st st (k 1 row, p 1 row) until 5½ inches from beg, end with a p row.

2. Crown Shaping, Row 1: K 3, * k 2 tog, k 4; repeat from * across, end k 2 tog, k 3. **Rows 2 through 4:** Work even in st st as established. **Row 5:** K 2, * k 2 tog, k 3; repeat from * across, end k 2 tog, k 3. **Rows 6 through 8:** Work even in st st. **Row 9:** K 1, * k 2 tog, k 2; repeat from * across, end k 2 tog, k 3. **Row 10:** Purl. **Row 11:** K 1, * k 2 tog, k 1; repeat from * across, end k 2 tog, k 2. **Row 12:** Purl. **Row 13:** * K 2 tog; repeat from * across. **Row 14:** Purl. **Rows 15 and 16:** Repeat Rows 13 and 14.

3. Finishing: Cut the yarn, leaving a 16-inch end. Draw the end through rem sts, pull snugly and secure. With rem of yarn, sew the back seam. **Duplicate St:** Following the chart in FIG. II, 6, with White work 16 to 18 snowflakes scattered around st st area of Cap. The snowflakes are scattered; there is no set pattern.

FIG. II, 6   LET IT SNOW! CAP TOP

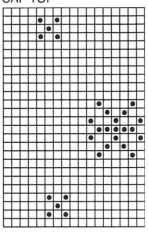

Weave the sewing elastic through the ribbing on the Cap. Adjust to fit and secure in place.

4. Right Mitten: With size 3 needles, cast on 36 sts. Work in k 1, p 1 ribbing for 2½ inches. Change to size 5 needles and work in st st for 4 rows, end with a p row.

5. Thumb Base Shaping, Row 1 (inc row): K 18, place marker, k 2 sts in next st (inc made), k 1, k 2 sts in next st (inc made), place marker, k 15. **Row 2:** Purl. **Row 3 (inc row):** K to marker, sl marker, inc in next st, k 3, inc in next st, sl marker, k 15. **Row 4:** Purl. **Row 5 (inc row):** K to marker, sl marker, inc in next st, k 5, inc in next st, sl marker, k 15. **Row 6:** Purl. **Row 7 (inc row):** K to marker, sl marker, inc in next st, k 7, inc in next st, sl marker, k 15. **Row 8:** Purl—

44 sts. *Next 4 Rows:* Work in st st, ending with a p row.

6. Thumb Row: K 18, sl them to a holder for back of hand, k 11 for thumb, sl rem sts to a holder for front of hand. Cast on 1 st, p 11, cast on 1 st—13 sts. Work in st st on these 13 sts until 1½ inches from cast-on sts, end on wrong side and dec 1 st on last row—12 sts. *Next Row:* * K 1, k 2 tog; repeat from * across. *Next Row:* Purl. *Next Row:* * K 2 tog; repeat from * across.

7. Finishing: Cut the yarn, leaving an 8-inch end. Draw the yarn through rem sts, pull snugly and secure. With remainder of yarn, working from wrong side, sew the thumb seam. Turn the thumb to the right side.

8. Hand: Sl 18 sts from the holder to the needle, pick up 2 sts at base of thumb, slip rem 15 sts to needle—35 sts. Work in st st until 5¼ inches above ribbing, end with a p row and dec 3 sts evenly spaced across last row—32 sts.

9. Top Shaping, Row 1: * K 2, k 2 tog; repeat from * across. *Row 2:* Purl. *Row 3:* * K 1, k 2 tog; repeat from * across. *Row 4:* Purl. *Row 5:* * K 2 tog; repeat from * across.

10. Finishing: Cut the yarn, leaving a 15-inch end. Draw the yarn through the rem sts, pull snugly and secure. Working from the wrong side, sew the seam with the remaining yarn.

11. Left Mitten: Work the same as the Right Mitten to beginning of thumb base shaping.

12. Thumb Base Shaping, Row 1 (inc row): K 15, place marker, inc 1 st in next st, k 1, inc 1 st in next st, place marker, k 18. Continue to work same as Right Mitten, reversing the shaping.

FIG. II, 7 LET IT SNOW! MITTENS

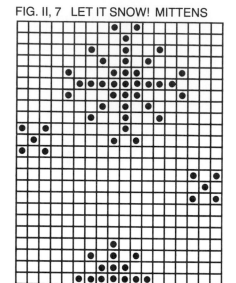

13. Duplicate St: Following the chart in FIG. II, 7, with White work several snowflakes around st st area of Mittens. The snowflakes are scattered; there is no set pattern.

$ [symbols]

KID'S LEG WARMERS

Average: For those with some experience in knitting.

Long and short versions. Directions are given for leg warmers for a 6 year-old child. Changes for 8 and 10 year-olds are in parentheses.

Materials: Yarns of various textures and colors (about 1 oz each of 16 different colors); 1 pair knitting needles, size to obtain gauge below, and 1 pair 2 sizes smaller, for ribbing.

Gauge: On larger needles in Stockinette Stitch (st st), 3½ to 4 sts = 1 inch.

Note: The leg warmers are worked in your choice of colors and patterns. Each pair is unique. The following are a few tips to help ensure a successful project: 1) Maintain the gauge; 2) Thinner yarns may be combined to form an average weight yarn, or may be worked in a pattern that tends to widen a bit, such as a seed stitch or garter stitch; 3) Heavy weight yarns should be used for a thin stripe or a pattern that pulls in, such as a bamboo stitch or pebble stitch; 4) Vary the widths of the stripes; 5) Use a very resilient yarn for the ribbing—if necessary, work in elastic later; 6) Work both leg warmers at the same time, or keep a record of the pattern on the first leg warmer to repeat on the second leg warmer.

Patterns for Average Weight Yarns: Stockinette stitch; reverse stockinette stitch; basketweave stitch; waffle rib; striped lace; 2 TW 2 by 4 stockinette stitch.

Patterns for Thinner Yarns: Garter stitch; seed stitch.

Patterns for Heavy Weight Yarns:
Pebble stitch; bamboo stitch.
Patterns for Loop or Fuzzy Yarns:
Garter stitch; reverse stockinette stitch.

See the knitting patterns be-low. When the number of stitches doesn't fit a pattern evenly, try to work the extra stitches as part of the pattern, or work the extra stitches in garter st or stockinette st as necessary.

Directions:
With the smaller needles and a resilient yarn, cast on 41 (43, 45) sts so the sts stretch. Work in k 1, p 1 ribbing for 2 inches. Change yarns, but not needles, and work across the first row of the pattern stitch you choose, increasing 10 (10, 12) sts. On the next row, change to the larger needles. Work even on 51 (53, 57) sts, changing yarns and pat-terns as desired until the total length measures: short version 10 (12, 14) inches; long version 13 (15, 17) inches. Work the last row of the last stripe on the smaller needles. Change the yarn to a resilient yarn for the ribbing and work in k 1, p 1 ribbing for 2 inches. Bind off loosely so the sts stretch. Sew the seams.

Basketweave Stitch:
Mult. of 10 sts plus 3. **Rows 1 and 3:** K 3, * p 7, k 3; repeat from *. **Row 2:** P 3, * k 7, p 3; repeat from *. **Rows 4 and 8:** Purl. **Rows 5 and 7:** P 5, * k 3, p 7 *; repeat *·to *, end k 3, p 5. **Row 6:** K 5, * p 3, k 7 *; repeat * to *, end p 3, k 5. Repeat Rows 1 to 8.

Waffle Rib:
Mult. of 3 sts plus 2. **Row 1:** * P 2, k 1; repeat from *, end p 2. **Row 2:** * K 2, p 1; repeat from *,

Kid's Leg Warmers

end k 2. **Row 3:** Knit. **Row 4:** Purl. Repeat Rows 1 to 4.

Striped Lace:
Odd number of sts. **Rows 1 (wrong side) and 2:** Purl. **Rows 3 and 4:** K 1, * yo, k 2 tog; repeat from *. **Rows 5 and 6:** Knit. Re-peat Rows 1 to 6.

2 TW 2 by 4 Stockinette Stitch:
Mult. of 4 sts. **Row 1 (wrong side):** Purl. **Row 2:** K 2, * 2 TW 2 (** knit 2nd st on left-hand nee-dle, then knit 1st st on left-hand needle, slide both sts off needle tog **; repeat ** to **), k 4;

repeat from *, end k 2. Repeat Rows 1 and 2.

Pebble Stitch:
Even number of sts. **Row 1:** Knit. **Row 2:** Purl. **Row 3:** K 1, k 2 tog to last st, k 1. **Row 4:** * K 1, pick up horizontal thread before next st and knit it; repeat from *, end k 2. Repeat Rows 1 to 4.

Bamboo Stitch:
Even number of stitches. **Row 1 (wrong side):** Purl. **Row 2:** K 1, * yo, k 2, pass yo over k 2 *; repeat * to *, end k 1. Repeat Rows 1 and 2.

CHECKERBOARD PULLOVER

Average: For those with some experience in knitting.

Directions are given for Women's Size Small (6-8). Changes for Sizes Medium (10-12) and Large (14-16) are in parentheses ( ). Immediately following the Women's Sizes are the Men's Sizes in brackets [ ]: Small [36-38], Medium [40-42] and Large [44-46].

Materials: Worsted weight yarn (1¾-oz/50-g ball): *Women:* 3 (3, 4, 5) balls of Turquoise (A), 2 (2, 3, 4) balls each of Dark Blue (B), Purple (C), Green (D), Green Tweed (E) and Red Tweed (F); *Men:* 3 (4, 5, 6) balls each of Turquoise (A) and Purple (C), 2 (3, 4, 5) balls each of Dark Blue (B), Green (D), Light Blue (E) and Medium Green (F); 1 pair each size 6 and size 8 knitting needles, OR ANY SIZE NEEDLES TO OBTAIN GAUGE BELOW; stitch markers; 1 set size 6 double-pointed needles (dp) for Women's Collar; tapestry needle.

Gauge: On size 8 needles in Stockinette Stitch (st st), 5 sts = 1 inch; 6 rows = 1 inch.

WOMEN'S SIZES

SIZES:	SMALL (6-8)	MEDIUM (10-12)	LARGE (14-16)
BODY BUST:	31½″	34″	38″
FINISHED MEASUREMENTS:			
BUST:	38″	41″	46″
WIDTH ACROSS BACK OR FRONT AT UNDERARMS:	19″	20½″	23″
WIDTH ACROSS SLEEVE AT UPPER ARMS:	16″	20″	22″

MEN'S SIZES

SIZES:	SMALL (36-38)	MEDIUM (40-42)	LARGE (44-46)
BODY CHEST:	38″	42″	46″
FINISHED MEASUREMENTS:			
CHEST:	41″	46″	50″
WIDTH ACROSS BACK OR FRONT AT UNDERARMS:	20½″	23″	25″
WIDTH ACROSS SLEEVE AT UPPER ARMS:	18″	20″	22″

Note 1: The pullover has no armhole shaping.

Note 2: When changing yarns while working the Checkerboard design (see FIG. II, 8, page 82), pick up the color to be used under the color previously used, twisting the yarns on the wrong side to prevent holes in the work. Carry the unused colors loosely on the wrong side of the work.

Directions:

1. Back: Starting at lower edge with size 6 needles and A [A], cast on 86 (92, 104), [92 (104, 116)] sts. Work in k 1, p 1 ribbing for 2 inches, increasing 10 sts evenly spaced across last row—96 (102, 114), [102 (114, 126)] sts. Cut A [A]; attach C [D]. Change to size 8 needles and with C [D], work in st st (k 1 row, p 1 row) until total length is 10 (11, 12) inches, [11 (12, 13)] inches from beg, ending with a p row. Beg Checkerboard design for both Women and Men, following FIG. II, 8 as follows: *Rows 1, 3, 5, 7:* * With A k 6 (6, 6), [6 (6, 6)], B k 6 (6, 6), [6 (6, 6)]; rep from * across, ending with A k 0 (6, 6), [6 (6, 6)]. *Rows 2, 4, 6, 8:* With A, p 0 (6, 6), [6 (6, 6)], * B p 6 (6, 6), [6 (6, 6)], A p 6 (6, 6), [6, (6, 6)]; rep from * across. Continue to follow FIG. II, 8 as established until Row 24 is completed. Cut

A and B; attach D [C]. *Mark each end of last row worked for beg of armhole.* With D [C], work in st st until 8 (9, 10) inches, [9 (10, 11)] inches from marked row, ending with a p row.

2. Shoulder Shaping: Bind off 32 (35, 38), [35 (38, 42)] sts at beg of next 2 rows for shoulders. Bind off rem 32 (32, 38), [32 (38, 42)] sts for back of neck.

3. Front: Work same as Back until 4½ (5½, 6¼) inches, [5½ (6¼, 7)] inches from marked row, ending with a p row.

4. Neck Shaping: Work across first 42 (44, 49) sts [44 (49, 54)] sts; join 2d ball of yarn and bind off center 12 (14, 16), [14 (16, 18)] sts for front of neck; work to end. Working both sides at once, dec one st at each neck edge every other row 10 (9, 11) times, [9 (11, 12)] times—32 (35, 38), [35 (38, 42)] sts. Work even in st st until same length as Back from marked row, ending with a p row.

5. Shoulder Shaping: Bind off 32 (35, 38), [35 (38, 42)] sts at each side for shoulders.

6. Sleeve One: Starting at lower edge with size 6 needles and B [B], cast on 48 (50, 56), [54 (56, 62)] sts. Work in k 1, p 1 ribbing for 2 inches, increasing 6 (6, 8), [6 (6, 8)] sts evenly spaced across last row—54 (56, 64), [60 (62, 70)] sts. Cut B [B]. Change to size 8 needles and work in st st. Inc one st each end every 7th (6th, 6th) row, [7th (6th, 6th)] row until there are 80 (90, 100), [90 (100, 110)] sts on needle, working as follows: With F [E], work for 6 (6½, 7) inches, [7 (7½, 8)] inches. Beg Checkerboard design following FIG. II, 8, working additional stitches into design. With E [F], work for

FIG. II, 8 CHECKERBOARD
PULLOVER

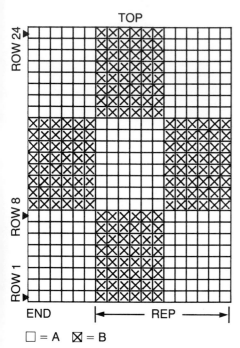

☐ = A   ☒ = B

6 (6½, 7) inches, [7 (7½, 8)] inches more. Bind off all sts.

7. Sleeve Two: Work ribbing same as Sleeve One. Continue to work the same as for Sleeve One in the following sequence: Work E [F] for 6 (6½, 7) inches, [7 (7½, 8)] inches, Checkerboard design, and then F [E] for 6 (6½, 7) inches, [7 (7½, 8)] inches more. Bind off all sts.

8. Finishing, Women's Collar (overlapped): Sew both shoulder seams. With right side facing and A, beg 2 rows below front neck bound-off sts and starting to the right of center Front 3 sts from start *(see photo, page 80),* with dp needles pick up and k 9 (10, 11) sts, working across rows, moving up until you are at bound-off front neck edge.

Tapering Right Edge: Pick up and k 75 (76, 87) sts around remainder of neck edge, ending to the left of center Front so that 3 sts will overlap at center Front—84 (86, 98) sts. Divide sts evenly between 3 needles. Work back and forth in rows in k 1, p 1 ribbing for 4 inches. Bind off loosely in ribbing. Sew in Sleeves from marker to marker. Sew side and Sleeve seams.

9. Men's Collar: Sew left shoulder seam. With right side facing, using size 6 needles and [A], starting at right back neck edge, pick up and k the following sts: [32 (38, 42)] sts along back neck edge, [13 (15, 17)] sts down left front neck edge, [14 (16, 18)] sts along front neck edge and [13 (15, 17)] sts up right front neck edge—[72 (84, 94)] sts. Work in k 1, p 1 ribbing for 6 rows; bind off loosely. Sew right shoulder and neckband seams. Sew in Sleeves from marker to marker. Sew side and Sleeve seams.

THE MAGIC OF MOVIES

Use your VCR to get everyone in the Christmas spirit.

A Christmas Carol　　　　　*It's a Wonderful Life*
Miracle on 34th Street　　*Mister Magoo's Christmas Carol*
Holiday Inn　　　　　　　*A Charlie Brown Christmas*
White Christmas　　　　　*How the Grinch Stole Christmas*
Rudolph the Red-Nosed Reindeer　*Frosty the Snowman*

DOUBLE-WARM SCARF
(9 x 67 inches, plus fringe)

Average: For those with some experience in knitting.

Materials: Bernat Berella Sport-spun yarn (1¾-oz skein): 4 skeins of Hunter Green (A) and 3 skeins of Natural (B); 1 pair size 6 knitting needles, OR ANY SIZE NEEDLES TO OBTAIN GAUGE BELOW.

Gauge: In Stockinette Stitch (st st), 22 sts = 4 inches; 30 rows = 4 inches.

Directions:

1. Starting at narrow edge with A, cast on 100 sts. Work in st st (k 1 row, p 1 row) in the following striped pattern: * 18 rows A, 18 rows B; rep from * 12 times more, end with 18 rows A. Bind off. Fold the scarf in half lengthwise so the long edges meet. Sew the seam.

2. Fringe: Wind A 4 times around a 9-inch piece of cardboard. Cut the yarn at one end, making 18-inch strands. Attach a fringe (using 4 strands) to every 3rd st along one narrow edge of the scarf for a total of 18 fringes. Repeat at the opposite edge. Trim the fringes evenly.

Did You Know . . .

The origin of the word "carol" is uncertain; some say that it is related to the carolare, meaning to sing, originally signifying a dance accompanied by singing. St. Francis of Assisi is considered the "Father of the Christmas Carol." In 1224, during a nativity celebration, he led his followers in songs of praise to the Christ Child and this "joyful noise" was adopted as part of the Christmas celebration.

BUTTON UP YOUR OVERCOAT!

Caroling from door to door is great fun, but staying warm and protected from the elements is essential. The following provides a guide to keeping toasty when Jack Frost is nipping at your nose!

Layer It On

• Use moisturizer freely to protect your skin from the cold and wind. Smooth it over your face, under your eyes, on elbows, knees and hands. This applies to both men and women.

• Use lip balm before going out, and carry it with you to reapply as necessary.

• A hat, optional in chilly weather, is a must when temperatures plummet. To restore flattened hair, brush it upside down and use a touch of hairspray.

Bundle Up

• Layer your clothing; multiple layers trap heat better than one very heavy garment.

• Stick to natural fibers; cotton, silk and wool provide warmth and still allow the skin to "breathe." Wear the softer fabrics (cottons, silks) next to the skin, and "itchy" wools over them.

• Wear tights or thermal underwear under slacks, and two pairs of socks to keep your legs and feet toasty.

• For safety when traveling the streets at night, wear bright colors.

• To keep your hands warm, use lined gloves or mittens, or wear two pairs.

COME TRIM THE TREE!

Is there any symbol more evocative of the season than the Christmas tree?

Whether you do it with family or friends (or both), decorating the Christmas tree is one of the most cherished traditions of the season. If you'd like to have a Trim-the-Tree party, you can approach it one of two ways:

• Bring out the ornaments you have collected over the years, buy tinsel or garlands and candy canes, and have everyone help decorate the tree.

• Start the party earlier in the day and have everyone help make the ornaments—string popcorn and cranberries, tie ribbon ties to gingerbread cookies (bake the gingerbread beforehand), make large bows out of red velvet ribbon, tie pine cones with ribbons, roll pine cones in glue and glitter, tie cinnamon sticks with baby's breath and bows. Or use a combination of store-bought and homemade ornaments to make the Christmas tree uniquely yours.

Did You Know . . .

The first recorded mention of a decorated Christmas tree dates back to 1605. The account tells of fir trees set up and hung with paper roses of different colors, with apples, flat wafers, gilded candies and sugar. One of the loveliest Christmas tree tales is that of Martin Luther and the fir tree: It is said that Luther, while walking through a forest one Christmas eve, beheld a tree illuminated by the stars. The beauty of the tree and stars inspired him to take home a small fir tree, to which he attached lighted candles. He felt this to be a recreation of the wonder of the night sky over the city of Bethlehem so long ago.

Remember that a holiday tree decorated with odds and ends and lots of love can be more beautiful than the most chic "designer" tree.

To further enhance the spirit of the season, you can place some of the following under the Christmas tree, before all the presents are wrapped:

• A miniature train set, complete with landscaping (use your imagination), houses, toy animals, and so on.

• A family of dolls, antique and new.

• A selection of antique toys.

• A menagerie of stuffed animals with bright bows around their necks.

• Favorite toys, such as an old red wagon, a special teddy bear, grandma's rocking horse or an antique doll cradle.

• A nativity scene.

Underneath it all, drape a brightly colored sheet as a background for your Christmas magic (and easy post-holiday clean-up)!

An Old-Fashioned Christmas Tree

"ANTIQUE" DOVE ORNAMENT

Easy: Achievable by anyone.

Materials: 24-gauge shiny tin; tin snips; medium-grade sandpaper; awl; acrylic paints; twine; hammer; cardboard; pencil; graphite paper; stylus or old ballpoint pen; scissors.

FIG. II, 9 "ANTIQUE" DOVE ORNAMENT

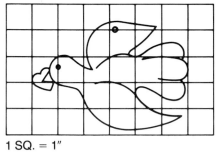

1 SQ. = 1"

Directions:
1. Enlarge the pattern in FIG. II, 9 onto the cardboard, following the directions on page 271.
2. Using the graphite paper and the stylus or old ballpoint pen, trace the pattern onto the tin. Cut out the pattern with the tin snips. Hammer out or sand down any sharp edges.
3. Paint the dove with several base coats of acrylic paint and let dry. Paint the accent features (contours, eyes, and so on).
4. Punch a hole with the awl for hanging. Run the twine through the hole and tie.

BEADED SNOWFLAKE ORNAMENT

Easy: Achievable by anyone.

Materials: Two 4-inch squares of needlepoint canvas; two 5½-inch squares of emerald green 14-count Aida cloth; glass beads: 1 tube each of gold, red and white *(see Materials Shopping Guide, page 274)*; 1½ yards of red middy braid; 1 yard of gold middy braid; thread to match fabric; glue-in-a-tube; needle: #10 crewel or #11 sharp.

Directions:
Note: *Counted bead embroidery is very similar to counted cross-stitch. It is worked with a half cross-stitch: Begin the stitch in the lower left corner of the thread intersection, attach the correct color bead, and finish the stitch in the upper right corner of this intersection. All stitches must go in the same direction or the beads will not be aligned properly. Do not "jump" more than 3 or 4 stitches without first securing the thread on the back of the work, or the last bead may be loose.*
1. Bead the design in FIG. II, 10, centered, on each of the two Aida cloth squares.
2. Baste together the two needlepoint canvas squares. Fringe ½ inch on each side of each beaded square. Place one beaded square, design facing out, on each side of the needlepoint

canvas squares. Stitch all the pieces together near the edges just inside the fringe.

3. Glue the red middy braid at the inner edge of the fringe. Glue the gold middy braid inside of, and very slightly overlapping, the red braid.

4. Cut a 5-inch length of the red middy braid. Wrap the cut ends with a piece of the gold braid to form a loop. Glue loop to corner of ornament for a hanger.

Beaded Snowflake Ornament

Did You Know . . .

Legend has it that on the night of Christ's birth, God sent three messengers, Faith, Hope and Charity, to select and light the first Christmas tree. The fir was chosen because each bough resembled a cross, with the twigs at right angles to the branches.

FIG. II, 10   BEADED SNOWFLAKE ORNAMENT

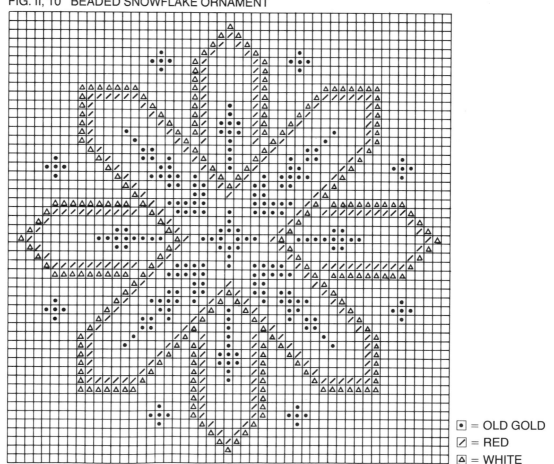

⊡ = OLD GOLD

☑ = RED

△ = WHITE

SEASONAL STORIES

These are just a few of the many classic stories that evoke the spirit of Christmas. Read them aloud to the whole family, year after year.

A Christmas Carol
   by Charles Dickens
Gifts of the Magi
   by O. Henry
A Child's Christmas in Wales
   by Dylan Thomas
How the Grinch Stole Christmas by Dr. Seuss
A Visit From St. Nicholas
   by Dr. Clement Clarke
   Moore
The Tailor of Gloucester
   by Beatrix Potter
A Christmas Memory
   by Truman Capote
little tree
   by e.e. cummings
The Best Christmas Pageant Ever by Barbara Robinson
The Fir Tree
   by Hans Christian Anderson
The Littlest Angel
   by Charles Tazewell
"Is There a Santa Claus?,"
   by Francis Church,
   The New York Sun

Did You Know . . .

In 1856, President Franklin Pierce put up the first decorated Christmas tree in the White House. Calvin Coolidge was responsible for the first outdoor tree at the White House, the lighting of which has become a yearly Christmas tradition.

Hearts A-Glow Ornament

HEARTS A-GLOW ORNAMENT

Easy: Achievable by anyone.

Materials: Glue-in-a-tube; small wooden heart-shaped box, about 3 inches long; gold paint; red, gold and copper sequins; 1 yard of gold soutache.

Directions:

1. Paint the box with the gold paint and let it dry.

2. Glue the gold soutache around the edge of the bottom of the box, and around the upper and lower edges of the box lid sides.

3. Beginning at the outer edge of the top of the lid, glue on the gold sequins: Place a tiny dab of glue where each sequin is to be placed and gently press the sequin on the glue. Overlap the sequins like fish scales. Repeat with a second, inner row of copper sequins *(see photo)* and let dry. Fill the center area with overlapping rows of the red sequins.

4. Glue a hanger loop of gold soutache to the top of the box.

LOVING BEAR ORNAMENT

(2½ inches tall)

Average: For those with some experience in crocheting.

Materials: Medium weight thread (250-yd ball): 1 ball of Ecru, or about 25 yards for each bear; size 13 steel crochet hook; stitch markers; darning needle; embroidery floss; scraps of Red, Brown and Green floss for facial features; polyester fiberfill.

Directions:

1. Head: Starting at tip of nose, ch 2. **Rnd 1:** 6 sc in 2nd ch from hook. **Do not join Rnds; mark beg of Rnds. Rnd 2:** (2 sc in next sc, sc in next sc) 3 times—9 sc. **Rnd 3:** Sc in each sc around. **Rnd 4:** (2 sc in next sc, sc in each of next 2 sc) 3 times—12 sc. **Rnd 5:** Sc in each sc around. **Rnd 6:** Sc in each of next 2 sc, 2 sc in each of next 8 sc, sc in each of next 2 sc—20 sc. **Rnd 7:** Sc in each of next 8 sc, 2 sc in each of next 4 sc, sc in each of next 8 sc—24 sc. **Rnds 8 and 9:** Sc in each sc around. **Rnd 10:** (Sc in each of next 5 sc, 2 sc in next sc) 4 times—28 sc. **Rnd 11:** Sc in each sc around. **Rnd 12:** (Sk next sc, sc in each of next 6 sc) 4 times—24 sc. **Rnd 13:** (Sk next sc, sc in each of next 5 sc) 4 times—20 sc. **Rnd 14:** (Sk next sc, sc in each of next 4 sc) 4 times—16 sc. Stuff Head firmly. **Rnd 15:** (Sk next sc, sc in each of next 3 sc) 4 times—12 sc. **Rnd 16:** (Sk next sc, sc in each of next 2 sc) 4 times—8 sc. **Rnd 17:** * Draw up a lp in each of next 2 sc, yarn over hook, draw through all 3 lps on hook; rep from * 3 times more. Sl st in next sc. Fasten off.

2. Ear (make 2): Starting at base of Ear, ch 5. **Row 1:** Sc in 2nd ch from hook, sc in each of next 3 ch—4 sc. Ch 1, turn. **Row 2:** Sc in each sc across. Ch 1, turn. **Row 3:** (Sk 1 sc, sc in next sc) 2 times—2 sc. Ch 1, turn. **Row 4:** Sl st in 2nd sc. Fasten off, leaving a 6-inch end for sewing. Sew the Ears' bases to Rnd 9 of the Head, ½ inch apart.

3. Body: Starting at neck edge, ch 8. Join with sl st to form ring. **Rnd 1:** 12 sc in ring. **Do not join Rnds; mark beg of Rnds. Rnd 2:** (2 sc in next sc, sc in each of next 2 sc) 4 times—16 sc. **Rnd 3:**

Loving Bear Ornament

(Sc in each of next 3 sc, 2 sc in next sc) 4 times—20 sc. **Rnd 4:** Sc in each sc around. **Rnd 5:** (Sc in each of next 4 sc, 2 sc in next sc) 4 times—24 sc. **Rnds 6 to 9:** Sc in each sc around. **Rnd 10:** Sc in each of next 12 sc (back edge); **do not** work rem sts. Ch 1, turn. **Rnd 11:** Sc in each of the 12 sc just worked. Ch 1, turn. **Rnd 12:** Sc in each of the 12 sc just worked, then work sc in each of the 12 sc (front edge) not worked on Rnd 10—24 sc. Fasten off. Stuff Body firmly. Sew front and back edges together. Sew Head to neck.

4. Leg (make 2): Starting at center of pad of foot, ch 2. **Rnd 1:** 6 sc in 2nd ch from hook. **Rnd 2:** 2 sc in each sc—12 sc. **Rnds 3 to 10:** Sc in each sc around. Fasten off, leaving a 6-inch end for sewing. Stuff firmly. Pinch top edge of Leg; using the darning needle and end of thread, sew opening flat. From back of Body, sew Legs to Body bottom seam.

5. Arm (make 2): Work same as Leg for 7 rnds. Stuff and sew opening flat as for Leg. Sew Arms to sides of Body.

6. Facial Features *(see photo):* Using 3 strands of embroidery floss throughout, embroider the nose in satin stitch over Rnd 1 of the Head; work a straight stitch under the center of the nose about ⅛ inch long; embroider a curved line below for the mouth. Working over Rnd 5 of the Head, embroider the eyes with French knots *(see page 272),* ⅜ inch apart. Work the heart on the left side of the Body in red satin stitch.

7. To form loop, attach crochet thread to top of Head and work a chain 2 inches long. Join with sl st to first ch. Fasten off.

CHRISTMAS TREE CARE

Follow these tips to keep your tree fresh throughout the holiday season.

- As soon as you get the tree home, cut the trunk on the diagonal and place the tree in a pail of water. Keep the tree outside the house until it's time to decorate.
- Before putting the tree in the tree stand, saw the trunk to make a straight flat edge. Place the tree firmly in the tree stand.
- The tree should *never* be placed near fireplaces, radiators, electric heaters or televisions.
- Once the tree is decorated, fill the container in the tree stand with water. Always keep the container filled.
- Make a firm rule that the tree is lighted *only* with an adult present.

MR. & MRS. CLAUS ORNAMENTS

Easy: Achievable by anyone.

Materials for Both: Two 25-mm wooden bead doll heads with rosy cheeks; two 38-mm round red beads; craft glue; white acrylic paint and brush; compass; 3-inch square of white felt for Mrs. Claus' sleeves and Mr. Claus' beard, moustache and cuffs; 1-inch square of flesh-colored felt for hands; 12 inches of cord to make hanging loops. *For Mr. Claus:* One 5-mm pearl; one ½-inch red pompon; one ¾-inch white pompon; 1½ x 2¼ inches of red felt for sleeves; 3 red seed beads and a tiny holly leaf for front of hat. *For Mrs. Claus:* One 1-inch white pompon; 5 inches of ⅛-inch-wide red ribbon; one 5-mm green sequin; 6½ inches of ¼-inch-wide scalloped lace edging; tiny pieces of green and brown felt for the Christmas tree she holds; 17 red seed beads.

Directions:

1. Using the compass and a piece of paper, draw a 2½-inch-diameter circle. Fold the circle in half and cut the circle exactly in half. Fold one of the halves in half, and cut in half. You now should have two pieces resembling one quarter of a pie. On one of these pieces, measure ½ inch from the point along one straight edge and draw a curved line from there toward the end where the other straight edge meets the outside curve of the

wedge. Cut along the curved line you just drew. The resulting shape should have two curved edges tapering to a point, and a straight edge measuring ¾ inch. This is the sleeve pattern. Cut out two red felt sleeves for Mr. Claus and two white felt sleeves for Mrs. Claus.

2. Mr. Claus: Glue a head bead over the hole of a red body bead. When the glue has dried, paint white hair and white eyebrows on the head bead. Cut a 6-inch length of cord and glue the cord ends to the top of the head bead to make a hanging loop. Glue the ¾-inch white pompon over the raw edges of the cord. On top of the white pompon, glue the ½-inch red pompon and glue the pearl on top of that. On the front of Mr. Claus' cap, glue the tiny holly leaf and three red seed beads. Glue the red felt sleeves around each side of the body, with the straight edges toward the front and ½ inch apart at the top of the cuffs. Glue flesh colored felt pieces, about ⅝ x ¼ inch and tapered at one end, under the ends of the sleeves for hands. Cut a 1½ x ⅛-inch strip of white felt. Cut the strip in half crosswise and glue one piece across the end of each sleeve for a cuff. Cut the white felt about ¾ inch wide and ½ inch deep for a beard, and ⅛ x ½ inch for a moustache. Trim to shape, and glue the beard and moustache on the face.

3. Mrs. Claus: Glue a head bead over the hole of a red body bead. When the glue has dried, paint on white hair and white eyebrows. Cut a 6-inch length of cord and glue the ends to the top of the head bead to make a hanging loop. Glue the 1-inch white pompon over the cord ends. Glue the white felt sleeves around the body bead as shown in the photograph, with flesh-colored felt hands glued just under the ends of the sleeves. Between the hands, glue a tiny, green felt Christmas tree, $5/16$ inch high, with a trunk of brown felt $1/16$ inch wide and $3/16$ inch long. Glue the scalloped lace edging around her head at the edge of the pompon, and around her neck for a ruffle. Tie a tiny bow of red ribbon for her hair and glue it over her left eye on the pompon "hair." Cut two $3/4$-inch lengths of red ribbon and glue them to the ends of the sleeves for cuffs. Leave a $1/8$-inch space and glue a row of eight red seed beads alongside each piece of ribbon. Glue the green sequin under her chin, and glue a red seed bead in the center of the green sequin.

Mr. & Mrs. Claus Ornaments

Did You Know . . .

Prince Albert, husband to Queen Victoria, popularized many German Christmas customs in England, including that of the Christmas tree. The palace tree was decorated with gingerbread, candy, fancy cakes, ribbons, toys and dolls, and an angel with outstretched wings at the top.

UNDER WRAPS

Make the most of your holiday gift giving with these hints to pretty up any package!

One of the most treasured childhood memories is peeking into the bottoms of closets and backs of cupboards to discover those mysterious bundles, gaily wrapped and beribboned. The following are a variety of ways to dress up and conceal oddly shaped gifts, as well as innovative trims to add something extra-special to boxed gifts.

THE BASIC BOX

• Place the box upside down on the wrong side of the wrapping paper. Allow for enough paper to let the ends meet with an inch overlap.
• Tape one end of the paper to the bottom of the box. Bring the other end around the box, turn the edge under and tape it.
• Fold down the top flaps. Crease the side flaps and fold them inward. Fold up the bottom flaps and tape them.

MAGIC TOUCHES

Ribbon Curls

Cut several pieces of curling ribbon 2 to 3 feet long, depending on the size of the gift. To create a curl, hold each piece tightly between a scissor blade and your thumb and pull gently but firmly. Cluster the curled pieces of ribbon and tape them to the center of the package.

Little Extras

For something special, decorate your packages with pieces of tinsel garland in silver or gold, or tuck miniature ornaments, figurines, stickers, cutouts from old Christmas cards, silk flowers or baby's breath around or in the center of the bow.

Unusual Wraps

Instead of using wrapping paper, substitute fabric scraps, wallpaper, aluminum foil, scarves, posters or even pages from newspapers, magazines or comic books to personalize packages for the holidays.

Under Wraps

SHARE THE SPIRIT

Christmas cards and letters are a wonderful way to let far-away friends and relatives share your holiday. But this year, why not try something a bit different? Take a series of photographs of your caroling and tree-trimming festivities, or videotape them, if possible. Your distant loved ones will feel as though they actually spent the season with you.

PRICELESS WRAPPINGS

Spread large rolls of plain white, red or green wrapping paper on the floor and supply the kids with crayons and marking pens. They will have a ball drawing Christmas designs and writing special messages on their own "designer" gift wrapping. Then help them wrap the gifts they are giving. Have lots of ribbons and bows handy. So what if a bow is a little crooked? These are boxes with "personality" written all over them—and fun to make too!

WRAPS FOR ODD SHAPES

Bottle Beauty
• Cut a circular piece of wrapping paper or fabric wide enough to cover the body of the bottle and be gathered around the bottle's neck.
• To create a bow, make several loops of yarn, all the same size. Pinch the loops together and secure them with a small piece of yarn.
• Stand the bottle in the center of the circle, gather the wrapping material around the neck of the bottle, and tie with the bow.

Chic Cylinder
• Trace both ends of a cylinder-shaped gift, such as a can of tennis balls, on wrapping paper.
• Cut out the circles and glue one to each end of the gift.
• Cut a piece of paper the length and girth of the gift. Center the cylinder on the edge of the paper, roll it up in the paper and tape the paper.

Candy Cane Umbrella
• Cut a piece of white fabric or paper 6 inches longer than the umbrella.
• Place the umbrella at the edge of the fabric and roll it up, leaving the handle free. Secure the fabric with tape or glue. Twist the ends of the fabric and tie them around the handle with wire, string or ribbon.
• Swirl red ribbon around the umbrella, securing the ribbon at the top and bottom with tape. Add a red bow at the top.

Christmas Jar
• Cut a circle of fabric 5 inches wider than the diameter of the jar lid, to create a ruffle effect.
• Secure the fabric over the lid with yarn or ribbon.

Cylinder Twist
• Cut a piece of paper twice the length of a cylinder-shaped gift. Center the gift at the edge of the paper, roll the paper around it and tape.
• Twist the paper at both ends and tie the ends with yarn, cord or ribbon.

Did You Know . . .

In ancient times, evergreen was the symbol of life during the cold, bleak winter months. People would adorn their homes with evergreen to bring the world of nature indoors. The Romans decorated their homes, streets, and even crowned their heads, with evergreen (and other types of greenery) during their winter festival. The use of evergreen in the celebration of the winter solstice was so popular that early Christian priests adopted its use in the celebration of Christmas.

TIME IT RIGHT! SENDING GIFTS BY MAIL

SELECT THE PROPER CONTAINER

Fiberboard containers (commonly found in supermarkets or hardware stores) generally are strong enough to mail items of average weight and size, up to 10 lbs. Paperboard cartons (similar to suit boxes) also can be used for items weighing up to 10 lbs. Some boxes have what is known as a "test board" rating, which indicates how strong they are. For example, a corrugated fiberboard box (125-lb test board) is good for mailing weights up to 20 lbs. High-density items, such as tools, require stronger containers (strength is indicated by a round imprint on a bottom corner of the box).

PACKAGE WITH CARE

• *Soft goods*, such as clothing, pillows or blankets, should be placed in a self-supporting box or tear-resistant bag, the box closed with reinforced tape, the bag sealed properly.

• *Perishables,* such as cheese, fruit, vegetables, meat or anything with an odor, must be placed in an impermeable container filled with absorbent cushioning and sealed with filament tape.

• *Fragile items*, such as glasses, dishes or photographic equipment, are safest packaged in fiberboard containers (minimum 175-lb test board) and cushioned with plastic foam or padding. Seal and reinforce the package with filament tape.

• *Shifting contents*, including books, tools and nails, should be packaged in fiberboard containers (minimum 175-lb test board). Make sure you use interior fiberboard separators or tape to prevent the contents of the parcel from shifting in transit. Seal and reinforce the package with filament tape.

• *Awkward loads*, such as some sports equipment or odd-shaped tools or instruments, require special packaging. Use fiberboard tubes or boxes with lengths not more than 10 times their girths. Cushioning must be of preformed fiberboard or foamed plastic shapes, and the closures should be as strong as the tubes themselves.

USE ADEQUATE CUSHIONING

If you are mailing several gift items in one package, wrap them individually and protect each one from the others with padding or plastic foam. To prevent one item from damaging another, make sure you fill the box completely with cushioning material, leaving no empty spaces. Polystyrene, shredded, rolled or crumpled newspaper, "bubble" plastic and fiberboard all are good cushioning materials. So are plastic foam chips, plastic egg cartons cut into pieces and packing straw. Commercially available foam shells or air-pocket padding also can be used, as well as padded mailing bags, which are good for small items.

SEAL THE CARTON PROPERLY

Use one of three recommended types of tape to secure your parcel: pressure-sensitive filament tape, nylon-reinforced Kraft paper tape or plain Kraft paper tape. All three types are available in stationery stores or five-and-dime stores. There's no need to wrap the container with brown paper—paper sometimes rips in handling. *Do not tie the package with string or twine!* This can become entangled in the mail-processing equipment.

REQUEST SPECIAL MARKINGS

Certain phrases printed on the outside of the parcel alert Postal Service employees to the nature of its contents. Mark breakable objects FRAGILE in three places: above the address, below the postage and on the reverse side. Packages of food or other items that can decay should be marked PERISHABLE in the same locations. The words DO NOT BEND on a package signal a fragile item, but the sender first must have protected this and similar articles with stiffening material. Ask the postal clerk to stamp your packages appropriately.

INSURE THE PACKAGES

Any gift sent by mail should be insured. You can insure a package for varying amounts up to $400. The cost is minimal and you have the added security of knowing that, in case anything happens to the package, you will be reimbursed. If you are mailing something that is worth more than $400, or if you are sending cash or an irreplaceable item through the mail, send it by registered mail.

USE ZIP CODES

The easiest ways to delay delivery of mail are to forget the ZIP Code or to use the wrong one. So, when addressing a package, be sure to include the ZIP Code in both the recipient's address and your return address.

TIME IT RIGHT

The Postal Service offers a wide range of delivery options for mailing packages, depending on the amount of money you want to spend and the time you've allowed for delivery. A good general rule to follow is to mail early in the day and early in the month. First-class letters and cards sent coast-to-coast should arrive within 3 to 4 days, those sent within a state should arrive within 2 to 3 days and those mailed to an address within a city should reach their destination in 2 days. However, as we all know, the Christmas season is the busiest time of the year for mail carriers, so it's best to allow at least two weeks for domestic delivery of holiday cards and gifts, just to be on the safe side.

DOMESTIC MAIL SERVICES

You can choose any one of three services to send packages up to 70 lbs. and 108 inches (length plus girth) by mail.

SERVICE	DESCRIPTION	COST	TIME
PRIORITY MAIL	Packages receive the same attention as first-class letters. Shipped by air, these parcels can be sent from any post office station or branch to any address in the U.S.	Determined by weight and distance traveled. A 2-lb. package from New York to Chicago: $2.40; a 5-lb. package: $4.86. A 2-lb. package from New York to Los Angeles: $2.40; a 5-lb. package: $6.37.	3 to 4 days
PARCEL POST	Takes longer than priority mail, but costs less. Packages can be mailed from any post office station or branch and are delivered directly to the addressee.	Determined by weight and distance traveled. A 2-lb. package from New York to Chicago: $2.24; a 5-lb. package: $3.29. A 2-lb. package from New York to Los Angeles: $2.35; a 5-lb. package: $6.25.	8 days
EXPRESS MAIL	Guaranteed to be delivered to the addressee by 3 P.M. the next business day. Packages automatically are insured for up to $500. If the mail is late, you can obtain a full postage refund by applying to the originating post office.	For direct delivery anywhere in the U.S., a ½-lb. package: $8.75; a 2-lb. package: $12.00; a 5-lb. package: $15.25. For recipient pick-up at post office, a 2-lb. package: $9.85; a 5-lb. package: $13.10.	Overnight

Note: Prices are accurate at time of press.

INTERNATIONAL MAIL

Destination	Air Parcels	Airmail Letter/Card
North and Northwest Africa	24 Nov	1 Dec
Australia	24 Nov	24 Nov
Caribbean/West Indies	12 Dec	12 Dec
Central and South America	5 Dec	5 Dec
Europe	1 Dec	5 Dec
Far East	1 Dec	5 Dec
Middle East	24 Nov	28 Nov
Southeast Asia	24 Nov	24 Nov
Southeast Africa	24 Nov	1 Dec
West Africa	24 Nov	1 Dec

Note: These dates are for mailing from the continental U.S. only. Check with your local post office after September 1 to confirm mailing dates if you wish to ship your packages.

Holiday Notes

Follow these additional pointers on mailing gifts so they arrive in perfect condition:

- **Use Heavyweight Wrapping Paper.** Thicker, heavier paper has a better chance of arriving without being torn.
- **Consider Using a Designed Gift Box.** Many boxes come decorated with holiday motifs.
- **Bows Don't Travel Well.** Instead, decorate packages with flat trims, stickers, yarn or tinsel ties.
- **Always Mail a Wrapped Present Inside Another Box.** Many gift boxes aren't meant to be used for shipping, so be sure to choose a box that is sturdy enough to support its contents and withstand the wear and tear of delivery.

Holiday Notes

See page 69 for pointers on sending food gifts.

New Mexican Pork Chili (recipe, page 100); Vegetarian Chili in Corn Tortilla Cups (recipes, pages 101 and 103); Christmas Chili Pie (recipe, page 102); Best Ever Carrot Cake (recipe, page 103)

CHILLY OUTSIDE? CHILI INSIDE!

New Mexican Pork Chili
Black Bean Chili with Ham and Turkey
Vegetarian Chili
Chili con Pollo
Mole Chili
Christmas Chili Pie
Corn Tortilla Cups
Best Ever Carrot Cake
Sangria, Beer, Milk and Soda

Note: All dishes in this menu except the Corn Tortilla Cups can be made ahead and frozen or refrigerated.

$ KK

NEW MEXICAN PORK CHILI (Hot)

Serve pinto beans on the side with this chunky pork chili, along with sour cream and chopped onions for garnish, if you wish. For a really "hot" chili, add the maximum number of jalapeño peppers indicated in the recipe.

Makes 6 servings.

- 2 tablespoons vegetable oil
- 4 strips bacon, cut into small dice (¼ cup)
- 2 pounds stewing pork (shoulder or butt), cut into ½-inch cubes
- ½ cup all-purpose flour
- 1 medium-size onion, finely chopped (about 1 cup)
- 3 cloves garlic, finely chopped (about 1 tablespoon)
- 3 tablespoons chili powder
- 1 to 3 pickled jalapeño peppers, stemmed, seeded and finely chopped (wear rubber gloves)
- 2 cups chicken broth
- ¼ teaspoon salt
- 3½ cups cooked pinto beans OR: 2 cans (15¼ ounces each) pinto beans, drained and rinsed

1. Heat the oil in a 10-inch skillet over medium-high heat. Add the bacon and cook until it is crisp, for about 5 minutes. Remove the bacon with a slotted spoon to paper toweling to drain, and set it aside. Set aside the skillet with the bacon drippings.
2. Shake the pork with the flour in a paper bag until the pork is coated. Remove the pork and shake off any excess flour.
3. Working in batches, sauté the pork in the bacon drippings in the skillet until the pork is evenly browned, for about 5 minutes. Remove the pork to a plate as it browns.
4. Lower the heat to medium. Return all the pork and the bacon to the skillet. Add the onion and the garlic, and cook until the onion is softened and transparent, for about 8 minutes. Add the chili powder, jalapeño peppers and broth. Bring the mixture to boiling. Lower the heat and

simmer, uncovered, stirring occasionally, for 2 hours, or until the meat is very tender and the sauce is thickened. If the sauce becomes too thick, thin it with a little water. Stir in the salt.
5. To serve, heat the pinto beans in a little water in a medium-size saucepan. Drain the pinto beans and serve them in a separate serving dish along with the chili.

KK N

BLACK BEAN CHILI WITH HAM AND TURKEY (Medium-Hot)

Makes 6 servings.

- 1 medium-size onion, finely chopped (1 cup)
- 4 cloves garlic, finely chopped
- 6 ounces boiled ham, cut into ¼-inch cubes (1 cup)
- 2 tablespoons vegetable oil
- 1 pound ground turkey, thawed if frozen
- 2½ tablespoons chili powder
- 1 can (35 ounces) whole tomatoes, drained and chopped (2½ cups)
- 1½ teaspoons cumin
- 2 bay leaves
- 2 cans (15 ounces each) black beans, drained and rinsed
- ¼ teaspoon salt

1. Sauté the onion, garlic and ham in the oil in a large saucepan over medium heat until the onion is softened and transparent, for about 8 minutes.
2. Add the turkey and raise the heat to medium-high. Brown the turkey for 2 minutes. Add the chili powder. Cook, stirring, for 1 minute more. Add the tomatoes, cumin and bay leaves, and cook for 20 minutes.
3. Add the black beans. Cook until the mixture is heated through, for about 10 minutes. Remove the bay leaves and stir in the salt.

💲 🗠

VEGETARIAN CHILI (Medium-Hot)

Makes 6 servings.

½ cup (3½ ounces) dried pinto beans
½ cup (3½ ounces) dried red kidney beans
8 cups cold water
1 large onion, finely chopped (about 1½ cups)
4 cloves garlic, finely chopped
1 small carrot, diced (⅓ cup)
1 small rib celery, diced (⅓ cup)
⅓ cup vegetable oil
1 cup (6½ ounces) dried lentils, picked over and washed
4 tablespoons chili powder
1 tablespoon leaf oregano, crumbled
2 teaspoons ground coriander
2 tablespoons sweet paprika
1 can (16 ounces) whole tomatoes, chopped and undrained
1 sweet red pepper, halved, seeded and diced (about 1 cup)
½ pound mushrooms, quartered (about 2½ cups)
¼ cup soy sauce
¼ teaspoon salt

1. Pick over and wash the pinto and red kidney beans. Combine the beans in a large bowl. Cover the beans with 5 cups of the cold water and soak them overnight. Rinse the beans, drain them and set them aside.
2. Sauté the onion, garlic, carrot and celery in the oil in a large saucepan over medium heat until the onion is softened and transparent, for about 8 minutes.
3. Add the drained beans, the lentils, chili powder, oregano, coriander, paprika, tomatoes with their liquid and the remaining 3 cups of cold water. Stir to combine all the ingredients. Bring the mixture to boiling. Lower the heat and simmer, uncovered, stirring occasionally, for 1½ hours.
4. Add the red pepper, mushrooms and soy sauce. Continue simmering, adding more water as needed if the chili becomes too dry, until the beans are very tender and the lentils are falling apart, for about 2 hours more. Stir in the salt.

🗠 ◣ ⌛

CHILI CON POLLO (Medium-Hot)

Makes 6 servings.

2 pounds boned, skinless chicken, preferably light and dark meats, cut into ½-inch cubes (about 4½ pounds on the bone)
¼ cup vegetable oil
1 medium-size onion, finely chopped (about 1 cup)
3 cloves garlic, finely chopped
1 sweet red pepper, halved, seeded and diced (about 1 cup)
1 can (4 ounces) mild green chili peppers, drained and chopped
1 can (16 ounces) whole tomatoes, chopped and undrained
1½ tablespoons tomato paste
3 tablespoons chili powder
1 teaspoon leaf oregano, crumbled
1 cup chicken broth
2 tablespoons cornmeal
¼ teaspoon salt

1. Sauté the chicken, working in batches, if necessary, in the oil in a large saucepan over medium-high heat, stirring frequently, for 4 minutes, or until the meat is white and firm to the touch.
2. Lower the heat to medium. Add the onion and the garlic and cook, stirring frequently, until the onion is softened and transparent, for about 8 minutes.
3. Add the red pepper, chili peppers, tomatoes with their liquid, tomato paste, chili powder, oregano, broth and cornmeal. Stir to mix all the ingredients well. Bring the mixture to boiling. Lower the heat and simmer, uncovered, stirring occasionally, for 30 minutes, or until the chicken is tender. Stir in the salt.

MOLE CHILI (Medium-Hot)

Unsweetened chocolate is the surprise ingredient that gives this chili its delicious, distinctive flavor.

Makes 6 servings.

- ⅓ cup raisins (2 ounces)
- ⅓ cup blanched almonds (1½ ounces)
- 2 tablespoons sesame seeds
- 4 tablespoons vegetable oil
- 5 tablespoons chili powder
- ½ cup water
- 1 medium-size onion, sliced
- 4 cloves garlic
- 2 teaspoons ground coriander
- 2 teaspoons ground cinnamon
- ½ teaspoon ground cloves
- 1 pound lean ground pork
- 1 pound lean ground beef
- 1 can (16 ounces) whole tomatoes, drained and chopped
- 1 cup beef broth
- 2 tablespoons red wine vinegar
- 1 can (15¼ ounces) red kidney beans, drained and rinsed
- ½ of a 1-ounce square unsweetened chocolate, chopped
- ¼ teaspoon salt

1. Sauté the raisins, almonds and sesame seeds in 2 tablespoons of the oil in a medium-size saucepan over medium heat. Cook, stirring constantly, until the raisins are puffy and the sesame seeds are lightly browned, for about 3 minutes. Add the chili powder and cook, stirring, for 1 minute more. Remove the mixture from the heat and add the water.
2. Transfer the mixture to the container of an electric blender or a food processor. Cover and whirl until the mixture is the consistency of coarse peanut butter. Add a little water, if necessary, to obtain the desired consistency. Add the onion and the garlic, and whirl until the mixture is a smooth purée. Mix in the coriander, cinnamon and cloves.
3. Sauté the pork and the beef, working in batches if necessary, in the remaining 2 tablespoons of oil in a large saucepan over high heat, breaking up the meat with a wooden spoon, for about 5 minutes, or until the meat is lightly browned.
4. Add the chili powder mixture, tomatoes and broth. Bring the mixture to boiling. Lower the heat and simmer, uncovered, stirring frequently, for 1 hour, or until the mixture is thickened. The mixture should not be too dry; add a little water, if necessary.
5. Add the vinegar and the red kidney beans. Cook, stirring occasionally, until the kidney beans are heated through, for about 10 minutes. Stir in the chocolate and the salt. Cook, stirring, until the chocolate is melted, for about 2 minutes.

CHRISTMAS CHILI PIE

Bake at 425° for 35 to 45 minutes.
Makes 6 servings.

- 5 cups cooked chili*
- 1 cup cornmeal
- 2 teaspoons baking powder
- 1 teaspoon salt
- 1 teaspoon sugar
- ⅔ cup milk
- 1 egg

1. Preheat the oven to hot (425°).
2. Spoon the chili into the bottom of an 8 x 8 x 2-inch or 9 x 9 x 2-inch baking pan.
3. Bake the chili in the preheated hot oven (425°) until it is hot and bubbly, for 10 to 15 minutes.
4. While the chili is heating, sift together the cornmeal, baking powder, salt and sugar into a medium-size bowl. Beat together the milk and the egg in a small bowl. Stir the milk mixture into the cornmeal mixture until the combined mixture is smooth. Pour it evenly over the hot chili.

5. Bake the pie in the hot oven (425°) for 25 to 30 minutes, or until the top is set and golden. Cut the pie into squares and serve them hot.

Note: Use any of our recipes for chili.

💲

CORN TORTILLA CUPS

*Use a tortilla basket fryer to make these festive, edible containers for chili.**

Makes 12 baskets.

> **Vegetable oil for deep frying**
> 1 **package 6-inch corn tortillas****
> **(10 ounces, 12 to a package)**

1. Pour enough oil into a deep-fat fryer or heavy casserole dish to cover a tortilla basket fryer. Heat the oil until a deep-fat frying thermometer registers 375°.
2. Place 1 corn tortilla in the larger wire basket of the tortilla fryer. Gently place the smaller basket on top of the corn tortilla. Lower the fryer into the hot oil. Deep fry until the tortilla is crisp and golden, for about 1 minute. Remove the fryer from the oil, carefully remove the smaller basket and turn out the tortilla basket onto paper toweling to drain. Repeat with the remaining tortillas.

*Notes: *Tortilla basket fryers can be found in the cookware section of many department stores or in specialty cookware stores.*
***Use only the pliable corn tortillas found in the refrigerator case. If the tortillas are a little dry, refresh them just before frying by steaming them for 20 to 25 seconds. Or place a tortilla on a sheet of microwave-safe paper toweling, cover it with another sheet and microwave at full power for 20 seconds.*

💲 🍴

BEST EVER CARROT CAKE

Bake at 325° for 1 hour and 20 minutes.
Makes 12 servings (one 10-inch tube cake).

> 3⅓ cups sifted all-purpose flour
> 2 cups sugar
> 1 teaspoon baking powder
> 1 teaspoon baking soda
> 1 teaspoon salt
> 1 teaspoon ground nutmeg
> 2 teaspoons ground cinnamon
> 4 eggs
> 1½ cups vegetable oil
> 2 teaspoons vanilla
> 2 cups coarsely shredded carrots
> 1 cup chopped walnuts
> Confectioners' Icing (recipe follows)

1. Preheat the oven to slow (325°). Grease a 10-inch Bundt® or angel cake tube pan.
2. Sift together the flour, sugar, baking powder, baking soda, salt, nutmeg and cinnamon into a large bowl. Make a well in the center of the dry ingredients. Add the eggs, oil and vanilla, and beat with a wooden spoon until the mixture is smooth. Stir in the carrots and the walnuts. Turn the batter into the prepared pan.
3. Bake the cake in the preheated slow oven (325°) for 1 hour and 20 minutes, or until the top springs back when lightly pressed with your fingertip.
4. Cool the cake in the pan on a wire rack for 10 minutes. Remove the cake from the pan and cool it completely before frosting.
5. Drizzle the cake with the Confectioners' Icing.

Confectioners' Icing: Gradually stir 1 to 2 tablespoons of milk or water into 1 cup of sifted 10X (confectioners' powdered) sugar, whisking constantly, to make a smooth icing that will flow easily from the tip of a spoon.

SCHEMATIC FOR CHRISTMAS COOKIE HITS

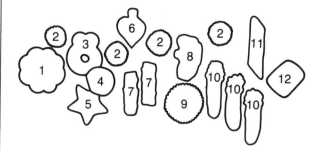

1. DOUBLE MOCHA WALNUT COOKIE
2. PECAN CUP COOKIES
3. MERRY CHRISTMAS WREATH
4. CHOCOLATE PECAN COOKIE
5. NOËL STAR
6. AMARETTO CREAM STRAWBERRY
7. ALMOND BUTTER FINGERS
8. STELLA
9. GERMAN HONEY-SPICE COOKIE
10. SWISS LEMON STRIPS
11. LOG JAM
12. NEAPOLITAN

CHRISTMAS COOKIE HITS

Double Mocha Walnut Cookies
Pecan Cup Cookies
Merry Christmas Wreaths
Chocolate Pecan Cookies
Noël Stars
Amaretto Cream Strawberries
Almond Butter Fingers
Stellas
German Honey Spice Cookies
Swiss Lemon Strips
Log Jams
Neapolitans
Spiced Coffee, Mulled Cider, Wassail Bowl

DOUBLE MOCHA WALNUT COOKIES

Bake at 400° for 8 to 10 minutes.
Makes about 3 dozen double cookies.

> 2   tablespoons instant coffee powder
> 2½ cups all-purpose flour
> 2½ teaspoons baking powder
> 1   cup very finely chopped or ground walnuts
> 1   cup (2 sticks) butter, softened
> 1½ cups sugar
> 2   eggs
>   Creamy Chocolate Frosting
>   (recipe follows)

1. Mash the instant coffee to a fine powder and set it aside. Sift together the flour and the baking powder onto wax paper and add the walnuts.
2. Beat together the butter, sugar, eggs and coffee powder in a medium-size bowl until smooth. Stir in the flour mixture until it is well blended.
3. Wrap the dough in aluminum foil. Chill it for 1 hour, or until firm enough to handle.
4. Preheat the oven to hot (400°). Grease 2 large baking sheets.
5. Divide the dough in half. Roll out each half on a floured surface to a ⅛-inch thickness. Cut with a floured 2¼-inch scalloped-edge cookie cutter. Transfer the rounds to the prepared baking sheets, ½ inch apart. Cut ½-inch rounds from the centers of half the cookies.
6. Bake in the preheated hot oven (400°) for 8 to 10 minutes, or until the cookies are lightly browned around the edges. Transfer the cookies to wire racks to cool. The cookies can be stored in a covered container for up to 2 weeks.
7. Sandwich two cookies together (1 whole with 1 cut out) with a thin layer of the Creamy Chocolate Frosting. Pipe frosting on each top following the scalloped edge.

Creamy Chocolate Frosting: Heat ⅓ cup of half and half and ¼ cup (½ stick) of butter in a small saucepan just until boiling. Stir in 1 package (6 ounces) of semisweet chocolate pieces and 1½ teaspoons of vanilla until the mixture is smooth. Beat in 2¼ cups of sifted 10X (confectioners' powdered) sugar until the frosting is a good spreading consistency.

PECAN CUP COOKIES

Bake at 350° for 20 minutes.
Makes about 4½ dozen cookies.

> ½   cup (1 stick) butter or margarine, softened
> ¼   cup granulated sugar
> 2   eggs, separated
> 1¼ cups all-purpose flour
> 1   cup ground or finely chopped pecans
> ¾   cup 10X (confectioners' powdered) sugar
> ½   teaspoon vanilla
>   Confectioners' Icing (recipe, page 103)
>   Red and green candied cherries

1. Beat together the butter or margarine, granulated sugar and egg yolks until the mixture is smooth.
2. Stir in the flour until it is well blended. Break off small pieces of the dough and press them into 1-inch tart or hors d'oeuvre pans, forming a shell about ⅛-inch thick. If you have only a few pans, refrigerate the remaining dough and the filling, and bake the cups in small batches.
3. Preheat the oven to moderate (350°).
4. To make the filling, combine the pecans, 10X (confectioners' powdered) sugar, vanilla and egg whites in a bowl. Beat until the mixture is well blended.
5. Spoon enough of the filling into each of the cups to come level with the edge of the shell. Place the cups on a baking sheet.
6. Bake the cups in the preheated moderate oven (350°) for 20 minutes, or until the filling is set and lightly browned. Transfer the tart pans to wire racks to cool for 5 minutes. Carefully remove the cups from the pans, gently easing them out with the tip of a paring knife; cool completely.
7. Decorate the tops with the Confectioners' Icing and the candied cherries.

MERRY CHRISTMAS WREATHS

Bake at 350° for 12 minutes.
Makes about 3⅓ dozen cookies.

1¾ cups all-purpose flour
½ teaspoon baking soda
½ cup (1 stick) butter, softened
½ cup sugar
1 egg
1 egg yolk
1 tablespoon grated orange zest (orange part of rind only)
1 egg white, slightly beaten
   Green sugar crystals
   Wedges of red and green candied cherries

1. Sift together the flour and the baking soda onto wax paper and set aside.
2. Beat together the butter, sugar, egg, egg yolk and orange zest until smooth.
3. Stir the flour mixture into the butter mixture until well blended. Wrap the dough in plastic wrap and chill it for 1 hour, or freeze the dough for 15 minutes.
4. Preheat the oven to moderate (350°). Lightly grease 2 baking sheets.
5. Divide the dough into 4 equal parts. Work with one quarter of the dough at a time, keeping the remaining dough refrigerated. Roll out one quarter of the dough with your hands on a lightly floured surface into a cylinder about ¼ inch in diameter. Cut the cylinder into 10 equal pieces. Repeat with the remaining dough.
6. Roll each piece into a strip 6 inches long. Holding each strip close to the baking sheet, quickly and gently form a small circle, overlapping the ends to form small tails. Place the circles on the prepared baking sheets ½ inch apart. Brush them with the egg white and sprinkle them with the green sugar crystals. Decorate the tails with the candied cherry wedges.
7. Bake in the preheated moderate oven (350°) for 12 minutes, or until the cookies are lightly browned. Transfer them to wire racks to cool. Store the cookies in a tightly covered container for up to 2 weeks.

CHOCOLATE PECAN COOKIES

A great make-ahead, nutty chocolate cookie. The dough can be kept frozen for up to 1 month.

Bake at 350° for 10 minutes.
Makes about 7½ dozen cookies.

3 cups all-purpose flour
½ cup unsweetened cocoa powder
1¼ cups (2½ sticks) butter, softened
1½ cups sifted 10X (confectioners' powdered) sugar
1 egg
1 teaspoon vanilla
1 cup finely chopped pecans
1 container (16½ ounces) milk chocolate frosting
   Pecan halves, for garnish

1. Sift together the flour and the cocoa powder onto wax paper and set aside.
2. Beat together the butter, 10X (confectioners' powdered) sugar, egg and vanilla in a large bowl until the mixture is smooth.
3. Stir in the flour mixture until it is well blended. Divide the dough in half and shape each half into a roll 1½ inches in diameter. Wrap the rolls in plastic wrap and chill them for 2 hours, or freeze them for 1 hour.
4. Roll each cylinder of chilled dough in the chopped pecans, shaping the rolls to be as round as possible. Freeze the rolls briefly if they become too soft.
5. Preheat the oven to moderate (350°).
6. Cut the rolls into ¼-inch slices. Place the slices on ungreased baking sheets, ½ inch apart.
7. Bake in the preheated moderate oven (350°) for 10 minutes, or until the cookies are firm. Store them in tightly covered containers for up to 2 weeks.
8. To serve, decorate the cookies with the milk chocolate frosting piped through a pastry bag or cake decorator. Garnish with the pecan halves.

NOËL STARS

Bake at 375° for 10 minutes.
Makes about 3 dozen cookies.

- 1 cup all-purpose flour
- ½ teaspoon ground cinnamon
- ¼ teaspoon salt
- ½ cup almond paste
- 1 egg yolk
- ½ cup (1 stick) butter, softened
- ¼ cup sugar
- ½ teaspoon vanilla
- ¼ cup toasted blanched almonds, finely chopped
  Confectioners' Frosting (recipe follows)
  Green food coloring
  Colored sprinkles OR: toasted whole almonds (optional)

1. Sift together the flour, cinnamon and salt onto wax paper and set aside.
2. Crumble the almond paste into a medium-size bowl. Add the egg yolk, butter, sugar and vanilla. Beat the mixture until it is smooth.
3. Stir the flour mixture and the almonds into the almond paste mixture until they are well blended. Wrap the dough in aluminum foil or plastic wrap and chill it for 2 hours.
4. Preheat the oven to moderate (375°). Grease and flour a large baking sheet.
5. Roll out half the dough at a time on a lightly floured board to a ⅛-inch thickness. Cut out the dough with a floured 2¼-inch star-shaped cookie cutter. Place the stars on the prepared baking sheet, ½ inch apart.
6. Bake in the preheated moderate oven (375°) for 10 minutes, or until the cookies are lightly browned around the edges. Transfer them to a wire rack to cool. Store the cookies in a tightly covered container for up to 2 weeks.
7. Tint the Confectioners' Frosting pale green with the food coloring. Fit a pastry bag or cake decorator with a small round tip. Pipe the frosting, outlining each star, ⅛ inch in from the edge, and pipe a small amount of the frosting in the center of each star. If you wish, decorate the stars with colored sprinkles or toasted almonds.

Confectioners' Frosting: Stir 1½ tablespoons of milk or water into 1⅓ cups of sifted 10X (confectioners' powdered) sugar. Add additional sugar, if necessary, to make a fairly stiff but spreadable frosting.

AMARETTO CREAM STRAWBERRIES

Bake at 350° for 10 minutes.
Makes about 6 dozen cookies.

1 **cup (2 sticks) butter, softened**
½ **cup sifted 10X (confectioners' powdered) sugar**
1 **teaspoon Amaretto (almond-flavored liqueur)**
2¼ **cups all-purpose flour**
⅔ **cup ground blanched almonds**
  Amaretto Butter Cream (recipe follows)
  Green food coloring
  Red sugar crystals

1. Beat together the butter, 10X (confectioners' powdered) sugar and Amaretto in a large bowl with an electric mixer at high speed until the mixture is smooth. Lower the mixer speed to low.
2. Stir in the flour and the almonds until they are well blended. Chill the dough for 1 hour.
3. Preheat the oven to moderate (350°). Grease 2 large baking sheets.
4. Roll out the dough, half at a time, on a floured surface to a ¼-inch thickness. Cut the dough with a floured small spade- or heart-shaped cookie cutter. Transfer the shapes with a spatula to the prepared baking sheets, spacing them ½ inch apart.
5. Bake in the preheated moderate oven (350°) for 10 minutes, or until the cookies are lightly browned around the edges. Transfer them to wire racks to cool. Store the cookies in tightly covered containers for up to 2 weeks.
6. Prepare the Amaretto Butter Cream. Reserve ½ cup untinted. Tint the remaining butter cream pale green with the food coloring and set it aside.
7. Frost the cookies with the untinted butter cream. Dip the frosted cookies in the red sugar crystals, or sprinkle the crystals heavily over the frosting, pressing them in slightly.
8. Make a wax paper cone and cut the tip off the cone to make a small opening. Or use a cake decorator with a small round tip. Fill the cone or decorator with the green butter cream. Pipe a green stem and long points to resemble a strawberry hull on top of each cookie.

Amaretto Butter Cream: Combine ¼ cup (½ stick) of softened butter, 2 tablespoons of Amaretto (almond-flavored liqueur), 1 tablespoon of heavy or whipping cream and 2 cups of sifted 10X (confectioners' powdered) sugar in a small bowl. Beat until the ingredients are well blended.

♪ Holiday Notes

DO THE SUGAR SIFT!

Lumps, the bane of confectioners' powdered sugar, sneak into frostings and glazes if they're not sifted out. For best results, use a fine sieve and press the sugar through it onto a piece of wax paper.

ALMOND BUTTER FINGERS

Bake at 350° for 15 minutes.
Makes about 4 dozen cookies.

- ½ **cup chopped blanched almonds**
- 1½ **tablespoons granulated sugar**
- ¾ **cup (1½ sticks) butter, softened**
- ⅓ **cup granulated sugar**
- 1 **teaspoon almond extract**
- 2 **cups all-purpose flour**
- 1 **egg white**
  **10X (confectioners' powdered) sugar
  (optional)**

1. Combine the almonds with the 1½ tablespoons of granulated sugar and set aside.
2. Beat together the butter, the ⅓ cup of granulated sugar and the almond extract in a medium-size bowl until the mixture is smooth. Stir in the flour until it is well blended.
3. Gather the dough into a ball and flatten it. Wrap the dough in aluminum foil or plastic wrap and chill the dough for 1 hour, or until it is firm enough to handle.
4. Preheat the oven to moderate (350°). Beat the egg white in a small bowl until it is frothy.
5. Divide the dough in half. Roll out each half on a floured surface to a rectangle ¼ inch thick and about 3 inches wide. Even the edges with a ruler to measure 2½ inches wide. Cut the rectangle crosswise into bars ¾ inch wide. Brush the tops with the egg white and sprinkle them evenly with the almond-sugar mixture. Lift the bars with a spatula to ungreased baking sheets, spacing the bars ¼ inch apart.
6. Bake in the preheated moderate oven (350°) for 15 minutes, or until the cookies are golden brown. Transfer them to wire racks to cool. Store the cookies in tightly covered containers for up to 2 weeks. If you wish, sprinkle the cookies with 10X (confectioners' powdered) sugar pressed through a fine sieve.

Did You Know . . .

The earliest carols are true folk poetry, simple and joyous. The subjects range from the sacred to the absurd, and there are carols that contain an odd mixture of both. Some carols celebrate the mystic, mythical aspects of Christmas; others are lively tunes that touch the hearts of "just plain folk." This variety is the key to the longevity and popularity of the Christmas carol.

STELLAS

Bake at 400° for 15 to 20 minutes.
Makes about 3½ dozen cookies.

- 1 **cup very finely chopped pecans**
- ½ **cup granulated sugar**
- ½ **teaspoon ground cinnamon**
- 3 **cups all-purpose flour**
- 1½ **cups (3 sticks) butter, softened**
- 1 **cup dairy sour cream**
- 2 **egg whites, slightly beaten**
  **Confectioners' Icing (recipe, page 103)
  OR: 10X (confectioners' powdered)
  sugar**

1. Combine the pecans, granulated sugar and cinnamon in a small bowl and set aside.
2. Sift the flour into a medium-size bowl. Cut in the butter until the mixture is crumbly. Stir in the sour cream. Work the dough with the spoon or your hands just until it holds together. Wrap the dough in aluminum foil or plastic wrap and refrigerate it for 6 hours.
3. Preheat the oven to hot (400°).
4. Divide the dough into 4 equal parts. Work with one quarter of the dough at a time, leaving the remaining dough refrigerated. The dough will be soft and sticky.
5. Lightly sprinkle the work surface with flour, then heavily with granulated sugar. Shape one quarter of the dough into a

ball. Roll out the ball to a round a little larger than 8 inches in diameter; the dough should be quite thin. Cut the dough into an 8-inch circle. Refrigerate the scraps. Divide the circle into 8 equal wedges.

6. Brush the circle with the beaten egg whites and sprinkle it with about ⅓ cup of the pecan mixture. Roll up each wedge from the wide end, tucking the point underneath. Place the cookies 1 inch apart on ungreased baking sheets. Repeat with the remaining dough and pecan mixture. Combine any leftover scraps of dough and form them into a ball. Roll out the dough, cut it into wedges and roll the wedges as above.

7. Bake in the preheated hot oven (400°) for 15 to 20 minutes, or until the cookies are lightly browned. Remove them to wire racks to cool. Store the cookies in a tightly covered container for up to 2 weeks.

8. To serve, drizzle the cookies with the Confectioners' Icing and let them stand to set the icing. Or, sprinkle them with sifted 10X (confectioners' powdered) sugar.

GERMAN HONEY SPICE COOKIES

Bake at 400° for 10 minutes.
Makes about 3¼ dozen cookies.

1   **cup honey**
3   **cups all-purpose flour**
½   **teaspoon baking soda**
1½ **teaspoons ground cinnamon**
½   **teaspoon ground nutmeg**
¼   **teaspoon ground cloves**
⅔   **cup firmly packed light brown sugar**
1   **egg**
2   **teaspoons grated lemon zest (yellow part of rind only)**
1   **tablespoon lemon juice**
½   **cup finely chopped candied citron**
½   **cup finely chopped blanched almonds**
⅓   **cup whole blanched almonds, split**
1   **container (3 ounces) candied red cherries, halved**
    Clear Sugar Glaze (recipe follows)

1. Heat the honey just to boiling in a medium-size saucepan and let it cool.
2. Sift together the flour, baking soda, cinnamon, nutmeg and cloves onto wax paper and set aside.
3. Combine the cooled honey, the brown sugar, egg, lemon zest and lemon juice in a large bowl. Beat together with a wooden spoon until the mixture is smooth.
4. Stir in the flour mixture until it is well blended. Stir in the citron and the chopped almonds. Form the dough into a ball and flatten the ball. Wrap the dough in aluminum foil or plastic wrap and chill it for at least 6 hours, or overnight.
5. Preheat the oven to hot (400°). Grease 2 large baking sheets.
6. Divide the dough in half. Roll out half at a time on a floured surface to a ¼-inch thickness. Cut the dough into rounds with a well-floured, 2½-inch round cookie cutter. Transfer the rounds to the prepared baking sheets, placing them ½ inch apart. Decorate the rounds with the almond and candied cherry halves.

7. Bake the cookies in the preheated hot oven (400°) for 10 minutes, or until the edges are lightly browned. Transfer the cookies to wire racks set over wax paper.
8. While the cookies bake, prepare the Clear Sugar Glaze.
9. Brush the warm cookies with the hot glaze and cool them completely. Store the cookies in a tightly covered container for at least 1 or 2 weeks.

Clear Sugar Glaze: Heat 1 cup of granulated sugar and ½ cup of water to boiling. Boil the mixture gently for 4 minutes, or until a candy thermometer registers 230°. Remove the mixture from the heat and let the bubbling subside. Stir in ¼ cup of sifted 10X (confectioners' powdered) sugar. If the syrup becomes cloudy, stir in a teaspoon of water and reheat the syrup until it is clear again.

SWISS LEMON STRIPS

Bake at 375° for 10 minutes.
Makes about 5 dozen cookies.

1½ cups (3 sticks) butter, softened
1   cup sugar
¼   teaspoon salt
3   egg yolks
2   teaspoons grated lemon zest (yellow part of rind only)
3   tablespoons lemon juice
1   tablespoon milk
3½ cups all-purpose flour plus additional for shaping cookies
    Lemon Butter Cream (recipe follows)
⅔   cup chopped skinned pistachio nuts*

1. Beat together the butter, sugar, salt and egg yolks in a large bowl until the mixture is smooth. Beat in the lemon zest, lemon juice and milk.
2. Stir in the flour until it is well blended.
3. Preheat the oven to moderate (375°).
4. Fit a large pastry bag with a ½-inch plain round tip. Fill the bag with one quarter of the dough. Press out the dough onto ungreased baking sheets in finger lengths

ZEST FOR FLAVOR

Zest is the colored part of the rind of citrus fruit. It's the part that contains all the fruit's flavorful oils. The white pith, directly underneath the zest, should not be used because it has a bitter taste.

To grate zest, use light pressure and stop grating just before you see the white part of the rind.

A quick way to grate zest is to remove strips with a sharp paring knife or swivel-bladed vegetable parer. Process the strips in the container of a food processor along with part of the sugar called for in the recipe.

about 3 inches long and ½ to ¾ inch wide, spacing them about ½ inch apart. Dip your finger in some flour and press down on each cookie where the pastry bag leaves a tail. Repeat with the remaining dough.
5. Bake the cookies in the preheated moderate oven (375°) for 10 minutes, or just until the edges are golden brown. Transfer the cookies to wire racks to cool completely. Store them in tightly covered containers for up to 2 weeks.
6. Frost one end of each cooled cookie with the Lemon Butter Cream and dip into or sprinkle the end with the pistachio nuts.

Lemon Butter Cream: Combine ¼ cup (½ stick) of softened butter, 1 teaspoon of grated lemon zest, 1 tablespoon each of lemon juice and milk, and 2 cups of sifted 10X (confectioners' powdered) sugar. Beat together the ingredients until smooth.

*Note: Rubbing off the skins from pistachio nuts can be done easily by pouring boiling water over the shelled nuts in a heatproof bowl, letting the nuts stand for 1 or 2 minutes, draining them on a towel and rubbing off the skins.

LOG JAMS

Bake at 350° for 17 minutes.
Makes about 4 dozen cookies.

2⅓ cups all-purpose flour
½ teaspoon baking powder
⅛ teaspoon salt
⅔ cup butter, softened
⅔ cup sugar
1 egg
2 teaspoons vanilla
1 cup apricot preserves
     OR: seedless red raspberry jam
     Confectioners' Icing (recipe, page 103)
⅓ cup chopped pistachio nuts

1. Sift together the flour, baking powder and salt onto wax paper and set aside.
2. Beat together the butter, sugar, egg and vanilla in a medium-size bowl until the mixture is smooth. Stir in the flour mixture until it is well blended.
3. Preheat the oven to moderate (350°).
4. Divide the dough into 4 equal parts. Shape each into a roll 10 inches long and 1 inch in diameter. Transfer the rolls to an ungreased large baking sheet, spacing them about 1 inch apart. Flatten the rolls slightly.
5. Press a ¼-inch-deep trough down the center of each roll with the handle of a wooden spoon, leaving the ends whole to keep the filling in place.
6. Spoon the preserves or jam into the troughs, filling them to the level of the dough.
7. Bake in the preheated moderate oven (350°) for 17 minutes, or until the rolls are light golden brown. Cut the warm rolls into ¾-inch-wide diagonal slices. Transfer the cookies to a wire rack to cool. Store them in tightly covered containers for up to 2 weeks.
8. To serve, drizzle the Confectioners' Icing over the edges of the cookies and sprinkle the pistachio nuts over the icing.

Did You Know . . .

The Christmas carol, unlike church hymns, was developed as a popular art form, a song about the Nativity, that usually was sung in the language of the surrounding countryside instead of Latin. In the 16th and 17th centuries, the Reformation so strongly discouraged such "frivolity" that caroling almost disappeared. In 1822, Davies Gilbert published the "Collection of Christmas Carols," which was a popular success, following on the heels of the general public's renewed interest in Christmas traditions.

NEAPOLITANS

Bake at 350° for 10 minutes.
Makes about 6 dozen cookies.

- 4 cups all-purpose flour
- 1 teaspoon baking powder
- 1/4 teaspoon baking soda
- 1/4 teaspoon salt
- 1 1/4 cups (2 1/2 sticks) butter, softened
- 1 cup firmly packed light brown sugar
- 1/2 cup granulated sugar
- 2 eggs
- 1/2 teaspoon vanilla
- 1/2 teaspoon almond extract
- 1 1/2 squares (1 ounce each) unsweetened chocolate, melted and cooled
  Red and green food coloring
- 2 tablespoons chopped pistachio nuts
- 2 tablespoons chopped candied red cherries
  Milk

1. Sift together the flour, baking powder, baking soda and salt onto wax paper and set aside.
2. Beat together the butter, brown and granulated sugars, eggs, vanilla and almond extract in a large bowl until the mixture is smooth.
3. Stir in the flour mixture until it is well blended. Divide the dough into 5 equal parts. Combine 2 parts to make 1 large portion. Place each portion in 4 small bowls.
4. Stir the chocolate into the large portion. Tint one small portion pink with the red food coloring. Tint a second small portion green with the green food coloring. Leave the third small portion plain. Stir the pistachio nuts into the green dough and the candied cherries into the pink dough. Leave the fourth portion of dough plain. Cover each of the bowls and chill the dough for 2 hours.
5. Shape the green dough into a long roll about 2 inches in diameter. Roll out the dough between 2 sheets of wax paper to a rectangle about 11 x 4 inches. Brush the top lightly with the milk. Repeat with the plain dough and place it on top of the green dough. Repeat with the pink dough and place it on top of the plain dough. With a ruler and a knife, trim the rectangle to exactly 11 x 4 inches. Wrap the layered dough in aluminum foil or plastic wrap and chill the dough for 1 hour, or freeze it for 30 minutes.
6. Divide the chocolate dough in half. Roll out each half between sheets of wax paper to an 11 x 6-inch rectangle. Divide the chilled layered dough in half lengthwise. Place one of the layered halves on one of the chocolate rectangles. Brush the layered dough with the milk and wrap the chocolate dough around the layered dough, pressing gently to form a long block. Repeat with the remaining chocolate and layered doughs. Wrap the dough blocks in aluminum foil or plastic wrap and freeze them for 1 hour. The dough blocks may be stored in the refrigerator for up to 1 week, or frozen for up to 1 month.
7. Preheat the oven to moderate (350°).
8. Cut the dough blocks into 1/4-inch slices. Place the slices on ungreased baking sheets 1/2 inch apart.
9. Bake in the preheated moderate oven (350°) for 10 minutes, or just until the cookies are set. To keep the colors bright, the cookies should not brown except on the bottom. Transfer the cookies to wire racks to cool completely. Store the cookies in tightly covered containers for up to 2 weeks.

SPICED COFFEE

Makes 6 servings.

- 3 cups extra-strong hot coffee
- 2 3-inch pieces stick cinnamon
- 4 whole cloves
- 4 whole allspice
   Softly whipped cream
   Ground nutmeg, to taste

1. Pour the hot coffee into a chafing dish with a flame underneath. Add the cinnamon, cloves and allspice. Steep the mixture over very low heat for 10 to 15 minutes. Strain the mixture.
2. Pour the coffee into heatproof wine glasses or cups. Top with the whipped cream and the nutmeg. Serve the coffee with sugar on the side.

MULLED CIDER

Makes 8 servings.

- 2 quarts apple cider
- 1½ teaspoons whole cloves
- ¾ teaspoon whole allspice
- 2 3-inch pieces stick cinnamon
- 1¼ cups California brandy
   Orange slices OR: lemon slices,
      for garnish (optional)

1. Combine the cider, cloves, allspice and cinnamon in a large saucepan. Slowly bring the mixture to boiling. Lower the heat and simmer the mixture for 15 minutes. Remove the spices and add the brandy.
2. Pour the cider into a 2½- to 3-quart punch bowl or individual cups. Garnish each cup with orange or lemon slices, if you wish.

WASSAIL BOWL

Bake apples at 350° for 10 minutes.
Makes 12 half-cup servings.

- 2 Red Delicious apples
- 2 whole cloves
- 2 whole allspice
- 2 whole cardamom pods, crushed
- 1 3-inch piece stick cinnamon
- 1 quart ale
- ½ teaspoon ground ginger
- ½ teaspoon ground nutmeg
- 1 cup sugar
- 1½ cups dry sherry
- 3 eggs, separated
   Additional cinnamon sticks, for garnish

1. Preheat the oven to moderate (350°).
2. Core the apples and cut them crosswise into ¼-inch-thick slices. Place the slices in a shallow baking pan.
3. Bake in the preheated moderate oven (350°) for 10 minutes, or until the apple slices are tender but still firm enough to hold their shape; set aside.
4. Tie the cloves, allspice, cardamom and cinnamon in a small piece of cheesecloth. Place the spice bag in a kettle or Dutch oven along with 1 cup of the ale, the ginger and nutmeg. Heat the mixture very slowly over low heat for 20 minutes (do not allow the mixture to boil). Remove the spice bag and stir in the remaining ale, ½ cup of the sugar and the sherry. Heat the mixture slowly for 20 minutes.
5. Beat the egg whites until foamy in a large bowl with an electric mixer. Slowly beat in the remaining ½ cup of sugar until soft peaks form.
6. Beat the egg yolks until light in a small bowl with an electric mixer and fold them into the beaten whites. Slowly beat the hot ale mixture into the egg mixture until the combined mixture is smooth.
7. Carefully pour the wassail into a heatproof punch bowl and float the baked apple slices on top. Serve in heatproof mugs, with a cinnamon stick in each.

Deck The Hall

Traditional

Old Welsh Tune

1. Deck the hall with boughs of hol-ly,
2. See the blaz-ing Yule be-fore us,
3. Fast a-way the old year pass-es.

Fa, la, la, la la, la, la, la, la,

'Tis the sea-son to be jol-ly.
Strike the harp and join the cho-res.
Hail the new, ye lads and lass-es.

Fa, la, la, la la, la, la, la, la,

Don we now our gay ap-par-el,
Fol-low me in mer-ry meas-ure.
Sing we joy-ous all to-geth-er

Fa, la, la, la, la, la, la, la la

Troll the an-cient Yule-tide car-ol
While I tell of Yule-tide trea-sure,
Heed-less of the wind and weath-er

Fa, la, la, la, la,

A PATCHWORK CHRISTMAS

Isn't every Christmas a patchwork Christmas? Old traditions remembered, new ones started, bits and pieces of nostalgia intermingled with today's lifestyle. Patchwork is uniquely American: as colonists used scraps of fabric to piece together quilts and clothing, so we piece together our Christmas traditions to blend old and new. This year, you can celebrate the holidays by creating a beautiful patchwork quilt and pillows for your bedroom. Or bring a touch of country to your kitchen with gingham café curtains and potholders. There's also a patchwork of presents to make, from a Sweet Dreams Sailboat Quilt for kids to our Padded Patchwork Hangers. If you'd like to treat friends to something special, try your hand at baking our old-fashioned breads. And for a family gathering, serve a hearty feast that features Green and White Stuffed Shells and luscious Chocolate Spumoni. Your family will agree: there's no place like home for the holidays!

THE PATCHWORK HOME

Fill your home with the charm and warmth of a country-style Christmas.

COUNTRY FLOWER BASKET ORNAMENT

Easy: Achievable by anyone.

Materials: Miniature woven basket; modeling clay; variety of small dried flowers and statice; lace; white glue; thin gold cord.

Directions:

1. Gently press a small amount of the modeling clay into the bottom of the miniature basket. Carefully insert the dried flowers and statice into the clay.

2. Measure the circumference of the body of the basket. Cut a piece of flat lace to that measurement. Glue the lace to the basket *(see photo).*

3. Thread the gold cord through the basket handle and tie the ends for a hanger.

Country Flower Basket Ornament

GINGHAM CHAIN

Easy: Achievable by anyone.

Materials: 1 yard of 44-inch-wide fabric (this makes about 24 feet of chain); matching thread or fabric glue.

Directions:

1. Cut 1½-inch-wide strips across the full width of the fabric.

2. At one long edge, fold ½ inch to the wrong side and press. At the opposite edge, fold a scant ¼ inch to the wrong side and press, then fold again to cover the raw edges. Pin through the four layers and topstitch along the fold (the center of the strip).

3. Cut the strip into 7-inch-long pieces. Overlap the cut ends ½ inch to form a ring and stitch or glue the ends together. Pass the next strip through the first ring and close the ends the same way. Repeat with the remainder of the strips.

Gingham Chain (directions, page 118); Cranberry Patchwork Ornaments (directions, page 120);
Big Cuff Christmas Stockings (directions, page 121)

Cranberry Patchwork Ornaments attached to a grapevine wreath

CRANBERRY PATCHWORK ORNAMENTS

Easy: Achievable by anyone.

Materials: Scraps of gingham or checked fabric; synthetic stuffing; embroidery floss or crochet thread for hanging.

Directions (¼-inch seams allowed):

1. Stuffed Bow: From the fabric, cut one 5 x 7-inch rectangle and two 2½ x 9½-inch strips.

2. Fold the larger piece in half (5 x 3½ inches) and stitch ¼ inch from the three raw edges, leaving 1 inch open at the center of the long seam. Turn the "bow" right side out and stuff it. Turn in the open edges and slipstitch.

3. Pin the two strips, right sides together, and cut a slant at each end. Seam the edges, leaving an opening on the long edge. Turn right side out. Turn under the open edges and slipstitch the opening closed. Wrap the piece tightly around the center of the bow. Sew through the tails against the bow to fasten.

4. Sew a loop of embroidery floss or crochet thread to the top center for a hanger.

5. Stuffed Animals: Enlarge the patterns in FIG. III, 1, following the directions on page 271. Cut one pair for each ornament from the fabric scraps.

6. Seam each pair together, right sides facing, leaving an opening about 1 inch long.

7. Turn the animal right side out and stuff it. Turn under the open edges and slipstitch the opening closed. Sew a long floss or thread loop at the top for a hanger.

FIG. III, 1 CRANBERRY
PATCHWORK ORNAMENTS

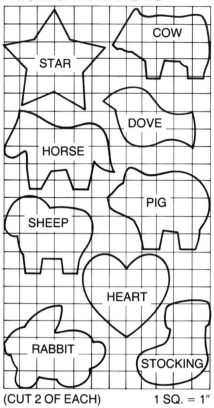

STAR

COW

DOVE

HORSE

PIG

SHEEP

HEART

RABBIT

STOCKING

(CUT 2 OF EACH)   1 SQ. = 1"

Did You Know . . .

*There's a patchwork of ways
to say "Merry Christmas"!
Joyeux Noël — French
Buon Natale — Italian
Feliz Navidad — Spanish
Fröhliche Weihnachten —
German
Glaedelig Jul — Danish
God Jul — Swedish
Wesotych Swiat — Polish
Böldog Karasconyi —
Hungarian
Noligh Math Tuth —
Scottish Gaelic
Any way you say it, say it with
a smile and you'll be
understood!*

BIG CUFF CHRISTMAS STOCKINGS

Easy: Achievable by anyone.

Materials: ½ yard of quilted fabric (makes 2 stockings); 5 x 12 inches of contrasting fabric for each cuff; matching thread.

Directions (¼-inch seams allowed):
1. Enlarge the pattern in FIG. III, 2, following the directions on page 271. From the quilted fabric, cut out the front and back stocking pieces.
2. With right sides together, seam the stocking pieces, leaving the top edge open. Seam the short ends of the cuff. Press the seam open and stitch a ½-inch hem at the long bottom edge.
3. Place the right side of the cuff against the wrong side of the stocking, with front seams matching and raw edges even. Stitch the top edges, holding in to create a slight fullness. Turn the cuff to the right side.

FIG. III, 2 BIG CUFF CHRISTMAS
STOCKING

1 SQ. = 1½"

Did You Know . . .

Just why, where and how the tradition of the Christmas stocking developed is uncertain. Throughout most of Western Europe, it is customary for little ones to put out their shoes on St. Nicholas Day (December 6), to be filled during the night with goodies and small gifts. One account of the origin of the Christmas stocking is a story about St. Nicholas. A nobleman had lost his money in an unsuccessful business venture and thus could provide no dowries for his three unmarried daughters. St. Nicholas heard of the plight of the dowerless young women and decided to help them. In the dark of the night, he went to their house and threw a bag of gold into the eldest daughter's room. Legend has it that the bag of gold fell into a stocking hung near the fire to dry — and so began the custom of hanging a stocking in hopes of receiving presents.

QUILT BASKET ORNAMENT

Easy: Achievable by anyone.

Materials: Graphite paper; dressmaker's carbon; pencil; child's holiday coloring book; stiff cardboard; 2 scraps of contrasting Christmas motif fabric; white glue; drill; narrow red ribbon.

Directions:

1. Using the graphite paper, trace a simple basket motif from the holiday coloring book onto the cardboard. Trace the bow separately. Cut out the basket and the bow.

2. Using the dressmaker's carbon and the cardboard patterns, trace the basket on one of the Christmas motif fabrics and trace the bow on the contrasting fabric. Cut the fabrics around the traced patterns, leaving a ¼-inch allowance.

3. Trace and cut another piece from the first fabric the exact size of the basket cardboard pattern (no cutting allowance), and a piece from the contrasting fabric the exact size of the bow cardboard pattern.

4. Spread glue on one side of the cardboard basket shape. Place the wrong side of the larger fabric basket piece on the glued side of the cardboard. Spread the fabric evenly so ¼-inch allowance extends beyond all the cardboard edges. Clip overlapping fabric at curves.

5. Spread more glue on the back of the cardboard basket shape and press the overlapping fabric onto the glue. Place the smaller fabric basket piece on the back of the basket, on top of the glued overlap.

6. Repeat Steps 4 and 5 for the bow fabric pieces and cardboard shape.

7. Glue the contrasting fabric bow on the front of the basket *(see photo).* Carefully drill a hole through the "knot" part of the bow. Thread the red ribbon through the hole, make a loop; tie ends in a bow for a hanger.

A PATCHWORK OF BASKETS

If you have an assortment of large and small baskets, consider using them in a holiday display. They can be filled with pine cones, cinnamon sticks, berries, ribbons and so on, and grouped in one area—the foyer, a cupboard, the coffee table. Or scatter the baskets around the house, but decorate all of them with the same ribbons so you have a theme recurring throughout the house.

COUNTRY CHRISTMAS WREATH

Average: For those with some experience in crafting.

Materials: ⅛-inch-thick craft wood for cutouts; 20-inch square of lattice wood; drill and ⅛-inch bit; 20- to 22-inch-diameter bleached grapevine wreath; tracing paper; graphite paper; white glue; red and green construction paper; Dremel saw; sandpaper; white spray paint; black spray paint; tie wire.

Directions:

1. Enlarge the partial patterns in Fig. III, 3, and the full patterns in Fig. III, 3a, onto tracing paper, following the directions on page 271.

FIG. III, 3 COUNTRY CHRISTMAS WREATH

QUILT BLOCK APPLIQUÉ PATTERNS

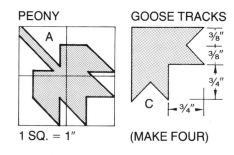

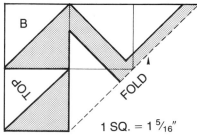

2. Square Motifs: Cut five 4-inch squares from the lattice wood. Spray the squares with the white paint.

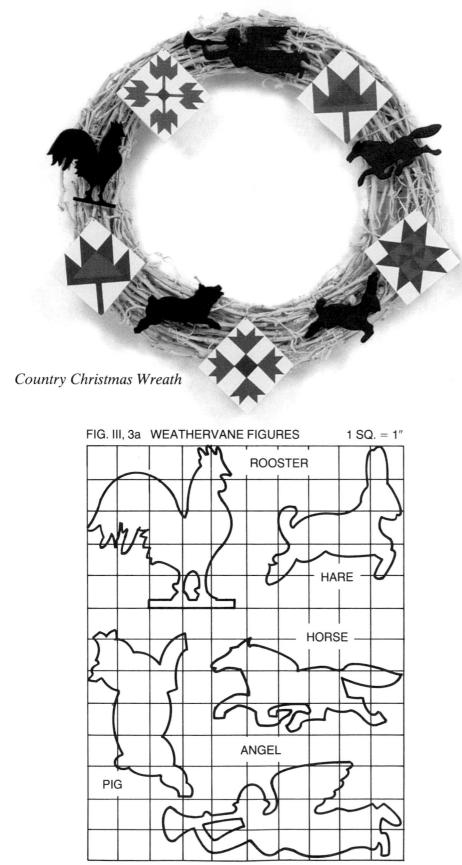

Country Christmas Wreath

FIG. III, 3a WEATHERVANE FIGURES   1 SQ. = 1″

ROOSTER

HARE

HORSE

ANGEL

PIG

3. Paper Appliqués *(glue the pieces to each 4-inch square):* Cut four pattern A pieces from the green paper and one ⅝-inch square from the red paper. Glue the pieces in place counterclockwise *(see photo).* Fold a piece of tracing paper in half and trace partial pattern B on one half of the folded paper. Retrace the pattern on the other half. Open the paper for the full pattern. Cut the background from the red paper and the triangle from the green paper. Glue the pieces in place *(see photo).* Cut four C patterns from the green paper and one 1-inch square from the red paper. Glue the pieces in place *(see photo).* For the D pattern *(not illustrated, see photo),* cut a 2-inch green paper square and glue it to the center of a white square. Cut four 1-inch squares from the red paper, cut the squares again on the diagonal and glue the triangles formed to the outside of the green square *(see photo).* Cut two ⅝-inch squares from the red paper, cut the squares on the diagonal and glue the triangles pinwheel-style in the center of the green square *(see photo).* For the last motif, reverse the colors for pattern B.
4. Drill a hole in one corner of each square, add tie wire and attach the square to the wreath.
5. Weathervane Figures: Using the tracing paper patterns and graphite paper, trace the figures onto the craft wood. Cut them out using the Dremel saw. Round all the edges with the sandpaper and spray the figures with the black paint. Drill holes ⅛ inch in diameter, add tie wires and attach the figures to the wreath, alternating them with the paper appliqué squares.

A PATCHWORK BEDROOM

Wake up to the warmth of a homespun holiday bedroom.

PATCHWORK PILLOW
(18 inches square)

Average: For those with some experience in quilting.

Materials: 18½-inch square of fabric for pillow back; scraps of red, green and off-white fabric; matching threads; synthetic stuffing or 18-inch square pillow form; piping *(optional)*.

Directions (¼-inch seams allowed):
1. Make a quilt block *(see Patchwork Quilt, Step 2, page 127, and* FIG. III, 4*)* for the pillow front.
2. If you wish, stitch piping to the edges of the quilt block, right sides together and raw edges even, clipping the piping seam allowance at each corner.
3. Pin the pillow back to the pillow front, right sides together and raw edges even. Seam around three sides and four corners. Turn the pillow right side out and stuff it. Turn under the open edges and slipstitch the opening closed.

PILLOW SHAMS
(for queen-size pillows)

Average: For those with some experience in sewing.

Materials for 2 Pillow Shams: 2 yards of 54-inch-wide fabric; matching thread.

Directions (½-inch seams allowed):
1. Cut the fabric in half lengthwise, making two 27 x 72-inch strips. Stitch a ½-inch hem along each short edge. Fold the strips in half, hemmed edges together, and pin-mark across the center.
2. Spread out each strip, right side up, and fold one end 2½ inches beyond the pin-marked center line. Repeat at the opposite end, overlapping the first by 5 inches. Pin across the overlaps and along the raw edges.
3. Stitch ½ inch from the raw edges. Turn the pillow sham right side out and press it.
4. Topstitch a border through both layers, 2 inches from each edge. Insert the pillow through the back opening.

*Patchwork Quilt (directions, page 126); Patchwork Pillows and Pillow Shams (directions, page 124);
Ruffled Pillow, Round Tablecloth and Square Tablecloth (directions, page 126)*

RUFFLED PILLOW
(16 inches square)

Average: For those with some experience in sewing.

Materials: ½ yard of 54-inch-wide fabric; matching thread; 2 yards of piping *(optional)*; synthetic stuffing or 16-inch square pillow form.

Directions (½-inch seams allowed):

1. From the fabric, cut two 17-inch squares and a 3-inch-wide ruffle strip, pieced as needed, to measure 96 inches long.

2. If you wish, pin the piping around the pillow front, right sides together and raw edges even, clipping the piping seam allowance at each corner. Using a zipper foot, stitch the piping in place around the front.

3. Ruffle: Seam the ruffle strip at the short edges to make a loop. Narrowly hem one long edge. Mark the other edge at the middle, then at the quarters. Pin the ruffle to the pillow top (over the piping), right sides together (the finished edge toward the pillow center) and raw edges even, with a quarter mark at each corner. Make shallow pleats as you pin, to take up the extra fullness. Stitch, using the zipper foot.

4. Stitch the pillow front to the pillow back along the previous stitching, with the ruffle between the pillow front and back. Stitch around three sides and four corners. Turn the pillow right side out and stuff it. Turn under the open edges and slip-stitch the opening closed.

ROUND TABLECLOTH
(about 100 inches in diameter)

Average: For those with some experience in sewing.

Materials: 6 yards of 54-inch-wide fabric; matching thread.

Directions (½-inch seams allowed):

1. Cut the fabric in half crosswise to make two pieces 54 inches wide by 3 yards long. Cut one piece in half, lengthwise, to make two pieces 27 inches wide. Seam one narrow piece to each long edge of the wide piece. Press the seams open.

2. Fold the cloth in half, crosswise, seams matching. Fold it again, lengthwise, to make a 53-inch square with four layers. From the center fold, mark off a quarter circle with a 50-inch radius. Pin the marked line through all the layers and cut out along the pins, saving all the scraps for appliqués. Narrowly hem the raw edge.

SQUARE TABLECLOTH
(53 inches square)

Easy: Achievable by anyone.

Materials: 1½ yards of 54-inch-wide fabric; matching thread; fabric scraps for appliqué; fusible webbing.

Directions:

1. Straighten the ends, if necessary, of the 54-inch square of fabric. Turn and stitch a ¼-inch hem at two opposite edges of the tablecloth, then hem the remaining edges of the tablecloth.

2. Enlarge the tree appliqué patterns in FIG. III, 8 *(page 129)*, following the directions on page 271. Trace four large trees and eight small trees onto the appliqué fabric. Pin the fabric to fusible webbing and cut out both layers together.

3. Pin a large tree appliqué with webbing, centered, at a corner of the tablecloth. Pin a small tree appliqué with webbing on either side of the large tree appliqué *(see photo, page 125)*. Fuse the appliqués with a hot iron. Repeat for the remaining three corners. When the appliqués are cool to the touch, zigzag stitch over the raw edges around the trees, if you wish.

PATCHWORK QUILT

Average: For those with some experience in quilting.

Materials: 45-inch-wide fabric: 1¼ yards of red, 3 yards of off-white and 4 yards of green; 6 yards of 44-inch-wide unbleached muslin, or a sheet, for the quilt backing; matching threads; masking tape; synthetic quilt batting; quilter's pins or No. 3 safety pins; darner or milliner's needle; between needle, for hand quilting *(optional)*; white sewing thread; green quilting thread.

Directions (¼-inch seams allowed):

1. Cutting: On the green fabric, draw the following: two 9 x 81½-inch and two 9 x 78-inch borders, three 3½ x 60½-inch and eight 3½ x 18½-inch lattice strips and twelve 3½-inch squares. Cut on the drawn lines. Then draw twenty-four 4½-inch squares, and across them draw both diagonals. Cut on the drawn lines (four triangles per square). *On the off-white fabric,* draw forty-eight each of 5⅜-inch, 5-inch and 3½-inch squares and twenty-four 4¼-inch squares. Across the 5⅜-inch squares draw one diagonal and cut on the drawn lines (two triangles per square). Cut out the 5-inch and 3½-inch squares. On the 4¼-inch squares draw four triangles, like the green pieces above, and cut them out. *On the red fabric,* draw forty-eight 5⅜-inch squares. Draw diagonally across each one and cut out two triangles per square.

2. Quilt Block (see FIG. III, 4*):* At a short edge, seam each green triangle to an off-white one to make a larger triangle. Seam two of these larger triangles together at the long edge (alternating the colors) to make a square. Repeat to make three more squares. Seam one of these squares, at the green edges, between two white ones. Repeat. Seam the green square between the remaining two patchwork squares at the white edges. Seam the three rows together to make the center of the

quilt block *(see* FIG. III, 4*)*. At the long edge, seam each red triangle to an off-white one to make a square. Then seam the two squares together at the white edges. Repeat to make three more pairs. Seam two of these pairs to opposite edges of the green and white patchwork *(see* FIG. III, 4*)*. Seam a white 5-inch square to each of the opposite ends of the two remaining pairs. Seam these two rows at opposite edges of the patchwork to complete the block.

3. Rows: Seam three quilt blocks alternately with two green 18½-inch lattice strips to make a horizontal row *(see* FIG. III, 5*)*. Repeat three times. Seam these four rows alternately with three green 60½-inch lattice strips to finish the patchwork.

4. Borders: Seam a longer border at each long edge of the patchwork *(see* FIG. III, 5*)*. Seam a shorter border at the top and bottom edges.

5. Quilt Backing: Cut the muslin or sheet in half crosswise (two 44-inch x 3-yard pieces) and seam them together at a long edge. Press.

6. Assembling: Spread the quilt backing, wrong side up, on the floor and tape down each corner. Spread the batting on top of the backing, smoothing it from the center out. Over the batting, spread the quilt top, right side up. With the quilter's or safety pins, pin together the three layers, from the center outward, straight to each edge and diagonally to each corner. Using the darner or milliner's needle, single lengths of the white thread and long stitches, baste through the three layers, from the center outward, straight to each edge and diagonally to each corner. Baste additional rows about 8

FIG. III, 4 PATCHWORK QUILT QUILT BLOCK

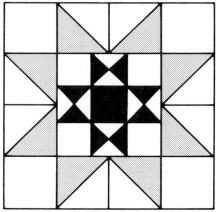

FIG. III, 5 PATCHWORK QUILT QUILT LAYOUT

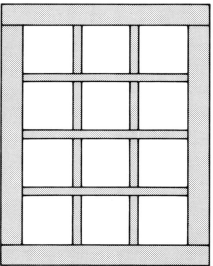

inches apart, stopping 1 inch from the raw edge.

7. Quilting: With the quilting thread, stitch in the ditch of the green lattice and border seams by hand, using the between needle, or by sewing machine.

8. Binding: Trim the quilt backing and batting ¾ inch inside the quilt top edges. Turn under the quilt top ¼ inch, then ½ inch, pin a hem at each edge and stitch all around.

9. Remove the basting.

A PATCHWORK CHRISTMAS KITCHEN

★

Bright touches of cheer for your holiday kitchen.

CAFÉ CURTAINS

Average: For those with some experience in sewing.

Materials: Fabric; curtain rod.

Directions (¼-inch seams allowed):

1. Install the curtain rod and measure the distance from the rod to the window sill. Then measure the width of the window. Cut two curtains, each the measured length and width (using a pair will give you double fullness). Cut two 3¼-inch-wide ruffle strips, pieced as needed, each twice as long as the width of one curtain. Hem the short edges of each.

2. Stitch a narrow hem at each side edge of the curtains. At each top edge, turn down ¼ inch and press. Then turn down 2 inches, press and stitch. Measure 1 inch from the top and stitch across the curtain, for the rod casing.

3. Stitch a ¼-inch hem at one long edge of each ruffle. Sew a gathering row ¼ inch from the raw edge. Pin a ruffle piece to the bottom edge of each curtain piece, right sides together, ends flush and raw edges even. Pull up the gathers to fit the width of the curtain and stitch over the gathering line. Turn over and press the ruffle downward.

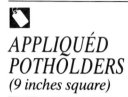

OVEN MITT

Average: For those with some experience in sewing.

Materials: 9½ x 24 inches of checked fabric; quilt batting or fleece interfacing.

Directions (¼-inch seams allowed):

1. Baste the batting or fleece to the wrong side of the fabric. Topstitch diagonal parallel lines (to connect the corners of the square checks) across the fabric. Repeat in the opposite direction (at right angles to the first stitchlines).

2. Enlarge the pattern in FIG. III, 6, following the directions on page 271. Cut out a front and a back for the mitt.

3. Right sides together, seam the two halves of the mitt, omitting the wrist edge. Double-stitch at the base of the thumb and clip the seam allowance to the stitchline. Turn up a ½-inch hem at the wrist edge and stitch. Turn the mitt right side out.

APPLIQUÉD POTHOLDERS
(9 inches square)

Average: For those with some experience in sewing and appliqué work.

Materials: Red and green fabric; quilt batting; fusible webbing.

Directions (¼-inch seams allowed):

1. Heart Potholder: Seam 1½-inch-wide strips of the red fabric to two opposite edges of a 7½-inch green fabric square. Trim the red edges flush with the green. Seam two more strips of the red fabric to the remaining green edges and trim the edges.

2. Enlarge the heart pattern in FIG. III, 7, following the directions on page 271. With the red fabric pinned to the fusible webbing, cut out a small heart. Pin the heart appliqué with webbing to the center of the green square and fuse them together with a hot iron. Machine stitch over the raw edges with a close zigzag (satin) stitch.

3. Cut a 1¼ x 5-inch strip. Turn under ¼ inch at each long edge and press. Fold the strip in half lengthwise, with edges matching, pin and edgestitch. Fold the tab in half and cross the ends.

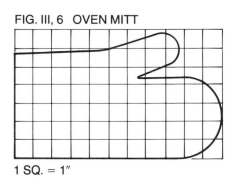

FIG. III, 6 OVEN MITT

1 SQ. = 1″

FIG. III, 7 HEART APPLIQUÉ

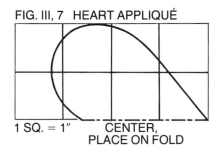

1 SQ. = 1″   CENTER,
PLACE ON FOLD

FIG. III, 8 TREE APPLIQUÉS

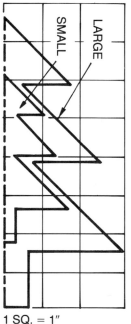

SMALL

LARGE

1 SQ. = 1″

*Café Curtains, Oven Mitt and Appliquéd Potholders
(directions, page 128)*

Pin the ends to one corner of the potholder top, with right sides together and raw edges even, and stitch.

4. Baste two layers of batting to the wrong side of the potholder front. Pin a 9½-inch potholder back to the potholder front, right sides together. Stitch around three sides and four corners. Turn the potholder right side out. Turn under the open edges and slipstitch closed. Topstitch ¼ inch from the edge.

5. *Diamond Potholder:* Follow the directions for the Heart Potholder, using a 4½-inch square piece at a diagonal instead of the heart appliqué.

6. *Tree Potholder:* Follow the directions for the Heart Potholder, omitting Step 1 and using the large tree appliqué in FIG. III, 8, instead of the heart appliqué.

PATCHWORK HEARTS PLACE SETTING

Sew up festive place settings for all your holiday meals!

NAPKIN
(17 inches square)

Average: For those with some experience in sewing.

Materials for 6 Napkins: 1 yard of 54-inch-wide green fabric; scraps of red fabric for heart appliqués; matching threads.

Directions:

1. For each napkin, cut an 18-inch square from the green fabric. Enlarge the appliqué heart pattern in FIG. III, 7 *(page 129)*, following the directions on page 271, and cut out a red heart for each napkin.

2. Stitch a ¼-inch hem at two opposite edges of each napkin, then hem the remaining edges of the napkin.

3. Baste a heart in one corner of each napkin. Machine stitch over the raw edges with a close zigzag (satin) stitch.

FIG. III, 9   HEART PLACE MAT

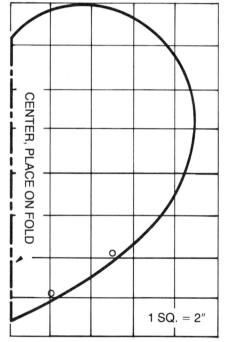

CENTER, PLACE ON FOLD

1 SQ. = 2"

REVERSIBLE PLACE MAT
(15 x 18 inches)

Easy: Achievable by anyone.

Materials for 6 Place Mats: 1 yard each of 45-inch to 54-inch-wide plaid and checked fabrics; matching thread; quilt batting.

Directions (¼-inch seams allowed):

1. Enlarge the heart place mat pattern in FIG. III, 9, following the directions on page 271. Cut out six hearts each from the plaid and checked fabrics.

2. Baste the batting to the wrong side of the plaid hearts. Pin each checkered heart to a plaid one, right sides together. Stitch around the heart, ¼ inch from the raw edges, leaving one side open between the circles on the pattern for turning.

3. Turn each place mat right side out. Turn under the open edges and slipstitch the opening closed. Topstitch ⅛ inch, then ⅜ inch, from the edge.

Napkin, Reversible Place Mat (directions, page 130); Tie-On Chair Backs (directions, below)

TIE-ON CHAIR BACKS

Easy: Achievable by anyone.

Materials: Fabric; quilt batting.

Directions (½-inch seams allowed):

1. Measure the width of the chair back. Decide on the desired depth of the pad. Add 1 inch to each of these two measurements and cut out two fabric rectangles of the desired measurements for the pad front and back. Cut four 1-inch-wide tie strips, 12½ inches long.

2. Baste the batting to the wrong side of the pad front. Pin the pad back to the pad front, right sides together, and stitch around one long (bottom) and two short edges. Turn the pad right side out. Turn under ½ inch at the top edge and press.

3. Ties (make 4): Turn under each tie strip edge ¼ inch and press. Fold the strip in half, lengthwise, with edges matching, pin and edgestitch. Slide the ends of two ties into the open top edge of the pad at one corner and pin the ties in place.

Repeat with the remaining two ties at the other open corner. Edgestitch over the ties and across the top edge of the pad.

A PATCHWORK OF PRESENTS

What could be more special than a gift crafted by loving hands?

PADDED PATCHWORK HANGERS

Average: For those with some experience in sewing.

Materials: Wooden coat hanger, full size or child's 10-inch; ¼ yard of 45-inch-wide fabric; matching thread; glazed batting; ½ yard of ribbon, about ⅜″ wide.

Directions:

1. Gathered Hook: Cut a 1½ x 14-inch strip of fabric. Turn each long edge ¼ inch to wrong side; press. Also turn under ¼ inch at one short end. Fold whole strip in half, wrong sides together; pin. Topstitch, ⅛ inch from folded edges. Slide strip over hanger hook with topstitched edges to the outside, gathering slightly. Hand sew against outside curve of hook to keep the pushed-up gathers in place.

2. Padding: Wrap the batting around half the hanger, starting at the hook, until its girth measures about 4¼ inches. Sew along batting edges, especially over the end, so it will stay in place while slipping on cover. Repeat with other hanger half.

3. Cover: Cut four 3-inch-wide strips of fabric, two of them 10 inches long and two 15 inches long. (For the child's hanger, cut four 2¾-inch-wide strips, two 6 inches long and two 9 inches long.) With the longest machine stitch, sew ⅜ inch from the two long edges and one short end of a 15-inch piece (9-inch piece for the child's hanger), rounding the two corners at the closed end. Pin this piece to a 10-inch piece (6-inch for the child's), right sides together, raw edges even, pulling up gathers so edges will match. Distribute fullness evenly, then stitch on gathering row. Turn sleeve right side out; slide it over one end of hanger. Repeat for other half. Turn under raw edges at center; slipstitch the sleeves together, catching in hook cover.

4. Bow: Tie ribbon into a double bow; tack at base of the hook.

PATCHWORK RIBBON FRAME

Easy: Achievable by anyone.

Materials: Inexpensive picture frame; white glue; variety of floral ribbon scraps.

Directions:

1. Working on one section at a time, spread a thin layer of glue over a small area of the frame.

2. Carefully lay down pieces of ribbon, one strip at a time, slightly overlapping the ends and sides of the ribbons. Try to vary the colors to make an interesting design.

3. Continue to glue down the ribbons until the entire frame front is covered. Extend the ribbons over the top, sides and bottom of the frame and attach the ribbon ends to the back of the frame with small dabs of glue. Let the glue dry completely.

CHRISTMAS KITTY TOWEL RACK

Easy: Achievable by anyone.

Materials: ½ yard of calico fabric; ¾ yard of toweling; lace appliqué; 1 yard of ribbon; one 12-inch dowel stick with knobs; small amount of fiberfill; 1 yard of cluny lace; ¾-inch-diameter bone ring.

Directions (¼-inch seams allowed):

1. Towel: Hem each end of the toweling fabric. Cut a 3-inch-wide strip from the calico fabric long enough to fit the width of the towel. Make a ¼-inch hem around the calico strip and sew the strip to the towel 3 inches from the towel's bottom hem, inserting the cluny lace close to the calico hem as you sew. Fold the towel into thirds and press.

2. Kitty: Enlarge the patterns for the cat body and tail in FIG. III, 10, following the directions on page 271. Pin the patterns to the calico fabric. Cut out a kitty front and back, and a tail front and back.

3. From the calico fabric cut out two tabs 2½ x 7 inches. Fold each tab in half, right sides together, and seam the long sides. Turn the tabs right side out and press them. Sew together the tail front and back, right sides together, leaving an opening where the tail will connect to the body. Turn the tail right side out and stuff it. Sew together the body front and back, right sides together, inserting the tail between the X's on the pattern and the tabs into the seam on the bottom edge. Leave about a 4-inch opening on the bottom. Turn the kitty right side out,

FIG. III, 10 CHRISTMAS KITTY TOWEL RACK

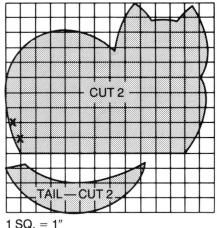

1 SQ. = 1"

stuff it firmly and slipstitch the opening closed. Trim the kitty's neck with the lace appliqué and the ribbon *(see photo)*.

4. Finishing: Sew the bone ring on the back of the kitty. Slide the dowel through the tabs.

133

MERRY CHRISTMAS BIB

Average: For those with some experience in sewing.

Materials: ¼ yard of green woven cotton or blend fabric; ¼ yard of red background Christmas print; purchased Christmas print for making stuffed ornaments, to be used for appliqué; 10 x 12 inches of cotton flannel; 66 inches of single-fold green bias tape to match green fabric; matching threads.

Directions (¼-inch seams allowed):

1. Wash and iron all the fabrics. Cut out one green 6½-inch square, three green 2½-inch squares, four red print rectangles 2 x 6½ inches, two red print 2-inch squares, one red print 2½-inch square and the Christmas print appliqué.

2. Cut the red 2½-inch square and green 2½-inch squares in half diagonally to make two red triangles and six green triangles.

3. Clip the seams of the Christmas ornament print appliqué, turn the edges under and press. Using a blind stitch, attach the appliqué to the center of the 6½-inch green square.

4. Sew a short side of a green triangle to each end of one red rectangle, right sides together, pressing the seams to the sides with an iron as you go. Center and sew the red rectangle to the bottom of the large green square. Sew a red print rectangle to the left and right sides of the large green square. Sew these red side rectangles to the green triangles for the bottom edge of the bib. Sew the long side of one green triangle to the long side of one red triangle to form a square. Repeat to form another square. Sew the resulting squares to the ends of the remaining red rectangle, with the green sides next to the rectangle. Center and sew the rectangle to the top of the large green square. Sew the remaining short sides of the green triangles to the side red rectangles. Sew a short side of the remaining two green triangles to each of the red squares, with a green triangle on the left of one red square and on the right of the other for the top edge of the bib. Sew the resulting two pieces to the top edge of the bib, placing a green triangle on each outside upper corner. The space in the upper center is for the neck.

5. Place the bib top on the flannel, right side up, and pin. If you want more absorbency, use two layers of flannel. Trim the flannel even with the bib edges. Pin the bias tape along the bib edges, right sides together; **do not** go around the neck. Sew along the fold of the tape. Turn the tape to the back of the bib and pin. Sew down the edge by hand, being sure not to go through the front of the bib.

6. The piece remaining from the bias tape should be about 31 inches long. Find the center of the tape and pin it to the center of the neck. Attach the tape as for the bib. Turn in the raw ends and sew close to the edge by machine, or overcast by hand.

THE FRIENDLY BEASTS

Easy: Achievable by anyone.

Materials: Cotton dish towel for each pillow; matching thread; synthetic stuffing; scrap of yarn for pig's tail; ½ yard of ⅜-inch-wide ribbon and a jingle bell for the cat.

Directions (¼-inch seams allowed):

1. Enlarge the patterns in FIG. III, 11, following the directions on page 271. The approximate finished sizes are: the cat and the pig, 12 inches long; the swan, 8 inches tall; the rabbit, 10 inches tall.

2. For each animal you choose to make, cut a front and back piece from the dish towel material. Turn over the pattern for the back piece. With right sides together, seam the front to the back, leaving an opening between the two circles indicated on the pattern. Clip almost to the seam at the inside curves and corners.

3. Turn the animal right side out and stuff it firmly. Turn under the raw edges of the opening; slipstitch the opening closed.

4. For the Cat: Thread the jingle bell onto the ribbon. Tie the ribbon into a bow with the bell in the center of the knot. Tie the ribbon around the cat's neck.

For the Pig: Thread a needle with the yarn. Draw the yarn through the pig at the top circle of the opening. Tie the yarn ends in a square knot.

FIG. III, 11 THE FRIENDLY BEASTS

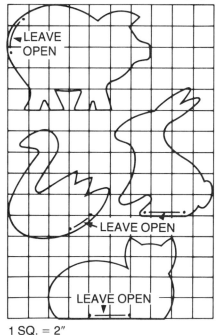

LEAVE OPEN

LEAVE OPEN

LEAVE OPEN

1 SQ. = 2"

PATCHWORK ART GALLERY

Designate the refrigerator or other large space as the "Christmas Art Center," and have the kids draw pictures with special holiday themes to be displayed during the season. If there's an abundance of art, you can rotate the works, the same way that the museums do.

Sweet Dreams Sailboat Quilt

SWEET DREAMS SAILBOAT QUILT
(about 36 x 51 inches)

Average: For those with some experience in quilting.

Materials: 42-inch-wide fabric: 1⅔ yards of small navy print for piecing, borders and binding, ½ yard of white print, ⅓ yard of medium-size navy print, 1 yard of light blue print for piecing, border and heart, ¼ yard of yellow print for sun, ¼ yard of red pin dot for boat, ½ yard of pale blue and white print for sail, 1⅔ yards of white and blue print for backing; 45 x 60 inches of extra loft bonded polyester batting; bonded batting to underline sails *(optional)*; ⅞ yard of ¾-inch-wide brown grosgrain ribbon for mast; ⅓ yard of ¼-inch-wide red velvet ribbon for flag; embroidery floss: 1 skein each of Brown, Navy, Red and Gold, plus small amount of Black and Pink; ¾-inch masking tape; cardboard for piecing templates; yardstick; quilter's or No. 3 safety pins; embroidery needle; darner or milliner's needle; between needle; white sewing thread; quilting thread to blend with fabrics.

Note: *The nine patch rectangle quilt is pieced, bordered, quilted and bound before sewing on the appliqués. The quilted surface gives a firm foundation for the large appliqué pieces. Thick bonded batting was used for the filler and the quilting was done by hand with a between needle. Use thin bonded batting if you will be machine quilting. Embroider the sun's face and the heart on the large pieces of fabric before cutting out the appliqués.*

Directions (¼-inch seams allowed):

1. Enlarge the patterns in FIG. III, 12 onto paper, following the directions on page 271.

2. On the yellow print fabric, embroider the sun face using outline and satin stitches. Then draw a 5¾-inch circle for the sun and cut it out.

3. Add the seams (½-inch on all sides if you wish to underline the sails with bonded batting; otherwise, ¼-inch seams) to the sail and the boat patterns. Cut a 2½ x 3½-inch pattern from the cardboard. Label each pattern piece and indicate the seam allowance.

4. Cutting: Cut the selvages from the small navy print fabric. Cut strips from the small navy print as follows: Cut four 60 x 2½-inch strips and label them A. Cut two 54½ x 2-inch strips and label them B. Cut two 48½ x 2-inch strips and label them C. Cut two 42½ x 2-inch strips and label them D. Cut two 33½ x 2-inch strips and label them E. A is for the binding, B is for the third side border, C is for the first side border, D is for the third top and bottom border, E is for the first top and bottom border. Use the remainder of the small navy print to mark and cut sixty-five 2½ x 3½-inch rectangles. Pin the sets of strips together and label them with pieces of masking tape, indicating the positions where they will be used. From the white print, cut fifty-two 2½ x 3½-inch rectangles. From the medium-size navy print, cut forty-eight 2½ x 3½-inch rectangles. From the light blue print, cut five strips across the folded fabric, selvage to selvage, 3½

FIG. III, 12 SWEET DREAMS SAILBOAT QUILT APPLIQUÉS

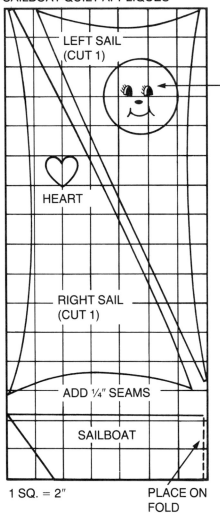

LEFT SAIL (CUT 1)

5¼" CIRCLE
ADD ¼" SEAM ALLOWANCE
EYES/NOSE — SATIN ST.
MOUTH — OUTLINE ST.

HEART

RIGHT SAIL (CUT 1)

ADD ¼" SEAMS

SAILBOAT

1 SQ. = 2"   PLACE ON FOLD

inches wide. Open up the remaining fabric and cut sixty 2½ x 3½-inch rectangles. Take two strips, remove the selvages, then measure and cut a 39½-inch-long strip from each. Sew the three remaining strips end to end with ½-inch seams, forming one long strip, and press the seams open. Cut off the selvages, fold the strip crosswise to measure 48½ inches and cut two strips of equal length.

5. Quilt Blocks: Refer to FIG. III, 12a *(page 138)* for piecing and the layout. Sew the rectangles into rows, then the rows into blocks, making 13 A blocks and 12 B blocks. Press the seams toward the darker color as you sew each third of a block.

6. Assembling Quilt Top: Starting with an A block, and alternating

Did You Know . . .

Charles Dickens once wrote that "Christmas is a good time; a kind, forgiving, charitable, pleasant time; the only time I know of, in the long calendar of the year, when men and women seem by one consent to open their shut-up hearts freely, and to think of other people below them as if they really were fellow passengers to the grave, and not another race of creatures bound on other journeys." Dickens in large part was responsible for the renewed interest in the celebration of the Christmas holiday. The publication of Dickens' "A Christmas Carol" in 1843 helped to popularize many of the traditions we still follow today.

FIG. III, 12a   SWEET DREAMS QUILT BLOCK LAYOUT

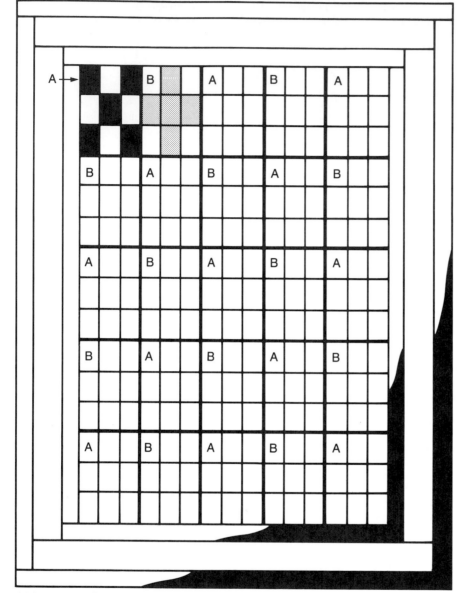

36" x 51"   PIECING CHART

BLOCK A
SMALL NAVY
PRINT/WHITE
13 BLOCKS

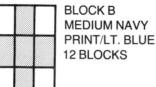

BLOCK B
MEDIUM NAVY
PRINT/LT. BLUE
12 BLOCKS

A and B blocks, seam the blocks to make a row five blocks wide. Start the second row with block B. Start the third row with block A, and so on. There will be five rows, each row having five blocks. On a piece of masking tape, label the upper left hand corner of each row of blocks with the row number and an arrow. The arrow on the first row points to the left, the arrow on the second row points to the right, and so on. Press the seams between the blocks in the direction indicated by the arrows. Now the block row seams are facing in opposite directions. Sew all the rows together.

7. Borders: Take the labeled borders and seam the small navy print C strips to the sides of the quilt. Then seam the E strips to the top and bottom of the quilt. Seam the longer light blue strips to the sides and the shorter light blue strips to the top and bottom. Finish with the small navy print B strips on the sides and the D's on the top and bottom. Press the seams outward after each set of borders is sewn. Lay the quilt backing on a large flat surface, wrong side up, and tape down the corners. Center the batting and the quilt top, right side up, on the backing. With the quilter's or safety pins, pin together the three layers, from the center outward, straight to each edge and diagonally to each corner. Using the darner or milliner's needle, single lengths of the white thread and long stitches, baste through the three layers, from the center outward, diagonally to each corner and straight to each edge. Baste additional rows 8 inches apart. Untape the corners.

8. Quilting: Stitch diagonally from corner to corner on each rectangle. On the light blue border, mark the quilting pattern with masking tape: Place a piece of ¾-inch masking tape next to each side of the light blue border, and one down the center. This gives two sets of narrow quilting lines in the center of the border. Also quilt next to the small navy print seam on each edge of the light blue border. Remove the basting stitches.

9. Binding: Fold the binding strips (A's) in half lengthwise, raw edges meeting, and press. Pin the binding to each longer side edge, right sides together and raw edges even. Stitch ⅜ inch from each edge and trim the ends flush. Turn the binding to the back of the quilt and slipstitch each fold to the seamline. Repeat at the top and bottom, leaving a 1-inch extension at both ends before you start sewing. After stitching the binding to the quilt top, turn under the extensions, bring the binding to the back and slipstitch.

10. Appliquéing Boat: Press the seams under and fold the boat in half, side to side. Center the fold line in the center of the middle bottom rectangle block and ¾ inch above the border. Pin the boat in place. Pin the brown ribbon in place through the center of the quilt, just above the boat. Slip the bottom end of the ribbon under the boat top and diagonally fold over the top of the ribbon to form the mast point. Using six strands of the Brown floss and a ladder stitch, embroider over the ribbon to secure it to the quilt top.

11. Making Sails: If you are not using batting to underline the

PERFECT PATCHWORK

The following tips will help to insure perfect results when quilting:
• In keeping with the American pioneer patchwork tradition, use fabric "seconds" for appliqué pieces. Check the fabric carefully for flaws; by taking care when laying out your pattern pieces, you can usually avoid the defects.
• Wash any cotton or cotton blend fabrics before you begin to preshrink them and to test for color fastness.
• Always press any fabric before laying out patterns or marking the fabric for cutting.

sails, turn under the seams and appliqué the sails in place, just above the boat and near the mast. Appliqué the boat in place. To underline the sails with batting, fold under the seams on the sail patterns and use them to cut one piece of batting per sail. Center the batting on each fabric sail, bring the edges of the sail up and over the batting and hand sew the sail to the batting. Pin the sails and appliqué the sails and boat in place. Using the pattern, embroider the heart on the remaining light blue fabric, cut it out and appliqué it on the bow of the boat. Appliqué a red velvet ribbon flag just behind the top of the mast.

12. Making Sun's Rays (Prairie Points): Cut ten 4-inch squares from the remaining yellow print fabric. Fold each square diagonally twice to make ten small triangles, and press. On each prairie point, sew a small running stitch ¼ inch from the raw edge through all the fabric layers. Leave a long end on every thread so they can be pulled to gather the points to fit around the sun. Turn under the edges of the sun and pin the sun to the upper left corner of the quilt, overlapping the block and border. Baste the sun in place. Place the prairie points around the edge of the sun, overlapping them slightly, and gather the points to fit. Keep the openings of the points all going in one direction so that each point following can be slipped into the opening of the preceding point. Using three strands of the Gold floss and a backstitch, sew down the sun ⅛ inch from the edge and sew the points at the edge of the sun. *Note: Make sure at least ¼ inch of the prairie points' seams is under the sun so no raw edges show.*

13. Finishing: With three strands of the Red floss, outline stitch around the boat. Use the Navy floss to outline the heart, bottom edge of the sail and inside edges of the sail near the mast, and to attach the sails to the top of the mast and to the ends of the boat.

A PATCHWORK OF BREADS

A delicious assortment of homemade breads to delight your family and friends.

ORANGE YOGURT BRAIDS

Bake at 350° for 25 minutes.
Makes 2 loaves.

    5   to 5½ cups all-purpose flour
    2   envelopes active dry yeast
    ½   cup (1 stick) butter
    1   cup plain yogurt
    1   teaspoon salt
    ½   cup sugar
    3   eggs, reserve 1 egg yolk
    1   teaspoon grated orange zest
          (orange part of rind only)
    ⅓   cup orange juice
    1   tablespoon milk

1. Combine 2 cups of the flour with the yeast in a large bowl.
2. Melt the butter in a small saucepan over low heat and stir in the yogurt, salt and sugar. Add the butter mixture to the flour mixture. Add the eggs, orange zest and orange juice, mixing well after each addition. Beat the butter-flour mixture for 2 minutes. Stir in enough of the remaining flour to make a soft dough.
3. Divide the dough in half and divide each half into 3 pieces. Roll each piece into a 16-inch-long rope. Braid the ropes loosely into two loaves. Place the loaves on greased baking sheets.
4. Cover the loaves and let them rise in a warm place, away from drafts, for 30 minutes, or until they are doubled in bulk.
5. Preheat the oven to moderate (350°). Mix together the reserved yolk and the milk. Brush the mixture over the loaves.
6. Bake in the preheated moderate oven (350°) for 25 minutes, or until the loaves sound hollow when tapped on the bottom with your fingertips. Cover the loaves loosely with aluminum foil for the last 10 minutes of baking to prevent the tops from over-browning.

OLD-FASHIONED WHITE BREAD

Fragrant and fresh from the oven — just like Grandma used to make.

Bake the rolls at 400° for 20 minutes; bake the loaf at 400° for 40 minutes.
Makes 1 loaf and 12 rolls.

    1   envelope active dry yeast
    ½   cup very warm water (120° to 125°)*
    3   tablespoons sugar
    2   cups milk
    2   tablespoons butter
    ¾   teaspoon salt
    7   to 8 cups all-purpose flour

Orange Yogurt Braid (recipe, page 140); Armenian Sesame Round (recipe, page 143); Dinner Rolls and Old-Fashioned White Bread (recipe, page 140); Savory Spiral Bread (recipe, page 144); Challah (recipe, page 142); Rye Round (recipe, page 143)

1. Sprinkle the yeast into the very warm water in a cup. Add ½ teaspoon of the sugar and stir until the yeast dissolves. Let the mixture stand until it is bubbly.
2. Combine the remaining sugar with the milk, butter and salt in a small saucepan. Heat just until the butter melts. Pour the butter mixture into a large bowl and cool it to lukewarm. Stir the yeast mixture into the cooled butter mixture.
3. Stir in 3 cups of the flour and beat until smooth. Gradually stir in enough of the remaining flour to make a soft dough.
4. Turn out the dough onto a lightly floured surface. Knead for 10 minutes, or until the dough is smooth and elastic, using only as much of the remaining flour as needed to keep the dough from sticking.
5. Place the dough in a greased bowl and turn the greased side up. Cover the bowl with a towel. Let the dough rise in a warm place, away from drafts, for 1 hour, or until it is doubled in bulk.
6. Punch down the dough, turn it out onto a lightly floured surface and knead it a few times. Let the dough rest for 10 minutes. Grease a 9 x 5-inch loaf pan and 12 muffin-pan cups.
7. Divide the dough in half and knead each half a few times. Shape one half into a loaf and place it, seam side down, in the prepared loaf pan. Shape the remaining half into 12 balls and place them in the prepared muffin-pan cups. Cover both the loaf pan and the muffin-pan cups with a towel.
8. Let the dough rise in a warm place, away from drafts, for 1 hour, or until it is doubled in bulk.
9. Preheat the oven to hot (400°).
10. Bake in the hot oven (400°) for 20 minutes for the rolls, 40 minutes for the loaf, or until the rolls are golden and the loaf sounds hollow when tapped with your fingertips. Remove the loaf and the rolls from the pans to wire racks to cool.

Note: Very warm water should feel comfortably warm on your wrist.

CHALLAH

The traditional Sabbath bread; sliced, day-old challah is wonderful to use in making French toast.

Bake at 350° for 30 minutes.
Makes 2 loaves.

- 1½ cups water
- ¼ cup sugar
- 3 teaspoons salt
- ⅓ cup butter
- 2 envelopes active dry yeast
- ½ cup very warm water (120° to 125°)*
- 3 eggs, beaten
- 7½ cups all-purpose flour
- 1 tablespoon water
- Poppy seeds (optional)

1. Combine the 1½ cups of water, the sugar, salt and butter in a small saucepan. Heat slowly until the butter melts, then cool the mixture to lukewarm.
2. Sprinkle the yeast into the ½ cup of very warm water in a large bowl. Stir the mixture until the yeast dissolves completely. Stir in the butter mixture and all but 2 tablespoons of the beaten eggs.
3. Beat in 4 cups of the flour until the mixture is smooth. Beat in enough of the remaining flour to make a soft dough.
4. Turn out the dough onto a lightly floured surface. Knead for 5 minutes, or until the dough is smooth and elastic, using only as much of the remaining flour as needed to keep the dough from sticking.
5. Place the dough in a greased large bowl and turn the greased side up. Cover the bowl and let the dough rise in a warm place, away from drafts, for 1½ hours, or until it is doubled in bulk.
6. Punch down the dough and let it rise for 30 minutes, or until it is doubled in bulk. Punch down the dough again. Turn out the dough onto a lightly floured surface and knead it a few times. Divide the dough into 6 even pieces. Roll each piece into a rope about 15 inches long.

7. Place 3 of the ropes on a greased baking sheet and braid them together. Pinch the ends of the ropes to seal them. Repeat with the remaining ropes. Let the braided loaves rise in a warm place, away from drafts, for 1 hour, or until they are doubled in bulk. Combine the remaining 2 tablespoons of beaten egg with the 1 tablespoon of water. Brush the egg-water mixture over the breads and, if you wish, sprinkle the tops with poppy seeds.
8. Preheat the oven to moderate (350°).
9. Bake in the preheated moderate oven (350°) for 30 minutes, or until the loaves are golden and sound hollow when tapped with your fingertips. Cool the loaves on wire racks.

Note: Very warm water should feel comfortably warm on your wrist.

ARMENIAN SESAME ROUNDS
Delicious loaves studded with toasted sesame seeds.

Bake at 350° for 30 minutes.
Makes 3 loaves.

 2 envelopes active dry yeast
2¼ cups very warm water (120° to 125°)*
 ¾ cup nonfat dry milk powder
 3 tablespoons sugar
 2 teaspoons salt
 3 tablespoons olive oil OR: vegetable oil
6½ cups all-purpose flour
 ¼ cup sesame seeds
 1 egg, beaten

1. Sprinkle the yeast into the very warm water in a large bowl. Stir the mixture until the yeast dissolves completely. Stir in the dry milk powder, sugar, salt and olive or vegetable oil.
2. Beat in 2 cups of the flour until the mixture is smooth. Beat in enough of the remaining flour to make a soft dough.
3. Turn out the dough onto a lightly floured surface. Knead for 10 minutes, or until the dough is smooth and elastic, using

only as much of the remaining flour as needed to keep the dough from sticking.
4. Invert a large bowl over the dough and let it rest for 20 minutes.
5. Divide the dough into quarters. Divide one quarter into 3 smaller pieces. Pat out a second quarter into a 9-inch round on a greased baking sheet. Make a 3-inch-wide dent in the center of the dough. Pat one of the smaller pieces of dough into a 3-inch round. Place the small round in the center of the dent. Repeat with the remaining dough to make 3 loaves. Cover each loaf with plastic wrap and chill the loaves for 2 to 6 hours.
6. Preheat the oven to moderate (350°).
7. Let the loaves stand at room temperature, uncovered, for 10 minutes.
8. Sprinkle the sesame seeds in a shallow baking pan. Toast the seeds in the preheated moderate oven (350°) for 5 minutes, or just until they are golden.
9. Brush the loaves with the beaten egg and sprinkle the tops with the sesame seeds.
10. Bake in the oven (350°) for 30 minutes, or until the loaves are golden and sound hollow when tapped on the bottom with your fingertips. Cool the loaves completely on wire racks.

Note: Very warm water should feel comfortably warm on your wrist.

RYE ROUND

Bake at 400° for 35 minutes.
Makes 2 loaves.

 2 envelopes active dry yeast
2½ cups very warm water (120° to 125°)*
 ¼ cup light molasses
 4 teaspoons salt
 2 tablespoons vegetable shortening
2½ cups rye flour
 1 tablespoon caraway seeds, crushed
5½ to 6 cups all-purpose flour
    Cornmeal

1. Sprinkle the yeast into ½ cup of the very warm water. Add 1 teaspoon of the molasses and stir until the yeast dissolves. Let the mixture stand for 10 minutes, or until it is bubbly and doubled in volume.
2. Combine the remaining water and molasses with the salt and the shortening in a large bowl. Stir in the yeast mixture, rye flour and caraway seeds. Add enough all-purpose flour to make a soft dough.
3. Turn out the dough onto a lightly floured surface. Knead for 10 minutes, or until the dough is smooth and elastic, using only as much of the remaining all-purpose flour as needed to keep the dough from sticking.
4. Place the dough in a greased large bowl and turn the greased side up. Cover the bowl with a towel and let the dough rise in a warm place, away from drafts, for one hour, or until it is doubled in bulk.
5. Grease a large baking sheet. Sprinkle the baking sheet with the cornmeal.
6. Punch down the dough, turn it out onto a lightly floured surface and knead it a few times. Invert the bowl over the dough and let the dough rest for 10 minutes. Halve the dough and knead each half a few times. Shape the halves into 2 rounds. Place the rounds 4 inches apart on the prepared baking sheet.
7. Let the rounds rise in a warm place, away from drafts, for 1 hour, or until they are doubled in bulk.
8. Preheat the oven to hot (400°).
9. Brush the rounds with water. Bake in the preheated hot oven (400°) for 35 minutes, or until the loaves are browned and sound hollow when tapped with your fingertips. Cool the loaves on a wire rack.

Note: Very warm water should feel comfortably warm on your wrist.

SAVORY SPIRAL BREAD
Serve this flavorful bread warm with soup or stew.

Bake at 350° for 45 minutes.
Makes 1 loaf.

 1 envelope active dry yeast
3½ teaspoons sugar
 1 cup plus 2 tablespoons very warm water (120° to 125°)*
 ¼ teaspoon salt
 2 eggs, slightly beaten
 2 tablespoons vegetable oil
 4 to 4½ cups all-purpose flour
 2 tablespoons butter
 4 large onions, coarsely chopped
 1 clove garlic, finely chopped
 ¼ teaspoon leaf basil, crumbled
 ¼ teaspoon leaf oregano, crumbled
 ¼ teaspoon leaf rosemary, crumbled
 1 cup grated Muenster cheese (4 ounces)
 ½ cup grated Parmesan cheese (2 ounces)
 ¼ cup finely chopped fresh parsley
    Salt and pepper, to taste
 1 tablespoon butter, melted
 1 small onion, sliced
 1 tablespoon poppy seeds
 ¼ teaspoon cracked pepper

1. Combine the yeast, ½ teaspoon of the sugar and 2 tablespoons of the very warm water in a small bowl. Let the mixture stand for 5 minutes, or until it is foamy.
2. Combine the remaining 1 cup of very warm water with the salt, eggs, oil and the remaining 3 teaspoons of sugar in a large bowl. Stir in the yeast mixture.
3. Beat in the flour, 1 cup at a time, until a stiff dough forms. Turn out the dough onto a floured surface and knead for 10 minutes, or until smooth and elastic.
4. Place the dough in a greased large bowl and turn the greased side up. Cover the bowl and let the dough rise in a warm place, away from drafts, until it is doubled in bulk, for 1½ hours.

TIPS FOR YULETIDE YEAST BREADS

• **Dissolving Yeast:** Combine the yeast with 1 teaspoon of sugar and very warm water. "Very warm" water should feel comfortably warm when dropped on your wrist.

• **Equal Measures:** You can substitute one cake (0.6 oz) of compressed yeast for one envelope of active dry yeast in most recipes. Use warm water to dissolve the fresh yeast. "Warm" water should feel tepid when dropped on your wrist.

• **Heating Milk for Yeast Breads:** Place the milk with the other ingredients in a small saucepan and warm slowly until the milk is hot, but not boiling.

• **Kneading the Dough:** Turn out the dough onto a lightly floured pastry board and knead until the dough is smooth and elastic.

• **Letting the Dough Rise:** Place the dough in a large bowl that has been greased with butter or margarine and turn up the greased side of the dough. Cover the bowl and let the dough rise in a warm place, away from drafts, until it is doubled in bulk. If you have an electric oven, warm it to 200°, turn it off and let it cool for 5 minutes with the door closed before you place the dough inside. A gas oven with the door left slightly ajar needs no preheating; the pilot light will keep the dough warm enough.

• **Checking the Volume:** Dough has doubled in bulk when a depression made with your fingertip remains. For an easy way to tell when dough has doubled, press the unrisen dough flat in the greased bowl and mark the dough's level. Remove the dough from the bowl. Fill the bowl with water to double the marked level and mark this second level. Return the dough to the bowl. When the dough has risen to the second marked level, it has doubled.

• **Shaping the Dough:** Punch down the dough on a lightly floured pastry cloth or board and follow the instructions in the individual recipes for shaping it.

• **Testing for Doneness:** Bread is fully baked when it turns golden and sounds hollow when lightly tapped with your fingertips.

• **Cooling Bread:** Cool bread in the pan on a wire rack for 5 minutes. Loosen the bread around the edges of the pan and invert the loaf onto the wire rack to cool completely.

• **Fast-Rising Active Dry Yeast:** Follow the package directions. In general, the water for dissolving this kind of yeast should be hotter and the rising time reduced compared to regular active dry yeast.

5. Melt the 2 tablespoons of butter in a small skillet over medium heat. Add the onion, garlic, basil, oregano and rosemary. Cook for 3 minutes, or until the onion has softened. Place the onion mixture in a bowl and let it cool to room temperature. Add the Muenster and Parmesan cheeses and parsley. Season with salt and pepper.

6. Punch down the dough and roll it out to form a 9 x 12-inch rectangle. Spread the onion mixture over the surface of the dough to within 1 inch of the edges. Roll up the dough, jelly-roll style, along a long side. Place the loaf on a greased baking sheet and cover it with a clean towel.

7. Let the loaf rise for 45 minutes, or until it is doubled in bulk.

8. Preheat the oven to moderate (350°). Brush the loaf with the 1 tablespoon of melted butter. Place the onion slices over the top of the loaf and sprinkle with the poppy seeds and the cracked pepper.

9. Bake the loaf in the preheated moderate oven (350°) for 45 minutes. Cool the loaf slightly on a wire rack.

Note: Very warm water should feel comfortably warm on your wrist.

Christmas Chocolate Spumoni (recipe, page 154); Green and White Stuffed Shells and Acorn Squash and Onion Marinara (recipes, page 152); Chicken and Wild Rice Salad (recipe, page 151); Antipasto Platter (recipe, page 150); Savory Bread Sticks and Spicy Tomato Christmas Cheer (recipes, page 149)

"WELCOME HOME" HOLIDAY BUFFET

(for 8 to 12)

Spicy Tomato Christmas Cheer
Savory Bread Sticks
Gorgonzola Spread
Antipasto Platter
Chicken and Wild Rice Salad
Acorn Squash and Onion Marinara
Green and White Stuffed Shells
Chocolate Marsala Poundcake
Christmas Chocolate Spumoni
New England Nutmeg Cookies
Assortment of Liqueur-and-Cream Coffees

WORK PLAN FOR "WELCOME HOME" HOLIDAY BUFFET

Up to One Month Ahead
- Prepare and freeze the Savory Bread Sticks, Christmas Chocolate Spumoni, Chocolate Marsala Poundcake and New England Nutmeg Cookies.

Up to Two Weeks Ahead:
- Prepare and freeze the Green and White Stuffed Shells.

The Day Before:
- Thaw all the frozen items except for the Savory Bread Sticks and the Christmas Chocolate Spumoni.

The Night Before or Early in the Day:
- Prepare the mushrooms and peppers for the Antipasto Platter.
- Prepare the Gorgonzola Spread and the Chicken and Wild Rice Salad; refrigerate.
- Assemble the Acorn Squash and Onion Marinara; refrigerate until 1 hour before serving time.

Several Hours Before:
- Unmold the Gorgonzola Spread.
- Unmold the Christmas Chocolate Spumoni onto a decorative, freezerproof platter, smooth the surface and return the spumoni to the freezer.
- Unmold the Gorgonzola Spread; return the spread to the refrigerator until serving time.

One Hour Before:
- Bake the Acorn Squash and Onion Marinara.
- Thaw the Savory Bread Sticks.
- Finish the Antipasto Platter.
- Start reheating the Green and White Stuffed Shells.
- Prepare the Spicy Tomato Christmas Cheer.
- Start reheating the Savory Bread Sticks.

During the Party:
- Whip the cream to garnish the Christmas Chocolate Spumoni.

Did You Know . . .

Just about every culture has its own favorite drink to toast the season in style. In England, the "wassail" bowl, a concoction of mulled cider and spiced ale, is the beverage of choice. Caraway-flavored Aquavit and spiced Burgundy wine are used in the making of "Glogg," the Scandinavian toasting treat. And eggnog, that frothy mixture of whipped eggs, brandy, sugar and cream, is a true American original; in the last century, it was served with a free restaurant lunch during Christmas week. It also was once a custom (many years ago of course) for any gentleman of standing, should he still be able to stand, to go "egg-nogging" around the town on New Year's Day.

💲 ⫷ ⬎ 🎆
SPICY TOMATO CHRISTMAS CHEER

You may wish to add a splash of vodka to this tasty drink.

Makes 12 servings (½ cup each)
or 8 servings (¾ cup each).

- 1 **can (46 ounces) vegetable cocktail juice**
- 2 **tablespoons brown sugar**
- 2 **tablespoons lemon juice**
- ¼ **teaspoon ground allspice**
- ¼ **teaspoon ground cinnamon**
- ⅛ **teaspoon ground cloves**
    **Lemon slices and cinnamon sticks,
    for garnish (optional)**

Combine the vegetable juice, brown sugar, lemon juice, allspice, cinnamon and cloves in a medium-size stainless-steel or enamel saucepan. Heat over medium heat until the mixture just starts to simmer. Reduce the heat to low and simmer for 3 minutes. Serve the drink in heatproof punch cups or mugs and, if you wish, garnish them with lemon slices and cinnamon sticks.

💲 ⬎
SAVORY BREAD STICKS

Bake at 375° for 20 minutes.
Makes 20 bread sticks.

- 4 **to 4½ cups unsifted flour**
- 2 **tablespoons leaf oregano, crumbled**
- 1 **tablespoon sugar**
- ½ **teaspoon salt**
- ½ **cup grated Parmesan cheese**
- 2 **packages rapid-rising dry yeast**
- 1½ **cups hot water (125° to 130°)**
- ¼ **cup grated Parmesan cheese, for topping**

1. Mix 3 cups of the flour with the oregano, sugar, salt, the ½ cup of Parmesan cheese and the yeast in a large bowl.
2. Stir the hot water into the dry mixture. Add enough of the remaining flour to make a soft dough.
3. Turn the dough out onto a lightly floured surface. Knead the dough, adding just enough of the remaining flour to keep the dough from sticking to the surface, for five minutes, or until it is smooth and elastic.
4. Grease a clean mixing bowl well. Shape the dough into a ball. Place the dough in the greased bowl and turn the greased side up. Cover the bowl with a buttered piece of wax paper and a towel. Lightly grease two large baking sheets.
5. Let the dough rise in a warm place, away from drafts, for about 25 minutes, or until it is doubled in bulk. Punch down the dough.
6. Turn out the dough onto a lightly floured surface. Knead the dough 10 times. Divide the dough into four equal parts. Cut each quarter into five equal pieces. Roll each piece between your hands to make a 10-inch-long rope. Place the ropes, 1½ inches apart, on the prepared baking sheets. Cover the ropes with a towel and let them rise in a warm place, away from drafts, for about 20 minutes, or until they are doubled in bulk. Preheat oven to moderate (375°).
7. Bake the bread sticks in the preheated moderate oven (375°) for 20 minutes, or until the tops are golden brown. Remove the bread sticks to wire racks to cool.
8. Wrap the bread sticks in heavy-duty aluminum foil, or place them in freezer-safe plastic bags and seal the bags. Label and date the foil packs or bags, and place them in the freezer.
9. When ready to serve, remove the bread sticks from the freezer and let them thaw at room temperature for 1 hour. Preheat the oven to hot (425°). Place the bread sticks on a baking sheet and brush them with cold water. Sprinkle the bread sticks with the ¼ cup of Parmesan cheese and bake them in the preheated hot oven (425°) for 4 minutes. The bread sticks should be crisp and the cheese should be melted. Serve the bread sticks hot, or at room temperature.

GORGONZOLA SPREAD

The tangy taste of Gorgonzola and the crunch of fresh red and green peppers combine beautifully in this colorful molded spread.

Makes about 5½ cups.

- 1 envelope unflavored gelatin
- 1 cup chicken broth
- ½ pound Gorgonzola cheese
- 2 packages (8 ounces each) cream cheese, softened
- ¾ cup thinly sliced green onion
- ¾ cup finely chopped sweet red pepper (1 medium-size pepper)
- ¾ cup finely chopped sweet green pepper (1 medium-size pepper)
- 1 round slice sweet red pepper, for garnish (optional)

  Thinly sliced green onion (green part only), for garnish (optional)

  Party-size rye bread OR: assorted crackers

1. Lightly grease a 6-cup mold. Sprinkle the gelatin over the broth in a small saucepan. Let the gelatin soften for 5 minutes. Gently warm the gelatin mixture over low heat, stirring, for about 3 minutes, or until the gelatin is melted. Cool the mixture.
2. Combine the Gorgonzola cheese with the cream cheese in a large bowl. Beat with an electric mixer at medium speed until the cheeses are well blended and smooth. Stir the gelatin mixture into the cheese mixture until thoroughly combined.
3. Stir the green onion and the red and green peppers into the gelatin-cheese mixture. Pour the mixture into the prepared mold. Refrigerate the spread until it is set, for 4 hours or overnight. To serve, unmold the spread onto a serving plate. Garnish with a round red pepper slice and sliced green onion, if you wish. Serve the spread with party-size rye bread or assorted crackers.

ANTIPASTO PLATTER

Makes 12 servings.

- 3 large sweet red peppers
- 2 cans (2 ounces each) anchovy fillets
- ½ cup olive oil
- 3 tablespoons lemon juice
- 2 tablespoons chopped flat-leaf Italian parsley
- 1 clove garlic, finely chopped
- ¼ teaspoon salt
- ⅛ teaspoon pepper
- 1 pound medium-size mushrooms, trimmed, washed and halved
- 1 small head chicory OR: green-leaf lettuce
- 1 fennel bulb, trimmed, cut lengthwise into ¼-inch-thick slices and each slice halved lengthwise

1. Preheat the broiler. Lay the red peppers in a single layer on the broiler pan. Broil them 2 inches from the source of the heat, turning frequently, for about 15 minutes, or until the red peppers are blackened.
2. Cool each red pepper under cold running water. Remove the blackened skin with a sharp knife and discard it. Core and seed the peppers, cut them into ¾- to 1-inch-wide strips and pat the strips dry on paper toweling. Place them in a large bowl.
3. Mash 3 of the anchovy fillets in a small bowl. Add the oil, lemon juice, parsley, garlic, salt and pepper. Whisk briskly to mix all the ingredients well.
4. Combine the mushrooms and the anchovy dressing with the red peppers. Toss lightly to coat the mushrooms and the peppers. Cover the bowl and refrigerate the mixture for several hours, or overnight.
5. To serve, arrange the chicory or lettuce leaves on a serving platter. Spoon out the mushrooms and mound them off-center on the platter. Arrange the red peppers and the fennel in alternating piles around the mushrooms. Roll up the remaining anchovy fillets and arrange them on the platter. Drizzle any remaining dressing over the antipasto.

⑤ ◁◁◁ ▥

CHICKEN AND WILD RICE SALAD

Allow a few hours for the flavors of this delicious salad to blend thoroughly.

Makes 12 servings.

6 boned, skinless chicken breast halves
     (2 pounds)
1 can (13¾ ounces) chicken broth
2 cups water
1 package (8 ounces) wild rice
⅓ cup olive oil
¼ cup lemon juice (2 lemons)
⅛ teaspoon pepper
1 medium-size sweet green pepper, cored
     and seeded
½ cup chopped red onion
¼ cup chopped flat-leaf Italian parsley
3 ounces pine nuts (pignoli) (about ⅔ cup)

♪ *Holiday Notes*

A PATCHWORK OF ORNAMENTS

Begin a family tradition: Every year, give each child his or her own ornament as a Christmas Eve gift. The children can place the current year's ornaments on the Christmas tree that night. When you take down the tree, pack each child's ornaments in a separate box (a plain carton can become a wonderful container when covered with Christmas wrapping paper) with his or her name on it. Through the years, your children will collect enough of these "special" ornaments to decorate their first trees away from home.

1. Combine the chicken with the broth in a medium-size saucepan and bring to boiling over medium-high heat. Reduce the heat to low and simmer, covered, for 10 minutes, or until the chicken is firm to the touch. Remove the chicken to a plate. Cover the plate and refrigerate the chicken for several hours, or until it is chilled completely.

2. Strain the chicken cooking liquid through a double thickness of cheesecloth into a 4-cup measure. Add the water to make 3½ cups of liquid. Pour the liquid back into the saucepan and bring to boiling over high heat. Add the rice. Return to boiling, stirring. Reduce the heat to low. Cover the saucepan and cook the rice, stirring occasionally, for 45 minutes, or until the rice is puffed open and tender, but not mushy. Pour the rice into a large bowl. Cover the bowl and refrigerate the rice for several hours.

3. Whisk together the oil, lemon juice and pepper in a small bowl.

4. When the chicken is chilled, cut it into 1-inch pieces.* Cut the green pepper lengthwise into ¼-inch-wide strips and cut the strips in half.

5. Add the chicken, green pepper, onion, parsley and pine nuts to the rice in the large bowl. Pour the lemon juice dressing over the salad and toss to combine all the ingredients. Arrange the salad on a serving platter. Cover the platter and refrigerate the salad for several hours to develop the flavors.

*Note: For the photo on page 146, we cut the chicken diagonally into 1-inch-thick slices. We arranged the chicken on the rice after the rice was tossed with the lemon juice dressing and other ingredients.

ACORN SQUASH AND ONION MARINARA

This vegetable dish is delicious served hot, directly from the oven, or an hour or two later at room temperature.

Bake at 425° for 45 minutes.
Makes 12 servings.

*1   can (14 ounces) Italian-style plum
       tomatoes*
2   teaspoons leaf oregano, crumbled
½   teaspoon salt
⅛   teaspoon pepper
4   acorn squash (4 pounds)
3   medium-size yellow onions (1 pound)
2   tablespoons olive oil

1. Preheat the oven to hot (425°).
2. Pour the tomatoes into a shallow, 4-quart, oven-to-table casserole dish. Mash the tomatoes with a wooden spoon to break them up. Sprinkle 1 teaspoon of the oregano, the salt and pepper over the tomatoes. Stir to combine the ingredients.
3. Wash the squash well and cut them in half lengthwise. Remove and discard the seeds. Cut the squash halves crosswise into ⅓-inch-thick slices.
4. Peel the onions and slice them into ¼-inch-thick rounds. Arrange the squash and the onions, overlapping, over the tomatoes in the casserole dish. Brush the tops with the oil and sprinkle the remaining teaspoon of oregano over all. Cover the casserole dish tightly with aluminum foil.
5. Bake in the preheated hot oven (425°) for 45 minutes, or until the onion and the squash are tender when pricked with a fork. Serve the casserole hot or at room temperature.

GREEN AND WHITE STUFFED SHELLS

A make-ahead marvel filled with creamy ricotta, this dish will please any crowd.

Bake, covered, at 425° for 30 minutes, then uncovered for 10 minutes.
Makes 12 servings.

Sauce:
1   cup finely chopped onion
2   tablespoons olive oil
2   cloves garlic, finely chopped
*2   cans (2 pounds, 3 ounces each) Italian-
       style plum tomatoes, undrained*
1   can (16 ounces) tomato sauce
2   teaspoons sugar
1   teaspoon salt
1   teaspoon leaf oregano, crumbled
½   teaspoon leaf basil, crumbled
¼   teaspoon pepper
¼   teaspoon fennel seeds
*2   tablespoons chopped flat-leaf Italian
       parsley*

Ricotta Filling:
2   containers (15 ounces each) ricotta cheese
*1   package (8 ounces) mozzarella cheese, cut
       into ¼-inch pieces*
½   cup grated Parmesan cheese
1   egg
¼   teaspoon pepper
*2   tablespoons chopped flat-leaf Italian
       parsley*
*1   package (10 ounces) frozen chopped
       spinach, thawed*

1   box (12 ounces) jumbo pasta shells
2   tablespoons olive oil

A PATCHWORK OF PLATES & GLASSES

If you have an uneven (or an excess) amount of holiday plates or glassware, consider these unusual uses for them:
• Place holiday potpourri in wide-mouth glasses or bowls.
• Place tiny glass balls in holiday tumblers and use these as part of a centerpiece.
• If you're giving a gift of goodies, include a holiday plate as part of the present.
• Display holiday plates and tumblers on a hutch or cupboard.

1. Prepare the Sauce: Sauté the onion in the oil in a large saucepan over medium heat until the onion is tender, for about 5 minutes. Add the garlic and sauté for 1 minute more.
2. Add the tomatoes with their liquid, breaking them up with a wooden spoon. Add the tomato sauce, sugar, salt, oregano, basil, pepper and fennel seeds. Cover the saucepan and cook over low heat, stirring occasionally, for 1 hour. Uncover the saucepan, and cook, stirring occasionally, for 1 hour and 20 minutes more, or until the sauce has thickened. Remove the saucepan from the heat and stir in the parsley.
3. Prepare the Ricotta Filling: Combine the ricotta, mozzarella and Parmesan cheeses with the egg, pepper and parsley in a large bowl.

4. Remove 1¾ cups of the filling to a medium-size bowl. Drain the spinach well and press it between layers of paper toweling to remove excess moisture. Stir the spinach into the 1¾ cups of filling.
5. Cook the pasta shells, following the package directions. You should have about 48 shells.
6. Meanwhile, divide the sauce between two 13 x 9 x 2-inch glass baking dishes, spreading the sauce evenly over the bottoms of the dishes.
7. Spoon the ricotta filling without the spinach into a pastry bag fitted with a very large (⅜- to ½- inch) plain tip. Pipe about 1 tablespoon of the filling into each of 24 cooked shells. Arrange the filled shells on the sauce, dividing them between the 2 dishes.
8. Spoon the spinach filling into the same bag. Pipe the spinach filling into the remaining shells and arrange the shells on the sauce, dividing them between the dishes. Brush the shells with the remaining 2 tablespoons of oil. Cover the dishes with aluminum foil and refrigerate the shells until 1 hour before serving. Or freeze the shells for up to 1 week; thaw the shells in the refrigerator for 8 hours, or overnight, before baking them.
9. When ready to bake the shells, preheat the oven to hot (425°).
10. Bake the shells, covered, in the preheated hot oven (425°) for 30 minutes. Uncover the dishes and bake for 10 minutes more or until the shells are heated through and the sauce is bubbly.

Note: For the photo on page 146, we used a smaller baking dish than the one called for in this recipe.

CHOCOLATE MARSALA POUNDCAKE

Bake at 325° for 1¼ hours.
Makes 16 servings.

3½ cups all-purpose flour
1 tablespoon baking powder
¾ teaspoon salt
1 cup (2 sticks) unsalted butter, softened
1⅔ cups sugar
5 eggs, separated
¾ cup milk
¼ cup sweet marsala wine
2 squares (1 ounce each) semisweet chocolate, grated

1. Preheat the oven to slow (325°). Grease and flour a 12-cup Bundt® pan.
2. Sift together the flour, baking powder and salt onto wax paper and set aside.
3. Beat together the butter and 1⅓ cups of the sugar in a large bowl until very light. Add the egg yolks, one at a time, beating well after each addition. Combine the milk with the marsala in a small bowl. Stir the dry ingredients into the creamed butter mixture alternately with the milk mixture, beginning and ending with the dry ingredients. Continue to mix until all the ingredients are well combined.
4. Beat the egg whites in a large bowl until soft peaks form. Gradually beat in the remaining ⅓ cup of sugar until stiff peaks form. Stir about one quarter of the egg whites into the batter to lighten it. Fold in the remaining egg whites and the chocolate until no streaks of white remain. Turn the batter into the prepared pan.
5. Bake the poundcake in the preheated slow oven (325°) for 1¼ hours, or until a wooden pick inserted in the center of the cake comes out clean. Cool the poundcake in the pan on a wire rack for 10 minutes. Remove the cake from the pan and cool it to room temperature on the wire rack.

A CACHE OF CHOCOLATE

Chocolate should be stored at a cool room temperature (60° to 75°). Stored in this way, it will keep for months. At warmer temperatures, some of the fat rises to the surface of the chocolate, resulting in a whitish coating called "bloom." While bloom detracts from the appearance of the chocolate, it has no effect on the flavor or texture of chocolate used in baking.

CHRISTMAS CHOCOLATE SPUMONI

Makes 16 servings.

3 pints chocolate ice cream
½ cup chopped mixed glacé fruits
2 tablespoons Grand Marnier OR: other orange-flavored liqueur
1½ cups heavy cream
¼ cup 10X (confectioners' powdered) sugar
½ cup chopped pistachio nuts
½ cup finely crushed chocolate-chocolate chip cookies
¾ cup heavy cream beaten with 1½ tablespoons 10X (confectioners' powdered) sugar until stiff, for garnish
1 teaspoon coarsely chopped pistachio nuts, for garnish (optional)

1. Line a 2-quart bowl with aluminum foil, smoothing the foil against the bowl. Chill the bowl in the freezer for 15 minutes.

2. Remove the ice cream from the freezer to soften slightly, for about 15 minutes. Place 1 cup of the ice cream in a small bowl, cover the bowl and reserve the ice cream in the freezer. Gently spread the remaining ice cream over the inside of the 2-quart bowl to form a shell. Place the bowl in the freezer until the ice cream is firm, for about 2 hours.

3. Meanwhile, combine the glacé fruits with the Grand Marnier or other orange-flavored liqueur in a small bowl. Set aside.

4. When the ice cream shell is firm, beat the 1½ cups of heavy cream with the ¼ cup of 10X (confectioners' powdered) sugar in a small bowl until stiff. Fold in the glacé fruit mixture and ¼ cup of the chopped pistachio nuts.

5. Remove the ice cream shell from the refrigerator. Sprinkle ¼ cup of the crushed cookies over the ice cream shell. Gently press the cookies into the ice cream with the back of a spoon. Spoon the whipped cream mixture into the shell, shaping a 1¼-cup cavity in the center. Place the bowl in the freezer until the whipped cream mixture is firm, for about 2 hours. Sprinkle the remaining ¼ cup of crushed cookies into the cavity and press them into the whipped cream mixture.

6. Soften the reserved 1 cup of ice cream in the refrigerator for 15 minutes. Stir the remaining ¼ cup of chopped pistachio nuts into the reserved ice cream. Spoon the ice cream-pistachio mixture into the cavity and smooth the top. Cover the bowl with plastic wrap and freeze the spumoni for at least 4 hours, or overnight.

7. To serve, remove the bowl from the freezer. Unmold the spumoni onto a serving platter and carefully peel off the aluminum foil. Smooth the surface of the spumoni with a spatula. Garnish with the sweetened whipped cream and, if you wish, sprinkle with a teaspoon of coarsely chopped pistachio nuts.

NEW ENGLAND NUTMEG COOKIES

These delicately spiced butter cookies are a perfect complement to hot tea.

Bake at 375° for 12 to 14 minutes.
Makes about 160 2-inch cookies.

- 1   cup (2 sticks) unsalted butter, softened
- 2   cups sugar plus extra for sprinkling
- 2   eggs
- ½   teaspoon vanilla
-      Pinch salt
- 1½   teaspoons baking soda
- ½   cup buttermilk
- ½   teaspoon freshly grated nutmeg, or to taste
- 5½   to 6 cups all-purpose unbleached flour

1. Beat together the butter and the sugar until light in a large bowl with an electric mixer at high speed. Beat in the eggs, one at a time, until well mixed. Beat in the vanilla and the salt.

2. Stir together the baking soda and the buttermilk. Sprinkle the nutmeg over the flour. Add the buttermilk and the flour alternately to the butter mixture, beginning and ending with the flour, to make a soft dough. Divide the dough into thirds and wrap each third in wax paper or plastic wrap. Refrigerate the dough for several hours or overnight.

3. Preheat the oven to moderate (375°). Grease several baking sheets.

4. Roll out the dough, one third at a time, on a lightly floured surface to a ⅛- to ¼-inch thickness. Cut the dough with 2-inch round cookie cutters and place the rounds on the prepared baking sheets. Sprinkle the rounds with the additional sugar.

5. Bake in the preheated moderate oven (375°) for 12 to 14 minutes, or until the cookies are golden brown. Using a metal spatula, immediately remove the cookies to wire racks. Cool the cookies completely before packing them in containers with tight-fitting lids.

The Holly And The Ivy

anonymous

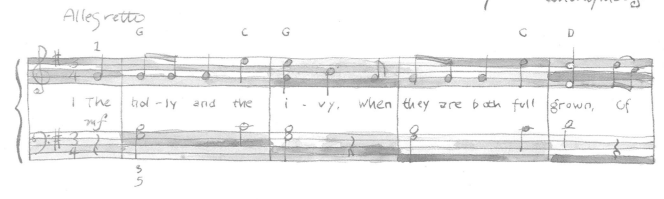

Allegretto

I The hol-ly and the i-vy, when they are both full grown, Of

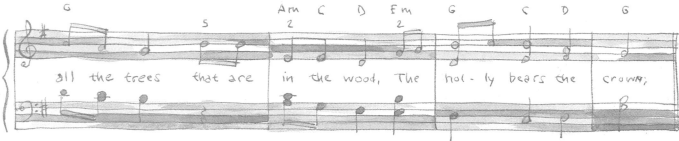

all the trees that are in the wood, The hol-ly bears the crown;

Chorus

The ris-ing of the sun, And the run-ning of the deer, The

play-ing of the mer-ry or-gan, sing-ing

THE MANY COLORS OF CHRISTMAS

Think of Christmas and you think of color: the bright red, green, yellow and blue lights that sparkle through the winter darkness; the silver and gold tinsel decorations of department stores and city streets; the gaily wrapped bundles under the tree. This year, try a Christmas of a different color—a room bedecked with lavender ribbons, lacy Victorian postcard ornaments and crystal chandelier drops. Those who fancy tartan will love our rhapsody of red and green plaid ornaments for the tree. If Christmas means elegance and sparkle to you, we bring you a room full of all that glitters. Or create a wonderland of winter white for your home. Tips on lighting inside and out, on canning homemade goodies, and two taste-tempting morning feasts will help color this and every Christmas beautiful.

A TOUCH OF LAVENDER

Soft shades of lavender lend a Victorian air to this romantic setting.

LAVENDER-COVERED BASKETS

Easy: Achievable by anyone.

You can make these by the dozen to fill with dried flowers, everlastings, or fresh flowers in a small vial of water. Use the completed basket with flowers as part of a centerpiece, on the mantel or anywhere you want to add a floral touch.

Materials: Small 4- to 6-inch-wide tightly woven basket(s) with handles; 1 pint of lavender flat latex paint and 1-inch-wide paintbrush, or 1 can of lavender spray paint; craft glue; up to ½ cup of dried lavender blossoms per basket (available at herb shops); dried flowers, or a small glass vial and fresh flowers, for each basket *(optional)*; lavender tissue paper *(optional)*.

Directions:
1. Place the basket on newspaper. Cover the outside of the basket and the handle with one light coat of paint. Let the paint dry completely.
2. Gently remove the lavender

blossoms from their stems, if necessary. Spread glue over the painted surface and sprinkle the blossoms over the glued area to cover it. Let the glue dry.
3. If you wish, place dried flowers, or a glass vial with fresh flowers, inside the basket, supported by crumpled tissue paper.

LACY VICTORIAN POSTCARDS

Easy: Achievable by anyone.

Materials: Gold spray paint; 6- or 8-inch-diameter paper doilies; Victorian-style postcards; craft glue; 1-inch-wide lavender ribbon; wire ornament hooks.

Directions:
1. Spread the doilies on newspaper and spray them with the gold paint. Let the paint dry.
2. Center a postcard on each dried doily and glue it in place.
3. Tie bows with the ribbon and glue one bow to the top of each doily, above the postcard. Use an ornament wire hook inserted into the top of the doily behind the knot of the bow as a hanger.

A tree bedecked with lavender ribbons, chandelier crystals, lavender-colored balls, and dried flowers.

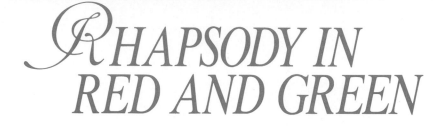

RHAPSODY IN RED AND GREEN

Traditional tartan adds cheery warmth to your celebration.

PLAID RIBBON ORNAMENTS

Easy: Achievable by anyone.

Materials: 2½-inch-diameter red and green glass balls; 3-inch-diameter Styrofoam® balls; ⅞-inch- and 2-inch-wide red-and-green plaid ribbons in various patterns; super-tacky glue; stiff-bristle brush; tracing paper; thin tie wire; hairpins; green floral tape; wire cutter; No. 10 jingle bells; stem wire.

Directions:

1. Wrapped Glass Ball, Version I: Cut two lengths of the ⅞-inch-wide ribbon that measure from the neck of a glass ball around and back to the neck. Glue the first ribbon in place, using the brush to smooth down the ribbon. Glue the second ribbon in place, crossing the first ribbon at a right angle at the bottom of the ball. Add two bows and a bell on one side of the neck, and repeat on the opposite side.

2. Version II: Glue ⅞-inch-wide ribbon around the center of a ball. Glue a bow to the ribbon

FIG. IV, 1 PLAID NOSEGAY ORNAMENT   ACTUAL SIZE

PETAL AND LEAF PATTERN

and a bell to the knot of the bow; repeat on the other side.

3. Plaid Flower Nosegay: Trace the actual-size patterns for the petal and leaf *(see* FIG. IV, 1*).* Using the 2-inch-wide ribbon throughout, cut a 4-inch-length for a center bud. Fold the piece in half lengthwise, fold both ends downward toward the center, then fold again and twist the bottom edge to hold the bud shape. Insert a hairpin and wrap it at the bottom with tie wire. Cut petals and leaves from ribbon. Add five petals around the bud, one at a time, securing each with tie wire. For some flowers, substitute three jingle bells, wired together to a hairpin, in place of a bud. Wrap the hairpin stem with floral tape. Wire together five flowers to form a nosegay. Add a leaf or two to each nosegay, taping each leaf to a separate stem.

4. Patchwork Plaid Ball: Cut 2-inch-wide ribbon into 1-inch lengths. Glue the pieces onto Styrofoam® balls, overlapping the edges, to cover the balls. Add a ribbon loop and jingle bells at the top of each ball, and a bow to the top of each loop.

160

SHAKER BOX TRIO

Easy: Achievable by anyone.

Materials: 3 miniature wooden Shaker boxes in decreasing sizes; green, red and white acrylic or poster paints; small paint brush; white glue; narrow red ribbon; gold metallic thread; small red wooden heart.

Directions:

1. Paint one Shaker box green, one red and one white. Let the paint dry completely.

2. Glue the boxes together in increasing order of size, from the smallest to the largest.

3. Wrap the ribbon around and over the stack of boxes, allowing the ribbon ends to extend a bit. Glue the ribbon to the top box. Measure a 3-inch length of gold thread and make it into a loop. Glue the heart over the glued ribbon at the top of the stack, catching part of the thread loop to make a hanger.

A tartan tree with Plaid Ribbon Ornaments (directions, page 160)

ALL THAT GLITTERS

*Capture the sparkle of the season
with ornaments of silver and gold.*

ALL THAT GLITTERS ORNAMENTS

Easy: Achievable by anyone.

Materials: Styrofoam® ornaments: 3-inch-diameter balls, 4-inch-diameter wreaths and 3½ x 3½-inch hearts; 2½-inch-diameter glass balls in silver and gold; 2½-inch-diameter sequins by-the-yard in gold and silver; rhinestone "diamonds" (loose); bugle beads by-the-yard in white and gold; 1-inch-long embossed metal leaves in gold and silver; gold and silver ribbon; straight pins; super-tacky glue; china marker; gold cord.

Directions:

1. Sequin- or Bugle Bead-Covered Shapes: Always make sure the sequins overlap each other in the same direction on their thread and that the bugle beads are not twisted. Cover the Styrofoam® shapes with glue, then apply the sequins, securing the first one with a straight pin.

Start at the bottom of the balls and at the center of the hearts. As you wind the sequins in place over the glue, be sure to overlap the edges of each previous row. Secure each end with another pin. Glue the bugle bead rows touching side by side, alternating the white and the gold. Pin a loop of gold cord at the top of each ornament for a hanger.

2. Wreaths: Cover the Styrofoam® shapes with glue. Wrap the wreaths with the silver or gold ribbon. Overwrap the ribbon with the sequins, spaced ¼ inch apart. On each front side, glue overlapping metal leaves at the stem end only, so the tips are free for a three-dimensional look. Pin a cord loop at the top of each ornament for a hanger.

3. Glass Ball Ornaments: Draw the desired motifs (leaves, spirals, and so on) with the china marker on each glass ball. When satisfied with your design, cover the design with glue. Gently press sequins, bugle beads and rhinestone "diamonds" into the glue as desired.

All That Glitters Ornaments (directions, page 162)

WINTER WHITE

Create a dream of a white Christmas with these snowy decorations.

THE 12 DAYS OF CHRISTMAS PAPERCUT

Average: For those with some experience in paper cutting or crafting.

Materials: 10 strips of lightweight white paper cut 5 inches wide and at least 36 inches long (shelf paper, craft paper or wrapping paper will work well); 5 x 18 inches of gold foil wrapping paper *(optional)*; tracing paper; pair of small scissors with pointed ends to cut small areas; pair of larger scissors; paper punch; pencil; heavy books or weight; ruler.

General Directions:
1. Making the "Blocks": First measure and carefully cut all the paper strips. Then measure and lightly draw a pencil line every three inches on each strip. Each of the rectangles formed is called a "block." The blocks will help you measure and fold the paper correctly for each pattern.
2. Transferring the Patterns: First, look at the patterns on

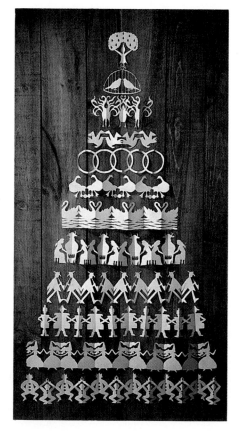

pages 166-167, Fig. IV, 2. Place a sheet of paper over a pattern; if you can't see through the paper well enough to trace the pattern, transfer it in the following way: Place the tracing paper over the pattern and carefully trace the outlines. Turn over the tracing paper and lightly cover the reverse side with the flat lead of the pencil. Place the tracing paper on top of the block, and carefully follow the tracing with the pencil, pressing down firmly. Lift the tracing paper; the pattern will be left on the block.
A Partridge in a Pear Tree:
Cut a strip two blocks long. Place one of the blocks over the pear tree pattern, with the tree trunk on the penciled-in fold line. Carefully trace the pattern. With the pattern on the block, fold the strip on the pencil line. The pattern has only half the picture you want to cut. By folding and cutting very carefully through both layers of paper, you'll create the whole picture. Cutting curves and corners is easier if you turn the paper toward the scissors instead of twisting your hand around the

A WINTER WONDERLAND TABLE SETTING

Make your Christmas Eve or Christmas dinner a snow queen's dream: Cover your table with an elegant brocade tablecloth (ours is cream with a gold paisley design). Then attach gold garland in graceful loops to the edge of the table. Set the table with white china and gold cutlery, and place small gold vases filled with white flowers at each setting. For the table centerpiece, trim a small white tree with framed photographs, locket-type ornaments, gold balls and ropes of imitation pearls. Make the meal a celebration of family and friends by decorating the table with personalized photo place cards. Use old photos (baby pictures are wonderful) or take Polaroids of your guests as they arrive, and slide the photos into ribbon-wrapped frames. These take-home treasures will add a special touch to any gathering.

FIG. IV, 2   THE 12 DAYS OF CHRISTMAS PAPERCUT - INCREASE ALL PATTERNS TO 3-INCH-WIDTH

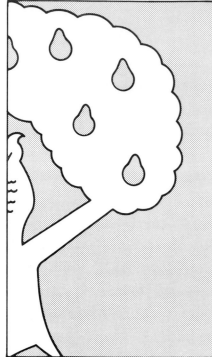

A PARTRIDGE IN A PEAR TREE

TWO TURTLE DOVES

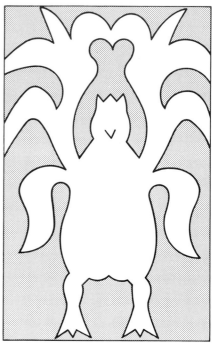

THREE FRENCH HENS

SEVEN SWANS A'SWIMMING

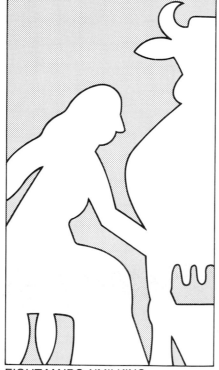

EIGHT MAIDS A'MILKING

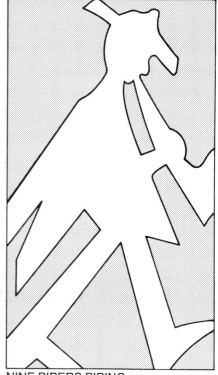

NINE PIPERS PIPING

FOUR CALLING BIRDS

FIVE GOLDEN RINGS

SIX GEESE A'LAYING

TEN DRUMMERS DRUMMING

ELEVEN LADIES DANCING

TWELVE LORDS A'LEAPING

paper to cut it. The pears on the pear tree are easy to make by using the paper punch. Punch out the holes and clip them into pear shapes using the tips of the small scissors.

Two Turtle Doves:

These kissing birds symbolize romantic love. Cut two blocks and transfer the pattern, placing the dove facing the pencil line. Fold the strip in half on the pencil line. Be very careful not to cut through the delicate cage. It will help to color lightly the part of the pattern you want to cut out. Use the paper punch to help get the scissors started in the small areas.

Three French Hens:

Cut three blocks and transfer the pattern to one of the end blocks. Accordion-fold the strip of paper, making sure you fold exactly on the lines. Cut around the pattern outline. Also cut through the lines on the hens' heads. When you open the cutting, lift the triangles formed by those lines and make the hens' beaks and combs. The three hens are exactly alike.

Four Calling Birds:

In the old English carol, the fourth day brought "colly birds," better known as blackbirds. Cut four blocks, transfer the pattern to an end block and accordion-fold the strip. Cut around the pattern outline, being very careful on the beaks. Unfold the strip and ruffle the feathers on the wings.

Five Golden Rings:

If you wish, use gold foil wrapping paper for this pattern. Cut a 5 x 18-inch strip of paper and mark it into 3-inch blocks on the reverse side. When a pattern contains the whole figure, you cut the same number of blocks as you need figures. When a pattern contains half figures, you need an extra block on the end. This strip will have six blocks instead of five. Transfer the pattern to the end block, on the reverse side. You can't trace through gold paper, so you'll have to use the alternate method *(see General Directions, Step 2).* Accordion-fold the paper with the gold side in. Cut around the pattern outline, being careful not to cut through the edges. Use the paper punch to open the center for cutting. Unfold the strip. There will be five locking rings and a half ring on each end. Carefully cut off each extra half ring.

Six Geese A'Laying:

Cut six blocks, transfer the pattern, accordion-fold very carefully and cut. The feet and the eggs are delicate.

Seven Swans A'Swimming:

Cut seven blocks, transfer the pattern, accordion-fold and cut. Be careful not to cut the waves in the water all the way through.

Eight Maids A'Milking:

Cut a strip ten blocks long, and transfer the pattern to an end block. The pattern has a whole maid, but only half a cow and pail. Accordion-fold and cut. Take your time; this is the hardest cut so far. Try not to let any of the paper layers slip out of line. Carefully open the cutting. Each cow has two maids milking her, and each maid is back-to-back with another. There will be maid with half a cow on each end. Cut off the extra ends. Flatten the strip under a weight.

Nine Pipers Piping:

This pattern is easier to cut than the maids and cows. Cut nine blocks, transfer the pattern, accordion-fold and cut. Take extra care to hold the paper layers together on this pattern. Narrow parts, such as the arms, legs and pipes, easily slip out of line.

Ten Drummers Drumming:

With so many drummers, we need some variety. So we'll alternate fat drummers with skinny drummers. Cut eleven blocks. Transfer the pattern. Take extra care in folding; it's harder to keep the paper straight as the number of folds increases. Cut around the pattern outline. The paper punch will help cut out the spaces between the arms and bodies.

Eleven Ladies Dancing:

The ladies dance together. Cut eleven blocks, transfer the pattern, accordion-fold and cut. The arms and veils are delicate, so take care in cutting and unfolding. Flatten the finished strip under a weight.

Twelve Lords A'Leaping:

This papercut shows action: as one lord leaps, another lands. Cut thirteen blocks, transfer the pattern, accordion-fold and cut. You can try to use the paper punch for the tight spaces, but the paper may be too thick.

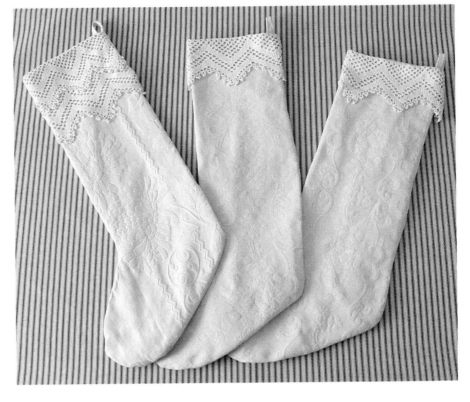

SNOW & LACE STOCKINGS

Average: For those with some experience in sewing.

Materials for One Stocking:
½ yard of white or off-white velvet, brocade, Marseilles spread, silk, old quilt top or fabric of your choice; ½ yard of unbleached muslin; 15 inches of lace trim of desired width.

Directions (½-inch seams allowed):

1. Enlarge the stocking pattern in Fig. IV, 3, following the directions on page 271. Cut out a full-size paper pattern for the stocking front and back.

2. Using the pattern, cut out two stockings each of the fabric and the muslin (flop the pattern to make a front and a back).

3. With right sides together, pin the fabric pieces and stitch around the sides and bottom, but not across the top. Trim the seam, clip the curves, turn the stocking right side out and press it. If using velvet, press on the wrong side of the fabric before turning the stocking. Then, with a cloth between the iron and the velvet, gently press around the edges of the turned stocking. Repeat with the muslin lining pieces, leaving a 3-inch opening in the toe seam. Trim the seam, clip the curves, but do not turn the muslin lining right side out.

4. Slide the fabric stocking inside the muslin lining so the right sides are together and the seams match. Stitch around the top, placing a fabric or ribbon loop for a hanger between the stocking and the liner so that it is attached in the rear seam. Turn the stocking right side out through the opening in the toe seam of the lining. Slipstitch the opening closed.

5. Position the muslin lining inside the stocking and press it. Pin the lace to the right side of the stocking, with the edge over and just inside the stocking, and slipstitch it in place.

FIG. IV, 3 SNOW & LACE STOCKINGS

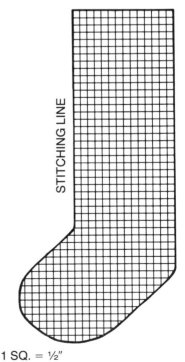

STITCHING LINE

1 SQ. = ½"

A LIGHT IN THE WINDOW

Easy: Achievable by anyone.

Materials: Strings of clear, white miniature lights; strings of amber-colored miniature lights; battery-operated candle lights; artificial doves; tie wire.

Directions:

1. Frame each window with the clear, white miniature lights. Place one battery-operated candle light in the center of each light-framed window.

2. Decorate indoor house plants with amber-colored miniature lights and the artificial doves.

Holiday Notes

A PERFECT MATCH!

Candles and candlesticks seldom match perfectly. Try putting a strip of self-stick foam weatherstripping tape around the base of each candle. The foam will adjust easily to the candlestick opening and keep the candle in place. Plus the foam won't show above the holder.

Did You Know . . .

Candles have been used for centuries in winter celebrations. During the Saturnalia, the festival of the winter solstice, the Romans fastened candles to trees as a symbol of the sun's return to the earth. Hanukkah, the Jewish "Festival of Lights" commemorating the rededication of the Temple by Judas Maccabeus in 165 B.C., is celebrated by lighting one candle on the first night and adding a lit candle each night for eight nights. Early Christians adopted candles for their Christmas feast as symbols of Christ, "The Light of the World." Durandas, a writer of that period, wrote that the wax represented Christ's body, the wick, his soul and the flame, his divine nature. In many cultures, tradition has been to place a candle in each window to guide the Christ Child, or weary travelers, to warmth, light and shelter.

Holiday Notes

VISIONS OF DE-LIGHT

Twinkling lights reaching out through the winter darkness is one of the loveliest sights of the season. Outdoor lighting is easy to vary, so you can use a different color scheme each year. Red and green are traditional, white or gold are elegant and striking, multi-colors give your home a bright, cheery look. Don't limit yourself to illuminating the rim of the roof—use the architecture of your home to its best advantage. If you're lucky enough to have bay windows, line the edges of the windows; if your front porch is particularly inviting, play up the area with strategically placed lights. Trees, shrubs, arches, columns, fences: let your imagination run wild.

• For a dramatic look to your outside lighting display, try floodlighting evergreens. Use blue, green, clear and deluxe white mercury lamps—these colors enhance the colors of evergreens. Avoid red, yellow, amber and pink lamps, which turn the trees a muddy brown color.

• Illuminate deciduous trees as well as evergreens. Flood a tree with a single spotlight to highlight its shape and pattern. Or place shiny ornaments on the tree and light it from below with several smaller spots.

• Get more sparkle and glitter by using transparent bulbs. These, unlike color-coated bulbs, allow the filament to show through.

• Wait until it's dark to set up your display, so you will be able to see the effects of your illumination; you can't get a true picture in daylight. Just be extra careful when using a ladder at night; have a helper steady the ladder while you work.

• Every year, before setting up your illumination display, check the light sets for cracked insulation, frayed wires or damaged sockets. Any one of these could cause a short circuit.

• Don't overload string sets. Check the instructions on each package to find out how many light sets can be connected to each other.

• Avoid overloading circuits. Most home circuits can take 15 amps, or 1,800 watts.

• Cover each outdoor plug and connector joint with plastic wrap to protect it from rain, sleet and snow; seal the wrapped joint with electrical tape.

• If you use staples instead of tape to secure lights, be sure that they're *insulated* staples.

• Make sure that your decorations pose no danger to children or pets: Don't leave cords dangling, loose on the floor or on the stairs.

Note: If you have questions about using decorative lights outdoors, call The GE Answer Center® information service 24 hours a day: 1-800-626-2000.

White Grape Juice Sparklers (recipe, page 175); Winter Fruit Compote (recipe, page 175);
Eggs Florentine in Tomato Cups (recipe, page 176); Spicy Ham Patties (recipe, page 177);
Banana Bran Muffins (recipe, page 178); Almond Coffee Cake (recipe, page 178)

COLORFUL CHRISTMAS BREAKFAST

(for 6 to 8)

White Grape Juice Sparklers
Winter Fruit Compote
Hearty Christmas Casserole
Eggs Florentine in Tomato Cups
Spicy Ham Patties
Bagels, Lemon Marmalade Muffins
Almond Coffee Cake, Banana Bran Muffins
Mixed Fruit Jam, Candied Fruit Scones
Spiced Apple Butter
Orange Currant Scones with Orange Butter
Raspberry Crumble
Coffee, Tea, Hot Cocoa

WORK PLAN FOR COLORFUL CHRISTMAS BREAKFAST

Up to Six Months Ahead:
- Prepare the Mixed Fruit Jam and the Spiced Apple Butter.

Up to One Month Ahead:
- Prepare and freeze the Lemon Marmalade Muffins, Almond Coffee Cake, Banana Bran Muffins, Orange Currant Scones, Orange Butter and Candied Fruit Scones.

Up to Several Days Ahead:
- Prepare and chill the Winter Fruit Compote, omitting the ginger.
- Prepare extra ice cubes for the White Grape Juice Sparklers.

The Day Before:
- Assemble and refrigerate the Hearty Christmas Casserole.
- Mix, shape and refrigerate the Spicy Ham Patties.
- Assemble and refrigerate the Eggs Florentine in Tomato Cups.
- Prepare the topping for the Raspberry Crumble.
- Unmold the ice cubes, place in plastic bags and return to the freezer.
- Prepare the dry ingredients for the Lemon Marmalade Muffins, Almond Coffee Cake, Banana Bran Muffins, Orange Currant Scones and Candied Fruit Scones, if they were not prepared ahead and frozen.

Early in the Day:
- Prepare the muffins, coffee cake and scones, if they were not prepared ahead and frozen; thaw them, if frozen.
- Prepare and refrigerate the Orange Butter, if it was not prepared ahead and frozen; thaw it, if frozen.

One Hour Before:
- Bake the Hearty Christmas Casserole.
- Bake the Eggs Florentine in Tomato Cups.
- Cut up the bagels.

30 Minutes Before:
- Cook the Spicy Ham Patties.
- Prepare the Raspberry Crumble.
- Reheat the muffins and scones.
- Slowly reheat the Winter Fruit Compote, adding the ginger now.

Just Before Breakfast:
- Sauté the spinach for the Eggs Florentine in Tomato Cups.
- Prepare the White Grape Juice Sparklers.

WHITE GRAPE JUICE SPARKLERS

Garnish each glass with a lemon wedge, or with grapes and kumquats threaded on skewers.

Makes 6 servings.

> *3   cups white grape juice*
> *3   cups club soda*

Combine the grape juice with the club soda in a large bowl. Fill six glasses with ice and divide the sparkling grape juice between them. Garnish each glass as you wish.

WINTER FRUIT COMPOTE

You can make this compote several days ahead. Add the ginger and reheat the compote just before serving.

Makes 6 servings.

> *1½   cups apple juice*
> *¼   cup pitted prunes*
> *½   cup dried pears*
> *¾   cup dried apricots*
> *½   cup golden raisins*
> *¾   cup brandy*
> *3   thin lemon slices*
> *2   Granny Smith or other tart apples,*
> *   unpeeled, cored and sliced*
> *2   pears, unpeeled, cored and cut into wedges*
> *2   teaspoons grated fresh gingerroot*

1. Mix together the apple juice, prunes, dried pears, apricots and raisins in a medium-size saucepan. Bring the mixture to boiling over medium heat.
2. Stir in the brandy and the lemon slices. Lower the heat and simmer the mixture for 15 minutes.
3. Add the apple and pear slices. Simmer for 5 minutes more, or until the fresh fruit is soft but still retains its shape.
4. Remove the lemon slices and stir in the ginger. Serve the compote warm.

RISE . . . AND SHINE!

There's so much to do on Christmas morning, especially if you have little ones in the house. Here are a few tips to help you face the morning with a smile:

• Do as much chopping, assembling and baking ahead of time as possible.
• Try to use cooking dishes that are attractive enough to go directly from the oven to the table.
• Make waffles or muffins ahead of time and freeze them, then just pop them into the microwave to warm.
• If you're planning to bake on Christmas morning, measure and mix the dry ingredients and the wet ingredients the day before, and store them separately, to reduce preparation time the next day.
• Be sure to set your breakfast table on Christmas Eve, and enjoy the feast!

Did You Know . . .

The bright red and green of the poinsettia have made it a cherished part of Christmas celebrations. This native of the American continent was discovered in Mexico in 1828 by Dr. Joel Roberts Poinsett. The Mexicans refer to the colorful plant as the "Flor de la Noche Buena," the Holy Night Flower. One legend about the poinsettia tells of a Christmas Eve long ago when the villagers of a Mexican town were laying gifts to the Holy Family before a crèche. A poor young boy, having nothing to offer, could only kneel in prayer outside the church. In the spot where he knelt, a beautiful plant with scarlet leaves sprang up, and the boy gave this as his gift to the Christ Child.

HEARTY CHRISTMAS CASSEROLE

This hearty Southwestern-style casserole can be made ahead of time, refrigerated and baked just before serving.

Bake at 325° for 35 to 45 minutes.
Makes 6 servings.

1 medium-size yellow onion, chopped
2 teaspoons safflower oil
1 tablespoon ground cumin
1 can (15 ounces) black beans, rinsed and drained
5 large eggs, beaten
2 cups canned low-sodium, cream-style corn (17 ounces)
1 cup lowfat milk
¾ cup shredded Monterey Jack cheese (about 2 ounces)
1 tablespoon Dijon-style mustard
   Pinch of ground hot red pepper
2 medium-size tomatoes, sliced
1 tablespoon chopped fresh cilantro
   OR: fresh parsley

1. Preheat the oven to slow (325°). Lightly grease a 9 x 11-inch baking dish.
2. Sauté the onion in the oil until the onion is translucent, for about 5 minutes. Add the cumin and cook for 2 minutes. Add the black beans, mix well and pour the mixture into the prepared baking dish.
3. Combine the eggs, corn, milk, Monterey Jack cheese, mustard and ground hot red pepper in a large bowl. Pour the egg mixture over the black bean mixture and top with the tomato slices.
4. Bake in the preheated slow oven (325°) for 35 to 45 minutes, or until the casserole is firm. Sprinkle the top of the casserole with the cilantro or parsley.

EGGS FLORENTINE IN TOMATO CUPS

This savory combination of sausage, spinach, eggs and cheese is made extra special by being served in scooped-out tomatoes.

Bake at 325° for 35 to 40 minutes.
Makes 6 servings.

½ pound turkey sausage (seasoned ground turkey without casings)
6 medium-size firm ripe tomatoes
6 small eggs
¾ cup grated low-sodium Swiss cheese (about 2 ounces)
1 teaspoon olive oil
2 cloves garlic, crushed
2 pounds fresh spinach, well-washed and drained

1. Preheat the oven to slow (325°).
2. Cook the sausage in a small skillet over medium-high heat just until it loses its pink color, for about 2 minutes. Drain off and discard the fat and liquid.
3. Core the tomatoes and remove the pulp. Spoon equal amounts of the sausage into the tomato shells. Crack an egg into each tomato cup. Top each egg with some of the Swiss cheese.
4. Bake the cups in the preheated slow oven (325°) for 35 to 40 minutes, or until the eggs are cooked and the tomatoes are tender. (Or prick the egg yolks and microwave the cups on full power for about 6 minutes.)
5. While the tomatoes bake, heat the oil in a very large skillet. Sauté the garlic in the oil. Working in batches, add the spinach to the skillet and sauté just until the spinach is wilted. Serve the tomato cups on a bed of the sautéed spinach.

SURPRISE! SURPRISE!

A surprise filling in muffins always is a treat. Besides the lemon marmalade suggested in our Lemon Marmalade Muffins, try using various other preserves and jams, a swirl of peanut butter, a chocolate kiss or chocolate morsels, or even half a strawberry. Always use about two thirds of the batter to top the filling in the muffin-pan cups.

SPICY HAM PATTIES

The patties can be mixed and shaped the day before. Turkey ham also can be used in this recipe.

Bake at 325° for 15 minutes.
Makes 6 servings.

2   cups cooked ham, cubed (10 ounces)
1   egg
2   tablespoons water
1   tablespoon coarse-grained mustard
¼   teaspoon ground hot red pepper
6   toast rounds
*   Chopped parsley, for garnish*

1. Preheat the oven to slow (325°).
2. Grind or finely chop the ham in a meat grinder or food processor. Mix the ham with the egg, water, mustard and ground hot red pepper until the ingredients are thoroughly combined.
3. Form the ham mixture into six 2-inch-thick patties. Place the patties on an ungreased baking sheet.
4. Bake in the preheated slow oven (325°) for 15 minutes, or until the patties are set and heated through. (Or pan-fry the patties in a teaspoon of butter or margarine in a nonstick frying pan.)
5. Place the patties, bottom side up, on top of the toast rounds. Garnish with parsley.

LEMON MARMALADE MUFFINS

Each muffin has a sweet surprise hidden inside.

Bake at 375° for 25 to 30 minutes.
Makes 12 muffins.

2   cups all-purpose flour
¼   cup sugar
1   tablespoon baking powder
1   large egg
1   cup lowfat buttermilk OR: lemon yogurt
¼   cup butter (½ stick), melted
1   teaspoon vanilla
¼   cup lemon marmalade

1. Preheat the oven to moderate (375°). Place paper or aluminum foil liners in 12 muffin-pan cups.
2. Sift together the flour, sugar and baking powder into a medium-size bowl.
3. In another bowl, mix together the egg, buttermilk or lemon yogurt, butter and vanilla. Pour the wet ingredients over the dry ingredients and fold just until the dry ingredients are moistened.
4. Fill the muffin-pan cups one third full. With the back of a spoon, form a well in the batter in each cup. Spoon 1 teaspoon of the marmalade into each well. Top the marmalade with the remaining batter.
5. Bake in the preheated moderate oven (375°) for 25 to 30 minutes, or until the muffins are golden brown. Serve warm.

◀◀ ALMOND COFFEE CAKE

This cake is made in minutes in the microwave. To reheat frozen cake, place one slice at a time on a plate in the microwave and reheat at half power for 3 to 3½ minutes.

Microwave at full power for 8 to 10 minutes.
Makes one 8-inch cake (8 servings).

Almond Filling and Topping:
- ¼ cup sugar
- ¼ cup sliced almonds
- 2 tablespoons unbleached all-purpose flour
- 1 teaspoon grated lemon zest (yellow part of rind only)

Cake Batter:
- 1 cup whole wheat flour
- ½ teaspoon baking powder
- ½ teaspoon baking soda
- ½ teaspoon ground allspice
- ½ teaspoon ground cinnamon
- ½ teaspoon ground nutmeg
- ¼ cup (½ stick) unsalted butter, softened
- ½ cup granulated sugar
- 1 egg
- ¾ cup plain nonfat yogurt
  10X (confectioners' powdered) sugar, for garnish

1. Grease an 8 x 8 x 2-inch microwave-safe baking dish.
2. Prepare the Almond Filling and Topping: Combine the sugar, almonds, flour and lemon zest in a small bowl. Mix the ingredients well.
3. Prepare the Cake Batter: Sift together the flour, baking powder, baking soda, allspice, cinnamon and nutmeg; set aside.
4. Beat together the butter, granulated sugar and egg in a medium-size bowl with an electric mixer at medium speed. Lower the mixer speed. Alternately add the dry ingredients and the yogurt to the butter mixture, beating until the ingredients are well mixed.
5. Spread half the batter in the prepared baking dish. Sprinkle with half the almond mixture. Top with the remaining batter and almond mixture.

6. Microwave, uncovered, at full power for 8 to 10 minutes, or until the top springs back when lightly pressed with your fingertip. Remove the cake from the pan and garnish it with a dusting of the 10X (confectioners' powdered) sugar.

💲⚡ BANANA BRAN MUFFINS

Wake up your family on Christmas morning with the wonderful aroma of warm muffins.

Bake at 375° for 20 to 25 minutes.
Makes 12 muffins.

- 1 large egg
- ¾ cup firmly packed light brown sugar
- 1 cup mashed bananas
- ½ cup golden raisins (optional)
- ⅓ cup safflower oil
- 1 teaspoon vanilla
- ¾ cup all-purpose flour
- ¾ cup whole wheat flour
- ½ cup oat bran
- 2 teaspoons baking powder
- ½ teaspoon baking soda
- ½ teaspoon ground allspice

1. Preheat the oven to moderate (375°). Place paper or aluminum foil liners in 12 muffin-pan cups.
2. Beat together the egg and the brown sugar in a small bowl until the mixture is smooth. Add the bananas, raisins if you wish, oil and vanilla.
3. Combine the all-purpose and whole-wheat flours, the bran, baking powder, baking soda and allspice in a large bowl. Add the banana mixture and stir just until the dry ingredients are moistened. Spoon the batter into the prepared muffin-pan cups.
4. Bake in the preheated moderate oven (375°) for 20 to 25 minutes, or until a wooden pick inserted in the center of a muffin comes out clean. Serve warm.

$ ⑆ MIXED FRUIT JAM

Makes six ½-pint jars.

1   stick cinnamon
10   whole cloves
2   navel oranges
1   cup water
3   tablespoons finely chopped peeled fresh
         gingerroot
1   package (12 ounces) cranberries, picked
         over and rinsed
1   can (8 ounces) crushed pineapple in its
         own juice, well-drained
1   package (1¾ ounces) powdered pectin
4   cups sugar

MUFFINS — EASY AS 1, 2, 3!

The perfect muffin has straight sides, a rounded top and a uniform grain texture. To insure tender, moist muffins, just follow these three mixing tips:
1. Add the wet ingredients to the dry ingredients with a few, quick strokes to just moisten the dry ingredients.
2. The mixed batter should be lumpy; if it pours smoothly from the spoon, you are guilty of overbeating.
3. You can recognize overbeaten muffins by the coarse texture and the tunneling throughout the muffin.

1. Tie together the cinnamon stick and the cloves in a small square of cheesecloth and set aside.
2. Remove the peel and the white pith from the oranges. Cut the peel into thin slivers.
3. Combine the spice bag, orange peel, water and ginger in a large saucepan or Dutch oven. Bring the mixture to boiling over high heat. Reduce the heat to low, cover and simmer for 20 minutes, or until the orange peel is tender.
4. Meanwhile, remove and discard any remaining white pith from the whole oranges. Section the oranges and coarsely chop the sections.
5. Add the chopped oranges, the cranberries and pineapple to the saucepan. Bring the mixture to boiling over high heat. Reduce the heat to low and simmer for 10 minutes, stirring the mixture occasionally.
6. Stir in the pectin. Return the mixture to boiling over medium-high heat. Add the sugar to the fruit mixture and return to a full rolling boil for 1 minute, stirring constantly.
7. Remove the saucepan from the heat. Skim off the foam and remove the spice bag. Let the jam stand for 15 minutes, stirring occasionally.
8. Spoon the jam into hot, sterilized, ½-pint jars to within ½ inch of the rim. Place hot, sterilized lids on the jars and screw on the rings. Process the jars in a hot water bath for 10 minutes, following the general directions on page 181. Cool the jars on a wire rack and test the seals. Store the labeled, dated jars in a cool, dark, dry place for up to 6 months.

CANDIED FRUIT SCONES

The secret to making light, luscious scones is not to overwork the dough. Bake these delicacies ahead of time and reheat them just before serving.

Bake at 400° for 15 to 18 minutes.
Makes 16 scones.

2 cups unsifted all-purpose flour
2 teaspoons baking powder
¼ teaspoon baking soda
2 tablespoons sugar
6 tablespoons butter or margarine
3 tablespoons chopped candied fruit
2 eggs, slightly beaten
6 tablespoons plain yogurt
 Milk
 Sugar (optional)

1. Preheat the oven to hot (400°).
2. Sift together the flour, baking powder, baking soda and sugar into a large bowl.
3. Cut in the butter or margarine with a pastry blender until the mixture resembles coarse cornmeal. Mix the candied fruit into the flour mixture.
4. Combine the eggs with the yogurt in a small bowl. Add the egg mixture all at once to the flour mixture. Stir with a fork just until a soft dough forms. Turn out the dough onto a lightly floured surface and knead it lightly.
5. Divide the dough into quarters. Flatten each quarter with your hand to a 4-inch-diameter round, about ½ inch thick. Place the rounds 2 inches apart on an ungreased baking sheet. With a floured knife, score each round into quarters about ¼ inch deep. Brush the rounds with the milk and, if you wish, sprinkle them with sugar.
6. Bake in the preheated hot oven (400°) for 15 to 18 minutes, or until the scones are puffed and golden. Transfer the scones to a wire rack to cool. To serve, separate each scone round into 4 wedges. Serve the scones warm.

BETTER THAN BUTTER

Fruit butters have no real butter in them. Rather, they're fruits that have been simmered slowly to a thick, butter-like consistency. Fruit butters are ideal on toast, muffins or bagels, and also are delicious as a glaze, spread on top of roasting ham (add them during the last 20 minutes or so of roasting time to avoid burning).

SPICED APPLE BUTTER

Serve this spicy-good spread on biscuits, toast, pancakes or waffles.

Makes five ½-pint jars.

4½ pounds cooking apples (about 7 to 9 apples), such as Granny Smith, cored and coarsely chopped
1½ cups apple juice
6 tablespoons firmly packed dark brown sugar
6 tablespoons dark molasses
2¼ teaspoons ground cinnamon
¾ teaspoon ground nutmeg
½ teaspoon ground cloves
½ teaspoon ground allspice
¼ teaspoon ground ginger
¾ cup golden raisins
½ teaspoon grated lemon zest (yellow part of rind only)

1. Combine the apples with the apple juice in a large, nonaluminum saucepan or Dutch oven. Bring the mixture to a gentle boil and cook, stirring frequently, for 15 to 20 minutes, or until the apples are tender.
2. Purée half the apples in the container of an electric blender or a food processor.

Return the apple purée to the saucepan. Repeat with the remaining apples.

3. Stir in the brown sugar, molasses, cinnamon, nutmeg, cloves, allspice and ginger. Bring the mixture to boiling and reduce the heat to low. Simmer, uncovered, stirring frequently to prevent sticking, for 1 to 1½ hours, or until the mixture is quite thick. Stir in the raisins and the lemon zest.

4. Spoon the apple butter into hot, sterilized, ½-pint jars to within ½ inch of the rim. Place hot, sterilized lids on the jars and screw on the rings. Process the jars in a hot water bath for 5 minutes, following the general directions below. Cool the jars on a wire rack and test the seals. Store the labeled, dated jars in a cool, dark, dry place for up to 6 months.

GENERAL DIRECTIONS FOR CANNING AND HOT WATER BATH PROCESS

Follow all the directions carefully and do not take any shortcuts.

1. Place the hot water bath canner on a surface burner. Add water to half-fill the canner (a tea kettle does this job easily), cover the canner and bring the water to a rapid boil while preparing the jars and food.

2. Wash the jars in hot sudsy water. Rinse them well and leave them in hot water until you are ready to use them.

3. Place new domed lids in a bowl and cover them with boiling water. Keep them in the water until you are ready to use them.

4. Follow individual recipe directions.

5. Remove the jars from the water, one at a time, and place them on paper toweling or a clean cloth. Pack and/or ladle the food into the jars, leaving the headroom specified in the individual recipe.

6. Wipe the tops and outside rims of the jars with a clean cloth. Place the domed lids on top and screw on the metal rings tightly, but do not use force.

7. Place the jars in the canner rack and lower the rack into the rapidly boiling water, adding additional boiling water to the canner if the water level is not 2 inches above Cover the canner and return the water to a full boil.

8. Process, following the time given in the individual recipe and calculating from the time the water comes to a second boil. *Note: For those who live at altitudes above sea level, when the recipe directions call for processing for 20 minutes or less, add 1 minute for each 1,000 feet; when processing for more than 20 minutes, add 2 minutes for each 1,000 feet.*

9. Remove the jars from the canner with tongs and place them, at least 3 inches apart, on a wire rack or cloth-lined surface until they are cool, for about 12 hours.

10. Test all the jars, to be sure they are sealed, by tapping them with a spoon. A clear ringing sound means a good seal. If a jar is not properly sealed, store it in the refrigerator and plan to use its contents within a month, or pour the contents of the jar into a bowl and process again from Step 5.

11. Remove the metal rings. Wipe the jars with a clean dampened cloth. Label, date and store the jars in a cool, dark, dry place.

ORANGE CURRANT SCONES WITH ORANGE BUTTER

Bake at 375° for 15 minutes.
Makes 22 scones.

2⅔ **cups whole wheat flour**
⅔ **cup unsifted all-purpose flour**
¼ **cup sugar**
2 **teaspoons baking soda**
2 **teaspoons cream of tartar**
½ **teaspoon salt**
½ **cup butter or margarine**
½ **cup currants**
3 **tablespoons grated orange zest (orange part of rind only)**
¾ **cup buttermilk**
⅓ **cup molasses**
1 **egg, slightly beaten**
    Orange Butter (recipe follows)

1. Preheat the oven to moderate (375°). Lightly grease 2 large baking sheets.
2. Combine the whole wheat and all-purpose flours with the sugar, baking soda, cream of tartar and salt in a large bowl. Stir to mix all the ingredients well.
3. Cut in the butter or margarine with a pastry blender until the mixture resembles coarse crumbs. Stir in the currants and the orange zest.
4. Add the buttermilk, molasses and egg. Stir the mixture lightly and quickly with a fork until a soft, puffy dough forms and all the dry ingredients are blended in.
5. Turn out the dough onto a lightly floured surface and shape it into a ball. Gently knead the dough a few times, then roll it out with a lightly floured rolling pin to a ¾-inch-thick circle. Cut the circle into diamond shapes using a 3½ x 2¼-inch diamond-shaped cookie cutter, dipping

the cutter in flour between cuts. Pinch the dough scraps together, re-roll and cut out more scones. Place the scones on the prepared baking sheets.

6. Bake in the preheated moderate oven (375°) for 15 minutes, or until the scones are lightly golden.
7. Meanwhile, prepare the Orange Butter.
8. Serve the scones warm or at room temperature, with the Orange Butter on the side.

Orange Butter: Combine ½ cup (1 stick) of unsalted butter or margarine, softened, with 1½ tablespoons of grated orange zest in a small bowl. Mix until the ingredients are thoroughly combined. Store the Orange Butter, covered, in the refrigerator.

Did You Know . . .

The glossy, dark green leaves and bright red berries of the holly tree have long been used in the celebration of Christmas. There are many legends associated with holly. One says that a holly tree was the "burning bush" from which Moses received God's message to become the leader of his people. In another legend, holly is a symbol of the Virgin Mary. Holly also is said to have sprung from the footprints of Christ when he walked the earth during his ministry. Yet a fourth legend says that Christ's crown of thorns was fashioned from holly leaves; at first its berries were white, but when the crown was pressed into Christ's forehead, the berries became red. Certainly, the evergreen holly tree has become a symbol of immortality, the promise of life everlasting.

RASPBERRY CRUMBLE

A Christmas morning delight that takes just minutes in the microwave.

Microwave at full power for 8 minutes.
Makes 6 servings.

- 3 cups fresh raspberries OR: 12 to 16 ounces frozen raspberries
- 2 tablespoons lemon juice
- ¼ cup firmly packed light brown sugar
- ½ cup whole wheat flour
- ⅔ cup quick-cooking oats
- ¼ cup slivered toasted almonds
- ¼ cup shredded coconut
- 1 teaspoon ground cinnamon
- ¼ cup (½ stick) unsalted butter, melted
  Vanilla lowfat yogurt, for serving

1. Spread the raspberries in an 8 x 8 x 2-inch microwave-safe baking dish. Sprinkle the raspberries with the lemon juice.
2. Toss together the brown sugar, flour, oats, almonds, coconut, cinnamon and butter in a small bowl. Sprinkle the mixture on top of the raspberries.
3. Microwave, uncovered, at full power for 8 minutes. Remove the baking dish from the microwave and let it stand on a heatproof surface for 10 minutes. Serve the crumble with the yogurt.

Red and Green Fruit Salad (recipe, page 187); Ham and Mushroom Puffs (recipe, page 188);
Hot Tomato Cocktail (recipe, page 186); Sesame Braid and Maple Nut Buns (recipe, page 187);
Irish Coffee Granita (recipe, page 189)

"HAPPY HOLIDAYS" BRUNCH

(for 6)

Hot Tomato Cocktail
Red and Green Fruit Salad
Sesame Braid and Maple Nut Buns
Ham and Mushroom Puffs
Irish Coffee Granita
Coffee, Tea, Hot Cocoa

WORK PLAN FOR HOLIDAY BRUNCH

Up to One Month Ahead:
- Prepare and freeze the Sesame Braid and the Maple Nut Buns.

Up to Several Days Ahead:
- Prepare the Irish Coffee Granita and the grated chocolate garnish; freeze them separately.

The Day Before:
- Prepare the puffs and filling for the Ham and Mushroom Puffs.
- Prepare the green onion curls for the Hot Tomato Cocktails; refrigerate them in a bowl of ice water.
- Prepare the dough for the Sesame Braid and Maple Nut Buns, if they were not prepared ahead and frozen; thaw them in the refrigerator, if frozen.
- Prepare and refrigerate the dressing for the Red and Green Fruit Salad.

In the Morning:
- Dress the Red and Green Fruit Salad.

- Chop the green onions for the Hot Tomato Cocktails.
- Bake the Sesame Braid and Maple Nut Buns, if they were not made ahead and frozen.
- Process the Irish Coffee Granita and return it to the freezer. Prepare and refrigerate the whipped cream garnish.

30 Minutes Before:
- Fill and reheat the Ham and Mushroom Puffs.
- Line a serving platter with the Red and Green Fruit Salad.
- Prepare the Hot Tomato Cocktails.
- Reheat the Sesame Braid and Maple Nut Buns, if they were made ahead and frozen.

Just Before Dessert:
- Beat the whipped cream, if it has separated; garnish the Irish Coffee Granita with the whipped cream and the grated chocolate.

HOT TOMATO COCKTAIL

Makes 6 servings.

>*6   small green onions*
>*2   cans (18 ounces each) tomato juice*
>*2   tablespoons lemon juice*
>*1   tablespoon Worcestershire sauce*
>*1   tablespoon chopped fresh dill*
>*   OR: ½ teaspoon dried dillweed, crumbled*
>*½   teaspoon leaf chervil, crumbled*

1. Slice a 1- to 2-inch piece from the bulb end of each green onion. Chop the slices and set them aside. To curl the green onions, make thin, lengthwise cuts through the tops of the green ends, leaving enough stalk uncut so that the onions don't separate.
2. Combine the tomato juice, lemon juice, Worcestershire sauce, dill, chervil and the chopped white portion of the green onion in a large saucepan. Bring the mixture to boiling over medium heat, stirring occasionally.
3. Pour the tomato mixture into the container of an electric blender or a food processor fitted with the metal blade. Blend until the mixture is smooth. Pour the tomato mixture into six glasses or mugs. Garnish the glasses with the onion curls.

💲 《《

RED AND GREEN FRUIT SALAD

Makes 6 servings.

3	large red apples
1	tablespoon lemon juice
1	pound red grapes
1	large red onion
2	bunches watercress, stems removed
2	tablespoons honey
⅔	cup lemon juice
¼	cup vegetable oil
½	teaspoon salt
⅛	teaspoon pepper
¼	cup finely chopped red onion

1. Wash, core and slice the apples. Toss the slices with the 1 tablespoon of lemon juice in a medium-size bowl. Divide the grapes into clusters. Peel the whole red onion and thinly slice it.
2. Arrange the watercress around the outer rim of a large serving platter or serving bowl. Arrange the apple slices, grapes and onion slices in the center of the platter. Set aside the platter.
3. Combine the honey, the ⅔ cup of lemon juice, the oil, salt, pepper and chopped red onion in a large, screw-top jar with a tightly-fitting lid. Shake the jar until the honey has dissolved completely. Spoon 3 tablespoons of the honey dressing over the apple and onion slices on the platter. Cover the platter tightly with plastic wrap. Refrigerate the salad and the dressing until ready to serve.

To Make Ahead: The dressing can be made a day ahead; the salad can be made several hours in advance.

《《

SESAME BRAID AND MAPLE NUT BUNS

Bake at 350° for 20 to 25 minutes.
Makes 1 bread loaf (12 servings) and 36 miniature sticky buns.

7	cups all-purpose flour
2	tablespoons granulated sugar
1	teaspoon salt
2	packages fast-rising dry yeast
2	cups hot water (125° to 130°)*
2	tablespoons butter, softened
½	cup honey
¼	cup maple syrup
3	tablespoons chopped candied ginger
½	cup currants
¾	cup chopped pecans
2	tablespoons poppy seeds
2	tablespoons sesame seeds
2	tablespoons wheat germ
1	egg white
1	teaspoon water
¾	teaspoon ground ginger
2	tablespoons light brown sugar

1. Reserve ½ cup of the flour. Combine the remaining flour with the granulated sugar, salt and yeast in a large bowl. Stir in the 2 cups of hot water and the butter. Beat the mixture until it is smooth. Gradually stir in enough of the reserved flour to make a soft dough.
2. Knead the dough on a floured surface until it is smooth and elastic, for about 3 to 5 minutes. Invert the bowl over the dough; let the dough rise for 15 minutes.
3. Grease and flour a 9-inch round layer cake pan. Combine the honey with the maple syrup. Pour the mixture into thirty-six 1-inch cupcake cups or a 13 x 9 x 2-inch baking pan. Combine the candied ginger, ¼ cup of the currants and ½ cup of the pecans. Sprinkle the pecan mixture equally over the maple syrup mixture in the cupcake cups or the pan.
4. Divide the dough in half. Set aside half the dough under the inverted bowl.

Divide the remaining dough into 3 equal pieces. Roll each piece into a 16-inch-long rope.

5. Cut 3 lengths of wax paper, each 18 inches long. Spread the poppy seeds on one, the sesame seeds on another and the wheat germ on the third. Beat together the egg white and the 1 teaspoon of water in a small bowl.

6. Brush one rope with the egg mixture and roll it in the poppy seeds. Brush another rope with the egg mixture and roll it in the sesame seeds. Brush the third rope with the egg mixture and roll it in the wheat germ. Set aside the remaining seeds and wheat germ.

7. Lay the ropes side-by-side on a flat surface. Gently braid the ropes together, trying not to shake off the seeds. Coil the braid into the prepared layer cake pan. Carefully spoon the remaining seeds and wheat germ onto the seedless areas of the braid. Cover the pan loosely and refrigerate the braid overnight.

8. Roll out the remaining dough into a 20 x 10-inch rectangle. Combine the remaining currants and pecans with the ground ginger and the brown sugar. Sprinkle the currant mixture over the dough and gently press it into the dough.

9. Roll up the dough from a long side and slice the roll into 36 pieces. Place 1 piece, cut side up, in each cupcake cup, or arrange the pieces in rows in the pan. Cover the cups or pan loosely and refrigerate the buns overnight.

10. Preheat the oven to moderate (350°).

11. Bake the braid and the buns in the preheated moderate oven (350°) for 20 to 25 minutes, or until they are firm to the touch and golden brown. Turn out the buns onto wax paper immediately, sticky side up. Cool the braid in the pan on a wire rack for 10 minutes. Turn out the braid onto the rack to cool completely.

Note: Hot water should feel comfortably hot to the touch.

HAM AND MUSHROOM PUFFS

Bake at 400° for 40 minutes.
Makes 6 servings.

Puffs:
- 1 cup water
- ½ cup (1 stick) unsalted butter
- ⅛ teaspoon salt
- ¼ teaspoon leaf marjoram, crumbled
- ¼ teaspoon leaf thyme, crumbled
- 1 cup sifted all-purpose flour
- 4 eggs

Ham and Mushroom Filling:
- ½ pound medium-size mushrooms, coarsely chopped
- 1 small onion, finely chopped
- ¼ teaspoon leaf thyme, crumbled
- 2 teaspoons unsalted butter
- ½ pound chicken breast cutlets, cut into ½-inch dice
- 1¼ cups dry white wine
- 2 tablespoons all-purpose flour
- ½ pound ½-inch-thick boiled ham, cut into ½-inch dice
- ¾ cup frozen small peas

1. Preheat the oven to hot (400°). Lightly grease a baking sheet.

2. Prepare the Puffs: Combine the water, butter, salt, marjoram and thyme in a saucepan. Bring the mixture to a full rolling boil over medium heat. Add the flour all at once. Stir the mixture vigorously with a wooden spoon to form a thick, smooth ball that leaves the sides of the pan clean. Remove the saucepan from the heat.

3. Add the eggs, one at a time, beating well after each addition, until the dough is shiny and smooth.

4. Spoon the dough into a large pastry bag fitted with a large star tip. Pipe the dough onto the prepared baking sheet in a solid 3-inch circle. Make a small circle of dough on top, ending in a point at the center. Repeat to make 5 more puffs.

5. Bake in the preheated hot oven (400°) for 40 minutes, or until the puffs are puffed and golden brown. Cool the puffs on a wire rack. When completely cool, horizontally slice each puff in half, three quarters through. Remove any filaments of soft dough that remain in the center.

6. Prepare the Ham and Mushroom Filling: Sauté the mushrooms, onion and thyme in the butter in a large skillet just until they are tender and golden brown. Add the chicken and 1 cup of the white wine. Simmer for 5 to 8 minutes, or just until the chicken is cooked through.

7. Stir the flour into the remaining ¼ cup of wine until smooth. Add the wine mixture to the chicken mixture. Cook, stirring, until the chicken mixture is thickened. Fold in the ham and the peas, and simmer for 1 minute more. Spoon the filling into the puffs.

To Make Ahead: The filling and the puffs may be made up to 24 hours ahead of time. Store the puffs in an airtight container in a cool, dry place. Refrigerate the filling separately. To serve, spoon the filling into the puffs. Place the puffs on a baking sheet and bake them in a preheated, hot oven (400°) for 15 to 20 minutes, or until heated through.

Microwave Instructions
(for a 650-watt variable power microwave oven)

Ingredient Changes: Reduce the amount of wine from 1¼ cups to ¾ cup.
Directions: Prepare the puffs as directed in the above recipe. To prepare the filling, combine the mushrooms, onion, thyme and butter in a microwave-safe, 2-quart casserole dish. Microwave at full power for 4 minutes, stirring once. Add the chicken and ½ cup of the wine. Cover and microwave at full power for 4 minutes, stirring once. Stir the flour into the remaining ¼ cup of wine until smooth. Stir the wine mixture into the casserole dish along with the ham and the peas. Microwave at full power for 5 minutes, stirring once. Spoon the filling into the puffs.

IRISH COFFEE GRANITA

Makes 6 servings.

> 4 cups freshly brewed hot espresso
>   OR: very strong regular coffee
> ½ cup granulated sugar
> ¾ cup Irish whiskey
> ½ cup heavy cream OR: whipping cream
> 2 teaspoons 10X (confectioners'
>   powdered) sugar
> ¼ teaspoon vanilla
> 1 square (1 ounce) semisweet chocolate,
>   coarsely grated

1. Combine the coffee, granulated sugar and whiskey in a 6-quart pitcher. Put the pitcher in the refrigerator until the mixture is cool.

2. Pour the cooled coffee mixture into ice cube trays or a 13 x 9 x 2-inch pan. Freeze the mixture until it is firm.

3. Unmold the coffee cubes or, if you used a baking pan, cut the mixture into 2-inch chunks. Place one quarter of the cubes or chunks in the container of a food processor fitted with the metal blade. Process until the frozen coffee mixture is a smooth purée. Spoon the purée into a freezer container. Repeat the process with the remaining cubes. Freeze the purée until it is firm.

4. Several hours before serving, return the frozen coffee purée to the container of the food processor. Process again just until smooth. Scoop the granita into individual dessert dishes or bowls. Freeze the granita until ready to serve.

5. Beat together the heavy or whipping cream, 10X (confectioners' powdered) sugar and vanilla until the cream is stiff. Refrigerate the whipped cream until ready to serve.

6. To serve, top the granita with the whipped cream and sprinkle the grated chocolate on top.

O Come, Little Children

J. P. A. Schulz

Simply, not too fast

1. O come, lit-tle chil-dren, O come, one and all. O come to the
2. O see, in the cra-dle, this night in the stall, O see how the

cresc.

man-ger in Beth-le-hem's stall; And see what our Fa-ther on
light daz-zles e-ven us all; In pure gleam-ing white lies this

cresc.

this ho-ly night, Has sent us from Heav-en for our de-light.
Child, heav-en's love, More beau-t'ous and ho-ly than an-gels a-bove.

FOR KIDS FROM 1 TO 92

There is something about the Christmas season that appeals to the child in all of us: the anticipation, the wonder, the delight. On the following pages, we celebrate that joy with magical decorations, a toyland of gifts and delectable kid-style munchies for the young, and the young-at-heart. You'll see visions of gingerbread dance before you with not one, but three gingerbread houses to make. Or you can dress up your tree with adorable Knit-Wits or calico dollies. For under the tree, there are stuffed dolls and travelin' trucks—even critter-type earmuffs! We've also got perfect party food for your little ones: smilin' sandwiches, a Christmas tree cake and colorful "stained-glass" cookies. And parents take note: There are tips on helping kids to be good—for goodness sake! Plus "kidsmart" guidelines to keep the whole family safe and happy throughout the holidays.

DISIONS OF GINGERBREAD

Enchant your family with a toy shop made entirely of gingerbread!

GINGERBREAD TOY SHOP

Average: For those with some experience in baking and cake decorating.

Materials:

- 2 batches Gingerbread Dough*
  (recipe, page 194)
  Egg whites
  Granulated sugar
- 2 batches Royal Frosting
  (recipe, page 194)
  Red, blue, green and yellow
  food colorings
- ½ package (1.65-ounce size)
  chocolate-coated coconut
  candy bar
  Red-colored decorating sugar
- 2 peppermint sticks
  Small red cinnamon candies
- 1 package (1 ounce) small
  chocolate nonpareil
  candies
- 2 packages (1 ounce each)
  square cherry-flavored
  hard candy
- 1 package (½ ounce) small
  green mint candies

- 1 package (1.72 ounces)
  colored candy-coated
  fruit gum
- 1 miniature chocolate bar
- 1 package (.90 ounce) cherry-
  flavored hard candy rings
- 1 package (8 ounces) small
  multi-flavored gumdrops
- 1 package (1.91 ounces) round
  wafer candies
  10X (confectioners'
  powdered) sugar

Paper for patterns; corrugated cardboard; thin cardboard; graphite or carbon paper; masking tape; construction or wrapping paper *(optional)*; glue *(optional)*; plastic wrap; aluminum foil; small round cookie cutters or coins, 2-inch round cookie cutter; small paintbrush; pastry bag; cotton; toothpicks; Christmas tree light in stand-up socket *(optional)*; semi-gloss polyurethane spray *(optional)*.

*Note: For the Gingerbread Plaza (optional; see page 195-196), make an extra half batch of the Gingerbread Dough; substitute an egg yolk for the whole egg.

Gingerbread Toy Shop (directions, pages 192-200)

GINGERBREAD DOUGH

Bake at 350° for 8 to 10 minutes.

5   cups unsifted all-purpose
    flour
½   teaspoon salt
1   tablespoon ground cinnamon
2   teaspoons ground ginger
1   teaspoon ground cloves
1   teaspoon ground nutmeg
1   cup vegetable shortening
1   cup granulated sugar
1   cup molasses
1   egg

Sift together the flour, salt, cinnamon, ginger, cloves and nutmeg onto wax paper. Beat together the shortening and the sugar until fluffy in a large bowl with an electric mixer. Beat in the molasses and the egg. Stir the flour mixture into the egg mixture to make a stiff dough. Chill the dough for 1 hour.

ROYAL FROSTING

1   box (1 pound) 10X
    (confectioners' powdered)
    sugar
3   egg whites
¼   teaspoon cream of tartar

Beat together the 10X (confectioners' powdered) sugar, egg whites and cream of tartar in a small bowl until the frosting is thick and fluffy. Keep the frosting at room temperature, covered with a damp towel to prevent it from drying out.

Directions for making the Gingerbread Toy Shop:

1. Prepare Gingerbread Dough: Refrigerate dough for 1 hour.
2. Paper Patterns: Draw and cut out the following paper patterns:
a. Side Walls: Cut out a 10½ x 7-inch rectangle. Label one 7-inch side "top," the other "bottom." Draw a line across the rectangle, 7 inches up from the bottom. Fold the rectangle in half lengthwise. Draw a diagonal line from the folded top corner to the cut edge of the line drawn across the rectangle. Cut along the diagonal line and open; label pattern "side." Cut out a 3-inch-square window in the center of the side wall, 2 inches from the bottom.
b. Front and Back Walls: Cut out an 11 x 7-inch rectangle and label it "front/back." Cut out a 5½ x 4-inch window 1¼ inches from the left side and 1½ inches from the bottom. Cut out a 3½ x 1½-inch door window 1¼ inches from the right side and ½ inch from the bottom. (The

back wall has no cutouts.)
c. Cardboard Roof pattern: Cut out an 11 x 5½-inch rectangle. Fold the rectangle in half crosswise to make a 5½-inch square. Label one end of the fold "top," the other "bottom." Turn the pattern so the folded corner marked "top" is the upper right corner of the square. Mark a point along the top edge of the square 4½ inches from the corner marked "top." Draw a diagonal line from the point to the bottom left corner of the square and cut along the line. Open the pattern and label it "roof." The top and bottom of the roof are already marked on the pattern.
d. Gingerbread Roof pattern: Trace cardboard roof pattern onto paper. Add ½ inch to each side and 1 inch on the bottom; do not add on to the top. Label this "gingerbread roof pattern."
e. Counters: Cut out the following patterns: The sides for counters 1 and 2 are both 2 x 1-inch rectangles. The front for

FIG. V, 1 GINGERBREAD
TOY PATTERNS

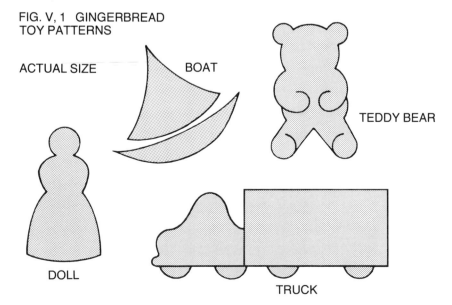

ACTUAL SIZE   BOAT

TEDDY BEAR

DOLL

TRUCK

counter 1 is a 3x2-inch rectangle. The top for counter 1 is a 3x1-inch rectangle. The front for counter 2 is a 5½x2-inch rectangle. The top for counter 2 is a 5½x1-inch rectangle. The sides for counter 3 are 2¾x1½-inch rectangles. The front for counter 3 is a 6x2¾-inch rectangle. The top for counter 3 is a 6x1½-inch rectangle.

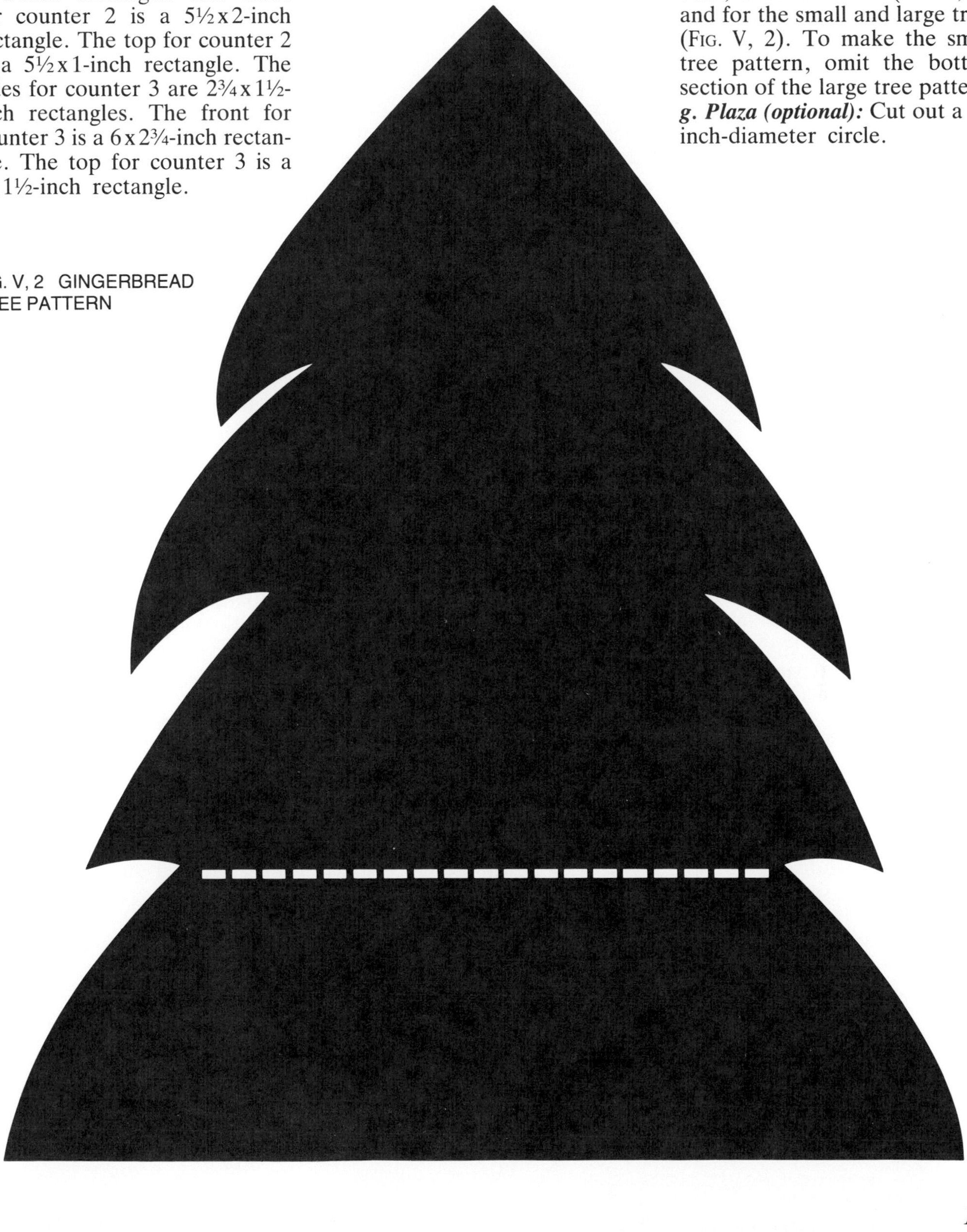

FIG. V, 2 GINGERBREAD
TREE PATTERN

f. Toys and Trees: Trace and cut out patterns for the doll, teddy bear, truck and boat (FIG. V, 1), and for the small and large trees (FIG. V, 2). To make the small tree pattern, omit the bottom section of the large tree pattern. *g. Plaza (optional):* Cut out a 16-inch-diameter circle.

3. Toy Shop Cardboard Pieces:
Trace the paper patterns onto the corrugated cardboard and cut out the following cardboard pieces:

a. 2 toy shop side walls. Score on the line drawn across the pattern, 7 inches up from the bottom. Cut out the windows.

b. 1 toy shop front wall with the window and the door window cut out.

c. 1 toy shop back wall, with no window or door window cut out.

d. 2 cardboard roof pieces.

e. Counters:

6 sides for counters 1 and 2
2 fronts for counter 1
2 tops for counter 1
1 front for counter 2
1 top for counter 2
2 sides for counter 3
1 front for counter 3
1 top for counter 3.

f. 3½ x 3-inch rectangle from the thin cardboard to hold the sign over the front window.

4. Assemble the Cardboard Pieces:

a. Shop frame: Lay the front of the shop on a flat surface with the large window to the right. Attach the side walls of the shop, taping them securely. Attach the back wall to the sides, taping it securely. Set the shop frame standing up and tape all the edges securely. Gently bend the top of the house sides inward along the scored lines.

b. Roof: Tape together the cardboard roof pieces along the top edge. Place the roof on top of the shop. Tape it securely at each edge.

c. Windows and Front and Side inside Walls: Place a piece of tape along each window edge and fold the tape over to the inside of the shop to cover the

cut edge. If you wish, cut construction or wrapping paper to fit over the inside of the front and side walls of the shop. (The back wall will be covered by toy shelves.) Glue the paper in place. Cut away any paper blocking the windows. Cut clear plastic wrap to cover the windows and extend ½ inch beyond on all sides. Cover one window on the outside and tape it at the top. Pull the wrap to the bottom and tape the bottom. Pull the wrap to one side and tape it, then pull it to the other side and tape it. Repeat for all windows.

d. Counters: Assemble two counter 1's and tape all the pieces securely. Assemble one counter 2 and tape it securely. Assemble one counter 3 and tape it securely.

e. Plaza (optional): Trace the paper pattern onto the corrugated cardboard. Place the toy shop on the cardboard, 9 inches back from the center front. Trace around the back part of the shop that extends beyond the circle. Cut out the plaza shape; it will be round in front, with a rectangular extension in back. If you wish, cut out a 3-inch square 1½ inches from the back of the rectangular extension for a tree light to illuminate the shop. Place the paper pattern on the cardboard piece. Set the shop in position and trace around the shop. Cut out, from the paper pattern only, the area the shop covers on the paper pattern.

5. Prepare the Gingerbread Dough for the Toy Shop Walls and Trees: Preheat the oven to moderate (350°). Cover several baking sheets with aluminum foil. Roll out half of one batch of the Gingerbread Dough on a prepared baking sheet, to a ⅛-inch thickness.

a. Side and Front Walls and Trees: Using the paper patterns, trace on the dough and cut out the front wall of the toy shop with the window and door window, 1 side wall, and as many trees as possible. You will need a total of 3 small trees and 3 large ones. Score 1 large and 1 small tree in half along their heights. Reserve any dough scraps. Leave the cut-out dough on the aluminum foil. Score the dough on the side and front walls to resemble bricks. Bake in the preheated moderate oven (350°) for 8 to 10 minutes, or until the gingerbread is firm and golden brown. Place the paper patterns on the gingerbread. If the gingerbread has expanded more than ⅛ inch beyond the patterns, trim off the excess while the gingerbread still is warm. Cool the gingerbread on the baking sheet for 5 minutes. Remove the pieces, still on the aluminum foil, to a wire rack. Cut the scored trees in half. Turn the cardboard shop frame on one side. Place the gingerbread side wall, still on the aluminum foil, on the side of the frame and mold it to the shape of the frame side. Cool the gingerbread completely. Remove the gingerbread and peel off the aluminum foil.

b. Side and Back Walls and remaining Trees: Roll out another half batch of dough on a prepared baking sheet. Cut out the second side wall, the back wall and trees. Do not cut out windows from the back wall. Score, bake, mold and cool the gingerbread as directed in Step 5, a.

6. Prepare the Gingerbread for the Shelves, Toys, Gift Packages, Counters, Roof, Awning, Sign and optional Plaza:

a. Shelves: Roll out another half batch of dough on a prepared baking sheet. Using the paper pattern, cut out another back wall; do not cut windows. Trim ¼-inch-wide strips from each side of the wall. Reserve the long strips. Add the short strips to the reserved dough scraps.

b. Toys and Gift Packages: Using the paper patterns, cut out 6 dolls, 6 teddy bears, 6 boats and 6 trucks from the dough with the point of a sharp knife. Cut out four 1 x ½-inch rectangles and four ¾-inch squares for gift packages. Cut out 8 balls of various sizes, using small cookie cutters or coins as patterns. Moisten 4 parallel lines, 1½

inches apart, across the length of the trimmed gingerbread back wall. Apply the two reserved ¼-inch strips to the back wall to resemble shelves. Cut and apply two more 10½ x ¼-inch strips of dough. Moisten the backs of enough toys to fit on the shelves and apply the toys to the back wall in an attractive arrangement. Reserve any dough scraps. Arrange the remaining toys, 1 inch apart, on the baking sheet with the toy wall. Bake in the preheated moderate oven (350°) for 8 to 10 minutes, or until the gingerbread is firm and golden brown. Cool the gingerbread on the baking sheet for 5 minutes. Transfer the gingerbread to a wire rack to cool.

c. Counters: Roll out the remaining half batch of dough on a prepared baking sheet. Cut out all the counter pieces and reserve the scraps. Position the counter pieces on the baking sheet, 1 inch apart. Score the counter pieces to resemble wood. Bake in the preheated moderate oven (350°) for 8 to 10 minutes, or until the gingerbread is firm and golden brown. Cool as in Step 6, b.

d. Roof: Knead together all the reserved dough scraps and reroll. Using the cardboard roof pattern, trace and cut out a piece of aluminum foil. Trace the gingerbread roof pattern on an aluminum foil-lined baking sheet. Center the cut-out aluminum foil piece on the traced roof piece, with the top lines meeting and equal spacing on all the other sides. The small piece of aluminum foil will remain attached to the gingerbread. Cut out a 13 x 1-inch rectangle of dough.

Place the rectangle at the bottom of the traced roof piece. Cut out forty 2-inch circles of dough with the 2-inch round cookie cutter. Place a row of circles, edges touching, on the aluminum foil, starting at the top of the dough strip. For the second row, start with half a circle, so the circles line up in a staggered pattern resembling tiles. Overlap the top of the first row slightly. Moisten the backs of the circles where they touch other dough pieces. Continue to make rows across the roof for a total of 6 rows. Trim off the sides and half the top row, using the gingerbread roof pattern as a guide. Brush the bottoms of the circles with the egg white and sprinkle with the granulated sugar. Bake in the preheated moderate oven (350°) for 8 to 10 minutes, or until the gingerbread is firm and golden brown. Cool as in Step 6, b. Repeat the whole process to make a second roof piece.

e. Awning and Sign: Cut a 2½-inch circle from the dough. Moisten the circle and fold it in half. Score, following the curve of the circle, to make the awning

Interior, Gingerbread Toy Shop

CHRISTMAS: THE UNTOLD STORY!

Let Mom or Dad become Santa Ford Coppola or Santa Spielberg for a family video production of the entire holiday season. Encourage the kids to take turns being in charge of the camera. Those wonderful memories captured on film will be a treasure for generations to come.

as pictured on page 193. Cut out a 5 x 1-inch rectangle from the dough. Roll one end under and the other over to make a 4-inch scroll for the sign. Bake in the preheated moderate oven (350°) for 8 to 10 minutes, or until the gingerbread is firm and golden brown. Cool as in Step 6, b.

f. Plaza (optional): If you wish, roll out the optional half batch of dough on an aluminum foil-lined baking sheet. Trace the plaza paper pattern on the dough. Cut out only the round portion that fits in front of and along the sides of the shop. Score in concentric arcs, starting from the front of the shop. Divide the arcs into segments resembling paving stones. Bake in the preheated moderate oven (350°) for 8 to 10 minutes, or

until the gingerbread is firm and golden brown. Cool as in Step 6, b.

7. Decorate the Toys and Gift Packages: Prepare 1 batch of the Royal Frosting. Spoon 1 tablespoon of the frosting into each of 5 small cups or dishes. Cover the remaining frosting with a damp cloth to prevent it from drying out. Using the food colorings, color the frostings pink, blue, green and yellow. Leave one of the cups of frosting white. Add ⅛ to ¼ teaspoon of water to each cup to thin the frosting. With the small paintbrush, paint the toys and gift packages (squares and rectangles). Spoon some white frosting into a pastry bag fitted with an adapter and writing tip. Outline the teddy bears on the shelves.

Pipe eyes and decorations on the dolls and teddy bears. Pipe dots, stripes and bows on the gift packages. Let the frosting decorations dry, then decorate the second side of the toys and gift packages.

8. Assemble the Toy Shop:

a. Walls: Spread the front, back and side walls of the shop cardboard frame with part of the remaining white frosting. Press the gingerbread pieces into place. Prop the gingerbread pieces with cans or boxes for 20 minutes, or until the gingerbread is secure.

b. Counters: Spread the cardboard counters with some of the remaining white frosting. Press the gingerbread pieces into place. Prop the pieces, if necessary, and set them aside to dry for 20 minutes.

c. Plaza (optional): Spread the round front portion of the cardboard plaza with some of the remaining frosting and apply the gingerbread piece.

9. Decorate the Cash Register, Awning, Sign, Counters and Windows:

a. Cash Register: Cut a 1-inch section from the end of the chocolate-coated coconut candy bar. Pipe a little frosting onto the cut end of the shorter piece. Set the shorter piece upright at the end of the larger piece of candy bar to make the cash register. Pipe frosting on the front for the keys, drawer and price indicator of the cash register. Frost the bottom and set the cash register on counter 3.

b. Awning: Pipe frosting over the scored lines on the awning.

c. Sign: Pipe the words "TOY SHOP" on the scroll sign. Sprinkle the letters heavily with the

red sugar. Gently shake off the excess sugar.

d. Counters: Change from the writing tip to a small star tip on the pastry bag. Pipe a star border along the top edges of the counters. Frost the toys onto the counters. Set aside the counters for 45 minutes, or until the frosting is completely dry.

e. Windows: With the small star tip, pipe molding onto the side windows, dividing each into 4 panes. Carefully lay the shop on its back. Pipe molding on the large front window, dividing it into 12 panes. Pipe molding on the door window, dividing it into 8 panes.

10. Attach the Toy Wall and Awning:

a. Toy Wall: Fit the toy wall onto the inside of the shop's back wall. Trim the toy wall, if necessary, to make it fit evenly; the toy wall should not extend beyond the bottom edge of the shop. Remove the toy wall, frost its back and press the toy wall into place.

b. Awning: Frost the back of the awning. Press the awning into place over the door. Trim the 2 peppermint sticks to fit beside the door. Pipe a double row of frosting on each side of the door. Press the peppermint sticks into the frosting. Pipe a row of frosting stars at the bottom of the awning. Set 5 small red cinnamon candies in the frosting stars.

11. Decorate the Toy Shop Front Corners, Make the Chimney and Position the Counters:

a. Decorate the Toy Shop Front Corners: Change from the small star tip to a medium star tip on the pastry bag. Pipe a shell border along the edge of each cor-

ner on the front of the shop. Set a small chocolate nonpareil candy into every other shell.

b. Make the Chimney: Frost together two stacks of 4 square cherry-flavored hard candies, and two stacks of 2 candies. Frost the stacks together, resting them on a flat surface, the 2 tall stacks on one side, and the 2 short stacks on the other side.

c. Position the Counters: Pipe a row of frosting on the open edge of counters 1 and 2. Press each counter 1 into place under the inside of a side window. Prop the counters with a box. Press counter 2 in place under the inside of the front window and prop it with more boxes. Let all the pieces dry completely, for several hours, or overnight. When you are ready to proceed again, prepare the second batch of Royal Frosting.

12. Position and Decorate the Sign, Roof, Toy Shop Back Corners and Chimney:

a. Position the cardboard Sign: Gently set the shop standing up. Tape the cardboard backing for the sign onto the cardboard roof, centering it over the front window. It should extend straight out at least 2 inches beyond the edge of the roof.

b. Position and decorate the Roof: Spread the cardboard roof with frosting. Press both of the gingerbread roof pieces (these pieces still have aluminum foil backing) into place on the cardboard. Prop the roof pieces with boxes at the front and back until they are secure.

c. Decorate the Toy Shop Back Corners: Spoon some of the frosting into the pastry bag fitted with the adapter and medium star tip. Pipe a shell border

HOME SWEET HOME

Just for fun, try to make a gingerbread house that resembles your own home. This makes a great gift for relatives who live far away or for a grown-up child who's moved out of the family home.

along the edge of the back two corners of the shop. Set a small chocolate nonpareil candy in every other shell. Pipe a shell border under the eaves on both sides of the shop. Decorate with a small green mint candy at the top and small red cinnamon candies along the sides.

d. Position the Gingerbread Sign: When the roof is secure, bend down the cardboard backing for the sign at the edge of the roof. Fit the gingerbread sign onto the cardboard, trimming the cardboard if necessary. Frost the back of the gingerbread sign. Pipe a row of frosting at the top of the sign. Press the sign into place. Prop the bottom of the sign with a box until it is secure.

e. Position and decorate the Chimney: Pipe a shell border along the point of the roof. Spoon 1 tablespoon of the frosting on the point of the roof, 1½ inches from the left side. Press the chimney into the frosting, flat end up, with the long side of the chimney toward the front of the roof and the short side resting on the point of the roof. Decorate the shell border along the roof point with the red and

green candies. Spoon a swirl of frosting on top of the chimney. Place a piece of colored fruit gum at each corner of the chimney. Push a fluff of cotton into the frosting in the center of the chimney for smoke.

13. Decorate the Front Door, Sign, Bushes and Trees:

a. Decorate the Front Door and Sign: Trim the miniature chocolate bar to fit between the peppermint sticks for the front door step. Fill in the center of the chocolate bar with frosting stars to make a doormat and set aside the chocolate bar. Change from the medium star tip to a medium writing tip on the pastry bag. Pipe a snowdrift over the awning, and icicles at the corners of the roof and the edge of the sign, as desired.

b. Decorate the Bushes and Trees: Color the remaining frosting green. Make two stacks of 3 cherry-flavored hard candy rings, and two stacks of 2 rings. Toothpick together two clusters of 8 green gumdrops to resemble bushes. Spoon some of the green frosting into the pastry bag fitted with a leaf tip. Pipe the frosting in leaves to fill the holes in the stacks of red ring candies and over the tops so the stacks resemble bushes. Cut small bits from the colored gumdrops and press the pieces into the green leaves for decorations. Pipe green leaves between the gumdrops to fill in the bushes. Set aside the bushes to dry. Mix the remaining green frosting with water until it is thin enough to be applied with the paintbrush. Paint the front of all the trees green and let them dry completely. Turn over the half-trees and paint their backs.

Paint a thick strip of green frosting down the center of each whole tree. Set the cut edge of a half-tree into the frosting. Prop on the dry side of the half-tree; let dry completely.

14. Set Up the Toy Shop: Position counter 3 in the center of the shop area on the plaza, if you are using a plaza. If you wish, install a Christmas tree light in a stand-up socket behind the counter. Set the shop in place over the counter. If you're not using a plaza, set up counter 3 and the shop on a tray or tablecloth. Place the doormat at the door. Arrange the bushes in front of the shop and the trees at the sides and back of the shop. Lay a path of round wafer candies to the front door. Sprinkle pieces of colored fruit gum around the bushes. Sift the 10X (confectioners' powdered) sugar over the roof and the trees.

15. To Preserve the Toy Shop: Tightly wrap the entire shop and plaza area in plastic wrap and store it in a cool, dry place. Or spray the entire shop and plaza area with semi-gloss polyurethane spray. Let the polyurethane dry completely and store the toy shop, tightly covered, in a cool, dark place.

LOLLIPOP DROP COTTAGE AND THATCHED COTTAGE

Easy: Achievable by anyone.

Makes one cookie cottage.

General Materials: 2 batches of Gingerbread Dough *(recipe, page 194)*; brown paper for patterns; two 16 x 12-inch pieces of ⅛-inch-thick foam core board; 1 batch of Royal Frosting *(recipe, page 194)*; poster board; colored tissue paper; masking tape.

General Directions:

1. Prepare the Gingerbread Dough and refrigerate it for at least 3 hours.

2. Enlarge and draw the patterns for the cottage pieces in FIG. V, 3 *(page 203)* on the brown paper, following the directions on page 271. Cut out the cottage pieces from the first piece of foam core board, as directed in the patterns.

3. Preheat the oven to moderate (350°).

4. Roll out the dough, one quarter at a time, on a well-floured pastry cloth or board to a ¼-inch thickness.

5. Using the brown paper patterns and a sharp knife, cut out a cottage front wall and back wall, and two side walls. Place the pieces 1 inch apart on large baking sheets.

6. Using the paper patterns, cut out the entrance front and side walls. Place the cut-out dough on a third baking sheet. Reroll the dough scraps as needed.

7. Bake one baking sheet at a time in the preheated moderate oven (350°) for 12 minutes, or until the gingerbread is firm.

Lollipop Drop Cottage (directions, page 201-203)

8. Cool the gingerbread on the baking sheets for 3 minutes. Loosen the gingerbread from the baking sheets with a long knife and slide the pieces onto wire racks to cool completely.

9. Prepare the Royal Frosting.

10. Spread a thin layer of frosting on the backs of all the gingerbread pieces and press them gently, but firmly, onto the cut-out foam core pieces. Allow them to dry for at least 1 hour.

11. Cover all the windows from the inside with colored tissue paper and tape the paper in place.

Thatched Cottage (directions, pages 201-203)

On the second uncut piece of foam core board, join the cottage front wall to a side wall with frosting. Hold the edges in place for 5 minutes, or until the frosting sets. Join the cottage back wall and remaining side wall to the first two walls with frosting. Allow the frosting to dry until firm, for 30 minutes.

12. Assemble the entrance front and side walls and join them with frosting. Allow the frosting to dry for at least one hour. Attach the entrance to the cottage front wall with frosting.

13. Fold a 9 x 14-inch piece of poster board in half crosswise to make two 9 x 7-inch sections. Spread the sections with frosting. Arrange and attach the roof-covering material, following the individual cottage directions, starting at the lower edges. Overlap the material to completely cover the poster board. Spread frosting along the top edge of the cottage front, back and side walls. Arrange the roof over the points of the tall walls and allow the frosting to dry until firm, for 30 minutes.

14. For the entrance roof, fold a 1 x 8-inch piece of poster board in half crosswise to make two 1 x 4-inch sections. Secure the entrance roof to the top of the entrance with frosting. Spread the entrance roof with frosting. Arrange and attach the entrance roof-covering material, following individual cottage directions.

Did You Know . . .

December 25 falls in the middle of the Australian summer, so Christmas celebrations tend to have a very different air than those in the Northern hemisphere. The great tradition is the Christmas Day picnic. During the Victorian era, women dressed all in white, carrying parasols to ward off the sun, and men sported straw "boater" hats. Families would celebrate on a holiday outing—replete with plum pudding and bottles of the locally produced wine. Trips to the beach were not uncommon on Christmas Day. Kite-flying, bathing and playing cricket all were acceptable activities. And while the traditional Christmas treats prevailed, there are accounts of braised kangaroo and parrot pie making an appearance at these celebrations "down under."

Lollipop Drop Cottage:
Materials: Round red cinnamon gummy candies for roof; red cinnamon candies for entrance roof; red and white peppermint sticks for columns; peppermint swirls for pastel trim and entrance window; jelly candies with centers cut out for wreaths.

Directions:
Using the photograph on page 201 as a guide, attach the decorative materials to the cottage with frosting.

Thatched Cottage:
Materials: Extra recipe of Royal Frosting to coat walls; pretzel rods and sticks for cross timbers; shredded wheat biscuits for roof; sliced natural almonds for entrance roof; spearmint leaves for base trim; jelly candies, evergreen sprig and narrow red ribbon for entrance trim.

Directions:
Frost all the walls to look like stucco. While the frosting still is soft, attach the pretzels to look like cross timbers. Cut the shredded wheat biscuits in half lengthwise with a sharp knife. Attach the biscuit halves to the roof with frosting, starting at the lower edges, and working up and over to create a "thatched" look. Continue to attach the decorations to the cottage with frosting, using the photograph on page 202 as a guide.

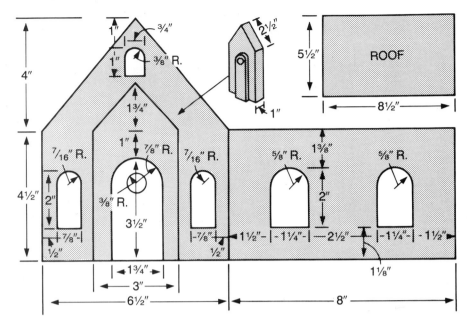

FIG. V, 3 LOLLIPOP DROP COTTAGE AND THATCHED COTTAGE PATTERNS

Holiday Notes

SECRET SANTA

If you have grown children and an enormously long family shopping list, try picking "Secret Santas" this year. Each person picks a name of a family member from a hat. For the rest of the holiday season, each Secret Santa leaves holiday messages, little gifts and goodies for his or her chosen person. Set a limit on spending so no one goes overboard. You also can have each Santa buy one special gift to give the chosen person Christmas Eve or morning, but it's a good idea to set a price limit on this, too.

Did You Know . . .

Some of the other names Santa Claus is known by:
Father Christmas, Kris Kringle,
St. Nicholas — England
Père Noël, le Petit Jésus,
le Petit Noël — France
Sankt Nikolaus — Germany
San Nicolaas, Sinter Klaas —
The Netherlands
Joulupukki (Old Man
Christmas) — Finland
Jultomten, St. Lucia — Sweden
Papa Noël — Brazil

YOUNG-AT-HEART TREE TRIMS

Decorations that will delight children of all ages.

💲 🏷️ KNIT-WITS
(3½ inches tall)

Average: For those with some experience in knitting.

Directions are given for six different ornaments.

Materials for Each Ornament: About 24 yards of leftover baby- or fingering-weight yarn in colors of your choice: we used White (A), Gray (B), Orange (C), Tan (D), Beige (E), Black (F), Red (G) and Green (H); embroidery floss: small amounts for facial features; 1 pair each size 1 and size 2 (for Stocking only) knitting needles, OR ANY SIZE NEEDLES TO OBTAIN GAUGE BELOW; tapestry needle; embroidery needle; polyester fiberfill; crochet hook *(optional)*.

Gauge: On size 1 needles in Stockinette Stitch (st st), 9 sts = 1 inch; 12 rows = 1 inch.

Note: *When changing colors, pick up the color to be used under the color previously used, twisting the yarns on the wrong side to prevent holes in the work. Carry the unused colors loosely on the wrong side of the work.*

General Directions:
1. Assembly: Leave a 12-inch length at the beginning and the end of the work. At the cast-on edge of the work, thread the tapestry needle with the 12-inch length and pull through each loop. **Do not** gather up yet.
2. To Form Neck: With matching yarn and the tapestry needle, pick up the front loop **only** of each stitch on the 25th row. **Do not** gather up yet. With right sides facing and with matching yarn, sew the two long edges together from the head to the toe. **Note:** *If applicable, first sew the ears and across the head.* Turn right side out and stuff

loosely. Gather the yarn at the cast-on edge and sew the opening closed. Gather the yarn at the neck and tie securely.
3. To Form Legs *(see photo)*: With matching yarn and the tapestry needle, work a running stitch up from the base, at the center front, for 8 rows, working through both thicknesses.
4. To Form Arms: Work a running stitch ⅜ inch in from the side edges and 8 rows up from the base for 10 rows. Add a 2½-inch hanging loop of yarn or wire to the top of the ornament.
5. Facial Features: With the embroidery floss and embroidery needle, work cross sts for the eyes and long sts for the nose and mouth. Add the whiskers.
6. Scarf: Cast on 4 sts and work in st st (k 1 row, p 1 row) in the colors of your choice for 7 inches. Bind off.

Gray Kitten:
1. With size 1 needles and A, cast on 32 sts. In st st (k 1 row, p 1 row), work 4 rows A, 16 rows B.
2. Bib, Row 21: K 15 B, 2 A, 15 B. **Row 22:** P 14 B, 4 A, 14 B. **Row 23:** K 13 B, 6 A, 13 B. **Row 24:** P 12 B, 8 A, 12 B. Cut A. **Next 10 Rows:** Work in st st with B.

3. Ears (attach 1 yard of A for each ear), Row 35: K 7 B, 2 A, 14 B, 2 A, 7 B. **Row 36:** P 6 B, 4 A, 12 B, 4 A, 6 B. **Row 37:** K 5 B; with A k 4, p 1, k 1; k 10 B; with A k 1, p 1, k 4; k 5 B. **Row 38:** P 4 B; with A p 5, k 2, p 1; p 8 B; with A p 1, k 2, p 5; p 4 B. **Row 39:** K 3 B; with A k 6, p 3, k 1; k 6 B; with A k 1, p 3, k 6; k 3 B. **Row 40:** P 2 B; with A p 7, k 4, p 1; p 4 B; with A p 1, k 4, p 7; p 2 B. **Row 41:** Bind off 1 B st, k 1 A and bind off remaining B st; with A k 6, p 5; with B bind off 3 sts, p 1 A and bind off remaining B st; with A p 4, k 7; with B bind off last 2 sts—24 sts. **Row 42 (left ear only):** With A p 2 tog, p 5, k 3, k 2 tog. Turn. **Row 43:** With A k 2 tog, bind off to last 2 sts, k 2 tog and pull yarn through. **Row 42 (right ear):** With A k 2 tog, k 3, p 5, p 2 tog. **Row 43:** Work same as Row 43 for left ear.

4. Tail: With B, cast on 4 sts. Work in st st for 2 inches, ending with a p row. With A, work 2 rows, turn; (k 2 tog) twice, turn; p 2, turn; k 2 tog.

5. Finishing: Follow the General Directions, Steps 1 to 6.

White Kitten:

Work the same as for the Gray Kitten with A only.

Striped Kitten:

With size 1 needles and A, cast on 32 sts. In st st, work 4 rows A, (3 rows C, 1 row A) 5 times, 10 rows C. **Rows 35 to 43:** Rep Rows 35 to 43 as for Gray Kitten, substituting C for B.

Panda:

1. With size 1 needles and F, cast on 32 sts. In st st, work 8 rows F, 12 rows A, 4 rows F, 4 rows A.

2. Eyes, Row 29: K 12 A, 2 F, 4 A, 2 F, 12 A. **Next 3 Rows:** In st

Knit-Wits (directions, page 204)

205

st, work 11 A, 4 F, 2 A, 4 F, 11 A. *Row 33:* Rep Row 29. *Row 34:* With A, p across.
3. Ears (attach 1 yard of F for each ear), Row 35: K 6 A, 4 F, 12 A, 4 F, 6 A. *Row 36:* P 5 A; with F p 4, k 2; p 10 A; with F k 2, p 4; p 5 A. *Row 37:* K 4 A; with F k 5, p 3; k 8 A; with F p 3, k 5; k 4 A. *Row 38:* P 3 A; with F p 6, k 4; p 6 A; with F k 4, p 6; p 3 A. *Row 39:* K 3 A; with F k 3, (sl 1, k 1, psso) twice, p 3; k 6 A; with F p 3, (k 2 tog) twice, k 3; k 3 A—28 sts. *Row 40:* P 3 A; with F p 2, (p 2 tog) twice, k 2; p 6 A; with F k 2, (p 2 tog through back of second st) twice, p 2; p 3 A—24 sts. *Row 41:* With A bind off 2 sts, k 1 F, pass A st on needle over, (sl 1, k 1, psso and pass first F st on needle over) twice. Bind off 2 F and 5 A, k 1 F, pass A st on needle over, (k 2 tog, pass st on needle over) twice. Bind off 2 F and 3 A sts. Gather ears and fasten off.
4. Finishing: Follow the General Directions, Steps 1 to 6.
Teddy Bear:
1. With size 1 needles and D, cast on 32 sts. Work in st st for 26 rows.
2. Muzzle, Row 27: K 14 D, 4 E, 14 D. *Next 3 Rows:* In st st, work 13 D, 6 E, 13 D. *Row 31:* Rep Row 27. *Next 3 Rows:* With D, work in st st.
3. Ears, Rows 35 to 41: With D only, rep Rows 35 to 41 of Ear for Panda.
4. Finishing: Follow the General Directions, Steps 1 to 6.
Santa:
1. With size 1 needles and F, cast on 32 sts. In st st, work 6 rows F, 4 rows G, 2 rows A, 12 rows G, 8 rows E, 2 rows A, 6 rows G. *Do not* cut yarn, but continue with G to end.

HIDE 'N GO SEEK ORNAMENTS

Borrow a bit of festive fun from Easter. On tree trimming day, hide non-glass ornaments all over the house. Searching for them will provide great entertainment for your kids and help keep them occupied while you hang the tree lights. For an extra-special touch, have a wrapped ornament at the end of the hunt for each child to add to his or her own collection.

2. Hat, Row 41: K 3, (k 2 tog, k 6) 3 times, k 2 tog, k 3—28 sts. *Row 42:* P 3, (p 2 tog, p 5) 3 times, p 2 tog, p 2—24 sts. *Row 43:* K 2, (k 2 tog, k 4) 3 times, k 2 tog, k 2—20 sts. *Row 44:* P 2, (p 2 tog, p 3) 3 times, p 2 tog, p 1—16 sts. *Row 45:* K 1, (k 2 tog, k 2) 3 times, k 2 tog, k 1—12 sts. *Row 46:* (P 1, p 2 tog) 4 times—8 sts. *Row 47:* (K 2 tog) 4 times. *Row 48:* (P 2 tog) twice; k last 2 sts tog.
3. Finishing: Follow the General Directions, Steps 1 to 5.
4. Pompon for Hat: Wind A yarn around two fingers at least six times, tie tightly at center and sew to top of Hat.
5. Beard: Wind A yarn 20 times around a 3 x ¾-inch piece of cardboard. Working at one edge of the cardboard, make a buttonhole stitch in each loop to hold the loops together. Slip the loops off the cardboard. Sew to the face, below the mouth, curving the sides upward.

Snowman:
1. With size 1 needles and A, cast on 32 sts. In st st, work 34 rows A, 6 rows H. *Do not* cut yarn; continue with H to end.
2. Hat, Rows 41 to 48: Rep Rows 41 to 48 of Hat for Santa.
3. Finishing: Follow the General Directions, Steps 1 to 6.
4. Pompon: Work same as pompon for Santa.

Stocking:
1. With size 2 needles and double strand of A, cast on 24 sts. Work in st st for 10 rows. Change to size 1 needles and in st st, work (6 rows G, 6 rows H) twice, then 2 rows G.
2. Heel, Next Row: With G k 8, turn; p 8, turn; k 7, turn; p 7, turn; k 6, turn; p 6, turn; k 5, turn; p 5, turn; k 4, turn; p 4, turn; k 3, turn; p 3, turn and k to end of row. *Next Row:* With G p 8, turn; k 8, turn; p 7, turn; k 7, turn; p 6, turn; k 6, turn; p 5, turn; k 5, turn; p 4, turn; k 4, turn; p 3, turn; k 3, turn and p to end of row. *Next 2 Rows:* With G, work in st st. *Next 6 Rows:* With H, k or p the first 2 sts of each row tog—18 sts. Cut yarn, leaving a 24-inch length. *Next 6 Rows:* With G, k or p first 2 sts of each row tog—12 sts. Cut yarn, leaving a 24-inch length.
3. Finishing: With the tapestry needle, thread the G yarn length through the last 12 sts and gather up to close the opening. Fasten off. With right sides facing, sew the two long edges together from the toe to the cuff, alternating G and H yarn, ending with A. Turn right side out and fold the stocking top down. *Optional:* With G and H yarns held tog, work a 20 st chain with a crochet hook and tack the loop to the inner side of the cuff.

OUR FINEST GIFTS

Teach your children the greatest joy of all—the joy of giving. Pick a family you know is having a tough time, or find one through the Christmas gift fund of your church or community center. Fill colorful shopping bags with holiday cookies, fresh fruit, warm gloves and socks, ornaments and a special Christmas message written by the kids. Allow your youngsters to stay up late one night (preferably Christmas Eve) and drop off the goodies without being seen. Everyone in the family will experience the wonder of being Santa for a night.

THE LITTLEST REINDEER

Easy: Achievable by anyone.

Materials: 4 flat wooden clothespins; saw; 2 brown pipe cleaners; white glue; 2 buttons for eyes; 1 red bead for nose; green felt; red felt; 3 tiny jingle bells.

Directions:

1. Saw the legs off one of the flat wooden clothespins to make the reindeer body; save the clothespin legs.

2. To make the head and ears, cut off the legs of a second clothespin 1 inch above the separation *(see photo for guide)*. Glue the brown pipe cleaners to the back of the ears for antlers. Glue the button eyes and bead nose to the face.

3. Glue a whole clothespin to each end of the body pin. Glue the head to the front of one of the whole clothespins. Glue a leftover leg for the tail to the other whole clothespin. Glue the other leg piece behind the head as a support.

4. Cut out a harness breast piece from the green felt *(see photo for guide)*. Cut a small diamond shape and a thin band from the red felt. Make a loop with the red band, slip the band over the reindeer's head and glue the ends together. Glue the green harness piece to the red band as shown. Glue the red diamond in the center of the green harness piece. Sew the tiny jingle bells to the red felt strip as shown in the photo.

A-DOUGH-ABLE ORNAMENTS

Easy: Achievable by anyone.

Bake at 375° for 20 to 40 minutes.
Makes about 20 ornaments.

Materials:

- 1 **cup water**
- ½ **cup (1 stick) butter or margarine**
- 1 **cup all-purpose flour**
- 4 **eggs**
  Buttercream Frosting (recipe, page 209)
  Assorted food colorings
  Cocoa
  Chocolate sprinkles, silver dragées, colored sugar crystals, candy canes, peanuts, green candied cherries

Sewing needle; metallic or nylon thread.

♪ Holiday Notes

A HUG A DAY . . .

On December 1, instead of (or in addition to) the usual mistletoe, hang holly or pieces of Christmas greenery in doorways around the house. Everyone who stands beneath the sprigs gets a hug: a "take them by surprise" hug, a "Yoo-hoo, I'm home" hug or just a "What you need is a hug" hug—a loving way to start off the season right.

Christmas Stocking

1. Bring the water and the butter or margarine to boiling in a medium-size saucepan. Stir in the flour with a wooden spoon until a ball forms. Remove the saucepan from the heat and cool the mixture slightly. Grease 2 large baking sheets. Add the eggs, one at a time, to the flour mixture, beating well after each addition. Be careful to keep the mixture smooth and glossy.

2. Preheat the oven to moderate (375°).

3. Fit a pastry bag with a ¼-inch round tip. Fill the bag with ⅓ of the dough. Pipe the dough onto the baking sheets, spacing the ornaments about 1 inch apart.

4. Christmas Stocking: Use one third of the dough. Pipe the outline of the stocking—about 3¾ inches long, 2½ inches from the heel to the toe. Fill in the stocking shape with the dough to a ¼-inch thickness.

5. Nutcracker: Use one third of the dough. Pipe the hat first, then a ball for the face, then the arms, body and legs.

6. Use the remaining third of the dough to make a second nutcracker or another stocking, depending on your preference.

7. Bake in the preheated moderate oven (375°) for 20 to 40 minutes, or until the ornaments are golden brown and firm. Remove the ornaments with a spatula to a wire rack to cool. Make a hole with a drinking straw in the body of the nutcracker while the ornament still is warm, to hold a peanut.

8. Make the Buttercream Frosting. Spoon about ¾ cup of the frosting into a pastry bag fitted with a small round tip. Divide the remainder of the frosting among 6 cups and tint each cup with the food colorings or the cocoa. You'll need about ½ cup of red, ½ cup of chocolate brown, ¼ cup of blue, ⅛ cup of yellow and a tablespoon each of green and pink frostings. Make 6 wax paper cones and fill each with a different color frosting. Cut off a tiny opening at the bottom of each cone for a tip and pipe the frostings to decorate the ornaments *(see photos, pages 208 and 209, for guide)*. Sprinkle the frosted ornaments with the candies, or decorate the stocking with green cherries cut into leaf shapes. Cut off the top ⅛ inch of the stocking; insert candies or a miniature candy cane in the stocking opening.

9. When the frosting is dry, thread the needle with the metallic or nylon thread and pierce through each ornament. Tie the ends of the thread together to form a loop for hanging.

Nutcracker

BUTTERCREAM FROSTING

Makes about 2¼ cups.

⅓   cup butter or margarine
1   teaspoon vanilla
1   package (1 pound) 10X
      (confectioners' powdered)
      sugar, sifted if lumpy
3   to 4 tablespoons milk

Beat together the butter or margarine and the vanilla until creamy in a small bowl with an electric mixer. Beat in the 10X (confectioners' powdered) sugar and 3 tablespoons of the milk until the frosting is smooth and stiff enough to spread, yet stands in soft peaks. Add more milk if the frosting is too stiff. Keep the surface of the frosting covered with plastic wrap to prevent it from drying out.

SAFETY FOR THE SEASON

• Be certain the toys you buy are appropriate for the age and personality of the child. Careful shopping will detect a toy that obviously is unsafe, but age and activity level are important factors to consider as well. For example, if there are infants or toddlers in the house, check all toys for small parts that might come off, and avoid toys with sharp edges or that are small enough to swallow.

• Check your Christmas tree for freshness before you buy it, and keep it watered to reduce the chance of fire. Check your tree lights annually to be sure the wires are not frayed or damaged in other ways, and don't leave the tree lit when you'll be away from the house.

• If you have small children, keep them in mind when you decorate the house: Place more delicate ornaments, or those with sharp edges, on the higher tree branches, out of the reach of curious little hands.

• A cozy fire is wonderful, but before the season begins, check to ensure your fireplace is in good working condition. You should never leave a fire burning unattended, and be sure to place a screen barrier between the fire and the rest of the room. Teach children that they should *never* play near the fireplace.

• Don't place the Christmas tree near the fireplace: The heat generated by the fire can cause the tree to ignite spontaneously.

• Remind children to be especially careful of outdoor traffic during the holidays.

• When entertaining family and friends, be sure children avoid alcoholic beverages; alcohol can be dangerous to small children. Have a second, non-alcoholic punch on hand for children and for those of your guests who don't drink. Then if little ones want "a taste," they can do so safely. (Be sure the non-alcoholic punch is easily differentiated from the spirited variety.)

Did You Know . . .

In some parts of Switzerland, the giving of the Christmas gifts is attributed to the Christ Child himself. The Child, dressed as an angel, rides around in a sleigh drawn by six reindeer and distributes fruit, candy, cookies and other little gifts. In other parts of Switzerland, it is a jolly, red-faced Father Christmas and his Wife who bring the presents; he to the boys and she to the girls.

Christmas Cherubs

CHRISTMAS CHERUBS AND ELFIN MAGIC ORNAMENTS

Easy: Achievable by anyone.

Makes about 6 cherubs and 6 elves. The cherubs and elves also can be used as table decorations or place markers.

Materials:

1   **can (8 ounces) almond paste**
2   **egg whites**
½   **teaspoon lemon extract**
1   **package (1 pound) 10X (confectioners' powdered) sugar, sifted if lumpy**
   Assorted food colorings
   Brandy

Small paint brush; toothpicks; sewing needle; metallic or nylon thread.

1. Break up the almond paste with your fingers in a medium-size bowl. Add 1 of the egg whites and the lemon extract. Mix the ingredients together with a fork until they are blended. Gradually add enough of the 10X (confectioners' powdered) sugar to form a soft dough.

2. Knead the dough with more of the 10X (confectioners' powdered) sugar in the bowl until a smooth, firm ball forms. Divide the dough into 12 pieces; keep the pieces covered with plastic wrap to prevent the dough from drying out.

3. Refer to the photos to help shape the cherubs and the elves. Each ornament is about 2½ inches tall. Divide each of the 12 dough pieces into smaller pieces

Did You Know . . .

In Scandinavia, there are different versions of who brings the Christmas gifts. Danish children believe that a little gnome wearing a grey suit and a pointed hat brings the goodies for the holiday. Accordingly, they set out a large portion of rice pudding (his favorite dish) to thank him. Tomtar or Julnissar, little men with long grey beards who live in dark corners or under the floorboards, are said to leave little surprises for boys and girls in Sweden. On Christmas Eve, the children, dressed in their very best, finally are allowed to see the Christmas tree and their father gives them their presents — each gift accompanied by an original verse!

for the body, head, arms, legs and other parts of each ornament. To color the dough, knead in a drop of food coloring until the desired shade is reached. Mold the smaller pieces between the palms of your hands into balls, pear shapes, ropes and so on. Shape all the parts of a figure first, then attach the parts using a little of the remaining egg white as glue at the points of attachment. If the dough is too dry to mold, knead a bit of the egg white into the dough to moisten it.

4. To paint colors on parts such as the candy cane or scarf, dilute the food colorings with the brandy and brush the colors onto the pieces with the small paint brush. To make the eyes and smiles on the cherubs, mark them with a toothpick, and paint the indentations with a bit of the diluted food coloring.

5. To make a sitting elf, mold the body and place it on the edge of an upside-down cup. Attach the legs so that they hang over the side of the cup.

6. Let the ornaments dry for about 1 hour. Thread the sewing needle with the metallic or nylon thread. Insert the needle and thread twice through the body of each ornament so that the thread ends meet at the same side. Let the ornaments dry until they are very firm. When firm, place each ornament directly onto a tree branch and tie it securely with the thread either to the branch above or below it.

Elfin Magic (directions, page 210)

Did You Know . . .

In Poland, after the Christmas Eve supper is finished, the "Star Man" appears and examines the children to see if they've learned their catechism (the teachings of the Catholic Church). Later in the evening, three children dress up as the Three Wise Men and travel about their village, knocking at the doors and leaving little gifts for the other children.

HELLO, DOLLIES!

Easy: Achievable by anyone.

Materials for Dolly: Two 6-inch squares of muslin; two 4x8-inch pieces of calico for dress; rug yarn: 2 yards of Chestnut, Gold or Brown for hair; ⅓ yard of lace or rickrack; ¼ yard of narrow ribbon; tiny buttons, beads or flowers; thread to match fabrics and trims; polyester fiberfill; extra-fine-point permanent marker; masking tape; crayons; tailor's water-soluble or disappearing-ink pen; hot glue gun and glue sticks, or thick craft glue. *For Treetop Angel:* Add two 4x8-inch pieces of muslin and 4x8 inches of quilt batting for halo and wings; use two 6x8-inch pieces of light print calico for dress; any additional trims of your choice.

FIG. V, 4 HELLO, DOLLIES!/TREETOP ANGEL

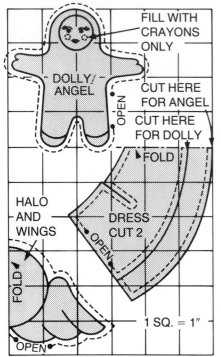

Directions for Dolly:

1. Enlarge the Dolly body and dress patterns in FIG. V, 4, following directions on page 271. Place the dress on folded paper. Cut out patterns. Open half pattern to make a full pattern.

2. Body: Place one muslin piece over Dolly pattern and secure muslin with masking tape. Trace Dolly outline and details (face, body) with the permanent marker. Lightly fill in details with crayons. Trace a stitching line with the tailor's pen. Iron muslin for one minute to set colors.

3. Pin remaining muslin piece over drawn piece, right sides facing. Sew around Dolly on stitch line, leaving an opening between the dots. Trim around Dolly with pinking shears, or clip all curves. Carefully turn

Dolly right side out. Fill Dolly with polyester fiberfill and slipstitch the opening closed.

4. Dress: Cut a dress front and back from calico and pin them together, right sides facing. Mark seam lines for armholes. Stitch around the dress. Trim corners, clip the curves and angles and slash the armhole lines. Turn dress right side out; press. Slipstitch opening closed. Stitch trims to hemline and at front neckline *(see photo, page 213).*

5. Assembly: Heat the glue gun. Glue dress to Dolly at the shoulders and back. Cut three or four 1-inch lengths of yarn and glue them to the top of Dolly's headline for bangs. Glue a wig to top of head, covering ends of bangs. Arrange hair in the style of your choice (we did some in braids, some in ponytails and left some straight). Tie off braids and ponytails with thread. Cut a 3-inch length of ribbon, form a loop and glue the loop to the back of the Dolly for a hanger.

Treetop Angel:

1. Enlarge the Angel body, dress, halo and wings patterns in FIG. V, 4, following the directions on page 271, using longer dress length on the pattern and placing dress and halo and wings patterns on folded paper. Cut out patterns. Open each half pattern to make a full pattern.

2. Construct the Angel body and dress following the directions for the Dolly.

3. Trace halo and wings pattern onto one of the 4 x 8-inch pieces of muslin. Pin remaining muslin piece over the drawn piece, right sides facing. Pin quilt batting to back. Stitch around halo and wings. Trim seams, corners

and angles. Turn halo and wings right side out and press. Slipstitch the opening closed. Glue lace or rickrack trims to halo.

4. Glue halo and wings piece to Angel's back. To make Angel a hanging ornament, form a ribbon loop, following directions for Dolly, and glue loop to the back of the wings for a hanger.

PAPER DOLL GARLAND

Easy: Achievable by anyone.

Materials: Lightweight white poster board; White rug yarn; hot glue gun and glue sticks.

FIG. V, 5 PAPER DOLL GARLAND PATTERN

ACTUAL SIZE

Directions:

Trace doll pattern shown in FIG. V, 5 and cut out pattern. Lightly trace pattern repeatedly on back of poster board. Carefully cut out dolls. Heat glue gun. Unwind yarn to length of garland you wish to have. Run a narrow stripe of glue across arms on back of each doll. Allow glue to cool slightly, then press yarn into glue. Continue along yarn, spacing dolls 1 inch apart.

Hello, Dollies! and Paper Doll Garland (directions, pages 211-212)

TOYLAND

Perfect presents for every child on your gift list.

PENCIL PALS

Easy: Achievable by anyone.

Materials: Pencil for each character; bread dough *(recipe, at right)*; craft glue; acrylic paints: brown, white, red, green, pink, black, blue, orange and yellow; toothpicks; size 00 and size 2 sable paint brushes; size 4 mm moveable eyes for each character; pair of small scissors.

Bread Dough Recipe:
- 3 **slices day-old bread, crusts removed**
- 3 **tablespoons white glue**
- 1 **tablespoon white acrylic paint**
- 3 **drops lemon juice**
- ½ **teaspoon glycerin**

Break the bread into small pieces. Mix together the bread pieces, the glue, paint, lemon juice and glycerin in a large mixing bowl. The dough will be very sticky; keep applying lotion to your hands to keep the dough from sticking. Knead the dough until it firms up, for about 5 minutes. Continue to knead the dough until it is soft and pliable.

General Directions:
When building a character, roll each part in your palms and

work in a small amount of paint until the desired color is reached and is uniform around the body part. Each character is formed by rolling small balls, log shapes, ovals and cones and attaching all the pieces with glue. The shapes should be flattened or sculpted to create the desired details. Refer to the photo for the placement of the different body parts. It would be impossible to create exact replicas of these characters; use your imagination to create your own unique characters.

Santa:

Santa is made with white, pink and red dough. Wrap a flattened 1-inch piece of red dough around the top of the pencil for Santa's suit and place a ball of pink dough on top of this for the head. Attach a pink nose to the face. Attach feet to the bottom of the suit and paint the feet black. Wrap a strip of white dough to the bottom of the suit, above the feet, for trim. Wrap a strip of dough around the middle of the suit for a belt and paint the belt black. Form two red arms and attach one to either side of the top of the suit. Form and attach white fur cuffs for trim on the arms, then attach two pink hands. Flatten a half circle of white dough and attach it to the back of the head for hair. Make a flat triangle of white dough for the beard and attach it to the face. Use a toothpick to carve details on the hair and beard, then poke a small hole through the beard for the mouth. Make the cap from a cone of red dough and wrap a piece of white dough around the bottom for trim. Add a ball of white dough to the top of the cap for a pompon. Glue on the eyes and paint a red circle around the toothpick hole for the mouth.

Snowman:

The snowman is made with white, blue and orange dough. Roll and flatten a piece of white dough so that it still is fairly thick, and wrap it around the top of the pencil for the body. Attach a round white head on top of the body. Form the arms from two logs of white dough that have indented ends for thumbs, and attach the arms to the body. Make the hat from a roundish piece of dough with a flattened piece of dough at the bottom for a brim, and paint the hat black. Wrap a log of blue dough, flattened slightly, around the neck of the snowman for a scarf. Paint pink stripes on the scarf. Roll a carrot shape from orange dough and attach the carrot to the face for a nose. Paint black dots for the smile and glue on the eyes.

Reindeer:

The reindeer is made with brown, red, white, yellow and orange dough. Wrap a 1-inch piece of flattened brown dough around the top of the pencil. Form the front legs from two logs of brown dough, each with a slit at one end for the hooves. Make two longer logs of brown dough for the hind legs and cut slits for the hooves. Curl the uncut end of each hind leg (see photo, page 114). Glue all the legs to the body and paint the hooves black. Make the head from a long oval of brown dough and attach a dot of red dough for a nose. Glue on the eyes. Roll small ovals of brown dough for the ears and attach them. Form a teardrop from the brown dough for the tail and attach the tail to the back of the reindeer. Paint a small white teardrop within the edges of the brown dough tail. Cut a slit for the mouth with a toothpick. To make the antlers, roll a small log of light brown dough and pinch out a small section from the side to form a Y. Make two antlers and attach them to the head. Roll a long, thin piece of red dough and flatten it slightly to make a collar. Glue the collar around the neck of the deer. Form several tiny bells from the yellow dough and glue them around the collar.

Elf:

The elf is made with green, pink yellow, white and red dough. Wrap a flattened 1½-inch piece of green dough around the top of the pencil for the elf's body. Flute the bottom half of the body and cut zigzags around the base with the scissors. Attach a round piece of pink dough to the top of the body for the head. Flatten a round piece of yellow dough and attach it to the head for hair. Make the ears from two flattened tear drops of pink dough. Attach a tiny, pointed cone of pink dough to the face for a nose. Form the arms from two logs of green dough with tiny pink hands attached at the ends. Form a square of white dough for the gift, paint lines on it to resemble ribbon, and place the gift between the hands. Roll a cone of red dough for the cap and cut zigzags around the bottom edge as for the base of the elf's outfit. Attach the cap to the head. Make two teardrops of red dough and curl up the tips for shoes. Attach the shoes to the bottom of the elf's outfit. Glue eyes onto the face; paint on a smile and rosy cheeks.

LITTLE BOY BLUE AND LITTLE BO PEEP

Challenging: Requires more experience in sewing and doll making.

Dolls:

Materials: ¾ yard of pink percale or chintz; matching thread; polyester fiberfill; rug yarn: 1 skein; thread to match rug yarn; embroidery floss: scraps of Blue and Red.

Directions:

1. Enlarge the doll pattern pieces in FIG. V, 6, following the directions on page 271. Cut out the fabric pieces according to the directions on the pattern. All the seams are sewn with right sides together unless otherwise noted.

2. Sew all the darts. Place the body back pieces together and sew the back seam, leaving an opening for stuffing as indicated. Attach the body back to the body front, sewing along all but the bottom edge. Turn the body right side out. Sew the leg pieces together in pairs. Sew along the side seams, but leave the top and bottom edges open. Sew a foot sole piece into each leg bottom opening and turn the leg right side out. Repeat the procedure with the arms, but leave only the tops open.

3. Stuff the legs firmly, keeping in mind that the seams are at the center front and back. Stitch across the top of each leg at the line indicated on the pattern. Turn up and baste the seam allowance on the body bottom opening. Insert the seam allowances of the leg tops into this opening and sew the opening

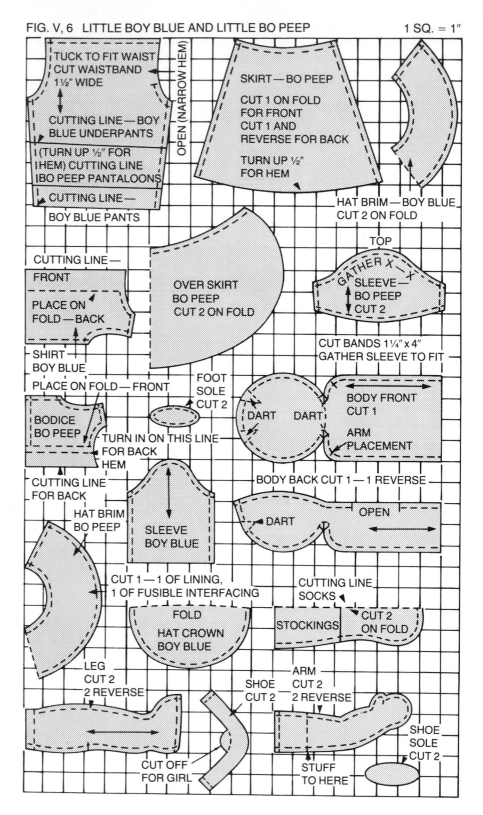

FIG. V, 6 LITTLE BOY BLUE AND LITTLE BO PEEP   1 SQ. = 1"

closed; be sure the stitching is very durable. Stuff the body firmly and slipstitch the back opening closed. Stuff the arms firmly up to the line indicated on the pattern. Sew across the arms at this line; the space above the line is not stuffed. Turn under seam allowance at the tops of the arms and sew it closed. Sew the arms to the body at the places indicated on the pattern, with half the arm width on either side of the side body seam.

4. To finish the doll, cut the yarn to the length desired for the hair. Cut enough yarn hair to cover the head. Drape the yarn across the head and sew the hair to the head by running the matching thread *through* the yarn and into the fabric of the head. The thread does not show because it does not cross over the yarn. Make the stitches at 1-inch to 1½-inch intervals. Arrange the hair as desired.

5. Draw a face on the doll, making half circles for the eyes and a curve for the mouth. Embroider the eyes with Blue floss using a satin stitch, and the mouth with Red floss using an outline stitch.

Little Bo Peep's Outfit:

Materials: ½ yard of white percale (also will make Boy Blue's underpants); 2½ yards of 1-inch-wide white lace; ¼ yard of print cotton fabric; ¼ yard of striped cotton fabric; ¼ yard of solid cotton fabric; ¼ yard of second color solid; scrap of brown felt or suede cloth; matching threads; 2½ yards of ⅜-inch-wide lace; ½ yard of ½-inch-wide ribbon; ½ yard of 1-inch-wide ribbon; 2 brown chenille stems; 1 pair Child's size 6-9 white knee socks; four ¾-inch-diameter

Little Boy Blue and Little Bo Peep (directions, pages 216-219)

snap fasteners; ¼ yard of fusible interfacing (also will make Boy Blue's hat interfacing).

Directions:

1. Enlarge the pattern pieces for Bo Peep's outfit, following the directions on page 271. Using the pattern as a guide, cut out the stockings from the pair of child's socks, leaving the ribbed cuff area for Little Boy Blue's socks. Sew the back seam and hem the top edge of each stocking. Cut out a pair of shoes from the brown felt or suede cloth. Sew the back seam of each upper shoe part and whipstitch a sole to each upper shoe.

2. Cut out the pantaloons from the white percale, following the directions on the pattern. Sew the center front seam and center back as indicated. Make a narrow rolled hem at the back opening and hem the leg bottoms. For each pantaloon leg, cut a piece of the 1-inch-wide lace twice the width of the leg and gather it to fit the leg width. Sew two rows of the 1-inch-wide lace to each leg, one extending below the hem edge and the other overlapping the first row. Sew the pantaloon leg seams. Pleat the top to fit the body.

3. For the petticoat, cut a

36 x 4¾-inch strip from the white percale. Turn up ¾ inch on one long edge to make a hem. Sew a piece of the 1-inch-wide lace over the hem, with ¼ inch of the lace width extending below the edge of the hem. Sew the short ends together to form the center back seam. This piece is the flounce of the petticoat. Now cut a 13½ x 2¾-inch strip from the white percale. Gather the unhemmed edge of the flounce and sew it to one long edge of the second piece. Hem the back opening for a placket. Gather the top edge of the petticoat to fit the top edge of the pantaloons, pinning the wrong side of the petticoat to the right side of the pantaloons. Cut a waistband 1½ inches wide from the white percale. Sew the waistband to the top of the petticoat/pantaloons and sew a snap fastener to the back opening.

4. For the dress and hat, cut the skirt pieces from the striped fabric, the overskirt and hat brim from the first solid color fabric, the bodice and hat crown from the print fabric, the apron (5¾ x 6¾ inches) and hat brim lining from the second solid color fabric. Sew the bodice shoulder seams. Gather the top of each sleeve and sew it to the bodice. Cut out 1-inch-wide strips for sleeve bands to fit the doll's arms loosely. Gather the lower edge of one sleeve and bind it with one of the bands. Repeat for the second sleeve. Sew the underarm seams. Turn under the back edges of the bodice. Cut a 1-inch-wide bias strip and bind the neck edge with it. Sew a piece of gathered ⅜-inch-wide lace to the neck and to the sleeve edges. Hem two long and

one short edge of the apron and sew ⅜-inch-wide lace around the three hemmed sides. Gather the unhemmed edge of the apron to measure 2½ inches. Sew the apron, centered, to the front of the bodice. Gather the top edges of the overskirt pieces, turning under the side seam allowances. Sew the top of the overskirt to the bodice bottom, placing the splits at the center front and the center back. Sew the skirt seams, leaving approximately a 4-inch opening in the back seam at the top of the skirt; hem the back opening. Hem the skirt, gather the top edge and sew the skirt top to the bodice bottom. Turn under the seam allowance on the overskirt and gather the overskirt to fit over the skirt; the bottom edges will turn under to form a puff. Sew a snap fastener to the skirt waistband, another at the neck line of the bodice and the last one midway between the other two.

5. Cut out the hat brim interfacing and fuse it to the brim. Place the brim and the lining together and sew along the outer curved edge. Sew the back seam and turn the brim right side out. Finger press the edge of the brim. Sew a piece of gathered ⅜-inch-wide lace around the edge. Gather the edge of the crown piece and sew the crown edge to the inner edge of the brim. Make a bow with the 1-inch-wide ribbon and sew it to the center front of the hat brim.

6. Make a shepherd's crook by twisting the 2 chenille stems together. Make a bow from the ½-inch-wide ribbon and sew the bow to the shaped crook.

Little Boy Blue's Outfit:
Materials: ¼ yard of blue percale; ¼ yard of blue and white gingham; scrap of white fabric; scrap of brown felt or suede cloth; matching threads; 2 small buttons; ½ yard of 1-inch-wide grosgrain ribbon; ¼ yard of ½-inch-wide red satin ribbon; three ¾-inch-diameter snap fasteners.

Directions:
1. Enlarge the pattern pieces for Little Boy Blue's outfit, following the directions on page 271.
2. Use the ribbed cuff of the child's sock for Little Boy Blue's socks. Make the socks following the directions for Little Bo Peep's stockings, but do not hem the tops. Make the shoes from the brown felt or suede cloth, following the directions for Little Bo Peep's shoes.
3. Make the underpants from the white percale, following the directions for Little Bo Peep's pantaloons, but omitting the lace. Attach the underpants directly to the waistband.
4. Make the shirt from the blue and white gingham, following the directions for Little Bo Peep's bodice, but placing the opening in the front. For the cuffs, cut two 4¼ x 2½-inch pieces from the white fabric. With raw edges even, fold each 2½-inch length in half, wrong sides together. Sew a cuff band to the wrong side of each sleeve edge, with raw edges even, then turn the cuff to the right side, using the seam as the fold line. Cut a 1¾ x 7-inch bias strip from the white fabric for the collar. Bind the neck with the collar band. Sew snap fasteners to the front opening. Make a bow with the 1-inch-wide ribbon; sew the bow to the front of the collar.

5. Cut out the pants from the blue percale. Make the pants following the directions for Little Bo Peep's pantaloons, adding a cuff to each leg end. Cut each cuff 2¾ x 6½ inches. Fold each cuff in half lengthwise, place it on the wrong side of a pant leg with all raw edges even and sew. Turn each cuff right side out. Tack the top of each cuff to the leg. Cut a waistband 1¼ inches wide and sew the waistband to the pants. Attach two pieces of the 1-inch-wide ribbon, crossing the ribbon on the back, for suspender straps. Sew a small button to the front of each strap.

6. Cut out the hat brim, crown and brim lining from the blue percale. Cut out the interfacing for the brim and fuse the interfacing to the brim. Sew the brim and brim lining together along the outer curved edge. Sew the back seam. Turn the brim right side out and press the seam edge. Leaving the crown folded, baste the curved edges together. Place the curved edges over the raw edge of the brim, overlapping the seam allowances. Stitch the brim to the crown, overlapping and stitching the crown's folded edges at the back. Sew ½-inch-wide red ribbon to cover the raw edges where the crown joins the brim.

"THINK PINK!" PIGLET
(16 inches tall)

Average: For those with some experience in crocheting.

Materials: 4-ply worsted weight yarn (3½-oz skein): 2 skeins each of Light Pink and Hot Pink, 1 skein each of White and Black; size I crochet hook, OR ANY SIZE HOOK TO OBTAIN GAUGE BELOW; polyester fiberfill; two ½-inch-diameter buttons; tapestry needle.

Gauge: With 2 strands of yarn held together, 3 sc = 1 inch; 3 rows = 1 inch.

Note: Do not join rounds, but use a marker to indicate the end of each round.

Directions:

1. *Head:* Starting at the tip of the nose with 2 strands of Light Pink, ch 4. Join with sl st to form ring. *Rnd 1:* 6 sc in ring. *Rnd 2:* 2 sc in each sc around—12 sc. *Rnd 3:* Using back lps only, sc in each sc around for nose ridge. *Rnd 4:* Using both lps, sc in each sc around. *Rnd 5:* (Sc in next sc, 2 sc in next sc) 6 times—18 sc. *Rnd 6:* Sc in each sc around. *Rnd 7:* (Sc in each of next 5 sc, 2 sc in next sc) 3 times—21 sc. *Rnd 8:* 2 sc in each of next 14 sc, sc in each of next 7 sc—35 sc. *Rnd 9:* Sc in each of next 7 sc, (2 sc in next sc, sc in next sc) 7 times, sc in each of next 14 sc—42 sc. *Rnds 10 to 13:* Sc in each sc around. *Rnd 14:* (Sc in each of next 6 sc, 2 sc in next sc) 6 times—48 sc. *Rnds 15 to 19:* Sc in each sc around. *Rnd 20:* (Sk next sc, sc in each of next 7 sc) 6 times—42 sc. *Rnd 21:* (Sk next sc, sc in each of next 6 sc) 6 times—36 sc. *Rnd 22:* Sc in each sc around. *Rnd 23:* (Sk next sc, sc in each of next 5 sc) 6 times—30 sc. *Rnd 24:* (Sk next sc, sc in each of next 4 sc) 6 times—24 sc. Stuff head firmly. *Rnd 25:* (Sk next sc, sc in each of next 3 sc) 6 times—18 sc. *Rnd 26:* (Sk next sc, sc in each of next 2 sc) 6 times—12 sc. *Rnd 27:* (Sk next sc, sc in next sc) 6 times. Fasten off. Weave the opening closed.

2. *Ears (make 2):* Starting at the tip of the ear with 2 strands of Light Pink, ch 2. *Row 1:* Sc in 2nd ch from hook. Ch 1, turn. *Row 2:* 2 sc in sc. Ch 1, turn. *Row 3:* 2 sc in each sc—4 sc. Ch 1, turn. *Row 4:* 2 sc in first sc, sc in each of next 2 sc, 2 sc in last sc—6 sc. Ch 1, turn. *Row 5:* 2 sc in first sc, sc in each of next 4 sc, 2 sc in last sc—8 sc. Ch 1, turn. *Rows 6 to 8:* Sc in each sc across. Ch 1, turn. Fasten off after Row

8. Sew the ears to the top of the head, 1½ inches apart, curving them slightly.

3. Body: Starting at the neck edge with 2 strands of Hot Pink, ch 18. Join with sl st to form ring. **Rnd 1:** 24 sc in ring. **Rnd 2:** Sc in each sc around. **Rnd 3:** (Sc in each of next 3 sc, 2 sc in next sc) 6 times—30 sc. **Rnd 4:** Sc in each sc around. **Rnd 5:** (Sc in each of next 4 sc, 2 sc in next sc) 6 times—36 sc. **Rnd 6:** Sc in each sc around. **Rnd 7:** (Sc in each of next 5 sc, 2 sc in next sc) 6 times—42 sc. **Rnds 8 to 13:** Sc in each sc around. **Rnd 14:** Change to White. Using 2 strands of yarn, and working in back lps only, sc in each sc around for start of underpants. **Rnds 15 to 21:** Using both lps, sc in each sc around. **Rnd 22:** (Sk next sc, sc in each of next 6 sc) 6 times—36 sc. **Bottom Shaping, Row 1:** Sc in each of next 10 sts. Do not work remaining sts. Ch 1, turn. **Row 2:** 2 sc in first sc, sc in each of next 8 sc, 2 sc in end sc—12 sc. Ch 1, turn. **Rows 3 to 5:** Repeat Row 2, increasing one st at each end every row—18 sc. Fasten off after Row 5 to complete flap.

4. Skirt: Join 1 strand of Hot Pink with sl st in outer lp of any st of Body Rnd 13. **Row 1:** 2 sc in each st around. Join with sl st to first sc. Ch 3. **Row 2:** Dc in same st as ch-3, * dc in next st, 2 dc in next st; rep from * around. Sl st to top of ch-3—126 dc. **Rows 3 to 6:** Ch 3. Dc in each st around. Sl st to top of ch-3. Fasten off

after Row 6. Sew the two buttons to the front of the dress. Stuff the body firmly and sew it closed. Sew the flap toward the front of the body.

5. Arms: Starting at the bottom of the hoof, with 2 strands of Light Pink, ch 4. Join with sl st to form ring. **Rnd 1:** 6 sc in ring. **Rnd 2:** 2 sc in each sc around—12 sc. **Rnd 3:** (Sc in next sc, 2 sc in next sc) 6 times—18 sc. **Rnd 4:** Using back lps only, sc in each sc around. **Rnds 5 to 14:** Using both lps, sc in each sc around. **Rnd 15:** Change to Hot Pink and sc in each sc around. **Rnd 16:** Using back lps only, sc in each sc around. **Rnds 17 to 20:** Using both lps, sc in each sc around. Fasten off after Rnd 20, leaving 10 inches of yarn to sew the top of the hoof. Using Black yarn and the tapestry needle, embroider 2 V's for the pig's nails on the edge of each arm, having the bottom of the nails touch the outer lp of Rnd 4. The nails are shaped like an upside-down V.

6. Sleeve Edge: Join 1 strand of Hot Pink with sl st in outer lp of any st of Rnd 15. Sc in same lp as sl st and in each lp around. Join with sl st to first sc. Fasten off. Stuff the arms and sew them to the sides of the neck edge, making sure the nails are facing you and towards the outer edge *(see photo, page 219)*. Sew the head to the top of the body.

7. Legs: Starting at the bottom of the sole, with 2 strands of Black, ch 8. **Row 1:** Sc in 2nd ch

from hook, sc in each of next 4 ch, hdc in next ch, 3 hdc in end ch. Working on opposite side of ch, hdc in first ch, sc in each of next 4 ch. Join with sl st to first sc. Ch 1. **Row 2:** Sc in each of first 4 sc, 2 sc in each of next 6 sc, sc in each of last 4 sc. Join with sl st to first sc. Ch 1. **Row 3:** Sc in each of first 7 sc, 2 sc in each of next 6 sc, sc in each of last 7 sc. Join with sl st to first sc. **Do not** ch 1. **Rnd 1:** Using back lps only, sc in each sc around—26 sc. **Rnd 2:** Using both lps, sc in each sc around. **Rnd 3:** Sc in each of next 7 sc, (sk next sc, sc in each of next 2 sc) 4 times, sc in each of next 7 sc—22 sc. **Rnd 4:** Sc in each of next 5 sc, (sk next sc, sc in each of next 2 sc) 4 times, sc in each of next 5 sc—18 sc. **Rnd 5:** Sc in each sc around. **Rnds 6 to 9:** Change to Hot Pink and sc in each sc around. Stuff the foot firmly after Rnd 7. **Rnds 10 to 19:** Change to Light Pink and sc in each sc around. Fasten off after Rnd 19, leaving 10 inches of yarn to sew with. Stuff the legs firmly and sew them to the seam of the body flap.

8. Tail: Using 2 strands of Light Pink, ch 12. Work 3 sc in 2nd ch from hook, * 2 sc in next ch, 3 sc in next ch; rep from * around to end of ch. Sew the tail to the back of the piglet's underpants.

9. Finishing: Using Black yarn, embroider the eyes, mouth and nostrils. With Hot Pink yarn, tie a bow at the top of the head.

LI'L CRITTER EARMUFFS

Average: For those with some experience in crocheting.

Materials: 4-ply worsted weight yarn: 1½ ounces of Gold, Gray or Tan for each pair, 1 ounce of Dark Brown for Lion's mane, small amount of Pink for Mouse's ears, small amount of Black for facial features; size F and size G crochet hooks, OR ANY SIZE HOOK TO OBTAIN GAUGE BELOW; 9 ounces of polyester fiberfill; 1 yard of ½-inch-wide orange ribbon; tapestry needle.

Gauge: With size G hook, 4 hdc = 1 inch; 4 rows = 1 inch.

Note: Do not join rounds, but use a marker to indicate the end of each round. Use size G hook unless otherwise stated.

General Directions:

1. Muffs (make 4): Ch 3. Join with sl st to form ring. Ch 1. *Rnd 1:* Work 6 hdc in ring. *Rnd 2:* Work 2 hdc in each st around— 12 sts. *Rnd 3:* *Work 1 hdc in next st, 2 hdc in next st; rep from * around—18 sts. *Rnd 4:* *Work 1 hdc in each of next 2 sts, 2 hdc in next st; rep from * around—24 sts. *Rnd 5:* *Work 1 hdc in each of next 3 sts, 2 hdc in next st; rep from * around—30 sts. *Rnds 6 to 8:* Continue to increase 6 sts evenly spaced around—48 sts. *Rnd 9:* Work sc around. Join with sl st to first sc. Fasten off, leaving about 10 inches of yarn to sew with. Sew two muff pieces together, stuffing them lightly. Repeat with the second pair of muff pieces.

2. Headband (make 1): Ch 8. *Row 1:* Hdc in 3rd ch from hook and in each ch across—6 sts. Ch 2, turn. *Rows 2 to 42:* Work 6 hdc across. Ch 2, turn. If you

Li'l Critter Earmuffs

wish, work fewer or more rows to adjust the fit. Fasten off, leaving about 6 inches of yarn to sew with. Sew each end to the top of a muff.

3. Ties (make 2): Ch 77. Hdc in 3rd ch from hook and in each ch across. Fasten off, leaving about 4 inches of yarn to sew with. Sew each tie to the bottom of a muff.

4. Eyes and Nose (make 6): With size F hook and Black, ch 2. Work 4 sc in 2nd ch from hook. Join with sl st to first sc. Fasten off, leaving about 10 inches of yarn to sew with. Sew on two

eyes at Rnd 2 of each muff, ¾ inch apart. If you wish, embroider an outline stitch around each eye. Sew on a nose at Rnd 2 of each muzzle *(see specific directions for the Lion, Mouse or Dog).*

Lion:

1. With Gold, follow the General Directions to make the muffs, headband, ties, eyes and nose.

2. Muzzle (make 2): With Gold, ch 3. Join with sl st to form ring. Ch 1. *Rnd 1:* Work 6 hdc in ring. *Rnd 2:* Work 2 hdc in each st around—12 sts. *Rnd 3:* * Work 1 hdc in each of next 2 sts, 2 hdc in next st; rep from * around—16 sts. *Rnd 4:* Work sc around. Join with sl st to first sc. Fasten off, leaving about 8 inches of yarn to sew with. Stuff and sew each muzzle to a muff, starting at Rnd 1.

3. Mane: Cut about two hundred 4-inch-long pieces of Dark Brown yarn. Tie two strands in each st of Rnd 8. Tie three strands at the end of each earmuff tie. Comb out the mane and tie tufts, and trim them to about 1 inch in length.

4. Facial Features: With Black and an outline stitch, embroider a smile under the nose, and connect the smile to the nose with a straight line of outline stitches.

Dog:

1. With Tan, follow the General Directions to make the muffs, headband, ties, eyes and nose. Work facial features following directions for the Lion's facial features. Make two bows from the orange ribbon; add one to each muff *(see photo, page 221).*

2. Muzzle (make 2): With Tan, ch 3. Join with sl st to form ring. Ch 1. *Rnd 1:* Work 8 hdc in ring. *Rnd 2:* * Work 1 hdc in next st, 2 hdc in next st; rep from * around—12 sts. *Rnd 3:* * Work 1 hdc in each of next 2 sts, 2 hdc in next st; rep from * around—16 sts. *Rnd 4:* Work sc around. Join with sl st to first sc. Fasten off, leaving about 8 inches of yarn to sew with. Stuff and sew each muzzle to a muff, starting at Rnd 1.

3. Ears (make 4): With Dark Brown, ch 12. *Row 1:* Hdc in 3rd ch from hook and in each of next 8 chs, 3 hdc in last ch. Work 9 hdc on other side of ch. Ch 2, turn. *Row 2:* Work 1 hdc in each of next 9 sts, 2 hdc in next st, 1 hdc in next st, 2 hdc in

next st, 1 hdc in each of next 9 sts. Fasten off, leaving about 6 inches of yarn to sew with. Sew on two ears at Rnd 7 of each muff.

Mouse:

1. With Gray, follow the General Directions to make the muffs, headband, ties, eyes and nose. With Gray, make the muzzle following the directions for the Dog's muzzle. Work the facial features following the directions for the Lion's facial features. Make two bows from the orange ribbon and add one to each muff *(see photo, page 221).*

2. Ears (make 4): With Pink, ch 3. Join with sl st to form ring. Ch 1. *Rnd 1:* Work 6 hdc in ring. *Rnd 2:* Work 2 hdc in each st around—12 sts. *Next Rnd:* Work sc around. Join with sl st to first sc. Fasten off. With Gray, rep Rnds 1 and 2. *Do not* fasten off. Hold the Gray and Pink pieces together, back to back. With Gray, work 2 hdc in each st around, working through both thicknesses—24 sts. *Last Rnd:* Work sc around. Join with sl st. Fasten off, leaving about 6 inches of yarn to sew with. Repeat from Rnd 1 three more times to make four ears. Sew on two ears at Rnd 7 of each muff.

TRAVELIN' TOYS
(truck: 3½ x 5½ x 12½ inches; ferryboat: 7¼ x 7¾ x 17 inches; engine: 3¾ x 3½ x 12 inches)

Challenging: Requires more experience in woodworking.

General Materials: Scraps of plywood *(see* FIGS. V, 7 *to* 9 *for the amount of wood needed for each toy);* jig or sabre saw; drill; hammer; nails; wood glue; non-toxic paints. *For Truck:* four 1½-inch-diameter wheels; four wooden pin axles. *For Ferryboat:* one 1-inch-diameter dowel; scrap of ¾-inch pine; two brass hinges. *For Engine:* four 1½-inch-diameter wheels; four wooden pin axles; 1½-inch end of Shaker peg.

Directions:
1. Using the jig or sabre saw, cut out the parts of the toys, following FIGS. V, 7 to 9.
2. For the vehicles on the Ferryboat, enlarge the patterns in FIG. V, 8a, following the directions

FIG. V, 7 TRUCK
(3½"W. x 5½"H. x 12½"L.)

A (LAT)   (1) ½" x 3½" x 12" BOTTOM
B (2 x 4)   (1) 1½" x 3½" x 3½" CAB
C (LAT)   (2) ½" x 1" x 10½" BODY
C1 (LAT)   (1) ½" x 1" x 2⅝" TAILGATE
D (LAT)   (4) ½" x 1" x 1¼" x CHASSIS
D1   (4) 1½" DIA. WHEELS
D2   (4) WOOD PIN AXLES
E (LAT)   (1) ½" x 1⅜" x 3½" BUMPER
F (LAT)   (1) ¼" x 1⅛" x 3½" BUMPER

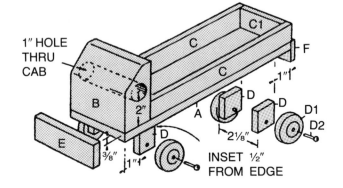

1" HOLE THRU CAB

INSET ½" FROM EDGE

on page 271. Using the jig or sabre saw, cut out the patterns from the ⅜-inch pine.

3. Sand the toy parts smooth. Using the photo as a guide, paint all the parts. Glue and/or nail all the parts together, as shown in the diagrams.

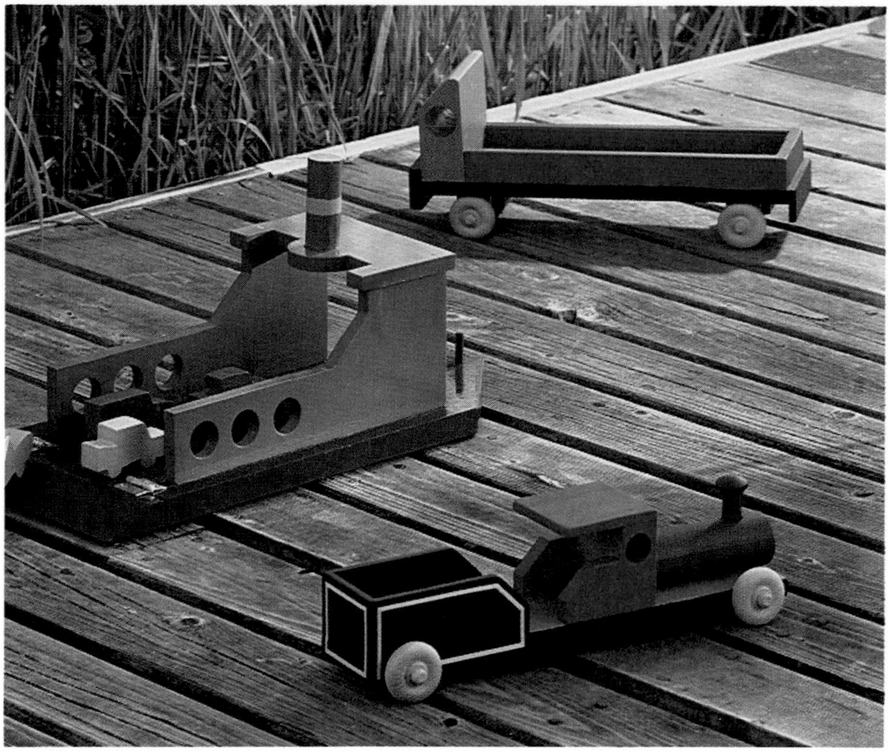

CARS AND TRUCKS THAT RIDE ON THE FERRYBOAT.

FIG. V, 8a 1 SQ. = ½″

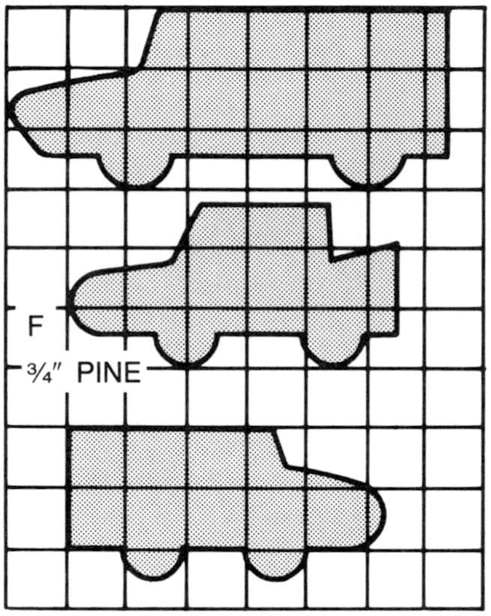
F
¾″ PINE

FIG. V, 8 FERRYBOAT
(7¼″W. x 7¾″H. x 17″L.)

A (1 x 8)	(1)	¾″ x 7¼″ x 15″ HULL
B (PLY)	(2)	½″ x 4″ x 10″ SIDES
C (PLY)	(1)	½″ x 3½″ x 6″ ROOF
D (DOWEL)	(1)	1″ Dia. x 2¾″ STACK
E (1 x 8)	(1)	¾″ x 2″ x 7¼″ RAMP
F (SCRAP)	(3)	(See FIG. V, 8a)

FIG. V, 9 ENGINE (3¾″W. x 3½″H. x 12″L.)

A (LAT)	(1)	½″ x 2½″ x 12″ BOTTOM
B (DOW)	(1)	1⅜″ DIA. x 4″ BOILER
C (LAT)	(1)	1″ x 2½″ x 2¼″ CAB
C1 (LAT)	(2)	½″ x 1⅜″ x 1½″ CAB SIDES
C2 (LAT)	(1)	¼″ x 2½″ x 2⅝″ CAB TOP
D (LAT)	(2)	¼″ x 1⅝″ x 4¼″ TENDER
D1 (LAT)	(1)	¼″ x 1⅝″ x 2½″ TENDER
D2 (LAT)	(1)	¼″ x ¾″ x 2″ TENDER
E	(4)	1½″ DIA. WHEELS
F	(4)	WOOD PIN AXLES
G		1½″ END OF SHAKER PIN—STACK

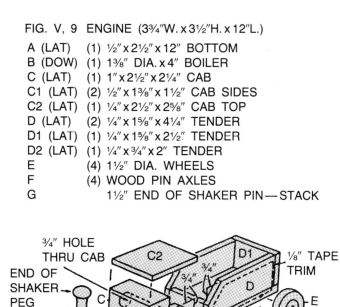

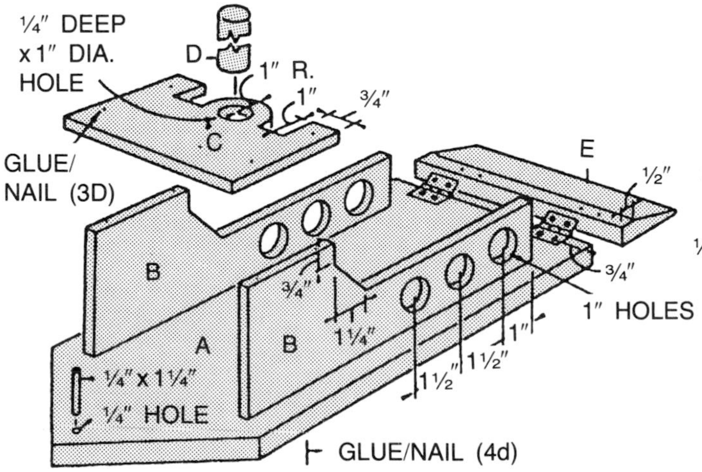
¼″ DEEP x 1″ DIA. HOLE
D
1″ R.
1″
¾″
C
GLUE/ NAIL (3D)
E
½″
B
¾″
1″ HOLES
A
B
¾″
1¼″
1½″
1½″
1″
¼″ x 1¼″
¼″ HOLE
GLUE/NAIL (4d)

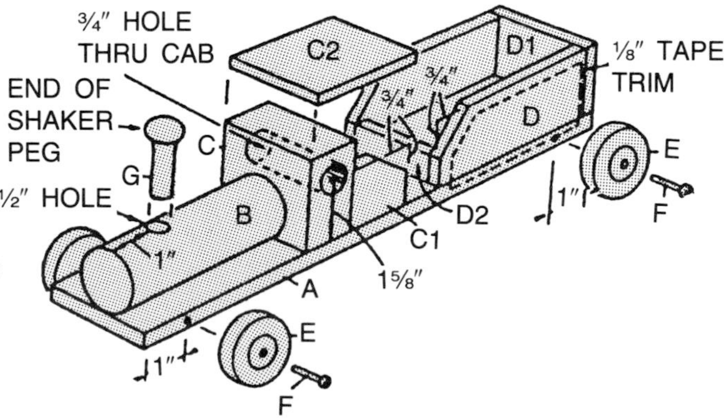
¾″ HOLE THRU CAB
C2
D1
⅛″ TAPE TRIM
END OF SHAKER PEG
C
¾″
¾″
D
E
G
½″ HOLE
B
D2
1″
F
C1
1″
A
1⅝″
E
1″
F

THE MANY FACES OF SANTA DOLL
(about 17 inches tall)

Average: For those with some experience in sewing and toy making.

Materials: ½ yard of unbleached muslin; matching thread; fluffy mohair yarn: 1 small skein of Creamy White; 1 x 1½ inches of red felt for mouth; 1-inch square of black felt; embroidery floss: small amounts of Light Blue and Light Pink for eyes; 6-inch embroidery hoop; White thread; embroidery needle; cotton or fiberfill to make firm stuffing; pencil; white craft glue; blush.

Directions (½-inch seams allowed):

1. Enlarge the pattern pieces in FIG. V, 10 *(page 227)*, #1 through #5, following the directions on page 271. Arrange the pattern pieces on the unbleached muslin except for #1, Santa's face, so there will be a leftover scrap on which you can draw a 2¼-inch-diameter circle. Cut out pieces #2 through #5 as indicated on the pattern; do not cut out Santa's face piece yet. Cut out an 8-inch square for the face and set it aside.

2. Pin together the body pieces, right sides together. Sew the body pieces, leaving an opening at the neck. Clip the curves, turn and stuff the body firmly with fiberfill. Pin and sew the two legs, right sides together; clip the curves, turn and stuff firmly. Turn in the seam allowance at the top of each leg. Stitch the legs to the bottom seam of the body. Sew the arms

together in the same way. Before stuffing each arm, hand-sew along the lines indicated on the arm pattern to outline the fingers and the thumb; stuff the fingers and thumb. Stitch a line to outline the crease between the fingers and the palm. Stuff fiberfill firmly into the remainder of the arm. Turn in the seam at the top of each arm and sew the arms to the body at the shoulders. Make the palms of the hands lie toward the body, with the thumbs up.

3. Draw Santa's face in the center of the 8-inch square of muslin and put the square in the embroidery hoop. Use the Light Blue embroidery floss and satin stitch to embroider the irises of the eyes. Use the Light Pink floss to embroider crow's feet at the outer corners of the eyes. Glue on ¼-inch circles of black felt for the pupils.

4. Cut out a 2¼-inch-diameter circle from the muslin and, by hand, run a line of stitching ¼ inch from the outside edge. Gather the circle and stuff it with fiberfill to make a firm ball. Flatten the ball and sew it tightly to close the opening. Glue or sew the ball to Santa's face to make a nose. Shape the mouth from the red felt and glue it in place. Using pattern piece #1, cut out Santa's face piece from the square of muslin. Place the face front and head back, right sides together.

5. Sew together the face and the back of the head, leaving an opening. Turn the head right side out and stuff it firmly with fiberfill. Use blush to color the cheeks and nose. Make loops of mohair yarn and sew the loops in rows around Santa's head for hair. Give him bushy eyebrows and a beard. Clip several strands of mohair and sew them between his nose and mouth to make a moustache; be sure the moustache is long enough to become part of the beard.

6. Turn the seam at the top of the body to the inside and slip-stitch the head to the body along the stitch line.

SANTA'S SUITS

Average: For those with some experience in sewing.

General Directions (½-inch seams allowed):

Enlarge the pattern pieces for Santa's clothes in FIG. V, 10 *(page 227)*, following the directions on page 271. Trace the pattern pieces onto tracing paper and number each piece. The front and back pieces are used for several different garments. You probably will find it easier to make a separate pattern for each outfit. Use fabric scraps instead of buying new fabrics.

Santa's Red Suit:

Materials: ¼ yard of red fabric; ⅛ yard or less of plaid wool fabric and green cotton fabric; matching threads; 16 inches of ¼-inch-wide elastic; ¾ yard of ½-inch-wide red braid trim; four ½-inch-diameter silver buttons.

Directions:

1. For the jacket, use pattern pieces #6, #7 and #8. Cut out four fronts (two are used as the facing), two backs and two sleeves. Sew the back pieces to the front pieces at the shoulders. Attach the sleeves to the jacket front and back at the shoulders. Seam the underarm of the sleeves and jacket. Stitch the facing to the jacket front along the raw edges, right sides together. Turn and clip the curves. Sew the back of the neckline. Hem the sleeves and the edge of the jacket. Attach braid trim to each sleeve. Make three buttonholes on the front of the jacket; attach buttons correspondingly.

2. For the pants, use pattern piece #11. Cut out four pieces, two for the front, two for the back; the pants front and back are the same. Pin the pants front to the pants back, right sides facing. Stitch the sides and the inseams. Clip and turn the pants right side out. Fold over ½ inch at the waistline and stitch to make an elastic casing. Adjust the elastic to fit Santa's waist.

3. For the vest, use pattern pieces #9 and 10. Cut out two vest fronts and one vest back from the plaid wool fabric (flop the vest front pattern piece to make the right and left sides of the vest front). Cut out two vest fronts and one vest back from the green cotton fabric for facing. Attach the plaid front pieces to the back pieces at the shoulders and side seams. Repeat for the facing pieces. Pin the plaid pieces to the facing pieces, right sides together, and seam around the outer edge, leaving a 2-inch opening in the

seam for turning. Clip the curves and turn the vest right side out. Clip the armhole to ease the curve, turn the seam to the inside and hand stitch together. Topstitch around the outside of the vest ¼ inch from the edges. Make a buttonhole on the vest front and attach the remaining button opposite.

4. For the boots, use pattern piece #12. Cut out four pieces, two for each boot. With right sides together, stitch the boots, leaving the top open. Clip the curves and turn the boots right side out. Hem the tops of the boots.

5. For the hat, use pattern piece #13. Cut out two pieces, for the hat front and back. With right sides together, stitch the front to the back, leaving the bottom edge open. Clip, turn and hem the hat. Attach braid trim to the edge of the hat.

Plaid Shirt:

Materials: ¼ yard of plaid cotton flannel; matching seam tape and thread; three ⅜-inch-diameter buttons, or three snaps.

Directions:

Use pattern pieces #14, #7, #8, #15, #16 and #17. Instructions are the same as for the red suit jacket. Stitch the collar (pattern #16), right sides together, clip and turn it right side out. Insert the collar between the shirt front and shirt facing and sew it in place. Add the cuffs (pattern #15) and a pocket (pattern #17). Finish the inside back neck edge with seam tape. Make buttonholes, or sew on snaps.

Jeans:

Materials: Denim (new or from old jeans); orange thread for detail stitching; 8 inches of ¼-inch-wide elastic; 4 brass studs.

Directions:

Use pattern piece #11. Instructions are the same as for the red suit pants. *Exceptions:* Add double rows of topstitching along the waistline *(see photo, page 225)* with the orange thread. Decorate the back pocket with topstitching as desired, then sew the pocket to the back of the jeans. Add the brass studs on the front and back. Insert elastic for the waistline only in the back half of the jeans.

Pajamas:

Materials: Striped cotton fabric; 12 inches of bias tape; 3 snaps or 4 green shirt buttons; 16 inches of ¼-inch-wide elastic.

Directions:

Use pattern pieces #14 (cut two only; there is no facing), #7, #8, #15 and #11. Instructions for the pajama pants and top are the same as for the red suit pants and jacket. *Exceptions:* Put a cuff on the end of each sleeve before sewing the sleeves to the pajama top. There is no facing. Finish the neck edge with the bias tape. Put on the snaps or buttons.

MAKING THE SEASON BRIGHT!

Sharing the Joy

Every community has a toy fund for underprivileged children. Take your child shopping and give him a budget to work with. Ask him to pick out something for himself that he thinks another child will love as well. He buys two, wraps both presents imaginatively and places one under the tree for himself. Take him to drop off the other gift at the toy fund. As your child opens his gift on Christmas morning, remind him that, thanks to him, another child is enjoying the same gift today.

Holiday "Hellos"

Arrange a visit to a local nursing home. Family and friends can pitch in to make Christmas cookies for the residents, or take baskets of fresh fruit, special jams and jellies or inexpensive toilet articles. Have plenty of Christmas carols photocopied to hand out so everyone can sing along. Even the staff members will be cheered by your thoughtfulness.

A Little Pet Pampering

Pets give us so much love throughout the year; this season, do something special for them. Let the kids plan a Christmas Eve feast for a beloved family pet. They can buy a different, maybe a bit more expensive, brand of dog or cat food, or help Dad and Mom make a super hamburger or tuna patty. Then tuck a custom-made Christmas card, some small presents (such as chewy toys for dogs; catnip mice for cats) and maybe a new collar into an inexpensive stocking for a special pet treat.

FIG. V, 10 THE MANY FACES OF SANTA DOLL AND SUIT PATTERNS   1 SQ. = 1"

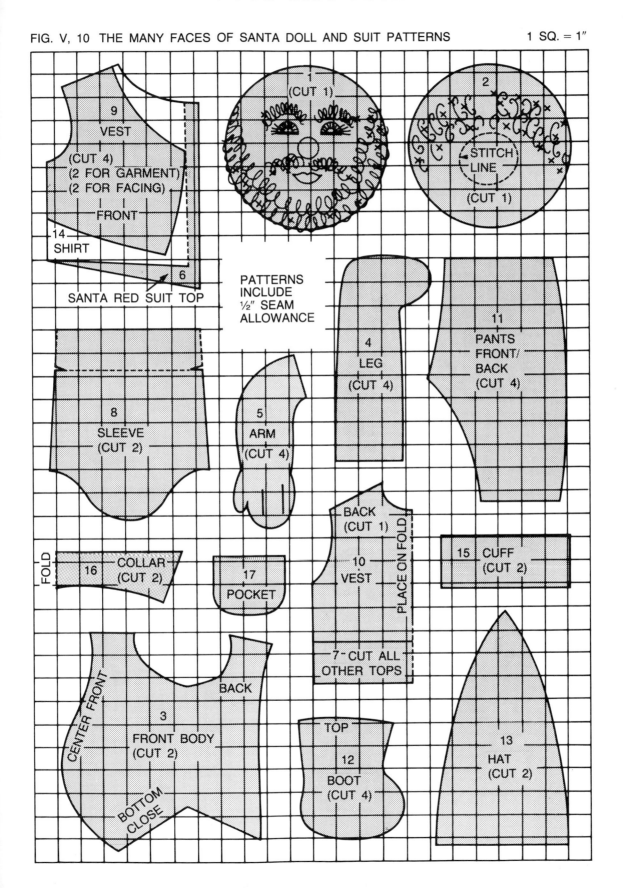

Smilin' Sandwiches (recipe, page 230); Christmas Tree Cake and Frosted Gingerbread Cookies (recipes, page 231); Cranberry Fizz Punch (recipe, page 232); Carrot and Cheese Sticks

CHRISTMAS KID-BITES

(for 12)

Smilin' Sandwiches
Carrot and Cheese Sticks
Frosted Gingerbread Cookies
Christmas Tree Cake
Cranberry Fizz Punch
Milk, Hot Cocoa

WORK PLAN FOR CHRISTMAS KID-BITES

Up to One Month Ahead:
- Prepare the dough for the Frosted Gingerbread Cookies the night before you plan to bake them. The following day, roll and bake the dough. Let the cookies cool completely and freeze them, tightly wrapped.
- Prepare, cool, cut, if necessary, and freeze the Christmas Tree Cake.

Up to Two Weeks Ahead:
- Decorate the Frosted Gingerbread Cookies. Store them in a tightly covered container.
- Prepare ice cubes. Unmold the cubes into plastic bags and return them to the freezer.

The Day Before:
- Prepare the fillings for the Smilin' Sandwiches.

- Thaw and decorate the Christmas Tree Cake. Refrigerate the decorated cake, or keep it in a cool place.
- Chill the cranberry juice cocktail and the soda or seltzer for the Cranberry Fizz Punch.
- Prepare the carrot sticks, place them in ice water and refrigerate them.

Early in the Day:
- Prepare the Smilin' Sandwiches. Layer them in a 9 x 13-inch baking pan or jelly-roll pan lined with damp paper toweling. Cover the sandwiches with more damp toweling, then with plastic wrap, and refrigerate them.
- Prepare the cheese sticks.

Just Before the Party:
- Prepare the Cranberry Fizz Punch.

SMILIN' SANDWICHES

An easy technique turns everyday food into party fare.

Makes 12 sandwiches.

> 1 loaf (24 slices) soft white bread
> Raisins
> Ham Filling (recipe follows)
> Cheese Filling (recipe follows)
> Sliced cooked ham
> American cheese

1. Use the open end of a 1-pound coffee can to cut out 24 large bread rounds. Press a "smile" onto 12 of the rounds by rolling a small glass about 1 inch above the edge of each round, making the smile as large as you wish. Cut through each indentation to make an open "mouth."

2. Cut the raisins in half and press the sticky sides down on the "face" rounds to make "eyes." Lightly toast all the bread rounds.

3. Spread the undecorated toasted rounds with the Ham Filling or the Cheese Filling. Top each with a "face" round. To indicate the type of spread used, place slices of ham or American cheese, cut in the shape of little tongues, in the open "mouths."

Ham Filling: Thoroughly combine 2 cans (4½ ounces each) of deviled ham with ¼ cup of mayonnaise and 1 teaspoon of prepared mustard. *Makes 1½ cups.*

Cheese Filling: Beat together 2 packages (3 ounces each) of softened cream cheese, 2 tablespoons of grated Parmesan cheese, 2 teaspoons of lemon juice and ¼ teaspoon of Worcestershire sauce until the mixture has a good spreading consistency. *Makes ⅔ cup.*

FROSTED GINGERBREAD COOKIES

Bake at 350° for 6 minutes.
Makes about 1½ dozen cookies.

- 1 **cup sifted all-purpose flour**
- ½ **teaspoon pumpkin pie spice**
- ¼ **teaspoon baking soda**
  Dash of salt
- 2 **tablespoons butter, softened**
- 2 **tablespoons firmly packed light or dark brown sugar**
- ¼ **cup molasses**
  Dried currants
  Canned and tube frostings
  Food coloring (optional)

1. Sift together the flour, pumpkin pie spice, baking soda and salt onto wax paper.
2. Beat together the butter and the brown sugar until light and fluffy in a medium-size bowl with an electric mixer at high speed. Beat in the molasses.
3. Add the flour mixture, one third at a time, blending the ingredients well to make a stiff dough. Wrap the dough in wax paper or plastic wrap. Chill the dough for several hours, or until it is firm enough to roll (overnight is best).
4. Preheat the oven to moderate (350°).
5. Roll out the dough, one quarter at a time, on a lightly floured board to a ⅛-inch thickness. Cut out the cookies with a floured 2- or 3-inch gingerbread man cookie cutter, or other cookie cutter of the same size. Place the cookies, 1 inch apart, on greased baking sheets. Gather the scraps into a ball, reroll and cut out. Decorate the unbaked cookies with cut-up currants for eyes, mouths and buttons.
6. Bake in the preheated moderate oven (350°) for 6 minutes, or until the cookies are firm. Remove the cookies from the baking sheets and cool them completely on wire racks. Decorate the cookies with the prepared frostings. If you wish, tint the frostings with food coloring. Store the cookies in a tightly covered container.

CHRISTMAS TREE CAKE

A specialty pan will save a step, although you can achieve the same results with a conventional pan.

Bake at 350° for 30 minutes.
Makes 12 servings.

- 1 **package (about 18 ounces) yellow cake mix**
- 2 **cans (about 16 ounces each) ready-to-spread vanilla frosting**
  Green food coloring
  Red cinnamon candies

1. Preheat the oven to moderate (350°).
2. Grease the bottom of an 8-cup Christmas tree-shaped pan or a 13 x 9 x 2-inch baking pan. Line the pan with wax paper and grease the paper.
3. Prepare the cake mix, following the package directions, and pour the mixture into the prepared pan.
4. Bake in the preheated moderate oven (350°) for 30 minutes, or until the center of the cake springs back when lightly touched with your fingertip. Cool the cake in the pan on a wire rack for 10 minutes. Run the tip of a small knife around the inside edges of the pan to loosen the cake, and invert the cake onto the wire rack. Peel off the wax paper and cool the cake completely. (If you used a 13 x 9 x 2-inch pan, cut the cake into a Christmas tree shape, using a sharp knife.)
5. Place 1 cup of the frosting in a small bowl and tint the frosting with the green food coloring. Set aside the green frosting.
6. Remove the cake from the wire rack to a serving platter or large cake plate. Brush the edges of the cake with a pastry brush to remove any loose crumbs. Spread the remaining white frosting around the sides and top of the cake. Decorate the frosted cake with the red cinnamon candies.
7. Fit a pastry bag with a large star tip. Fill the bag with the green frosting and pipe a border around the edge of the cake on the platter.

CRANBERRY FIZZ PUNCH

This may look like a sparkling Sangria, but it's really non-alcoholic punch for kids of all ages.

Makes 6 servings.

1 *bottle (16 ounces) cranberry juice cocktail, chilled*
1 *bottle (12 ounces) lemon-lime soda OR: seltzer, chilled*
1 *lemon, sliced*
1 *lime, sliced*

Just before serving, mix together the cranberry juice cocktail and the soda or seltzer in a large pitcher. Add the lemon and lime slices.

Holiday Notes

TOYING—WITH AFFECTION

For kids, or the young at heart, a grouping of dressed-up dolls at play is a delightful holiday scene. Teddy bears, stuffed animals and the like can be set up at tea, waiting for Santa or setting up a Christmas tree.

Holiday Notes

THE KIDS' PARTY LINE

- A special invitation adds to a child's sense of anticipation.
- For a quick cleanup, use festive paper plates and cups.
- Stick to serving finger foods—no knives or forks are needed.
- Keep the napkins handy! Kids often wind up with more food on them than in them.
- Serve fun foods, such as hero sandwiches or pizza. Keep the pâté for *your* party.
- Cut foods into fun shapes using holiday cookie cutters and use edible garnishes on serving platters. *Don't use toothpicks*—it's too easy to swallow them accidentally.
- Bake or buy a special cake in the shape of a toy or a favorite cartoon character.
- Have walk-away goodies at hand for young guests to take home—a delicious way to remember the fun.
- Make something for the party together with your child. It will make him or her feel involved and provide you with some "private" time together.
- Take Polaroids throughout the party and be sure to get at least one shot of each child. As the kids leave, present each one with their own personal party favor.
- The busier, the better! Musical chairs and pin the tail on the donkey still are popular with small children. For older kids, try a trivia game or charades.
- As soon as the kids show signs of boredom, move on to the next activity.
- For easy-on-you entertaining, check at a local college for students who do clown acts, sing-alongs or magic.
- Balloons and streamers are fairly inexpensive but can help put folks in a party mood.
- Have a goodie scavenger hunt. Remember to hide treats where little hands can reach them easily.
- Keep the number of kids to a minimum. A too-large group is overwhelming for the kids and for you.
- Have enough adult helpers—two adults for every six children.

BE GOOD—FOR GOODNESS SAKE!
By Letitia Baldrige

Here are a few pointers to help your children to be on their best behavior for Christmas.

Q: What's the most important thing to keep in mind about children's holiday manners?

A: Not to make too many demands on your children or expect too much. Over-tired children are unable to mind their manners. Never plan a visit to Santa, a shopping trip and a party on one day—it's too much to handle.

Q: How can I teach my child to be tactful about the gifts he receives?

A: Teach him to withhold any feelings of disappointment or dislike while the giver is present so he doesn't hurt their feelings. Later, try playing a game called "Find the Good Points." Ask him to try think of something he likes about his gift. For instance, he doesn't love the style of sweater Uncle Ed gave him, but he does like the color.

Q: Are there any table manners I can practice with my child?

A: Here are the five most important rules to teach your child about table manners:

• Your napkin is your friend. As soon as you sit down, unfold it, place it on your lap and keep it there as though it were attached. If you drop it, pick it up and put it back. When dinner is over, fold the napkin and place it on the table, next to your plate.

• Never use your thumb to push food onto your fork. It is difficult to get some food, such as green peas, onto your fork, but the more you practice, the better you become.

• If you don't like the taste of something you have just put in your mouth, keep that fact a secret. Swallow what's in your mouth and don't eat any more of that particular dish. Always take very small bites of any unfamiliar food on your plate, just in case.

• After you finish eating, place your knife and fork side by side on your plate.

• Praise the food you've liked best. "Mr. and Mrs. Eaton, I loved the sweet potatoes with marshmallow topping." That will make the Eatons happy. And they'll probably invite you back for more sweet potatoes!

Q: Have you any good rules for children to follow when greeting guests?

A: A child should rise, extend a hand and say, "Hello, Mr. and Mrs. Smith." Teach your children how to make guests feel at home if you're occupied with other hosting duties: "Would you like to come and see our Christmas tree, Mr. Oliver?" With gentle prompting these responses will become automatic.

Q: How can I help my children enjoy visiting relatives' homes for the holidays?

A: It's important for children to understand that obeying the rules in a household makes things easier for everybody.

• Explain that they may find themselves faced with situations that require resourcefulness and a lot of patience. For example, they will have to be careful of their personal belongings because Grandma's house is small.

• Tell them that they may be meeting new people and eating unfamiliar foods. If you explain in advance the types of situations they're likely to encounter, they may come up with ways of their own to minimize any problems.

Q: Is there anything I should keep in mind about children and etiquette?

A: That it's tough being young and having to sit quietly in someone else's house when everyone else is talking about things that are of no interest to you at all. Bring along a bag of games, books or small toys when visiting. After your children have said their hellos, let them be excused to play quietly in an area designated by your hosts.

Q: At what age should my child be expected to write her own thank-you letters?

A: A child in the first or second grade should be able to write a simple thank-you note drafted by a parent. (As a courtesy to postal workers, parents should address all envelopes until their children's handwriting is in reasonably good shape.) By the time she's in the fourth or fifth grade, she should be able to write a brief note without any help.

CANDY COOKIES

*Lovely to look at, delicious to eat—
these cookies are sure to be a
hit with everyone!*

STAINED GLASS COOKIES

Sour ball candies melt to form the "glass" in the cookies.

Bake at 350° for 10 minutes.
Makes about 5 dozen cookies.

- 5 **cups all-purpose flour**
- 1 **teaspoon baking powder**
- 1 **teaspoon salt**
- 1 **cup (2 sticks) butter or margarine**
- 2 **cups sugar**
- 2 **eggs**
- 2 **teaspoons vanilla**
- 1 **teaspoon lemon extract**
- **Vegetable oil**
- 1 **pound assorted sour ball candies**

1. Sift together the flour, baking powder and salt onto wax paper.
2. Beat together the butter or margarine and the sugar until fluffy in a large bowl with an electric mixer at high speed. Beat in the eggs, one at a time, then the vanilla and the lemon extract until all ingredients are thoroughly blended.
3. Stir in the flour mixture to make a stiff dough. Wrap the dough in wax paper and refrigerate it for 3 hours, or overnight.
4. Preheat the oven to moderate (350°).
5. Brush baking sheets generously with the oil (this makes the cookies easier to remove from the sheets after baking).
6. Roll out the dough, one quarter at a time, on a lightly floured pastry cloth or board to a ¼-inch thickness. Cut the rolled dough into hearts, flowers or other shapes with 3-inch cookie cutters. Cut out the centers with 1 to 1½-inch cookie cutters.
7. Place the cookies, no more than 4 or 5 at a time, on the prepared baking sheets. Place a sour ball in the hole in the center of each cookie.
8. Bake in the preheated moderate oven (350°) for 10 minutes, or until the candy melts and the cookies are golden. Cool the cookies on the baking sheets on wire racks for 2 minutes. Gently loosen around each cookie with a long sharp knife and transfer the cookies with a metal spatula to the wire racks to cool completely.

Note: If the candy centers become too firm, return the cookies to the oven for 2 minutes, or until the candy melts slightly, then remove the cookies from the baking sheets at once.

Stained Glass Cookies (recipe, page 234); Toffee Toppers and Chocolate Mint Thins (recipes, page 236); Peanut Brittle Triangles and Chocolate Caramel Squares (recipes, page 237)

TOFFEE TOPPERS

Bake at 350° for 10 minutes.
Makes about 4 dozen cookies.

5 cups all-purpose flour
1 teaspoon baking powder
1 teaspoon salt
1 cup (2 sticks) butter or margarine
2 cups sugar
2 eggs
2 teaspoons vanilla
12 soft chocolate-covered toffee bars
    (1⅛ ounces each), crushed*
    Canned frosting (optional)
    Sugar decorations, such as nonpareils or
    confetti (optional)

1. Sift together the flour, baking powder and salt onto wax paper.
2. Beat together the butter or margarine and the sugar until fluffy in a large bowl with an electric mixer at high speed. Beat in the eggs, one at a time, then the vanilla until all the ingredients are well blended.
3. Stir in the flour mixture to make a stiff dough. Remove 1⅓ cups of the dough to a small bowl and stir in the toffee. Wrap the plain and toffee doughs in wax paper and chill them for 3 hours, or overnight.
4. Preheat the oven to moderate (350°).
5. Roll out the plain dough, one quarter at a time, on a lightly floured surface to a ¼-inch thickness. Cut out the rolled dough with 3-inch cookie cutters. Place the cookies on baking sheets and top each with a dollop of the toffee dough.
6. Bake in the preheated moderate oven (350°) for 10 minutes, or until the cookies are golden. Remove the cookies to wire racks to cool completely. Store them in a tightly covered metal container.
7. If you wish, decorate the cookies by dipping their tops in frosting, then in sugar decorations. Let frosting set; store.

Note: Toffee can be crushed in a food processor. It may form a paste; this is fine for the recipe.

CHOCOLATE MINT THINS

You also can use peanut brittle pieces, rather than mint patties, in this recipe.

Bake at 375° for 10 minutes.
Makes about 2 dozen cookies.

1½ cups all-purpose flour
¼ cup cocoa powder (not a mix)
½ teaspoon baking soda
¼ teaspoon salt
¾ cup sugar
½ cup (1 stick) butter or margarine, at room
    temperature
1 teaspoon vanilla
1 egg
1 package (6 ounces) chocolate-covered
    mint patties
    Canned frosting
    Green food coloring
    Tube of green decorator icing

1. Sift together the flour, cocoa powder, baking soda and salt onto wax paper.
2. Beat together the sugar and the butter or margarine until well blended in a medium-size bowl with an electric mixer at high speed. Beat in the vanilla and the egg. Reduce the mixer speed to low.
3. Gradually beat the flour mixture into the butter mixture until all the ingredients are well blended. If the dough is very soft, refrigerate it for 30 minutes.
4. Preheat the oven to moderate (375°).
5. Divide the dough into thirds. Combine 2 of the thirds and shape this larger portion of the dough into mounds equal in number to the number of mint patties. Top each mound with a mint patty, then with a piece of the remaining third of the dough. Carefully shape the dough around each mint patty so that the patty is completely covered. If the dough becomes too soft while you are working with it, refrigerate it until it is stiff. Place the cookies, 2 inches apart, on greased baking sheets. Score the cookies with a fork to flatten them slightly.

6. Bake in the preheated moderate oven (375°) for 10 minutes, or until the cookies are firm on top. Cool the cookies on the baking sheets on wire racks for 3 minutes, then carefully remove the cookies to the wire racks to cool completely.

7. Top the cookies with frosting tinted green, then decorate with swirls of the green decorator icing; let the frosting set. Store the cookies between layers of wax paper in a tightly covered container.

PEANUT BRITTLE TRIANGLES

Bake at 375° for 20 minutes.
Makes about 3 dozen triangles.

2¼ cups all-purpose flour
1 teaspoon baking soda
1 teaspoon salt
1 package (8 ounces) peanut brittle
1 cup (2 sticks) butter or margarine
1 cup peanut butter
½ cup granulated sugar
½ cup firmly packed brown sugar
1 teaspoon vanilla
2 eggs
   Canned vanilla frosting (optional)
   Whole peanuts (optional)

1. Preheat the oven to moderate (375°). Grease a 15 x 10 x 1-inch jelly-roll pan.
2. Sift together the flour, baking soda and salt. Crush the peanut brittle.
3. Beat together the butter or margarine and the peanut butter until well blended in a large bowl with an electric mixer at high speed. Beat in the granulated and brown sugars, the vanilla and eggs. Gradually add the flour mixture to the butter mixture. Stir in 1¼ cups of peanut brittle.
4. Spread the dough in the pan. Sprinkle the remaining peanut brittle on top.
5. Bake in the preheated moderate oven (375°) for 20 minutes. Cool in the pan on a wire rack. Cut into 2-inch triangles and decorate the triangles with the frosting and the peanuts, if you wish.

CHOCOLATE CARAMEL SQUARES

Melted chocolate candy bars are folded into a brownie batter for a delectable treat.

Bake at 350° for 37 minutes.
Makes about 2½ dozen squares.

1 cup all-purpose flour
½ cup firmly packed light brown sugar
⅓ cup (about ¾ stick) butter or margarine, at room temperature
5 bars (2.1 ounces each) chocolate-coated caramel and marshmallow bars
¼ cup milk
2 eggs, slightly beaten
1 teaspoon vanilla
2 tablespoons all-purpose flour
½ teaspoon baking powder
1 can (3½ ounces) blanched sliced almonds
   Canned frosting (optional)
   Candied cherries (optional)

1. Preheat the oven to moderate (350°). Grease a 13 x 9 x 2-inch baking pan.
2. Combine the 1 cup of flour with the brown sugar in a small bowl. Cut in the butter or margarine until the mixture becomes a crumbly dough. Press the mixture into the prepared pan.
3. Bake in the preheated moderate oven (350°) for 12 minutes, or until the crust is a light golden brown. Cool the crust in the pan on a wire rack while preparing the filling.
4. Melt the candy bars with the milk in a small saucepan over medium-low heat. Cool the mixture slightly, then very slowly beat the mixture into the eggs in a small bowl, beating constantly to prevent curdling. Beat in the vanilla, then the 2 tablespoons of flour mixed with the baking powder. Pour the filling over the crust. Sprinkle the almonds over the top.
5. Bake in the preheated moderate oven (350°) for 25 minutes, or until the top is firm. Cool in the pan on a wire rack. Cut into squares or bars with a sharp knife. Decorate the squares with frosting and candied cherries, if you wish.

237

We Wish you a Merry Christmas
(and a happy New Year!)

Allegretto — anonymous

1. We wish you a Mer-ry Christ-mas, We wish you a Mer-ry Christ-mas, We

wish you a Mer-ry Christ-mas, And a Hap-py New Year!

Chorus

Good ti-dings we bring for you and your kin, We

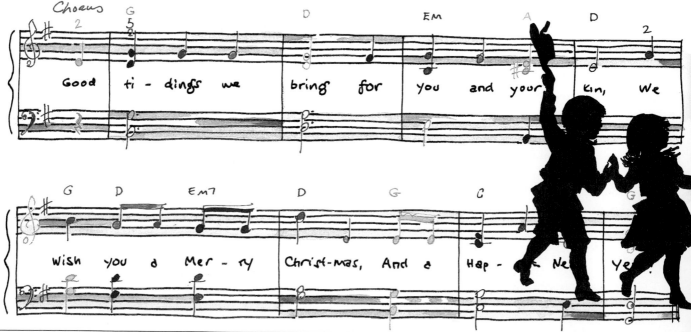

wish you a Mer-ry Christ-mas, And a Hap-py New Year!

238

CHEERS FOR THE NEW YEAR

Welcome the new year with a night to remember! After all, we're beginning a new decade—what better reason to pull out all the stops for your New Year celebration? Choose your style—cozy and elegant, or glitzy and glamourous. We'll help you plan the party right down to the centerpiece on your table. Our delicious party menus start the evening off right. The festive feasting includes a "Black Tie Optional" buffet with stuffed mushrooms, caviar dip, shrimp in cilantro sauce and a macadamia pear tart. For a more intimate New Year's Eve gathering, try a spinach ricotta roulade, salmon pâté and individual Grand Marnier chocolate soufflés. By the time the champagne corks are popping, you and your guests will be on your way to a joyous new year. All the best in 1990, from our Family to yours.

SPARKLE PLENTY!

Welcome the New Year with glitter galore.

CELEBRATION CENTERPIECE

Easy: Achievable by anyone.

Materials: Large glass or cut glass bowl; gold, silver and pale blue glass ball ornaments.

Directions:
Fill the large glass bowl with the glass ball ornaments. Use the arrangement as a centerpiece for the dining table or as a decorative touch anywhere in the house.

Variations:
• Combine tiny balls in a variety of colors with all-silver or all-gold large balls.
• Fill the bowl with red and green apples. Place the bowl in the center of a wreath tied with a few bright red and green bows.

Did You Know . . .

The giving of gifts in celebration of the New Year is a far older custom than that of the Christmas present. Early Romans gave branches from sacred trees for good luck in the coming year. They called such gifts "strenae," derived from the name of the goddess of luck. In later years, Roman New Year's gifts included gilded nuts, and coins with the two faces of the god Janus, for whom January was named. In Persia, eggs, the symbol of fertility, were given at the New Year; ancient Egyptians gave pottery, and the Druids gave mistletoe, the plant they considered most holy.

ALL THINGS BRIGHT AND BEAUTIFUL

Easy: Achievable by anyone.

Materials: Mirrored mat or tiles; white poinsettia; candles of differing heights, in complementary shades of pink and lavender; silver candlesticks; several votive candles in glass holders; assorted baskets; pink glass ornaments (we used ornaments blown to look like bunches of grapes); dried and/or fresh cut flowers in pink and lavender; pine cones; ribbons as desired.

Directions:

1. Place the white poinsettia on the mirrored mat or tiles, either centered or slightly off center.

2. Fill the baskets with pine cones and dried or cut fresh flowers, and arrange the baskets around the poinsettia. Decorate the basket handles with ribbons, if you wish.

3. Place the candles in the candlesticks and arrange them among the baskets.

4. Place the votive candles, along with the ornaments and the remaining pine cones and flowers, to fill in around the poinsettia, basket and candlestick arrangement. Drape or tie the ribbons as you wish.

Did You Know . . .

Family reunions and gift-giving for adults are the main activities during New Year's Day celebrations in France. On this day, children often give small, homemade presents to their parents, and it is traditional to remember those who give service to the family with some show of appreciation.

241

LET THE GOOD TIMES ROLL

*Try one of our entertaining ideas
to help you ring in the New Year.*

HOME FILM FESTIVAL

*For New Year's Eve, host a silver-screen bash.
Invite movie buffs for a viewing of a "golden
oldie" or a recent hit—and make the evening
memorable by recreating the film's ambience.*

• Set the mood for a romantic comedy, such as
Arthur or *It Happened One Night*, with a
candlelight dinner, and tell your friends to come
prepared to share their funniest dating memories.
• Love the Marx Brothers? Invite your friends to
a triple bill of the brothers' funniest films. No
guests admitted unless dressed like Groucho,
Harpo, Chico or Zeppo.
• Bring to life a classic Western (John Wayne's
The Rio Grande, for instance) with cowboy hats,
a hot and hearty chili feed, and trail-mix snacks.
• Blow up a beach ball, throw a blanket on the
floor and recapture summer with fruity tropical
drinks and a beach party video. *Where the Boys
Are* or *Clambake*, with Elvis, will liven things up.
• Stage a Leading Lady or Leading Man Look-
Alike Contest. How about a Scarlett O'Hara and
Rhett Butler party to go with a screening of *Gone
With the Wind?*
• Don't forget the kids! Hold a Disney matinée at
your house featuring one of the classics, such as
Mary Poppins or *Lady and the Tramp*. *(See
"Family Flicks," at right).*
• If you have slightly older kids, have a "monster
party." Tell the kids to come dressed as their
favorite movie monsters, and have a festival of
favorite old-time chillers—*Frankenstein* or *The
Crawling Eye*, for example.

FAMILY FLICKS

*If you're trying to find a movie that will satisfy the
whole family, take a look at our list. A good
"family" movie should work on several levels, and
be as enjoyable to Mom and Dad as it is to the
kids. Many of the following films are based on
classic books, and should prove entertaining to
both children and adults.*

FULL-LENGTH ANIMATION

Charlotte's Web (1972) E.B. White's wonderful
story of the friendship between a spider and a pig
comes vividly to life in this first-rate film.
Dumbo (1941) An endearing Disney movie about
a flying elephant.
The Hobbit (1977) The timeless adventures of
Bilbo Baggins, by J.R.R. Tolkien (first published
in 1937), are too good to miss reading or seeing.
Lady and the Tramp (1955) A canine love story
with enough action and adventure to keep
everyone glued to their seats (great songs, too).
Pinocchio (1940) A Disney classic, based on the
19th century book by Carlo Collodi, about the
wooden puppet who wants to become a real boy.
The Secret of N*I*M*H (1982) This lively
adaptation of Robert O'Brien's book, *Mrs.
Frisby and the Rats of NIMH*, tells how some
field mice rescue rats from a science job.
Watership Down (1978) Richard Adams' story
tells about a group of rabbits seeking a better life.

FULL-LENGTH FEATURE FILMS

The Black Stallion (1979) An appealing, gripping
story about a young boy and his love for a horse.
E.T. (1982) Steven Spielberg's now-classic tale of
the lost, lovable extra-terrestrial and the kids who
help him to go "home."

He Makes Me Feel Like Dancin' (1983) This delightful documentary tells how ballet dancer Jacques D'Amboise's labor of love transforms New York City youngsters into performers.

The Incredible Journey (1963) Based on Sheila Bumford's bestseller, this is the story of two dogs and a cat who journey more than 200 miles to find their owners.

Mary Poppins (1964) Based on the books by P.L. Travers, this light-hearted musical is family entertainment at its best.

The Never Ending Story (1984) A young boy becomes part of the fairy tale he's reading—based on Michael Ende's book.

Willie Wonka and the Chocolate Factory (1971) Based on Roald Dahl's book, this musical tells the story of Willie Wonka, his fabulous factory and the very nasty children (and one nice one) who visit it—and are never the same.

The Wizard of Oz (1939) L. Frank Baum's story of Dorothy Gale from Kansas and her journey through the Land of Oz. Both the book and the film have become classics.

Old Yeller (1957) Fred Gipson's 1956 book about two Texas boys and a stray dog became a Disney hit that still inspires and moves one to tears.

THE POPPING GOURMET

Popping the corn is half the fun of having popcorn, and you don't need a popcorn popper; a pot with a heavy bottom will do just fine. Measure out 1 part vegetable oil to 3 parts popcorn. Cover the pot, set the heat to medium, start shaking the pot and listen to the corn pop. Remember to keep shaking the pot or the corn may burn.

For a change of flavor from the standard salt and butter, try one of these "gourmet" variations:

• Grated Parmesan cheese with chopped chives.

• Onion salt or garlic salt with chopped parsley.

• One tablespoon of olive oil, one tablespoon of grated Parmesan cheese, ¼ teaspoon each of basil and thyme.

• One tablespoon each of olive oil, tomato paste and grated Parmesan cheese, ¼ teaspoon of oregano, ⅛ teaspoon of garlic salt and a third cup of shredded mozzarella cheese.

• For a real treat, combine freshly popped kernels with nuts, raisins, toasted coconut and a dash of curry powder.

GUYS & DOLLS

For a fun and elegant New Year's Eve, ask guests to come dressed in '30's and '40's garb:

• The men can wear double-breasted suits, smoking jackets, lace-up shoes and fedoras.

• The women can wear clingy, floor-length gowns, preferably cut on the bias. (Now's the time to make use of bridesmaids gowns collecting dust in the closet!) Accessories can include elbow-length gloves, rhinestone jewelry, seamed stockings and small beaded clutch purses.

• Play such toe-tapping classics as "Satin Doll" and "Take the A-Train." Of course, anything by Glenn Miller or Benny Goodman is just what the maestro ordered.

• No New Year's Eve is complete without a sing-along finale of "Auld Lang Syne" (preferably with Guy Lombardo and his orchestra).

GO, TEAM, GO!

Hold a Rose Bowl (or other football game) indoor tailgate party. Feature lots of cold weather foods and drinks. Decorate the TV room with plaid blankets and memorabilia from your favorite college, pro, or high-school team. Plan a buffet, and space out the courses so that people can munch during the pre-game, half time and post-game periods.

ARUBA, JAMAICA . . . KOKOMO?

Plan a "Beat the Winter Blahs" party. Tell guests to come wearing hot-weather clothes: t-shirts, skimmy tops, shorts, lightweight pants, boat shoes, sneakers, thongs, sandals. (Remember to turn up the thermostat!) Serve cold pasta salads, hot dogs, potato chips, any fresh vegetables you can find, soda, fruit juices and so on. Choose whatever music makes you think of your favorite summertime days from childhood or the present. From "Lazy, Hazy, Crazy Days of Summer" to the Beach Boys' "Kokomo," the selections are varied and wonderful. Get out beach balls and blankets for decorations. And don't forget ice cream and sherbet for dessert!

Rosy Punch (recipe, page 247); Hot Cheddar Puffs (recipe, page 248); Savory Stuffed Mushrooms (recipe, page 247); Shrimp in Cilantro Sauce (recipe, page 249)

"BLACK TIE OPTIONAL" BUFFET

(for 16)

Rosy Punch
Savory Stuffed Mushrooms
Hot Cheddar Puffs
Shrimp in Cilantro Sauce
Caviar Dip with Crudités
Tricolor Pizza
Macadamia Pear Tart

WORK PLAN FOR
"BLACK TIE OPTIONAL" BUFFET

Up to Two Weeks Ahead:
- Bake the Hot Cheddar Puffs; cool them completely before freezing.

Up to Three Days Ahead:
- Prepare the Macadamia Pear Tart and refrigerate it, covered.

The Day Before:
- Prepare the Shrimp in Cilantro Sauce and refrigerate it.
- Prepare the base for the Rosy Punch and refrigerate it.
- Prepare the filling for the Savory Stuffed Mushrooms and refrigerate it, along with the mushroom caps.
- Hard-cook the eggs for the Caviar Dip and refrigerate them. Cut up and refrigerate the vegetables to be served with the dip.

Several Hours Before:
- Prepare and refrigerate the sautéed leeks and prosciutto for the Tricolor Pizzas. Cut up the red pepper strips and shred the cheese; refrigerate them.
- Prepare and decorate the Caviar Dip; refrigerate it, loosely covered with plastic wrap.
- Sauté and stuff the mushroom caps for the Savory Stuffed Mushrooms; refrigerate them in a single layer on a baking sheet.
- Rinse the watercress for the Savory Stuffed Mushrooms, pat it dry, place it in a plastic bag and refrigerate it.
- Prepare the dough for the Hot Cheddar Puffs, if they were not prepared ahead and frozen; cover the bowl and set aside the dough.

One Hour Before:
- Assemble the Tricolor Pizzas.
- Remove the Macadamia Pear Tart from the refrigerator. Whip the cream to serve with the tart; cover and refrigerate the cream.

Just Before the Party:
- Spoon the Hot Cheddar Puff dough onto prepared baking sheets and bake for 35 to 40 minutes, if the puffs were not prepared ahead and frozen. Or reheat the frozen puffs for about 15 minutes.
- Complete the Rosy Punch.
- Heat the Savory Stuffed Mushrooms and garnish them with the watercress.
- Bake the Tricolor Pizzas, one at a time.

During the Party:
- Reheat the Macadamia Pear Tart. Whip the cream a bit if it has separated.

ROSY PUNCH

This delightful punch will bring a glow to the heart and a sparkle to the eye.

Makes 16 servings.

  3   **cups water**
  3   **cinnamon sticks**
  8   **slices fresh gingerroot, each ⅛ inch thick, unpeeled**
10   **whole cloves**
  6   **cups cranberry juice cocktail**
1½ **cups orange juice**
  3   **tablespoons fresh lemon juice**
  2   **cups crème de cassis (black currant liqueur)**
 ½ **cup apple schnapps**
  4   **thin orange slices, quartered, for garnish**
      Cinnamon sticks and cranberries, for garnish (optional)

1. Combine the water, cinnamon sticks, ginger and cloves in a large, nonaluminum saucepan. Bring the mixture to boiling over medium heat. Reduce heat to low.
2. Simmer the spice mixture, uncovered, for 30 minutes, or until the liquid is reduced to about half (1½ cups). (The recipe can be made ahead up to this point. Cover and refrigerate the spice mixture. When you're ready to finish the punch, bring the mixture back to boiling before proceeding with the recipe.)
3. Add the cranberry juice cocktail, orange juice, lemon juice, crème de cassis and apple schnapps to the spice mixture. Simmer just until the punch is heated through; do not boil the punch.
4. Ladle the punch from a large punch bowl into glass mugs. Garnish each mug with a quarter of an orange slice and, if you wish, a cinnamon stick and some cranberries.

CRÈME DE LA CRÈME

Crème de cassis liqueur is made from French black currants. It is purple-blue in color, sweet and syrupy—perfect for a special drink. You already may have tasted cassis in a Kir or Kir Royale, made with white wine or champagne, respectively.

SAVORY STUFFED MUSHROOMS

These delicious hors d'oeuvres are wonderful hot or cold.

Makes 36 mushrooms.

1½ **pounds white button mushrooms, 1¼ to 1½ inches in diameter**
  6   **tablespoons olive oil**
 ¼ **teaspoon plus ½ teaspoon salt**
  6   **large cloves garlic, sliced crosswise**
 ½ **cup chopped shallots**
 ¼ **cup brandy**
 ⅔ **cup walnuts**
  2   **bunches watercress**

1. Gently wipe the dirt and sand from the mushrooms with paper toweling. Separate the stems from the caps. Trim any woody or rough parts from the stems. Reserve 2 cups of the stems for the stuffing.
2. Heat 4 tablespoons of the oil in a skillet. Sauté the mushroom caps for 2 to 3 minutes, or until they are cooked but not too soft. Remove the caps with a slotted spoon and place them, round side up, on a plate. Sprinkle the caps with ¼ teaspoon of the salt and set them aside.
3. In the same skillet, heat the remaining 2 tablespoons of oil. Sauté the garlic for about 1 minute, or until it begins to turn golden. Add the reserved mushroom stems and the shallots. Cook over medium

"DRY CLEAN" ONLY

Mushrooms never should be soaked in water. A wipe with a damp cloth usually will remove the small amount of dirt and sand that coats them. If the mushrooms really are dirt-imbedded, run them very quickly under lukewarm running water, lightly brushing them with a piece of paper toweling.

heat for 5 to 8 minutes, or until the mushroom stems are soft and well cooked. Be careful not to burn the garlic; it should be golden in color.

4. Add the brandy to the skillet. Cook the mixture, stirring constantly, until all the liquid has evaporated.

5. Very finely chop the mushroom stem mixture, along with the walnuts, using a knife or placing the walnuts in the container of a food processor. Stir in the remaining ½ teaspoon of salt.

6. Stuff each mushroom cap with about 1 teaspoon of the walnut filling. Serve the mushrooms hot or cold on a bed of watercress. (To heat the mushrooms, place the caps in a single layer in a baking dish. Bake in a preheated moderate oven (350°) for 20 minutes.) Garnish each stuffed cap with a watercress leaf.

WET STORAGE

As its name suggests, watercress is best kept with its stems immersed in water. Cover the sprigs with a plastic bag and refrigerate the watercress until you are ready to use it.

HOT CHEDDAR PUFFS

Known as Gougères, these are similar to cream puffs, but are made with spiced cheese. Dry white wine can be used for all or part of the water in this recipe.

Bake at 375° for 35 to 40 minutes.
Makes 48 puffs.

1½ **cups water**
½ **cup (1 stick) butter**
½ **teaspoon ground hot red pepper**
½ **teaspoon salt**
1½ **cups unsifted all-purpose flour**
6 **eggs**
½ **pound coarsely shredded sharp Cheddar cheese (2 cups)**

1. Preheat the oven to moderate (375°). Grease four baking sheets.

2. Combine the water, butter, ground hot red pepper and salt in a large saucepan. Bring the mixture to boiling over medium heat. Boil until the butter has melted.

3. Remove the mixture from the heat. Add the flour all at once and stir briskly with a wooden spoon just until the dough leaves the sides of the pan. Do not overbeat.

4. Let the dough cool in the pan for 2 minutes. Add the eggs, one at a time, beating with the wooden spoon after each addition, until the dough is completely smooth. Stir in the Cheddar cheese.

5. Drop the dough by heaping teaspoonfuls onto the prepared baking sheets, about 1½ inches apart. (You should have about 48 puffs.)

6. Bake in the preheated moderate oven (375°) for 35 to 40 minutes, or until the puffs are lightly browned and crisp. Remove the puffs to a wire rack to cool completely. Serve the puffs immediately, or wrap them well and freeze them; refrigerating the puffs makes them soggy.

7. Reheat frozen puffs directly from the freezer. Place them on greased baking sheets and bake in a preheated moderate oven (350°) for 15 minutes, or until the puffs are heated through.

SHRIMP IN CILANTRO SAUCE

Makes 16 servings.

- 4 cups firmly packed, coarsely chopped fresh cilantro OR: parsley
- 2 pickled jalapeño peppers, seeded (wear rubber gloves)
- 1 teaspoon salt
- ½ cup olive oil
- 3 tablespoons fresh lime juice
- 1 tablespoon salt
- 2 pounds large shrimp (about 44 shrimp) OR: 2 pounds medium-size shrimp (about 92 shrimp), shelled and deveined

1. Combine the cilantro or parsley, the jalapeño peppers and the 1 teaspoon of salt in the container of a food processor. Cover and whirl until the mixture is finely chopped. Add the oil and whirl for a few seconds, or until all the ingredients are well blended.
2. Pour the sauce into a large bowl. Stir the lime juice into the sauce, cover the bowl and refrigerate the sauce.
3. Bring 4 quarts of water to boiling in a large saucepan. Add the 1 tablespoon of salt. Add the shrimp to the boiling water and cook for about 2 minutes, or until the shrimp are pink and opaque. Drain the shrimp thoroughly.
4. Toss the warm shrimp in the cilantro sauce. Refrigerate the mixture until well chilled, for 5 hours or overnight.
5. Serve the shrimp in a shallow dish with wooden picks.

A NEW LEAF

Cilantro, also known as Chinese parsley or fresh coriander, figures prominently in Chinese, Indian and Mexican cuisines. It resembles parsley, but its flavor is sharper and more pungent; some people liken it to soap. It definitely is an acquired taste, but one many people crave!

Did You Know . . .

In medieval England, New Year's Day was celebrated as the Feast of Fools. The townspeople performed parodies of court and church rituals, and even the clergy joined in the singing and the satires. This sort of frivolity proved to be unpopular with the ruling class and was condemned by the Council of Basil in 1431.

CAVIAR DIP WITH CRUDITÉS

Let your imagination run wild and make your own design on top of the dip with the caviar, green onion and chopped egg yolk.

Makes 16 servings.

4	hard-cooked eggs
1	bunch green onions, trimmed, white and green parts divided and sliced separately
2	containers (16 ounces each) dairy sour cream
4	ounces salmon caviar
4	ounces black caviar, such as beluga, sevruga or lumpfish*
	Assorted vegetables, such as broccoli flowerets, cucumber, carrot and celery sticks, radishes, blanched snow peas and Belgian endive leaves, for crudités

1. Separate the egg whites from the egg yolks. Chop the egg whites (you should have about 1 cup). Press the egg yolks through a fine sieve and set aside. Measure ⅔ cup each of the white and the green parts of the green onion; reserve the remainder for another use.
2. Combine the sour cream, white part of the green onion, egg whites and 1 tablespoon each of the salmon and black caviars. Spoon the mixture into a shallow serving dish at least 12 inches in diameter.
3. Spoon the remaining caviars, the green part of the green onion and the egg yolks on top of the sour cream mixture in a decorative design. Cover the dish and refrigerate the dip until serving time. Serve the caviar dip with the crudités.

*Note: If you're using lumpfish caviar, rinse it in a fine sieve under cold running water to wash off the dye. Gently pat the rinsed caviar with paper toweling.

TRICOLOR PIZZA

An elegant version of a fun favorite — in holiday colors!

Bake at 425° for 20 minutes.
Makes 16 servings.

⅓	cup olive oil
10	cups thinly sliced leeks, both white and green parts (8 medium-size or 6 large leeks)
½	teaspoon salt
½	pound thinly sliced prosciutto OR: smoked ham, cut into ¼-inch strips
2	tubes (10 ounces each) refrigerated pizza dough
2	large sweet red peppers, cored and cut into strips
½	pound coarsely shredded mozzarella cheese (about 3 cups) Freshly ground black pepper

1. Preheat the oven to hot (425°). Place the oven rack in the lowest position.
2. Heat the oil in a large skillet over medium heat. Add the leeks and the salt to the skillet and toss to coat the leeks with the oil. Cover the skillet and simmer the mixture, stirring occasionally, for 8 minutes, or until the leeks are tender. Stir in the prosciutto or ham. Set the mixture aside, uncovered.
3. Place the dough in two 14-inch pizza pans. Pat the dough with your hands to stretch it to the edges of the pans.
4. Spread the leek mixture over the dough. Top with the red pepper strips.
5. Bake the pizzas, one at a time, in the preheated hot oven (425°) for 15 minutes. Sprinkle half the mozzarella cheese on top of each pizza. Continue baking each pizza for 5 minutes more, or until each crust is lightly browned on the edges. Sprinkle the black pepper over the mozzarella cheese. Cut each pizza into 8 wedges and serve the wedges hot.

MACADAMIA PEAR TART

Bake at 350° for 35 to 40 minutes.
Makes 16 servings.

1 *cup unsifted all-purpose flour*
1 *cup plus 2 teaspoons sugar*
1 *cup coarsely chopped macadamia nuts*
   (about 5 ounces)
1 *teaspoon baking powder*
½ *teaspoon salt*
1 *cup milk*
2 *eggs*
2 *teaspoons vanilla*
6 *ripe Bartlett pears (2 to 2½ pounds),*
   peeled, halved and cored
   Whipped cream (optional)

1. Preheat the oven to moderate (350°).
   Butter two 9½- to 10-inch round ceramic
   tart or quiche pans.
2. Combine the flour, 1 cup of the sugar, the
   macadamia nuts, baking powder and salt
   in a large bowl. Stir with a large spoon
   until all the ingredients are well blended.
3. Stir together the milk, eggs and vanilla in a
   medium-size bowl until the ingredients are
   blended. Add the milk mixture to the
   flour mixture and stir until smooth.
4. Place each pear half, cut side down, on a
   cutting board. Cut crosswise into ¼-inch
   slices. Slide a spatula under the sliced pear
   half to keep it in its original shape and
   place the pear half in one of the prepared
   pans, with the stem end toward the center.
   Repeat with the remaining halves. Press
   down on the pear halves to fan the slices
   slightly toward the center.
5. Pour the batter over the pears, dividing
   the batter evenly between the two pans.
   Sprinkle the tops of the pears with the
   remaining 2 teaspoons of sugar.
6. Bake in the preheated moderate oven
   (350°) for 35 to 40 minutes, or until a
   wooden pick inserted in the center of each
   tart comes out clean, and the tops are
   golden brown.
7. Cool the tarts completely on wire racks.
   Cover the tarts and refrigerate them until
   they are well chilled.
8. Serve the tarts chilled and, if you wish,
   topped with whipped cream.

*Note: The tarts can be stored in the
refrigerator for up to 3 days.*

Did You Know . . .

*You can see elaborate costumes, remarkable
pageantry and hundreds of string bands—all
on New Year's Day in Philadelphia, when
thousands of Mummers march up Broad
Street in the city's biggest annual parade. The
Mummers' Parade dates to pre-colonial
times, and blends Northern European,
British and Black-American heritages. The
ancient practice of mumming comes from the
British Isles. In pre-colonial America,
groups of costumed men performed plays
from house to house in the hopes of
receiving holiday gifts or goodies. The
Germans added the Belsnickle, the
forerunner of Santa Claus, who spawned
additional comic masqueraders. Southern
plantation life also made significant
contributions to this event. The parade's
theme tune, "Oh! Dem Golden Slippers,"
was composed by Philadelphian James
Bland in 1879. And the famed Mummers'
Strut may have been an offshoot of the
popular 19th-century cakewalk dance. The
Parade, which officially began in 1901,
includes competitions in four areas: string
bands, fancies, fancy brigades and clowns.*

Hot and Spicy Chutney with Cream Cheese and Crackers (recipe, page 257); Salmon Pâté (recipe, page 259); Mushroom Turnovers (recipe, page 258); Sesame Shrimp (recipe, page 258); Baked Sweet Pepper Wedges (recipe, page 257); Spinach Ricotta Roulade (recipe, page 256)

COZY AND ELEGANT NEW YEAR'S EVE

(for 6 to 8)

Peach Blossom Sunrise

Spinach Ricotta Roulade

Hot and Spicy Chutney

with Cream Cheese and Crackers

Baked Sweet Pepper Wedges

Sesame Shrimp

Mushroom Turnovers

Salmon Pâté

Grand Marnier Chocolate Soufflés

Coffee, Tea or Cappuccino

WORK PLAN FOR COZY AND ELEGANT NEW YEAR'S EVE

Up to One Month Ahead:
- Prepare the Grand Marnier Chocolate Soufflés.

Up to a Week Ahead:
- Prepare extra ice cubes for the Peach Blossom Sunrise; unmold the cubes into plastic bags and store in the freezer.
- Prepare and refrigerate the Hot and Spicy Chutney.
- Prepare and freeze the Mushroom Turnovers, baked or unbaked; layer the turnovers with wax paper between them to avoid sticking.
- Prepare the Salmon Pâté; refrigerate.

The Day Before:
- Prepare and refrigerate the orange segment garnish for the Grand Marnier Chocolate Soufflés. Pour the remaining melted chocolate over the soufflés and return them to the freezer.
- Prepare the orange juice and peach schnapps mixture for the Peach Blossom Sunrise; cover and refrigerate the mixture. Also refrigerate the champagne or club soda.
- Prepare the spinach filling for the Spinach Ricotta Roulade; cover and refrigerate the filling.
- Prepare the marinade for the Sesame Shrimp, but do not coat the shrimp; cover and refrigerate the marinade separately. Prepare and refrigerate the dipping sauce.

Early in the Day:
- Prepare the Spinach Ricotta Roulade and refrigerate it.
- Shell and devein the shrimp; refrigerate.
- Cut up and assemble the Sweet Pepper Wedges; cover them lightly.
- Assemble and refrigerate the Mushroom Turnovers on baking sheets, if they were not prepared ahead and frozen.
- Make cucumber rounds to serve with the Salmon Pâté, if you wish.

No More than One Hour Before:
- Marinate the shrimp for the Sesame Shrimp.
- Slice the Spinach Ricotta Roulade and arrange the slices on a platter; cover them lightly.

Just Before the Party:
- Bake the Sweet Pepper Wedges.
- Sauté the Sesame Shrimp; serve the shrimp with the dipping sauce.
- Bake the Mushroom Turnovers. If the turnovers were prepared ahead and frozen, place them, still frozen, in single layers on baking sheets and bake at 350° for 15 to 20 minutes.
- Toast bread for toast points to serve with the Salmon Pâté, if you wish.

Just Before Dessert:
- Garnish the Grand Marnier Chocolate Soufflés with the chocolate-dipped orange segments.

PEACH BLOSSOM SUNRISE

Makes 8 servings.

5   cups orange juice
⅔ cup peach schnapps
    Ice cubes
1½ to 2 cups champagne OR: club soda,
    chilled
4   to 5 teaspoons grenadine syrup
    Peach slices OR: orange slices,
    for garnish (optional)

1. Combine the orange juice with the peach schnapps in a pitcher or jug. Cover the pitcher and chill the mixture for at least 2 hours, or overnight.
2. For each serving, pour ½ cup of the chilled juice mixture into an 8- to 10-ounce footed glass. Add 2 to 3 ice cubes and 3 to 4 tablespoons of the champagne or club soda. Drizzle ½ teaspoon of the grenadine syrup over each drink; do not stir. Garnish each glass with a peach or orange slice, if you wish.

Did You Know . . .

Champagne, named for an area in the north of France, is one of the great discoveries of the Middle Ages. Dom Perignon was the keeper of the wine cellar for a monastery. One day he discovered a hitherto forgotten cache of wine. Upon close inspection, Dom Perignon found that the bottles were filled with tiny bubbles. Curious about the effect of the mysterious effervescence, he took a sip — and ran outside crying, "O, come quickly, I am drinking stars!" Only wines produced in the Champagne region of France may truly be called "champagne"; all others must be titled "sparkling wines."

♪ Holiday Notes

COLOR IT ELEGANT

For an instant touch of elegance, tie a ribbon bow around the stem of each wine or champagne glass you use. Our Peach Blossom Sunrise *(recipe, above)* has been brightened by a ribbon of gold to add a shimmery New Year's touch. Try scarlet red and pine green ribbons for Christmas, autumnal hues for Thanksgiving — whatever colors and patterns fit the occasion.

SPINACH RICOTTA ROULADE

Bake at 400° for 15 minutes.
Makes 8 servings.

Spinach Ricotta Filling:
- 1 medium-size onion, finely chopped
- 2 tablespoons olive oil
- 1 medium-size sweet red pepper, cored, seeded and cut into ½-inch dice
- 1 package (10 ounces) frozen chopped spinach, thawed and squeezed dry
- 1 teaspoon grated lemon zest (yellow part of rind only)
- ¼ teaspoon salt
- ⅛ teaspoon sugar
- ⅛ teaspoon pepper
- ¾ cup ricotta cheese, drained

Egg Roulade:
- ¼ cup (½ stick) unsalted butter
- ⅓ cup unsifted all-purpose flour
- 1⅓ cups milk, warmed
- ¼ teaspoon pepper
- 6 eggs, separated, plus 1 egg white
- 1¼ cups grated Parmesan cheese

1. Prepare the Spinach Ricotta Filling: Sauté the onion in the oil in a large skillet, stirring often, for about 8 minutes, or until the onion is soft and golden. Add the red pepper and cook for 4 minutes more. Add the spinach, lemon zest, salt, sugar and pepper. Transfer the mixture to a medium-size bowl. Stir in the ricotta cheese and set aside the filling.
2. Preheat the oven to hot (400°). Grease the bottom of a 15½ x 10½-inch jelly-roll pan. Line the bottom of the pan with wax paper; grease and lightly flour the paper, tapping out any excess flour. Set aside.
3. Prepare the Egg Roulade: Melt the butter in a heavy saucepan over low heat. Stir in the flour. Cook, stirring, until the mixture is smooth and lightly colored. Gradually whisk in the warm milk. Raise the heat to medium. Cook over medium heat, stirring, for 4 to 5 minutes, or until quite thick. Stir in the pepper and remove the saucepan from the heat.
4. Beat the egg yolks, one at a time, into the milk mixture. Stir in ¾ cup of the Parmesan cheese and transfer the mixture to a large bowl.
5. Beat the egg whites in another large bowl until stiff peaks form. Carefully fold the egg whites into the milk mixture. Spoon the egg-milk mixture into the prepared pan, smoothing the top with a spatula. Sprinkle the top evenly with the remaining ½ cup of Parmesan cheese.
6. Bake in the preheated hot oven (400°) for 15 minutes, or until the roulade is golden and a cake tester inserted in the center comes out clean. Carefully invert the roulade onto a kitchen towel or wax paper. Remove the paper from the top of the roulade. Starting with a long side, roll up the roulade and towel together. Place the roll, seam side down, on a wire rack. Cool at room temperature for 20 minutes.
7. Carefully unroll the roulade and remove the towel. Spread the filling down the length of the roulade, leaving a 2-inch border on one long side and a 1-inch border at each short end. Roll up the roulade again, jelly-roll fashion, starting with the long side without the border. Wrap the roll tightly with plastic wrap and refrigerate it. To serve the roulade, unwrap it, cut it crosswise into slices and serve the slices chilled or at room temperature.

HOT AND SPICY CHUTNEY

Serve this "as is" on crackers or toast, or mix 2 tablespoons of chutney into 3 ounces of cream cheese for a variation.

Makes 2 cups.

3/4 **pound sweet red peppers, cored, seeded and cut into 1/4-inch dice (1½ cups)**
1/2 **pound dried apricots, cut into 1/4-inch dice**
1/2 **cup raisins**
1 **medium-size onion, finely chopped**
3 **cloves garlic, thinly slivered**
1 **2-inch piece fresh gingerroot, peeled and thinly slivered (1½ tablespoons)**
3/4 **teaspoon salt**
1/2 **to 3/4 teaspoon crushed red pepper flakes, or to taste**
1/2 **teaspoon cumin seeds**
1/2 **teaspoon mustard seeds**
1/2 **cup sugar**
1/4 **cup plus 2 tablespoons red wine vinegar**

1. Combine the red peppers, apricots, raisins, onion, garlic, ginger, salt, red pepper flakes, cumin seeds, mustard seeds and sugar in a medium-size saucepan.
2. Cook the mixture, uncovered, over medium heat, stirring occasionally, for about 5 minutes, or until the sugar dissolves.
3. Add the vinegar to the pepper mixture. Cook, stirring often, for 30 to 35 minutes, or until the mixture is shiny and thick. Remove the saucepan from the heat and cool the chutney. Cover the chutney and refrigerate it.

Did You Know . . .

In an effort to keep the faithful from pagan celebrations of the year's end, the ancient Byzantine and Gallican churches designated New Year's Day as the first of a three day fast in commemoration of the Circumcision. This day eventually became known as St. Basil's Day, and still is celebrated as such in Greece and Romania.

BAKED SWEET PEPPER WEDGES

Bake at 375° for 35 to 40 minutes.
Makes 8 servings.

2 **medium-size sweet red peppers**
2 **medium-size sweet yellow peppers**
1 **medium-size onion, finely chopped**
1 **can (28 ounces) crushed tomatoes, well drained**
1/4 **cup chopped fresh parsley**
1/4 **cup plus 2 tablespoons olive oil**
3 **tablespoons pine nuts (pignoli)**
4 **cloves garlic, finely chopped**
1 **teaspoon salt**
1/4 **teaspoon pepper, or to taste**
1/4 **cup fresh bread crumbs**

1. Preheat the oven to moderate (375°). Lightly oil a 13 x 9-inch baking pan.
2. Trim the tops off the red and yellow peppers. Discard the stems and finely chop the tops. Cut each pepper lengthwise into sixths. Place the wedges, cut side up, in the prepared pan and set aside the pan.
3. Combine the pepper tops, onion, tomatoes, parsley, 1/4 cup of the oil, the pine nuts, garlic, salt and pepper in a medium-size bowl. Spoon an equal amount of the mixture into each of the pepper wedges.
4. Bake in the preheated moderate oven (375°) for 25 to 30 minutes, or until the wedges are just tender. Sprinkle the bread crumbs and the remaining 2 tablespoons of oil over all the wedges. Bake for 10 minutes more.

SESAME SHRIMP

Makes 8 servings.

Marinade:
- 2   tablespoons sesame seeds
- 1   2½-inch piece fresh gingerroot, peeled and coarsely chopped
- 1   tablespoon rice wine vinegar
- 1   tablespoon Oriental sesame oil
- ¼   cup cold water
- 2   teaspoons honey
- ½   teaspoon salt
- ⅛   teaspoon ground hot red pepper

- 1¼   pounds large shrimp (about 19 shrimp), shelled and deveined (1 pound cleaned)

Dipping Sauce:
- 2   tablespoons honey
- 2   tablespoons rice wine vinegar
- 2   tablespoons soy sauce
- 4   teaspoons Oriental sesame oil
- ½   teaspoon Dijon-style mustard

- 3   tablespoons peanut oil for cooking shrimp

1. Prepare the Marinade: Combine the sesame seeds with the ginger in the container of an electric blender or a food processor. Cover and whirl until the ingredients are blended. Add the vinegar, Oriental sesame oil, cold water, honey, salt and ground hot red pepper.
2. Transfer the marinade to a large bowl. Add the shrimp and toss to coat. Cover the bowl with plastic wrap and marinate the shrimp in the refrigerator for at least 45 minutes, but no more than 60 minutes.
3. Prepare the Dipping Sauce: Whisk together the honey, vinegar, soy sauce, Oriental sesame oil and mustard in a small bowl. Set aside the bowl.
4. To cook the shrimp, heat the peanut oil in a large skillet over medium-high heat. Working in batches, lift the shrimp from the marinade with a slotted spoon or spatula to the skillet. Sauté for 1 to 3 minutes, or until the shrimp just begin to curl. Serve with the dipping sauce.

MUSHROOM TURNOVERS

Bake pecans at 350° for 10 minutes; bake turnovers at 375° for 12 to 15 minutes. Makes 16 turnovers.

- ¼   cup pecans (about 1 ounce)
- 2   small leeks, well-washed and finely diced (¾ cup)
- 3   tablespoons butter
- ½   pound mushrooms, trimmed, halved and thinly sliced (about 2½ cups)
- 1   tablespoon chopped fresh mint OR: ½ teaspoon leaf mint, crumbled
- ¼   teaspoon salt
- ⅛   teaspoon pepper
- ¼   cup dairy sour cream
- 4   13 x 9-inch sheets phyllo dough (from an 8-ounce package)
- 3   tablespoons melted butter

1. Preheat the oven to moderate (350°).
2. Bake the pecans on a baking sheet in the preheated moderate oven (350°) for about 10 minutes, or until the pecans are toasted. Cool the pecans and coarsely chop them. Raise the temperature to 375°. Place the oven rack in the lowest position.
3. Sauté the leeks in 2 tablespoons of the butter in a large, heavy skillet over medium heat for about 20 minutes, or until the leeks are soft and lightly browned. Add the mushrooms and the remaining 1 tablespoon of butter. Cook until the mushrooms are soft and the moisture has evaporated, for about 15 minutes more. Stir in the mint, salt and pepper. Remove the skillet from the heat and stir in the sour cream and the toasted pecans. Cool the mixture slightly.
4. Lightly grease a baking sheet.
5. Working with one sheet of phyllo dough at a time and keeping the others covered with plastic wrap, brush a sheet with the melted butter. Cut the sheet lengthwise into 4 equal pieces. Place a measuring tablespoonful of the filling on the bottom corner of one strip, leaving a 1-inch border

at the bottom. Fold the corner up over the filling to form a triangle, then fold the triangle up and over. Keep flipping the triangle up and over to the end of the strip. Trim off any excess dough. Repeat with the remaining sheets and filling.

6. Place the turnovers on the prepared baking sheet. Lightly brush the tops with the remaining melted butter.

7. Bake in the preheated moderate oven (375°) for 12 to 15 minutes, or until the turnovers are crisp and golden.

◀◀

SALMON PÂTÉ

This mixture keeps for a week in the refrigerator. Serve it with toast points or cucumber rounds.

Makes about 2 cups.

2	*tablespoons heavy cream*
	OR: whipping cream
2	*tablespoons dairy sour cream*
3	*cups cold water*
1	*carrot, peeled and thinly sliced*
1	*small onion, thinly sliced*
1	*bay leaf*
3	*thin lemon slices*
1	*fresh red chili pepper*
½	*pound fresh salmon fillets, with skin*
2	*shallots, finely chopped*
1	*tablespoon plus ¼ cup (½ stick) unsalted butter, at room temperature*
4	*ounces smoked salmon, diced*
1	*tablespoon lemon juice*
½	*teaspoon salt*
⅛	*teaspoon white pepper*
1	*tablespoon finely chopped fresh dill*
	Few sprigs fresh dill, for garnish
1	*bay leaf, for garnish (optional)*
	Thin sweet red pepper strips, for garnish (optional)
3	*tablespoons butter, clarified**

1. Whisk together the heavy or whipping cream and the sour cream in a small bowl. Refrigerate the cream mixture.

2. Combine the cold water, carrot, onion, bay leaf, lemon slices and chili pepper in a skillet large enough to hold the salmon fillets in one layer. Bring the mixture to boiling over medium heat and boil for 10 minutes. Reduce the heat to medium-low. Add the salmon fillets, skin side up. Simmer very gently over medium-low heat for about 10 minutes, or until the salmon is just cooked; do not overcook the salmon. Remove the salmon from the poaching liquid; remove and discard the skin. Cool the salmon fillets completely.

3. Sauté the shallots in 1 tablespoon of the butter in a small skillet over medium heat, stirring, for about 5 minutes, or until the shallots are golden. Transfer the shallots to the work bowl of a food processor.

4. Add the salmon fillets, smoked salmon and cream mixture to the food processor. Cover and purée until the mixture is smooth. With the processor running, add the remaining ¼ cup of butter, bit by bit, until the mixture is smooth. Add the lemon juice, salt and white pepper. Fold in the chopped dill.

5. Spoon the mixture into a 2-cup soufflé dish or decorative serving dish. Smooth the top with a rubber spatula. Garnish with a few fresh dill sprigs and, if you wish, a whole bay leaf and thin red pepper strips. Pour the clarified butter over the top of the pâté to cover it completely. Refrigerate the pâté for 4 hours to set it.

*Note: To clarify butter, melt the butter in a saucepan over medium heat. Remove the saucepan from the heat and skim off the foam from the top of the butter. With a small ladle, spoon the clear liquid butter into a dish, leaving the milky solids behind. Discard the milky solids. Use the clear butter.

GRAND MARNIER CHOCOLATE SOUFFLÉS

Makes 10 servings.

1   package (10¾ ounces) frozen poundcake, thawed
¼   cup Grand Marnier OR: other orange-flavored liqueur OR: orange juice
1   package (6 ounces) semisweet chocolate pieces
1   cup heavy cream OR: whipping cream
½   envelope (1½ teaspoons) unflavored gelatin
3   eggs, at room temperature
3   tablespoons sugar
1   can (11 ounces) mandarin orange segments, for garnish
3   squares (1 ounce each) semisweet chocolate, for garnish
1   tablespoon vegetable shortening

1. Remove the poundcake from its aluminum foil pan. Cut the cake horizontally into four equal layers. Lay two of the layers on a flat surface, short ends together and cut them into 5 circles, using a 2½-inch cookie cutter, with the center circle overlapping both layers of cake. Repeat with the remaining 2 layers of cake. Place a round in the bottom of each of ten 3 x 1½-inch individual soufflé dishes. Drizzle the rounds with 2 tablespoons of the Grand Marnier, other orange-flavored liqueur or orange juice. Place the dishes on baking sheets and set them aside.

2. Melt the chocolate pieces with ¼ cup of the heavy or whipping cream in a medium-size saucepan over low heat, stirring constantly, until the mixture is smooth. Set aside the mixture.

3. Sprinkle the gelatin over the remaining 2 tablespoons of Grand Marnier in a small saucepan and let stand for 5 minutes to soften the gelatin. Heat the mixture over low heat, stirring constantly, until the gelatin dissolves.

4. Beat the eggs until frothy in a medium-size bowl with an electric mixer at high speed. Gradually beat in the sugar. Continue to beat until the mixture is thick and pale yellow. Reduce the mixer speed to low and beat in the gelatin mixture, then the melted chocolate, until all the ingredients are well mixed. Refrigerate the chocolate mixture while beating the cream.

5. Beat the remaining ¾ cup of cream in a small bowl until stiff peaks form. Fold the whipped cream into the chocolate mixture and divide the cream-chocolate mixture evenly among the prepared soufflé dishes (about ⅓ cup each). Freeze the soufflés until they are firm. When the soufflés are firm, cover them with plastic wrap and return them to the freezer.

6. The day before serving, drain the orange segments and arrange them on a tray lined with paper toweling. Refrigerate the orange segments for 1 hour. Meanwhile, melt the chocolate squares with the shortening in a custard cup placed in a small saucepan of simmering water. Stir until the melted chocolate is smooth.

7. Dip each chilled orange segment halfway into the melted chocolate. Place the dipped orange segments on an aluminum foil-lined tray and refrigerate them until serving time. Unwrap the soufflés and evenly drizzle any leftover melted chocolate over the tops. Return the soufflés to the freezer until serving time.

8. Just before serving, garnish each soufflé with a chocolate-dipped orange segment.

CHASE AWAY THE JANUARY BLUES

*Some great ideas to prevent a
post-holiday slump.*

THE DATE:
JANUARY 1, 1990!

Whether you've spent the previous evening quietly or partying, there's no better way to welcome the New Year than with a noontime brunch featuring make-ahead foods, fruit juices and coffee. Put the emphasis on casual. If you have last year's resolutions written down, bring them out. Or jot down this year's resolutions and save them to read next New Year's Day.

UN-TRIMMING THE TREE PARTY

Turn this most dreaded task into a festive one by inviting friends the week after Christmas to help you *un*decorate. Serve a hearty soup, casserole or chili, a tossed salad, crusty bread and mulled cider. Your tired tree will disappear effortlessly, your home will be filled with friends and your Christmas spirit will soar well into the New Year.

BACK ON THE (DIET) TRACK

Wrap up New Year's Day with a small gathering of friends and a "back on the diet" dinner. Serve dishes that emphasize fruits and vegetables, fresh fish and grilled chicken. Use the occasion as a chance for quiet conversation with those you may not have seen for a while because of the holiday rush. Or make it a "family only" gathering, and discuss the highlights of the holidays, as well as ways to make them even better next year.

PHOTO FINISH

Does January loom before your family as a time of "nothing to do?" Designate the first month of the New Year as "Family History Month." Gather the family together and sort through those boxes filled with old family photos. Organize them into piles: Mom, Dad, brother, sister, grandparents and so on. Then place the photos chronologically in keepsake albums, with short stories about the pictures or messages to future generations. Your kids will get a real sense of family history as Mom and Dad answer questions about known and unknown relatives.

WHAT WAS IT LIKE IN THE OLD DAYS?

Give your children the priceless gift of history. Compile an audio family history by visiting relatives, particularly the elderly, and tape-record their answers. Ask them questions about their childhoods, their parents and grandparents, and the changes in the country they've witnessed. Children will enjoy learning from first-hand sources about the "good old days."

THANK YOU!

Set aside one night in the week between Christmas and New Year's, and make a list of the thank-you notes that need to be written. Let the kids illustrate blank postcards with stickers, messages and drawings. The note-writing task will be accomplished quickly and enjoyably.

CRAFTS BASICS & ABBREVIATIONS

HOW TO KNIT

THE BASIC STITCHES

Get out your needles and yarn, and slowly read your way through this special section. Practice the basic stitches illustrated here as you go along. Once you know them, you're ready to start knitting.

CASTING ON: This puts the first row of stitches on the needle. Measure off about two yards of yarn (or about an inch for each stitch you are going to cast on). Make a slip knot at this point by making a medium-size loop of yarn; then pull another small loop through it. Place the slip knot on one needle and pull one end gently to tighten (FIG. 1).

FIG. 1

• Hold the needle in your right hand. Hold both strands of yarn in the palm of your left hand securely but not rigidly. Slide your left thumb and forefinger between the two strands and spread these two fingers out so that you have formed a triangle of yarn.

Your left thumb should hold the free end of yarn, your forefinger the yarn from the ball. The needle in your right hand holds the first stitch (FIG. 2).

FIG. 2

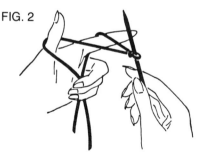

You are now in position to cast on. See ABBREVIATIONS (page 263) for explanations of asterisk (*).
• Bring the needles in your right hand toward you; slip the tip of the needle under the front strand of the loop on left thumb (FIG. 3).

FIG. 3

• Now, with the needle, catch the strand of yarn that is on your left forefinger. (FIG. 4).

FIG. 4

• Draw it through the thumb loop to form a stitch on the needle (FIG. 5).

FIG. 5

• Holding the stitch on the needle with the right index finger, slip loop off your left thumb (FIG. 6). Tighten up the stitch on the needle by pulling the freed strand back with your left thumb, bringing the yarn back into position for casting on more stitches (FIG. 2 again).

FIG. 6

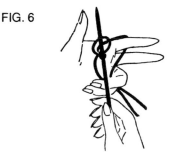

• *Do not cast on too tightly.* Stitches should slide easily on the needle. Repeat from * until you have cast on the number of stitches specified in your instructions.

KNIT STITCH (k): Hold the needle with the cast-on stitches in your left hand (FIG. 7).

FIG. 7

• Pick up the other needle in your right hand. With yarn from the ball in *back* of the work, insert the tip of the right-hand needle from *left to right* through the front loop of the first stitch on the left-hand needle (FIG. 8).

FIG. 8

• Holding both needles in this position with your left hand, wrap the yarn over your little finger, under your two middle fingers and over the forefinger of your right hand. Hold the yarn firmly, but loosely enough so that it will slide through your fingers as you knit. Return the right-hand needle to your right hand.

• With your right forefinger, pass the yarn under (from right to left) and then over (from left to right) the tip of the right-hand needle, forming a loop on the needle (FIG. 9).

FIG. 9

• Now draw this loop through the stitch on the left-hand needle (FIG. 10).

FIG. 10

KNITTING ABBREVIATIONS AND SYMBOLS

Knitting directions are always written in standard abbreviations. They look mysterious at first, but you'll soon know them: **beg**—beginning; **bet**—between; **bl**—block; **ch**—chain; **CC**—contrasting color; **dec(s)**—decrease(s); **dp**—double-pointed; " or **in(s)**—inch(es); **incl**—inclusive; **inc(s)**—increase(s); **k**—knit; **lp(s)**—loop(s); **MC**—main color; **oz(s)**—ounces(s); **psso**—pass slipped stitch over last stitch worked; **pat(s)**—pattern(s); **p**—purl; **rem**—remaining; **rpt**—repeat; **rnd(s)**—round(s); **sk**—skip; **sl**—slip; **sl st**—slip stitch; **sp(s),**—space(s); **st(s)**—stitch(es); **st st**—stockinette stitch; **tog**—together, **yo**—yarn over; **pc**—popcorn stitch.

* (asterisk)—directions immediately following * are to be repeated the specified number of times indicated in addition to the first time—i.e. "repeat from * 3 times more" means 4 times in all.

( ) (parentheses)—directions should be worked as often as specified—i.e., "(k 1, k 2 tog, k 3) 5 times" means to work what is in ( ) 5 times in all.

• Slip the original stitch off the left-hand needle, leaving the new stitch on right-hand needle (FIG. 11).

FIG. 11

Keep stitches loose enough so that you can slide them along the needles, but firm enough so they do not slide when you don't want them to. Continue until you have knitted all the stitches from the left-hand needle onto the right-hand needle.

• To start the next row, pass the needle with stitches on it to the left hand, reversing it, so that it is now the left-hand needle.

PURL STITCH (p): Purling is the reverse of knitting. Again, keep the stitches loose enough to slide, but firm enough to work with. To purl, hold the needle with the stitches in your left hand, with the yarn in *front* of your work. Insert the tip of the right-hand needle from *right to left* through the front loop of the first stitch on the left-hand needle (FIG. 12).

FIG. 12

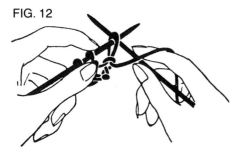

• With your right hand holding the yarn as you would to knit, but in *front* of the needles, pass the yarn over the tip of the right-hand needle, then under it, forming a loop on the needle. (FIG. 13).

FIG. 13

• Holding the yarn firmly so that it won't slip off, draw this loop through the stitch on the left-hand needle (FIG. 14).

FIG. 14

• Slip the original stitch off the left-hand needle, leaving the new stitch on the right-hand needle. (FIG. 15).

FIG. 15

SLIPSTITCH (sl st): Insert the tip of the right-hand needle into the next stitch on the left-hand needle, as if to purl, unless otherwise directed. Slip this stitch off the left-hand needle onto the right, *without working it* (FIG. 16).

FIG. 16

BINDING OFF: This makes a finished edge and locks the stitches securely in place. Knit (or purl) two stitches. Then, with the tip of the left-hand needle, lift the first of these two stitches over the second stitch and drop it off the tip of the right-hand needle (FIG. 17).

FIG. 17

One stitch remains on the right-hand needle, and one stitch has been bound off.

• Knit (or purl) the next stitch; lift the first stitch over the last stitch and off the tip of the needle. Again, one stitch remains on the right-hand needle, and another stitch has been bound off. Repeat from * until the required number of stitches have been bound off.

• Remember that you work two stitches to bind off one stitch. If, for example, the directions read, "k 6, bind off the next 4 sts, k 6 . . ." you must knit six stitches, then knit *two more* stitches before starting to bind off. Bind off four times. After the four stitches have been bound off, count the last stitch remaining on the right-hand needle as the first stitch of the next six stitches. When binding off, always knit the knitted stitches and purl the purled stitches.

• Be careful not to bind off too tightly or too loosely. The tension should be the same as the rest of the knitting.

• To end off the last stitch on the bound-off edge, if you are ending this piece of work here, cut the yarn leaving a six-inch end; pass the cut end through the remaining loop on the right-hand needle and pull snugly (FIG. 18).

FIG. 18

SHAPING TECHNIQUES

Now that you know the basics, all that's left to learn are a few techniques which will help shape whatever it is you are making.

INCREASING (inc): This means adding stitches in a given area to shape your work. There are several ways to increase.

1. To increase by knitting twice into the same stitch: Knit the stitch in the usual way through the front loop (FIG. 19), but *before* dropping the stitch from the left-hand needle, knit *another* stitch on the same loop by placing the needle into the back of the stitch. (FIG. 20). Slip the original stitch off your left-hand needle. You have made two stitches from one stitch.

FIG. 19

FIG. 20

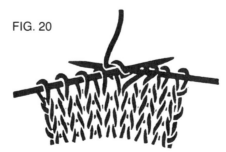

2. To increase by knitting between stitches: Insert the tip of the right-hand needle under the strand of yarn *between* the stitch

you've just worked and the following stitch; slip it onto the tip of the left-hand needle (FIG. 21).

FIG. 21

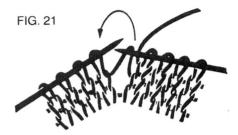

Now knit into the back of the loop (FIG. 22).

FIG. 22

3. To increase by "yarn-over" (yo): Pass the yarn over the right-hand needle after finishing one stitch and before starting the next stitch, *making an extra stitch* (arrow in FIG. 23). *If you are knitting,* bring the yarn under the needle to the back. *If you are purling,* wind the yarn around the needle once. On the next row, work all yarn-overs as stitches.

FIG. 23

DECREASING (dec): This means reducing the number of stitches in a given area to shape your work. Two methods for decreasing are:

1. To decrease by knitting (FIG. 24) **or purling** (FIG. 25) **two stitches together:**

FIG. 24

FIG. 25

Insert the right-hand needle through the loops of two stitches on the left-hand needle at the same time, complete the stitch. This is written as "k 2 tog" or "p 2 tog."

• If you work through the **front** loops of the stitches in the usual way, your decreasing stitch will slant to the right. If you work through the **back** loops of the stitches, your decreasing stitch will slant to the left.

2. Slip 1 stitch, knit 1 and psso: Insert the right-hand needle through the stitch on the left-hand needle, but instead of working it, just slip it off onto the right-hand needle (go back to FIG. 16). Work the next stitch in the usual way. With the tip of the left-hand needle, lift the slipped stitch over the last stitch worked and off the tip of the right-hand needle (FIG. 26).

FIG. 26

Your decreasing stitch will slant to the left. This is written as "sl 1, k 1, psso."

Pass Slipped Stitch Over (psso): Slip one stitch from the left-hand needle to the right-hand needle and, being careful to keep it in position, work the next stitch. Then, with the tip of the left-hand needle, lift the slipped stitch over the last stitch and off the tip of the right-hand needle (FIG. 26).

ATTACHING THE YARN

When you end one ball of yarn or wish to change colors, begin at the start of a row and tie the new yarn with the previous yarn, making secure joining. Continue to work (FIG. 27).

FIG. 27

HOW TO CROCHET

DIRECTIONS FOR RIGHT-HANDED AND LEFT-HANDED CROCHETERS

Most crochet stitches are started from a base of chain stitches. However, our stitches are started from a row of single crochet stitches which gives body to the sample swatches and makes practice work easier to handle. When making a specific item, follow the stitch directions as given.

Holding the crochet hook properly (see FIG. 1), start by practicing the slip knot (see FIG. 2) and base chain (see FIG. 3, page 268).

FIG. 2 THE SLIP KNOT (BASIS FOR CHAIN STITCH)

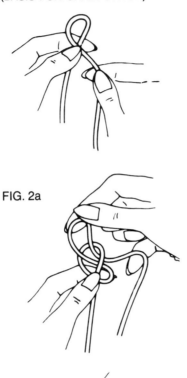

FIG. 2a

FIG. 2b

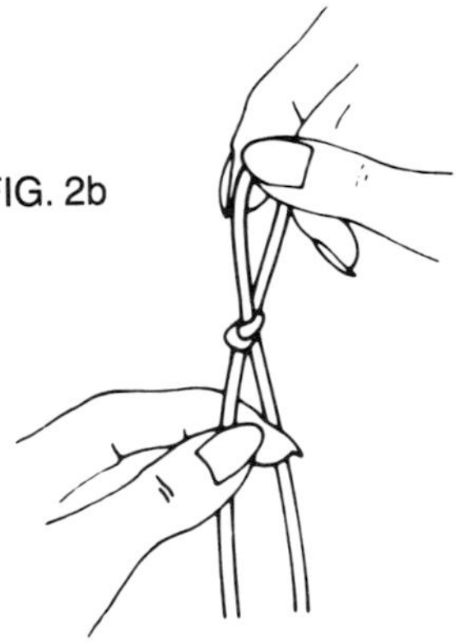

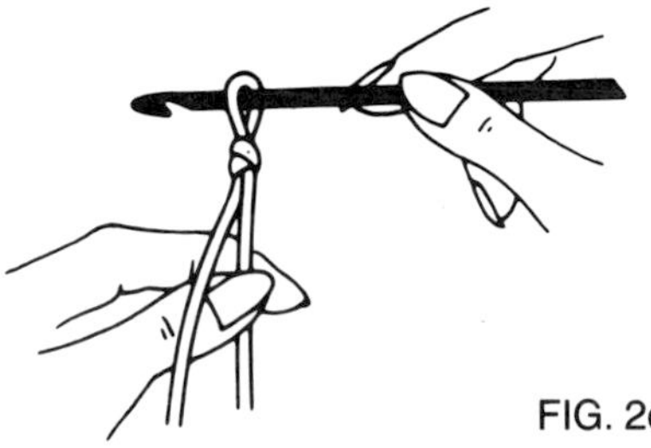

FIG. 2c

FIG. 1 HOLDING THE HOOK

CROCHET ABBREVIATIONS

Following is a crochet abbreviations listing, with definitions of the terms given. To help you become accustomed to abbreviations used, we have repeated them through our stitch instructions.

beg—begin, beginning; **ch**—chain; **dc**—double crochet; **dec**—decrease; **dtr**—double treble crochet; **hdc**—half double crochet; **in(s)** or ″—inch(es); **inc**—increase; **oz(s)**—ounce(s); **pat**—pattern; **pc**—picot; **rem**—remaining; **rnd**—round; **rpt**—repeat; **sc**—single crochet; **skn(s)**—skein(s); **sk**—skip; **sl st**—slip stitch; **sp**—space; **st(s)**—stitch(es); **tog**—together; **tr**—triple crochet; **work even**—continue without further increase or decrease; **yo**—yarn over; * (asterisk)—repeat whatever follows * as many times as indicated; ( )—do what is in parentheses as many times as indicated.

CHAIN STITCH (ch): Follow the steps in FIG. 3. As you make the chain stitch loops, the yarn should slide easily between your index and middle fingers. Make about 15 loops. If they are all the same size, you have maintained even tension. If uneven, rip them out by pulling on the long end of the yarn. Practice making chains and ripping out until you have a perfect chain.

FIG. 3 CHAIN STITCH (CH)

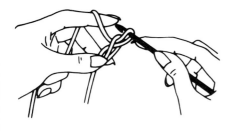

YARN OVER (YO)

FIG. 3a

FIG. 3b

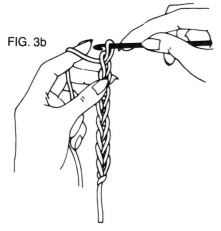

FOR LEFT-HANDED CROCHETERS

FIGS. 1 to 3 are for right-handed crocheters and are repeated in FIGS. 1 Left to 3 Left for left-handed crocheters.

LEFT-HANDED CROCHETERS
FIGS. 1 LEFT TO 3 LEFT

FIG. 1L
HOLDING THE HOOK

FIG. 2L

FIG. 2La

FIG. 2Lb

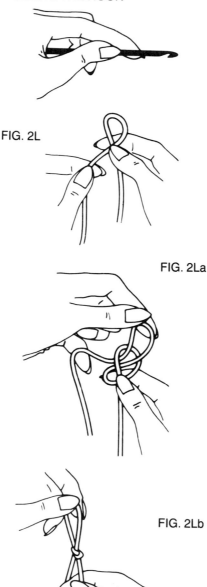

FIG. 2Lc

CHAIN STITCH (CH)

FIG. 3L

FIG. 3La

FIG. 3Lb

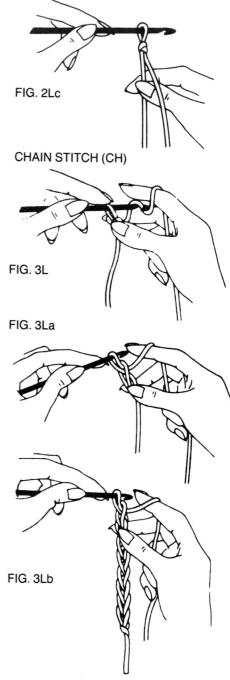

From here on, we won't be showing hands—just the hook and stitches. Left-handed crocheters can use all the following right-handed illustrations by simply turning the book upside down and using a mirror (with backstand) that will reflect the left-handed version.

SINGLE CROCHET (sc): Follow the steps in FIG. 4. To practice, make a 20-loop chain (this means 20 loops in addition to the slip knot). Turn the chain, as shown, and insert the hook in the second chain from the hook (see arrow) to make the first sc stitch. Yarn over (yo); for the second stitch, see the next arrow. Repeat to the end of the chain. Because you started in the second chain from the hook, you end up with only 19 sc. To add the 20th stitch, ch 1 (called a turning chain) and pull the yarn through. Now turn your work around (the "back" is now facing you) and start the second row of sc in the first stitch of the previous row (at the arrow). Make sure your hook goes under both of the strands at the top of the stitch. Don't forget to make a ch 1 turning chain at the end before turning your work. Keep practicing until your rows are perfect.

ENDING OFF: Follow the steps in FIG. 5. To finish off your crochet, cut off all but 6″ of yarn and end off as shown. (To "break off and fasten," follow the same procedure.)

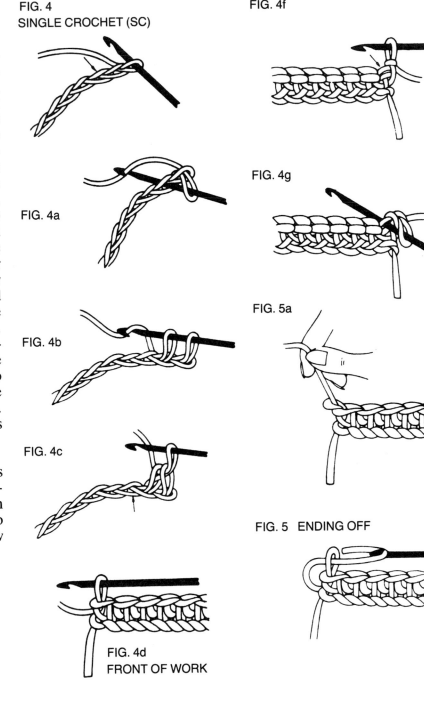

FIG. 4
SINGLE CROCHET (SC)

FIG. 4a

FIG. 4b

FIG. 4c

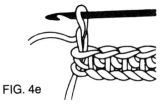

FIG. 4d
FRONT OF WORK

FIG. 4e

FIG. 4f

FIG. 4g

FIG. 5a

FIG. 5 ENDING OFF

DOUBLE CROCHET (dc): Follow the steps in FIG. 6. To practice, ch 20, then make a row of 20 sc. Now, instead of a ch 1, you will make a ch 3. Turn your work, yo and insert the hook in the second stitch of the previous row (at the arrow), going under both strands at the top of the stitch. Pull the yarn through. You now have three loops on the hook. Yo and pull through the first two, then yo and pull through the remaining two—one double crochet (dc) made. Continue across the row, making a dc in each stitch (st) across. Dc in the top of the turning chain (see arrow in FIG. 7). Ch 3. Turn work. Dc in second stitch on the previous row and continue as before.

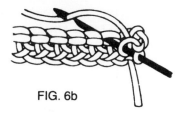

FIG. 6b

FIG. 6c

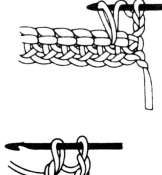

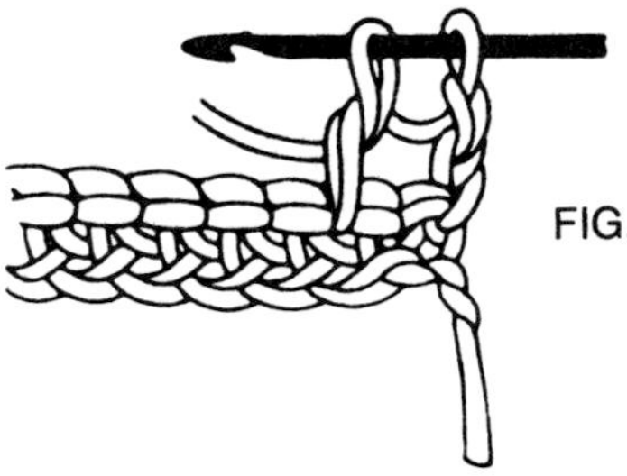

FIG. 6d

Note: You may also start a row of dc on a base chain (omitting the sc row). In this case, insert the hook in the fourth chain from the hook, instead of the second (see FIG. 8).

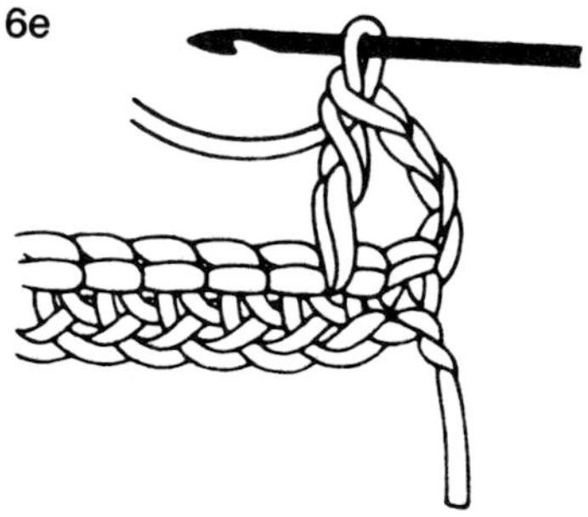

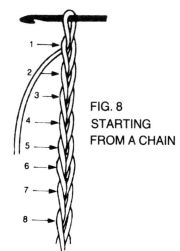

FIG. 8
STARTING
FROM A CHAIN

FIG. 6
DOUBLE CROCHET (DC)

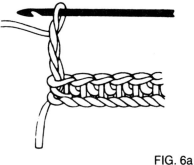

FIG. 6a

FIG. 6e

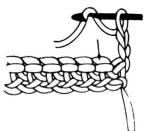

FIG. 7

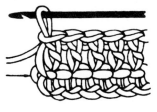

SLIP STITCH (sl st): Follow the steps in FIG. 9. This is a utility stitch you will use for joining, shaping and ending off. After you chain and turn, *do not yo.* Just insert the hook into the *first* stitch of the previous row (see FIG. 9A), and pull the yarn through the stitch, then through the loop on the hook—the sl st is made.

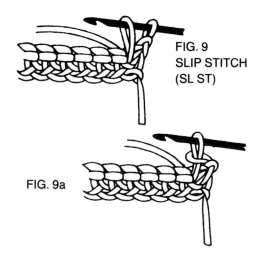

FIG. 9
SLIP STITCH
(SL ST)

FIG. 9a

HALF DOUBLE CROCHET
(hdc): Follow the steps in Fig. 10 and 10A.

FIG. 10
HALF DOUBLE CROCHET (HDC)

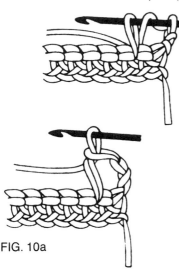

FIG. 10a

To practice, make a chain and a row of sc. Ch 2 and turn; yo. Insert the hook in the second stitch, as shown; yo and pull through to make three loops on the hook. Yo and pull the yarn through *all* three loops at the same time—hdc made. This stitch is used primarily as a transitional stitch from an sc to a dc. Try it and see—starting with sc's, then an hdc and then dc's.

TECHNIQUES OF CROCHETING

Now that you have practiced and made sample squares of all the basic stitches, you are ready to learn about adding and subtracting stitches to change the length of a row whenever it's called for. You do this by increasing (inc) and decreasing (dec).

To increase (inc): Just make two stitches in the same stitch in the previous row (see arrow in Fig. 11). The technique is the same for any kind of stitch.

FIG. 11 INCREASING (INC)
FOR SINGLE CROCHET

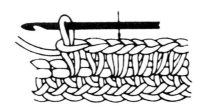

To decrease (dec) for single-crochet (sc): Yo and pull the yarn through two stitches to make three loops on the hook (see steps in Fig. 12). Pull the yarn through all the loops at once— dec made. Continue in regular stitches.

FIG. 12 DECREASING (DEC)

FOR SINGLE CROCHET   FIG. 12a

To decrease for double crochet (dc): In a dc row, make the next stitch and stop when you have two loops on the hook. Now yo and make a dc in the next stitch. At the point where you have three loops on the hook, pull yarn through all loops at the same time. Finish the row with regular dc.

HOW TO ENLARGE DESIGNS

If the design is not already marked off in squares, make a tracing of it. Mark the tracing off in squares: For a small design, make squares ¼″; for larger designs, use ½″ or 2″ squares, or the size indicated in the directions. Decide the size of enlargement. On another sheet of tracing paper, mark off the same number of squares that are on the design or original tracing. For example, to make your design, each new square must be 6 times larger than the original. Copy the outline from your original tracing to the new one, square by square. Use dressmaker's carbon and a tracing wheel to transfer the design onto the material you are decorating.

EMBROIDERY STITCH GUIDE

BLANKET STITCH

Work from left to right, with the point of the needle and the edge of the work toward you. The edge of the fabric can be folded under or left raw. Secure the thread and bring out below the edge. For the first and each succeeding stitch, insert the needle through the fabric from the right side and bring it out at the edge. Keeping the thread from the previous stitch *under* the point of the needle, draw the needle and thread through, forming a stitch over the edge. The stitch size and spacing can be uniform or varied.

BLANKET STITCH

FEATHER STITCH

CROSS STITCH

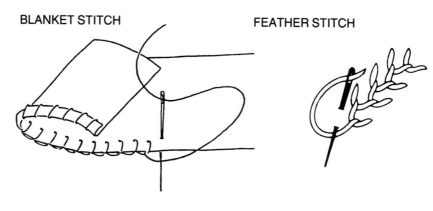

FRENCH KNOT

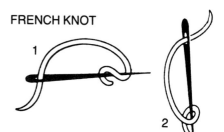

CHAIN STITCH

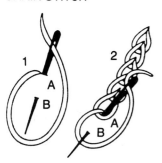

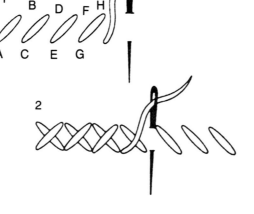

FLY STITCH

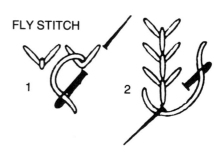

BLIND STITCH

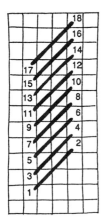

STRAIGHT STITCH

TENT OR CONTINENTAL STITCH
OR PETIT POINT

SLANTED GOBELIN STITCH
(worked vertically)

LONG AND SHORT STITCH

INTERLOCKING GOBELIN STITCH

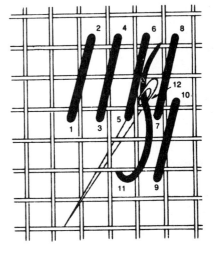

MOSAIC STITCH

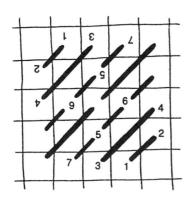

SCOTCH STITCH

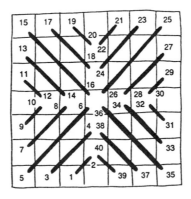

SCOTCH STITCH VARIATION

MATERIALS SHOPPING GUIDE

*Some of the projects in this book suggest using specific
manufacturers' products.
Here's a list of those products with the names and addresses of
their manufacturers.*

PROJECTS AND PRODUCTS

Chapter I *(page 45):* Wreath-making materials and forms from Kelco Industries, Milbridge, ME 04658 (1-800-343-4057 or 207-546-7541).

Chapter I *(page 47):* Yarn in Reindeer Sweater, "Rugger" Bulky Yarn by Brunswick.

Chapter I *(page 55):* Yarn in Reindeer and Snowflake Pillows, Reynolds Icelandic Lopi.

Chapter I *(page 56):* Hat boxes from Sample House, 4722 Bengal, Dallas, TX 75235, Attention Retail Sales Department (214-688-0751).

Chapter II *(page 74):* Yarn in Frosty 'N Friends Pullover, "Red Heart" Sport Yarn by Coats & Clark.

Chapter II *(page 78):* Yarn in Checkerboard Pullover, "Royal" and "Royal Tweed" Worsted Weight Yarn by Aarlan.

Chapter II *(page 81):* Yarn in Double-Warm Scarf, Berella Sportspun by Bernat.

Chapter II *(page 86):* Beads in Beaded Snowflake Ornament, from Mil Hill Graphics, Inc., Box 7343, High Point, NC 27264.

Chapter III *(pages 120-131):* All fabrics from Waverly.

MANUFACTURERS AND ADDRESSES

Aarlan Yarns
  Wooly West
  208 S. 13th East, Salt Lake City, UT 84102
  (801) 583-9373
Bernat
  Art Needlecrafts
  P.O. Box 394, 29 Mendon St., Oxbridge, MA 01569
  (508) 278-2458
Brunswick
  The Mill Store
  P.O. Box 581, Pickens, SC 29671
  (803) 878-6375
Coats & Clark
  Dept. C.S., Box 1010, Toccoa, GA 30577
  (404) 886-7562
Glass Beads
  York Novelty Import, Inc.
  10 West 37th St., New York, NY 10018
  1-800-223-6676
  (No Gold, but Bronze)
Reynolds Icelandic Lopi
  Needlecraft House, 1-800-225-6340
  or
  Johnson Creative Arts, 445 Main St., West Townsend, MA 01474
Waverly Fabrics
  for a store nearby call: 1-800-423-5881

INDEX

Italicized page numbers refer to photographs